IFIP Advances in Information and Communication Technology

665

Editor-in-Chief

Kai Rannenberg, Goethe University Frankfurt, Germany

Editorial Board Members

TC 1 – Foundations of Computer Science
  Luís Soares Barbosa⬤, University of Minho, Braga, Portugal

TC 2 – Software: Theory and Practice
  Michael Goedicke, University of Duisburg-Essen, Germany

TC 3 – Education
  Arthur Tatnall⬤, Victoria University, Melbourne, Australia

TC 5 – Information Technology Applications
  Erich J. Neuhold, University of Vienna, Austria

TC 6 – Communication Systems
  Burkhard Stiller, University of Zurich, Zürich, Switzerland

TC 7 – System Modeling and Optimization
  Fredi Tröltzsch, TU Berlin, Germany

TC 8 – Information Systems
  Jan Pries-Heje, Roskilde University, Denmark

TC 9 – ICT and Society
  David Kreps⬤, National University of Ireland, Galway, Ireland

TC 10 – Computer Systems Technology
  Ricardo Reis⬤, Federal University of Rio Grande do Sul, Porto Alegre, Brazil

TC 11 – Security and Privacy Protection in Information Processing Systems
  Steven Furnell⬤, Plymouth University, UK

TC 12 – Artificial Intelligence
  Eunika Mercier-Laurent⬤, University of Reims Champagne-Ardenne, Reims, France

TC 13 – Human-Computer Interaction
  Marco Winckler⬤, University of Nice Sophia Antipolis, France

TC 14 – Entertainment Computing
  Rainer Malaka, University of Bremen, Germany

IFIP – The International Federation for Information Processing

IFIP was founded in 1960 under the auspices of UNESCO, following the first World Computer Congress held in Paris the previous year. A federation for societies working in information processing, IFIP's aim is two-fold: to support information processing in the countries of its members and to encourage technology transfer to developing nations. As its mission statement clearly states:

IFIP is the global non-profit federation of societies of ICT professionals that aims at achieving a worldwide professional and socially responsible development and application of information and communication technologies.

IFIP is a non-profit-making organization, run almost solely by 2500 volunteers. It operates through a number of technical committees and working groups, which organize events and publications. IFIP's events range from large international open conferences to working conferences and local seminars.

The flagship event is the IFIP World Computer Congress, at which both invited and contributed papers are presented. Contributed papers are rigorously refereed and the rejection rate is high.

As with the Congress, participation in the open conferences is open to all and papers may be invited or submitted. Again, submitted papers are stringently refereed.

The working conferences are structured differently. They are usually run by a working group and attendance is generally smaller and occasionally by invitation only. Their purpose is to create an atmosphere conducive to innovation and development. Refereeing is also rigorous and papers are subjected to extensive group discussion.

Publications arising from IFIP events vary. The papers presented at the IFIP World Computer Congress and at open conferences are published as conference proceedings, while the results of the working conferences are often published as collections of selected and edited papers.

IFIP distinguishes three types of institutional membership: Country Representative Members, Members at Large, and Associate Members. The type of organization that can apply for membership is a wide variety and includes national or international societies of individual computer scientists/ICT professionals, associations or federations of such societies, government institutions/government related organizations, national or international research institutes or consortia, universities, academies of sciences, companies, national or international associations or federations of companies.

More information about this series at https://link.springer.com/bookseries/6102

Luis M. Camarinha-Matos ·
Luis Ribeiro · Leon Strous (Eds.)

Internet of Things

IoT through a Multi-disciplinary Perspective

5th IFIP International Cross-Domain Conference, IFIPIoT 2022
Amsterdam, The Netherlands, October 27–28, 2022
Proceedings

 Springer

Editors
Luis M. Camarinha-Matos 🆔
NOVA University of Lisbon
Monte Caparica, Portugal

Luis Ribeiro
Linköping University
Linköping, Sweden

Leon Strous
De Nederlandsche Bank
Amsterdam, The Netherlands

ISSN 1868-4238   ISSN 1868-422X (electronic)
IFIP Advances in Information and Communication Technology
ISBN 978-3-031-18874-9   ISBN 978-3-031-18872-5 (eBook)
https://doi.org/10.1007/978-3-031-18872-5

This Springer imprint is published by the registered company Springer Nature Switzerland AG
The registered company address is: Gewerbestrasse 11, 6330 Cham, Switzerland

Preface

The fifth IFIP Internet of Things (IoT) conference (IFIPIoT 2022), that took place in Amsterdam, the Netherlands, during October 27–28, 2022, had an overall theme of "IoT through a multi-disciplinary perspective". As in the previous editions of this annual event, the topics presented reflected the variety of aspects with respect to IoT, aspects covered by IFIP's Domain Committee on IoT which organizes this conference.

The Technical Program Committee for this edition consisted of 46 members from 15 countries who considered 36 submissions. Each paper was refereed by at least three reviewers with more than half of the papers having four or more reviews. The single-blind review principle was applied. Committee members had to indicate in the review system for each assignment whether they had a conflict of interest. Where conflicts of interest where disclosed or identified the conflicted committee member did not take any decision regarding the revision, acceptance, or management of the respective manuscripts.

In total, 20 full papers were selected for presentation resulting in an acceptance rate of 56%. The papers were selected on the basis of originality, quality, and relevance to the topic. As expected, the peer-reviewed papers covered a wide array of topics that were clustered into the following themes:

- IoT for Smart Villages
- Security and Safety
- Smart Home
- Development, Engineering, Machine Learning
- Applications

The conference featured two keynote speakers. The first keynote was given by Michael Beigl of the Karlsruhe Institute of Technology (KIT) in Germany on "Wearable computing". The second keynote on "The Internet of Secure Things" was given by Sandro Etalle from the Eindhoven University of Technology in the Netherlands.

There was also a panel session addressing the relationship between AI and IoT. What is, can be, should be the impact of AI on the Internet of Things? What do we need to enhance the security, reliability, efficiency of IoT?

We thank the authors and presenters, the panel members, the session chairs, the organizers of special sessions, the Program Committee, and the external reviewers for their hard work and contributions and look forward to their continued involvement.

We feel that all contributions make this book a rich volume in the IFIP AICT series and we trust that the reader will be inspired by it.

August 2022

Luis M. Camarinha-Matos
Luis Ribeiro
Leon Strous

Organization

General Co-chairs

Paul Havinga   University of Twente, The Netherlands
Srinivas Katkoori   University of South Florida, USA

Program Co-chairs

Luis M. Camarinha-Matos   NOVA University of Lisbon, Portugal
Luis Ribeiro   Linköping University, Sweden

Organizing Chair

Leon Strous   De Nederlandsche Bank, The Netherlands

Web Chair

Omkar Dokur   University of South Florida, USA

Technical Program Committee

Carmelo Ardito*	Politecnico di Bari, Italy
Suzan Bayhan	University of Twente, The Netherlands
Elisa Bertino	Purdue University, USA
Luis M. Camarinha-Matos*	NOVA University of Lisbon, Portugal
Augusto Casaca*	INESC-ID/IST, Portugal
Jose Neuman De Souza*	Federal University of Ceará, Brazil
Gordon Fletcher*	Salford University, UK
Paul Havinga	University of Twente, The Netherlands
Geert Heijenk	University of Twente, The Netherlands
Chenglu Jin	CWI Amsterdam, The Netherlands
Stamatis Karnouskos	SAP, Germany
Srinivas Katkoori*	University of South Florida, USA
Mehran Mozaffari Kermani	University of South Florida, USA
Arianit Kurti	Linnaeus University, Sweden
Maryline Laurent	Institut Mines-Telecom, France
Paulo Leitão	Instituto Politécnico de Bragança, Portugal
Tiziana Margaria	Lero, Ireland
Peter Marwedel	TU Dortmund, Germany
Vincent Naessens	KU Leuven, Belgium
Mário Nunes	INOV, Portugal
A. Luís Osório	Instituto Politécnico de Lisboa, Portugal

Fabio Paterno*	ISTI-CNR, Italy
Joachim Posegga	University of Passau, Germany
Franz Rammig	University of Paderborn, Germany
Luis Ribeiro	Linköping University, Sweden
Kay Roemer	TU Graz, Austria
Carmen Santoro	ISTI-CNR, Italy
Susana Sargento	University of Aveiro, Portugal
Damien Sauveron*	XLIM, CNRS/University of Limoges, France
Jürgen Schönwälder	Jacobs University Bremen, Germany
Abbas Shahim	Vrije Universiteit Amsterdam, The Netherlands
Krassen Stefanov*	University of Sofia, Bulgaria
Leon Strous*	De Nederlandsche Bank, The Netherlands
Jean-Yves Tigli	Université Côte d'Azur/CNRS, France
A Min Tjoa*	TU Wien, Austria
Damien Trentesaux	Université Polytechnique Hauts-de-France
Venkanna U.	IIIT Naya Raipur, India
Rainer Unland	University of Duisburg-Essen, Germany
Sebastiaan von Solms*	University of Johannesburg, South Africa
Ulrika H. Westergren*	Umeå University, Sweden
Marco Winckler*	Université Côte d'Azur, France
Li Da Xu*	Old Dominion University, USA
Venkata P. Yanambaka	Central Michigan University, USA
Hui Zhao	University of North Texas, USA
Hao Zheng	University of South Florida, USA
Alois Zoitl	Johannes Kepler University Linz, Austria

Additional Reviewers

Alisson De Souza	Federal University of Ceará, Brasil
Johannes Köstler	University of Passau, Germany
Gérald Rocher	Université Côte d'Azur/CNRS, France
Stef Schinagl	Vrije Universiteit Amsterdam, The Netherlands

*members of the IFIP Domain Committee on IoT

Contents

Smart Home

Development, Engineering, Machine Learning

Applications

IoT for Smart Villages

aGROdet: A Novel Framework for Plant Disease Detection and Leaf Damage Estimation

Alakananda Mitra[1] , Saraju P. Mohanty[1(✉)] , and Elias Kougianos[2]

[1] Department of Computer Science and Engineering, University of North Texas, Denton, USA
alakanandamitra@my.unt.edu, saraju.mohanty@unt.edu
[2] Department of Electrical Engineering, University of North Texas, Denton, USA
elias.kougianos@unt.edu

Abstract. By 2050, 60% more food will be required to feed a world population of 9.7 billion. Producing more food with traditional agriculture will stress the earth's limited natural resources. To avoid such a scenario, greener, sustainable, and modern agricultural practices should be followed. More efficient food production along with a reduction of food wastage at different levels of the food supply chain will ease our ecosystem. Plant disease outbreaks are one of the major causes of crop damage, which is essentially one of the causes of food wastage. Hence, plant disease detection and damage estimation are important to prevent crop loss. However, until now, not much work has been done to estimate the damage caused by the disease. In this paper, we propose a novel method, *aGROdet*, to detect plant disease and to estimate the leaf damage severity. *aGROdet* is aimed at being implemented at the edge platform of IoT systems in the proposed Agriculture Cyber Physical System. A convolutional neural network-based model has been proposed to detect different plant diseases. The model has been trained with large publicly available datasets. More than 97% accuracy has been achieved in the initial phase of the experiment. A pixel-based thresholding method has been used for estimating the severity of the damage. Damage estimation limiting factors, such as on the leaf and around the leaf shadows, have also been addressed.

Keywords: Smart agriculture · Smart villages · Internet of Agro Things (IoAT) · Agriculture Cyber Physical System (A-CPS) · Plant health · Plant disease · Crop damage · Convolutional neural network

1 Introduction

Agriculture is one of the major industries of today's society. It is complex and is affected by various unpredictable factors such as climate change, population explosion, natural resource limitation, and plant diseases. Due to the recent advancements in information and communication technology (ICT), breakthrough hardware innovations, and the computing paradigm shift from cloud-based computing to more edge-oriented computing, various issues in agriculture are being addressed. The inclusion of automation in agriculture through Artificial Intelligence (AI)/Machine Learning (ML)/Deep Learning Technologies (DLT) has welcomed *Agriculture 4.0* [19], and *Agriculture 5.0* is knocking at the door. The need for initiatives for agriculture cyber physical systems (A-CPS)-based solutions is greater than ever. Figure 1 shows some of the agricultural problems which can be solved using A-CPS concepts.

© IFIP International Federation for Information Processing 2022
Published by Springer Nature Switzerland AG 2022
L. M. Camarinha-Matos et al. (Eds.): IFIPIoT 2022, IFIP AICT 665, pp. 3–22, 2022.
https://doi.org/10.1007/978-3-031-18872-5_1

Fig. 1. Agricultural problems solvable using agriculture cyber physical systems

Plants, like all living things, are prone to diseases. Disease inhibits a plant from reaching its full capacity [2]. It varies with seasons and plant types. External conditions or living organisms can cause diseases. Nutritional deficit, heat, flooding, and freezing are some examples of external agents that cause non-infectious or abiotic diseases, whereas plant pathogens like fungi, bacteria, viruses, and algae cause biotic diseases. The occurrence of a biotic disease is illuminated by the *"Disease Triangle"* [32] shown in Fig. 2. Disease occurs when all three factors-favorable environment, vulnerable host, and harmful pathogens-are present concurrently. The red region in the Venn diagram of Fig. 2 represents the occurrence of the disease. However, certain factors, such as pathogen genetic variation, local micro-climate, and host plant immunity at a specific stage of its life cycle, may alter this fact [2]. To develop a disease in a plant, the pathogen needs to complete its life cycle in the host.

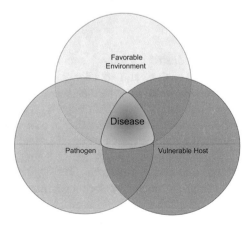

Fig. 2. Disease triangle [32]

1.1 Research Problem

Diseases prevent the growth of plants. They affect the quality of the crop and reduce the final yield. Billions of dollars in crop losses happen per year. The food supply chain is also gravely impacted [3]. Hence, farmers need to:

- Detect the disease early.
- Identify the disease.
- Know about the severity of the disease.
- Determine the extent of damage.

Regular monitoring of plants is necessary for a successful disease management system. According to [25], speedy detection of plant disease at early stages of outbreak and its prevention will become the two major goals of agricultural research by 2030. In this paper, three of the four points are addressed.

1.2 Proposed Solution

We propose a novel automatic method, *aGROdet*, to detect plant disease and estimate corresponding leaf damage. However, the damage due to diseases can be present in different stages of plant growth and at different parts of a plant. A convolutional neural network-based method for the identification of the disease and a novel pixel-based thresholding method for estimating the leaf damage severity are proposed. Regular monitoring of fields and checking the conditions of the plants through *aGROdet* can detect the disease early.

The paper is organized in the following way: Sect. 2 discusses the significance of the work in the context of a smart village. Section 3 reviews recent work on plant disease detection. The proposed A-CPS is described in Sect. 4. Section 5 provides an overview of *aGROdet*, detailed methodology, and experimental details. Section 6 evaluates the performance of *aGROdet* and compares our work with existing work. Finally, the paper concludes with future work direction in Sect. 7.

2 Significance of aGROdet in a Smart Village Context

Today, close to 3.4 billion people live in rural areas. The majority of villages lack technology, innovation, energy, and industry even today. However, the modernization of villages with Internet connectivity, smart agriculture, smart healthcare, smart grid, and education is required. A holistic approach is needed for rural areas to ensure the sustainable development of society. To implement that goal, various smart village movements have recently emerged across the globe in various sectors. For example, Fig. 3 shows the smart energy project sites of IEEE Smart Village initiatives [1].

The application of heterogeneous technologies centered on the Internet-of-Things (IoT) can shape rural areas as smart villages [8]. As the financial backbone of the smart village is agriculture industry, it is one of the most important areas of research for smart villages. To transform the traditional agriculture to an efficient, sustainable, and green agriculture, digital transformation is the key. In this context, our proposed method aGROdet is appropriate.

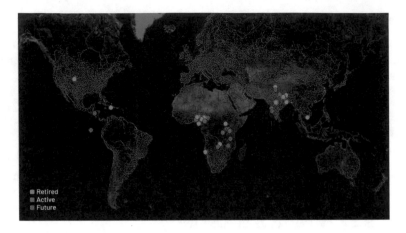

Fig. 3. IEEE smart village map for smart energy projects [1]

- Plant disease is a major challenge for sustainable agriculture. It is a nightmare for farmers as disease can destroy the plants and cause huge losses. The common method of plant disease detection in developing countries even today is manual observation. It is an arduous process. It needs expertise, and the service is so expensive that it is not always affordable for farmers [31]. In such a scenario, the farmer can have an overall idea of the disease and its severity through the proposed method, *aGROdet*.
- It automatically and accurately detects plant diseases and estimates damage. Significantly less effort is needed from the farmers' perspective to use *aGROdet*. It is accessible through a mobile app. To get the results, farmers only need to take a photo of the diseased leaf. The rest of the process is automatic.
- It is an edge-based Internet of Agro Things (IoAT) method that can detect plant disease and estimate the damage even without an Internet connection. If an Internet connection is not available for any reason, the damage estimation procedure will not be affected. An Internet connection is used to store data in the cloud. This stored data is used for future training of the model.
- This is a very useful tool for farmers who can detect plant diseases with an estimation of plant damage on their own. No expert knowledge is required.
- We hope that *aGROdet* will help farmers take proper control measures and save time, money, and secondary plant losses.

3   Related Works

During a review of the literature, two types of papers addressing plant or crop diseases stand out: the first addresses multi-crop disease solutions, while the second focuses on a specific crop or plant type. In the last decade, mostly traditional image processing algorithms and hand-picked features with machine learning (ML) classifiers have been used to detect plant and crop diseases. Those approaches have their own difficulties, along with not so great accuracy [18]. In recent studies, mostly computer vision-based methods with deep learning networks are being proposed for this purpose. The use of deep learning networks, mostly convolutional neural network (CNN)-based approaches, makes the disease identification automatic, reduces manual intervention, and performs better in detecting plant diseases.

Complex features are obtained automatically in deep learning network-based solutions via various layers and types of neural networks, particularly CNN. Different CNNs have been used for different purposes, such as feature extractor [10], classification network [35], and disease localization network [38].

3.1 Single Plant/Crop Diseases Detection

Non-parametric ML classifiers are used in various works, along with the recent trend of deep learning networks for detecting plant/crop diseases. For example, the K-means algorithm is used in [24] for paddy leaf diseases. Several studies have been conducted on cotton diseases. The K-nearest neighbors (KNN) algorithm has been used in [28] for cotton leaf diseases. Ramularia leaf blight cotton disease has been identified using non-parametric classifiers from multi-spectral imagery of an UAV in [39]. A decision tree classifier has been used for detecting cotton crop diseases [7]. Cotton leaf spot disease has been detected in [5] using Support Vector Machines (SVM). Cucumber's powdery mildew has been segmented using U-Net at pixel level with high accuracy in [17].

A combination of InceptionV3 and ResNet50 networks has been used to identify grape leaf diseases with 98.57% testing accuracy [13]. A shallow 3D CNN structure has been used on hyperspectral images to identify a soil-borne fungal disease, charcoal rot, for soybean [23]. An improved AlexNet model has been used to identify fragrant pear diseases and insect pests [37]. A typical accuracy of 96.26% has been achieved. In [26], a Faster RCNN has been used to detect sugar beet leaf spot disease with 95.48% accuracy. Northern maize leaf blight detection has been done in [34] using multi-scale feature fusion method with improved SSD. Mask R-CNN has also been used to segment UAV images in [33] for northern maize leaf blight detection. In [4], a YOLOv3 network was used to detect pests and diseases in tea leaves. Using SegNet, four categories of grape vine diseases have been identified in [14] from UAV images.

3.2 Multi Plants/Crops Diseases Detection

Deep learning techniques are popular in the research community for multi-plant detection. A convolution neural network-based Teacher-Student network has been utilized to detect plant diseases [6]. A sharper visualization of the diseased leaf has been achieved with the PlantVillage dataset [11]. Another deep convolution neural network-based on GoogleNet and AlexNet has been used to detect crop diseases with 99.35% accuracy [22] using the earlier mentioned dataset. In [30], Single Shot MultiBox Detector (SSD) model has been chosen among three different deep learning models for plant disease detection. It shows 73.07% mean average precision (mAP) with the Adam optimizer on the Plant Village dataset. In [12] severity of crop leaf disease has been estimated along with crop type and crop disease prediction with an 86.70% accuracy using binary relevance (BR) multi-label learning algorithm and Convolutional Neural Network. Another

CNN-based structure, built from a ResNet50 network with shuffle units, has been used to detect plant disease and estimate the severity of the disease in [16] with an accuracy of 91%, 99%, and 98% for disease severity, plant type, and plant disease classification, respectively. In [9] several networks have been tested and finally an accuracy of 99.53% in identifying plant disease has been achieved. Disease prediction has also been done along with crop selection and irrigation [36]. In this work, a CNN-based plant disease detection network has achieved an accuracy of 99.25%.

From the above discussion, it is clear that the majority of papers address various diseases for different plants or crops. However, it is highly important to estimate the disease-related damage. Without that knowledge, plant disease management and prevention is not possible.

4   Proposed A-CPS

Figure 4 shows the agriculture cyber physical system (A-CPS) [21] for plant disease detection and damage severity estimation. It is developed through the proposed IoAT-based method *aGROdet*.

The A-CPS consists of two systems - physical systems and cyber systems. Physical systems consist of "things", stakeholders, and computing devices. In our case, the "things" are UAV cameras and phone cameras, the computing devices are single board computers and mobile phones, and the "stakeholders" are microbiologists, plant pathologists, agriculture companies, farmers, and the Agriculture Research Service. Cyber systems comprise deep learning models, software, efficient data storage, and blockchain for data security. It is distributed in two different platforms. Deep learning models and software are present both at the edge and in the cloud, whereas the rest are mainly in the cloud. Physical systems and cyber systems are connected through the network fabric. Depending on the location and range, the network fabric can be Sigfox, ZigBee, LoRa, Wi-Fi, 4G, or 5G.

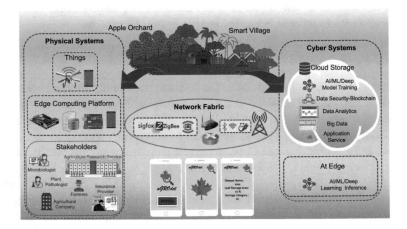

Fig. 4. Agriculture cyber physical system

As *aGROdet* performs two jobs - plant disease identification and damage severity estimation-we divide the work into two parts. The methods have been described in the following Sect. 5.

5 aGROdet: Proposed Method

5.1 Detection of Plant Disease

Methodology. This section describes the proposed deep learning-based method for identifying plant diseases from images of leaves. It is a multi-class image classification problem wherein the model learns to label images through supervised learning techniques and predicts the label of an unknown image. The model learns the features of the labeled images during training and classifies the unknown and unlabeled images with a confidence score. The success of accurate prediction depends on the classifying skill of the model, which in turn depends on how well the model has learned.

Network Architecture: Convolutional neural networks (CNN) are state-of-the-art architectures for image classification. Various CNN structures are being used for image classification in the literature. Here, a custom CNN has been used for plant disease detection purposes, as shown in Fig. 5. It has 5 convolutional blocks. Each block comprises a *Convolutional* layer with *ReLU* activation followed by a *BatchNormalization* layer and a *MaxPooling* layer. There are 32 filters in the first Conv2D layer, 64 filters in the Conv2D layers of the next three blocks, and the final block Conv2D layer consists of 128 filters. The kernel sizes of the convolutional layers are kept the same as (3×3) with stride 1 and no zero padding. *BatchNormalization* layers only normalize the previous layer output during inference after being trained on a similar type of images as testing data. A *MaxPooling* layer has been used to reduce the spatial dimensions. The kernel size of the *MaxPooling* layer is 2×2 with stride 2. The final block is followed by a *Flatten* layer which is succeeded by two *Dense* layers. The first *Dense* layer uses *ReLU* activation and 1280 nodes, whereas the last one has 39 nodes and a *Softmax* activation function. $6, 117, 287$ of the $6, 117, 991$ parameters are trained. Table 1 describes the output shapes of the layers in detail.

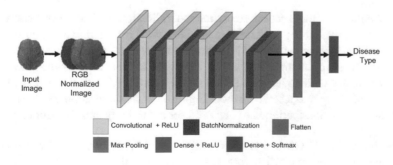

Input Image · RGB Normalized Image · Disease Type

Convolutional + ReLU · BatchNormalization · Flatten
Max Pooling · Dense + ReLU · Dense + Softmax

Fig. 5. Plant disease detection network

Table 1. *aGROdet* CNN architecture for plant disease detection

Layers	Output shape
Conv2D (f = 32, k = 3, s = 1, p = 0) Activation: ReLU BatchNormalization	(254, 254, 32)
Maxpooling2D (k = 2, s = 2)	(127, 127, 32)
Conv2D (f = 64, k = 3, s = 1, p = 0) Activation: ReLU BatchNormalization	(125, 125, 64)
Maxpooling2D (k = 2, s = 2)	(62, 62, 64)
Conv2D (f = 64, k = 3, s = 1, p = 0) Activation: ReLU BatchNormalization	(60, 60, 64)
Maxpooling2D (k = 2, s = 2)	(30, 30, 64)
Conv2D (f = 64, k = 3, s = 1, p = 0) Activation: ReLU BatchNormalization	(28, 28, 64)
Maxpooling2D (k = 2, s = 2)	(14, 14, 64)
Conv2D (f = 128, k = 3, s = 1, p = 0) Activation: ReLU BatchNormalization	(12, 12, 128)
Maxpooling2D (k = 2, s = 2)	(6, 6, 128)
Flatten	(4,608)
Dense (u = 1280)	(1280)
cre Dense (u = 39)	(39)

Experimental Validation

Dataset Details: In this section, experimental validation of disease detection is presented. Publicly available plant leaf data has been used for training and evaluating purposes. The PlantVillage dataset [11] has been used for training the system. The dataset has 55, 448 images of 39 different classes. 38 classes are related to plants' leaves, and 1 class is for images with no leaves. 49, 886 images were used for training and validation whereas 5, 562 images to test the method. Figure 6 shows some sample images from the dataset. 80%–20% distribution has been used for the training and validation.

Dataset Processing: RGB images of size 256×256 have been used for training. The images have been normalized before sending them to the network to avoid slowing down during training by limiting computation with large numbers. Data augmentation has been performed on training and validation data for better and more accurate performance. Figure 7 shows samples of augmented data. Image processing techniques,

Fig. 6. Sample images from PlantVillage dataset [11]

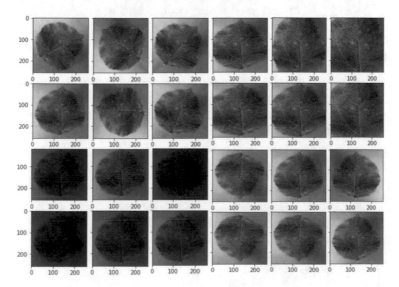

Fig. 7. Sample augmented data. Data is augmented on the fly for different rotation, zoom, brightness, horizontal and vertical flip.

e.g., rotation, zoom, brightness, horizontal and vertical flip, have been used to generate augmented data on the go.

Experiment: Figure 8 shows the plant disease detection workflow. The augmented and preprocessed data is used for training the network. The Adam optimizer [15] has been used with an initial learning rate of 0.001. The model has been trained for 75 epochs, meaning 75 times the network iterated through the total dataset during training. The model has been trained with and without a reduced learning rate of factor 0.1. Then the trained model is saved for future inference. The model is evaluated using the 5, 562 images that were kept aside. The disease detection network in *aGROdet* has been implemented in Keras with TensorFlow back end.

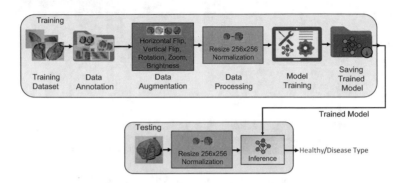

Fig. 8. Plant disease detection workflow

5.2   Estimation of Leaf Damage Severity

This section describes the leaf damage severity estimation process. To estimate damage severity, leaf area and damage area are calculated. The ratio of these two areas gives the percentage of leaf damage. Finally, a rule-based system predicts the damage severity. Figure 9 shows the pipeline of the method.

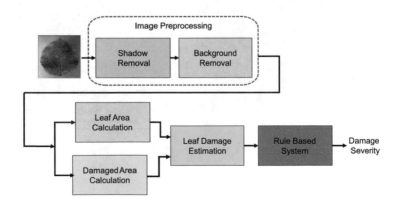

Fig. 9. Leaf damage estimation workflow

Leaf Area Detection. This is the first step to estimating leaf damage severity. First, the leaf area is detected and a mask is created for the leaf. Background segmentation and thresholding have been used to create the mask. Finally, the area of the mask is calculated to obtain the leaf area.

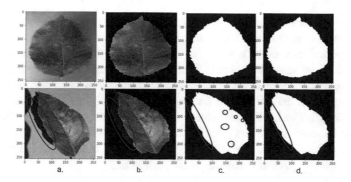

Fig. 10. Leaf area detection by creating leaf mask. a. Input Image b. Background Segmentation c. Mask Creation for the Leaf d. Noise Reduction from the Mask. Red large ovals show the shadow around the foreground object and small circles highlight the shadows on the foreground object. (Color figure online)

Background Segmentation: The leaf image consists of two parts- foreground object and the background. Our object of interest is the foreground object, or leaf. To segment the background from the leaf, the GrabCut [29] algorithm has been used. When different foreground objects are present, the number of iterations and the parameters of the algorithm need to be changed manually. But as in our case, only a specific type of object, i.e., leaf, is detected, no manual adjustment is necessary.

In this method, an initial rectangle is drawn over the foreground object. The outside of the rectangle is considered the confirmed background. The inside of the rectangle consists of the foreground and some parts of the background. In our work, we kept the image size of 256×256 as in Fig. 10(a) and chose to draw a large rectangle of size 226×226. A large rectangle is drawn to ensure that the whole foreground object or leaf stays within the Region of Interest (ROI).

Once the ROI is defined, the GrabCut algorithm applies a Gaussian Mixture Model (GMM) to the ROI. The pixels are grouped based on their similarity in color. A graph is created based on the pixel distribution where each pixel forms a node. Two additional nodes work as the references. The pixels attached to the *Source* node are considered foreground pixels. However, background pixels are connected to the *Sink* node. The probabilities of connecting to *Source* or *Sink* nodes decide the weights of the edges of the graph. Similar pixel nodes are connected by edges with higher weight values. Finally, the foreground pixels are segmented from the background pixels by minimizing a cost function, which is the summation of the weights of the cut edges. We iterated the process 5 times to segment the leaf from its background. After segmentation, the background pixels are turned black for the next step of processing, as shown in Fig. 10(b).

Thresholding and Leaf Area Detection: Shadows can be present on and around the leaves. They have an impact on accurate leaf detection. The outer shadow increases the leaf area, whereas the on-leaf shadows hinder the creation of a perfect mask for the leaf. The large red ovals in Fig. 10 show around the leaf shadows, and smaller circles denote on the leaf shadows.

As HSV color space separates image color (hue) from the color intensity (value), we transform the leaf images from RGB color space to HSV color space. The thresholding is then performed over black color, as in Fig. 10(c). As the foreground object, a leaf, is our object of interest, the mask is inverted. But several masks have noise due to specular reflection and shadows on the leaf. This noise has been shown in small red circles in Fig. 10(c). To get a noise-free mask, we selected the largest contour of the foreground object. The healthy leaf consists of a large contour, whereas a damaged leaf has a larger contour and several smaller contours depending on the damage. Hence, the largest contour, selected from the foreground image, is drawn over the mask as in Fig. 10(d). It gives a perfect noise-free mask for the leaf.

Around the Leaf Shadow Removal: Around the leaf shadows have been removed before *background segmentation*. As shown in Fig. 11(b), pixel-based thresholding is performed to select the shadow. The area around the leaf shadow part is then segmented from the foreground leaf during background segmentation, as in Fig. 11(c). It is removed through contour selection during final mask generation as in Fig. 11(d). Finally, the final mask is made noise free in Fig. 11(e).

Fig. 11. Removal of shadow around the leaf. a. Input Image b. Detection of Shadow around the Leaf c. Shadow Removal d. Leaf Mask Creation e. Noise Reduction from the Mask. Red large ovals show shadow around the leaf and brown ovals highlight the shadow on the leaf. (Color figure online)

Damage Area Detection. Leaf damage area calculation is also necessary to estimate the leaf damage severity. The process is shown in Fig. 12. First, around the leaf shadow is detected and removed, as in Fig. 12(b) and Fig. 12(c). As shown in Fig. 12(d), a mask is generated for the green portion of the leaf and is bit-wise merged with the input image, as shown in Fig. 12(e). Next, the black background of the image is segmented from the merged image and recolored with any other color to differentiate it from the damage, as in Fig. 12(f). Next, pixel-based thresholding is performed on the black color to generate the mask for the damage, as in Fig. 12(g).

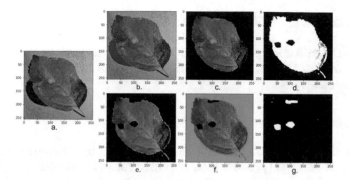

Fig. 12. Leaf damage area detection. a. Input Image b. Detection of Shadow around the Leaf c. Shadow Removal d. Leaf Mask Creation e. Merging of Mask and Input Image f. Recoloration of the Black Background to Differentiate them from the Damage g. Damage Mask Creation.

Leaf Damage Estimation. For estimating leaf damage, the areas of the leaf mask and damage mask are calculated. Pixels, present in the masks, are counted to calculate the area. Figure 13 shows a sample area calculation and the estimated percentage damage of a leaf.

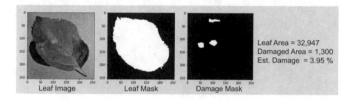

Fig. 13. Leaf damage estimation

Then, a rule-based system decides the severity of the damage to the leaf. The damage severity grade scale is suggested in Table 2. If there is no damage detected, the system predicts the leaf as healthy. However, if the percentage of damage is greater than 0, it grades the damage severity into different tiers depending on the values. According to Table 2, the damage severity grade of the damaged leaf in Fig. 13 is *Gr-1* as the damage is between 0 and 5%.

Table 2. Damage severity grade scale

Estimated damage (%)	Damage severity grade
0	Healthy
>0 and ≤5	1
>5 and ≤10	2
>10 and ≤25	3
>25 and ≤50	4
>50	5

6 Performance Evaluation of aGROdet

This section describes the performance of *aGROdet* for disease detection and disease severity estimation. Unseen images from the PlantVillage Dataset [11] have been used for evaluation purposes.

6.1 Disease Detection

The performance of the model has been evaluated through various metrics. 5, 562 unseen images of the [11] dataset have been used for validating the model. Figure 14 shows the *confusion matrix* for this multi-class problem. Different performance metrics [20] have been calculated as in Eqs. 1, 2, 3, and 4.

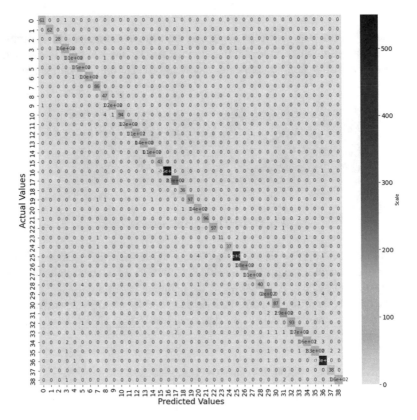

Fig. 14. Confusion matrix for disease detection network (Trained without reduced learning rate). Classes are denoted by numbers instead of the class names to fit into the figure space.

$$Accuracy = \frac{TP + TN}{TP + TN + FP + FN} \tag{1}$$

$$Precision = \frac{TP}{TP + FP} \tag{2}$$

$$Recall = \frac{TP}{TP + FN} \tag{3}$$

$$F1 - score = \frac{2}{\frac{1}{Precision} + \frac{1}{Recall}} \tag{4}$$

TP is *True Positive*, TN is *True Negative*, FP is *False Positive*, and FN is *False Negative*. Two other diagnostic curves-*ROC* curves and *Precision-Recall* curves-are drawn too. Figure 15(a) and Fig. 15(b) show such curves for only 8 classes. These evaluating tools are originally defined for binary class problems. However, for multi-class problems, these metrics and curves have been obtained by utilizing the *one vs. all* method. A weighted average precision of 98% has been achieved.

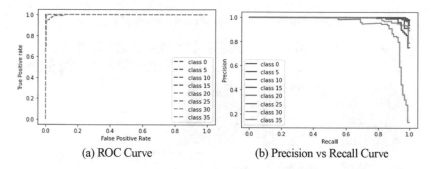

(a) ROC Curve   (b) Precision vs Recall Curve

Fig. 15. Performance evaluation curves for disease detection (Trained without reduced learning rate)

Table 3 shows the accuracy of the model for two different training scenarios. When the model is trained with a reduced learning rate of factor 0.1, better accuracy is obtained.

Table 3. Accuracy for disease detection network

Training type	Accuracy (%)		
	Training	Validation	Testing
Without reduced learning rate	97.62	97.42	97.68
With reduced learning rate	98.89	98.41	98.58

6.2 Leaf Damage Severity Estimation

The method has been validated with part of the PlantVillage dataset [11]. No experiment has been done with corn leaf images in the dataset. Estimation of damage will not be correct in those cases, as the whole leaf is not visible in the image. Table 4 shows some sample results. The first column shows the tested images, whereas the second and third columns present leaf and damage masks, respectively. The results are stated in columns four and five. The estimated leaf damage presented in the fourth column of the table matches with the leaf and mask damage images of columns two and three. The shadows on and around the leaves impact the damage estimation negatively. However, damage estimation by *aGROdet* is not affected as damage masks in column three of Table 4 are accurately generated even in the presence of shadows. Even if there is some specular reflection in the image, *aGROdet* can still correctly estimates the damage of leaves.

There are certain scenarios when *aGROdet* will not estimate leaf damage correctly, e.g., for variegated plants. In those plants, the healthy leaves have other colors, e.g., yellow or white, along with green. Abelia, Azalia, Boxwood, Cape Jasmine, Hydrangea, and Lilac are such variegated plants. However, our area of interest is mainly crops, fruits, and vegetable plants or trees where the color of the leaves is usually green. They may turn yellow if they are under abiotic stress due to lack of nutrients in the soil, over or under watering, over use of fertilizers, extreme cold, and absence of enough light. However, *aGROdet* can detect those yellow parts as damage.

Table 4. Damage severity prediction through aGROdet

Image	Leaf Mask	Damage Mask	Estimated Damage (%)	Damage Severity Grade
			3.95	1
			2.97	1
			53.49	5
			10.69	3
			9.49	2

6.3 Comparative Analysis

Table 5 shows a comparative analysis between *aGROdet* and other existing works. The majority of the papers did not address the disease severity issue. [12] has addressed the disease severity issue, but lower accuracy has been obtained. However, an accurate leaf damage percentage has been achieved in our work along with the disease type. *aGROdet* gives a better perspective of leaf damage.

Table 5. A quantitative analysis of the current paper with existing works

Works	Disease type	Accuracy (%)	Damage estimation
Ji et al. [12]	Multi Disease	86.70	Yes
Mohanty et al. [22]	Multi Disease	99.35	No
Ji et al. [13]	Single	98.57	No
Wang [37]	Single	96.26	No
Ozguven et al. [26]	Single	95.48	No
Pallagani et al. [27]	Multi Disease	99.24	No
Current paper	**Multi Disease**	**98.58**	**Yes**

7 Conclusion and Future Work

Plant disease is one of the major causes of crop damage. It stalls a plant's growth and prevents plants from reaching their full potential. Hence, plant disease detection is important. However, to prevent the disease, farmers need to know the severity of the disease. Hence estimation of the damage is another important area of research to know the severity of the disease. Our proposed *aGROdet* could be a useful component to smart village initiatives. In this paper:

– We proposed a plant disease detection system, *aGROdet*, for plant disease detection and leaf damage estimation.
– We evaluated our system through various performance metrics. *aGROdet* has a very high success rate in detecting disease and estimating leaf damage.
– Even when there are shadows in the image, *aGROdet* accurately calculates the damage.
– *aGROdet* accurately estimates damage, even in the presence of some specular reflection.

However, there are limitations to *aGROdet* which need further experimentation. In future work, these limitations are required to be addressed.

– [11] has images of single leaves. In reality, when the images are taken with a mobile phone camera or UAV, there will be several leaves in the same image. Hence, a single leaf image needs to be detected from the shot image before applying *aGROdet*.

- As previously stated, *aGROdet* does not estimate damage in variegated leaves. Inclusion of these plants' damage estimates would be a good addition.
- Extent of damage is another area that needs attention.
- Disease can appear in any part of the plant. Here, only the top of the leaves are considered. In the future, other parts of the plants affected by disease need to be considered too.
- More work on the removal of shadows and specular reflections is needed. This will increase the accuracy of damage estimation.
- The presence of pests on the leaf has not been considered. Inclusion of damage estimation in the presence of the pest would be an interesting task too.
- Finally, more publicly available datasets will be an important addition to this research. Clean and more informational datasets will orchestrate the progress of data-centric AI initiatives.

References

1. IEEE Smart Village Map. https://smartvillage.ieee.org/our-projects/. Accessed 6 Apr 2022
2. Plant Disease: Pathogens and Cycles. https://cropwatch.unl.edu/soybean-management/plant-disease. Accessed 31 Mar 2022
3. Plant Diseases. https://www.ars.usda.gov/crop-production-and-protection/plant-diseases/docs/action-plan-2022-2026/. Accessed 4 Apr 2022
4. Bhatt, P.V., Sarangi, S., Pappula, S.: Detection of diseases and pests on images captured in uncontrolled conditions from tea plantations. In: Autonomous Air and Ground Sensing Systems for Agricultural Optimization and Phenotyping IV, vol. 11008, p. 1100808. International Society for Optics and Photonics (2019)
5. Bhimte, N.R., Thool, V.: Diseases detection of cotton leaf spot using image processing and SVM classifier. In: Proceedings of the Second International Conference on Intelligent Computing and Control Systems (ICICCS), pp. 340–344 (2018)
6. Brahimi, M., Mahmoudi, S., Boukhalfa, K., Moussaoui, A.: Deep interpretable architecture for plant diseases classification. In: Proceedings of the Signal Processing: Algorithms, Architectures, Arrangements, and Applications (SPA), pp. 111–116 (2019)
7. Chopda, J., Raveshiya, H., Nakum, S., Nakrani, V.: Cotton crop disease detection using decision tree classifier. In: Proceedings of the International Conference on Smart City and Emerging Technology (ICSCET), pp. 1–5 (2018)
8. Degada, A., Thapliyal, H., Mohanty, S.P.: Smart village: an IoT based digital transformation. In: Proceedings of the IEEE 7th World Forum on Internet of Things (WF-IoT), pp. 459–463 (2021)
9. Ferentinos, K.P.: Deep learning models for plant disease detection and diagnosis. Comput. Electron. Agric. **145**, 311–318 (2018)
10. Hasan, M.J., Mahbub, S., Alom, M.S., Nasim, M.A.: Rice disease identification and classification by integrating support vector machine with deep convolutional neural network. In: Proceedings of the 1st International Conference on Advances in Science, Engineering and Robotics Technology (ICASERT), pp. 1–6 (2019)
11. Hughes, D.P., Salathé, M.: An open access repository of images on plant health to enable the development of mobile disease diagnostics through machine learning and crowdsourcing. CoRR abs/1511.08060 (2015). https://arxiv.org/abs/1511.08060
12. Ji, M., Zhang, K., Wu, Q., Deng, Z.: Multi-label learning for crop leaf diseases recognition and severity estimation based on convolutional neural networks. Soft. Comput. **24**(20), 15327–15340 (2020)

13. Ji, M., Zhang, L., Wu, Q.: Automatic grape leaf diseases identification via unitedmodel based on multiple convolutional neural networks. Inf. Process. Agric. **7**(3), 418–426 (2020)
14. Kerkech, M., Hafiane, A., Canals, R.: Vine disease detection in UAV multispectral images using optimized image registration and deep learning segmentation approach. Comput. Electron. Agric. **174**, 105446 (2020)
15. Kingma, D.P., Ba, J.: Adam: a method for stochastic optimization (2014). https://doi.org/10.48550/ARXIV.1412.6980
16. Liang, Q., Xiang, S., Hu, Y., Coppola, G., Zhang, D., Sun, W.: PD2SE-Net: computer-assisted plant disease diagnosis and severity estimation network. Comput. Electron. Agric. **157**, 518–529 (2019)
17. Lin, K., Gong, L., Huang, Y., Liu, C., Pan, J.: Deep learning-based segmentation and quantification of cucumber powdery mildew using convolutional neural network. Front. Plant Sci. **10** (2019). https://doi.org/10.3389/fpls.2019.00155
18. Liu, J., Wang, X.: Plant diseases and pests detection based on deep learning: a review. Plant Methods **17**(22) (2021). https://doi.org/10.1186/s13007-021-00722-9
19. Mitra, A., et al.: Everything you wanted to know about smart agriculture. arXiv Computer Science arXiv:2201.04754, p. 45 (2022)
20. Mitra, A., Mohanty, S.P., Corcoran, P., Kougianos, E.: A machine learning based approach for Deepfake detection in social media through key video frame extraction. SN Comput. Sci. **2**(2), 98 (2021). https://doi.org/10.1007/s42979-021-00495-x
21. Mitra, A., Singhal, A., Mohanty, S.P., Kougianos, E., Ray, C.: eCrop: a novel framework for automatic crop damage estimation in smart agriculture. SN Comput. Sci. **3**(4), 1–16 (2022)
22. Mohanty, S.P., Hughes, D.P., Salathé, M.: Using deep learning for image-based plant disease detection. Front. Plant Sci. **7** (2016). https://doi.org/10.3389/fpls.2016.01419. https://www.frontiersin.org/article/10.3389/fpls.2016.01419
23. Nagasubramanian, K., Jones, S., Singh, A.K., et al.: Plant disease identification using explainable 3D deep learning on hyperspectral images. Plant Methods **15**, 98 (2019). https://doi.org/10.1186/s13007-019-0479-8
24. Narmadha, R., Arulvadivu, G.: Detection and measurement of paddy leaf disease symptoms using image processing. In: Proceedings of the International Conference on Computer Communication and Informatics (ICCCI), pp. 1–4 (2017)
25. National Academies of Sciences, Engineering and Medicine and others: Science breakthroughs to advance food and agricultural research by 2030. National Academies Press (2019)
26. Ozguven, M.M., Adem, K.: Automatic detection and classification of leaf spot disease in sugar beet using deep learning algorithms. Physica A **535**, 122537 (2019)
27. Pallagani, V., Khandelwal, V., Chandra, B., Udutalapally, V., Das, D., Mohanty, S.P.: DCrop: a deep-learning based framework for accurate prediction of diseases of crops in smart agriculture. In: Proceedings of the IEEE International Symposium on Smart Electronic Systems (iSES), pp. 29–33 (2019)
28. Parikh, A., Raval, M.S., Parmar, C., Chaudhary, S.: Disease detection and severity estimation in cotton plant from unconstrained images. In: Proceedings of the IEEE International Conference on Data Science and Advanced Analytics (DSAA), pp. 594–601 (2016)
29. Rother, C., Kolmogorov, V., Blake, A.: "GrabCut": interactive foreground extraction using iterated graph cuts. ACM Trans. Graph. **23**(3), 309–314 (2004). https://doi.org/10.1145/1015706.1015720
30. Saleem, M.H., Khanchi, S., Potgieter, J., Arif, K.M.: Image-based plant disease identification by deep learning meta-architectures. Plants **9**(11) (2020). https://doi.org/10.3390/plants9111451. https://www.mdpi.com/2223-7747/9/11/1451
31. Singh, V., Misra, A.: Detection of plant leaf diseases using image segmentation and soft computing techniques. Inf. Process. Agric. **4**(1), 41–49 (2017)

32. Stevenson, J.A.: Plant Pathology: An Advanced Treatise. Horsfall, J.G., Dimond, A.E. (eds.), vol. 3. Academic Press, New York (1960)
33. Stewart, E.L., et al.: Quantitative phenotyping of Northern Leaf Blight in UAV images using deep learning. Remote Sens. **11**(19), 2209 (2019)
34. Sun, J., Yang, Y., He, X., Wu, X.: Northern maize leaf blight detection under complex field environment based on deep learning. IEEE Access **8**, 33679–33688 (2020)
35. Thenmozhi, K., Reddy, U.S.: Crop pest classification based on deep convolutional neural network and transfer learning. Comput. Electron. Agric. **164**, 104906 (2019)
36. Udutalapally, V., Mohanty, S.P., Pallagani, V., Khandelwal, V.: sCrop: a novel device for sustainable automatic disease prediction, crop selection, and irrigation in internet-of-agro-things for smart agriculture. IEEE Sens. J. (2020)
37. Wang, B.: Identification of crop diseases and insect pests based on deep learning. Sci. Program. **2022**, 10, Article ID 9179998 (2022). https://doi.org/10.1155/2022/9179998
38. Wiesner-Hanks, T., et al.: Millimeter-level plant disease detection from aerial photographs via deep learning and crowdsourced data. Front. Plant Sci. **10**, 1550 (2019)
39. Xavier, T.W.F., et al.: Identification of ramularia leaf blight cotton disease infection levels by multispectral, multiscale UAV imagery. Drones **3**(2) (2019). https://doi.org/10.3390/drones3020033. https://www.mdpi.com/2504-446X/3/2/33

PUFchain 3.0: Hardware-Assisted Distributed Ledger for Robust Authentication in the Internet of Medical Things

Venkata K. V. V. Bathalapalli[1], Saraju P. Mohanty[1(✉)] [iD], Elias Kougianos[2] [iD], Babu K. Baniya[3], and Bibhudutta Rout[4]

[1] Department of Computer Science and Engineering, University of North Texas, Denton, USA
VenkatakarthikvishnuvardBathalapalli@my.unt.edu,
saraju.mohanty@unt.edu
[2] Department of Electrical Engineering, University of North Texas, Denton, USA
elias.kougianos@unt.edu
[3] Department of Computer Science and Digital Technologies, Grambling State University, Grambling, USA
Baniyab@gram.edu
[4] Department of Physics, University of North Texas, Denton, USA
bibhudutta.rout@unt.edu

Abstract. This paper presents a Hardware-assisted security primitive that integrates Physically Unclonable Functions (PUF) and IOTA Tangle for device authentication in the Internet-of-Medical-Things (IoMT). The increasing market and scope for the IoMT is due to its potential in enhancing and improving the efficiency of health services across the globe. As the applicability of IoMT is increasing, various security vulnerabilities are surfacing and hindering its adoption. Device and data security are pivotal for Healthcare Cyber-Physical Systems (H-CPS) since a vulnerable working ecosystem in healthcare to various security attacks could risk the patient's lives. To ensure the authenticity of IoMT, the proposed security scheme uses Masked Authentication Messaging (MAM), which is the second level communication protocol for secure data storage, retrieval and sharing in IOTA Tangle. MAM works in three modes: Public, Private and Restricted. The proposed security primitive has been developed in *Restricted mode* for ensuring the utmost security by storing the PUF key of the IoMT in Tangle using MAM. PUFs are one of the most widely adopted hardware security primitives which work based on nanotechnology to build a secure fingerprint that guarantees the integrity of consumer electronic devices. For validating PUFchain 3.0, a strong arbiter PUF module, which supports higher number of Challenge Response Pairs (CRP), has been configured on two FPGA boards on both the IoMT and the edge server sides for validation. The proposed security scheme has taken less than 1 min to upload the transaction onto Tangle through MAM and less than 2 s to retrieve the data, which substantiates its robustness and potential for sustainable and secure Smart Healthcare.

Keywords: Internet-of-Medical-Things (IoMT) · Distributed Ledger Technology (DLT) · Physically Unclonable Function (PUF) · Hardware-Assisted Security (HAS) · Security-by-Design (SbD) · Masked Authentication Messaging (MAM) · Blockchain

ⓒ IFIP International Federation for Information Processing 2022
Published by Springer Nature Switzerland AG 2022
L. M. Camarinha-Matos et al. (Eds.): IFIPIoT 2022, IFIP AICT 665, pp. 23–40, 2022.
https://doi.org/10.1007/978-3-031-18872-5_2

1   Introduction

IoMT devices generate large amount of fragmented data for different applications in Smart Healthcare. These fragmented data are being used for various clinical experiments and research [21]. Wearable and implantable medical electronic devices are placed inside and on the body to monitor various physiological parameters and generate data for analysis which are processed in cloud and edge computing systems [11,16]. In order to address the privacy issues in smart healthcare, many researchers have adopted Distributed Ledger Technology (DLT) based solutions which provide immutability and confidentiality. Blockchain has been one of the most widely explored DLT for financial transactions since its inception in 2008 [18]. However, resource constrained IoT devices cannot sustain the computational resource requirements of blockchain. The IoT devices are vulnerable to various types of physical attacks where the authorized nodes can be replaced by the fake ones [5,19,24]. Authenticity of IoT devices at the Physical layer of H-CPS is also important, along with data confidentiality and privacy which can be addressed using PUFs. PUF-based security solutions can be embedded onto a chip and generate keys from the PUF design using process variations inside an Integrated Circuit (IC) [5,9,22] which can be used as security keys.

Using asymmetric keys for encryption and decryption of data can sometimes restrict access to medical professionals or patients. At the same time, a universal access key for encryption and decryption defeats the whole purpose of using security protocols. Hence a simple scalable approach for the authenticity of IoMT devices is needed [5]. PUFs do not require a database for key storage. The PUF keys can be generated instantly by taking advantage of micro manufacturing process variations [9,14,17,20]. Tangle is a DLT based solution which is a Directed Acyclic Graph (DAG) and has similar fundamental working principles as the Blockchain such as immutability, and irreversibility while being simple [2,27]. Tangle also addresses the fundamental challenges in Blockchain which have been hindering its application in resource constrained decentralized and distributed Fog and Edge computing systems. It does not require miner and transaction fees to validate a transaction and add it to the Tangle DAG.

The rest of the paper is organized in the following manner: Sect. 2 presents the novel contributions of this paper. Section 3 presents the security schemes and various DLT based security solutions in SC. Section 4 explains MAM and its working. The working flow of device authentication and transaction validation in the proposed PUFchain 3.0 is explained in Sect. 5. Section 6 outlines the implementation details and Sect. 7 presents the conclusion and directions for future research.

2   Novel Contributions

In motivation to propose a novel approach for sustainable cybersecurity in IoMT, we propose a device authentication method by including PUF key of IoMT inside IOTA Tangle using MAM which reduces the chance for its vulnerability to various kinds of security attacks. The broad overview of PUFchain 3.0 is illustrated in Fig. 1.

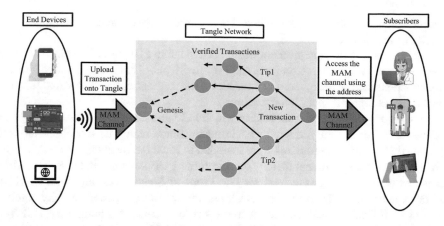

Fig. 1. Tangle DLT for a secure H-CPS using MAM.

The novel contributions of this paper include the following:

- Providing a minerless, low cost decentralized DLT for device authentication using PUFs and creating a secure channel for communicating IoMT data through MAM.
- A DLT that utilizes Proof of Work requiring minimal amount of computational resource requirements.
- A PUF based security approach where a PUF module can be integrated inside wearable and implantable IoMT devices and can generate a unique device fingerprint.
- A system that doesn't require transaction fees and allows secure communication through MAM.
- A robust multi level device authentication system for edge computing driven SC.
- A sustainable security solution which works in the Restricted mode of MAM where an authorization key is created to restrict unauthorized access to the MAM channel.

3   Related Research Overview

The success of Blockchain in financial transaction has increased its applicability in IoT based applications. However, the rate of transaction approval and time taken to append blocks in the Blockchain have driven researchers to explore the possibilities for other DLT based solutions that could address the aforementioned issues.

An approach for IoMT data sharing through Tangle was proposed [27] using MAM. Different sensors were interfaced with a Raspberry pi and the corresponding data was published in MAM restricted mode. This work however doesn't include a device authentication mechanism.

A scalable approach for integrating DLT with Blockchain was proposed [13] where IoT devices could be integrated with Tangle which could then connect to Blockchain in the backend through a connector node. In this approach, IoT devices have been classified as full and light nodes depending on their functionality. These devices can also function offline and upload transactions onto Tangle once they are approved by peers. Blockchain in this approach is proposed to be working in the cloud and IoT devices are integrated with Tangle through edge computing which reduces latency and facilitates data processing capability at the source. This method however does not emphasize the security of IoT devices.

A mutual authentication protocol was proposed using PUF and Blockchain for multi server systems using Smart Contracts and Proof of Work. This approach uses one-way hash functions and a fuzzy extractor for biometric authentication. However this approach requires high computational resources.

Authors in [8] proposed a method in which PUF and Blockchain have been linked together for IC traceability in supply chain management using the Inter Planetary File System (IPFS). Various protocols were included to trace the ownership of a chip using PUF key and smart contracts thereby storing these PUF keys in the IPFS. To address the issues with consensus mechanisms like Proof of Stake (PoS) and with an objective of exploring Blockchain technology's use for hardware assisted security, a robust Proof of PUF-Enabled Authentication consensus mechanism for integrating PUF with Blockchain was implemented in [18]. The result, PUFchain, works by authenticating the PUF key of the device and its properties before uploading the data onto a database.

Most of the aforementioned approaches for HAS are utilizing Blockchain protocols like PoW, PoS and Ethereum Smart Contracts. PoW is a computationally intensive consensus algorithm which requires block validators or miners to achieve a nonce value to validate a block of transactions.

Proof of Stake (PoS) on other hand is a stake-based block validation process where the miner having higher amount of stake most probably is delegated with the responsibility of validating the transaction. To address the above issues, a Proof of Quality of Service based DAGs-to-Blockchain (PoQDB) consensus mechanism was proposed in [3]. In this approach, the IoT devices can upload the data onto Cobweb ledger where each transaction is authenticated using digital signature algorithm. After uploading data in Cobweb using the MQ Telemetry Transport (MQTT) protocol, the Edge server will upload the JSON data onto the Blockchain. However using private and public keys for authentication makes this protocol vulnerable to network and spoofing attacks.

4   Tangle DLT

4.1   IOTA Tangle

Tangle is a DLT which is based on a DAG, where a transaction validates two previous transactions to become part of the network. As the number of incoming transactions increases, the transaction validation rate also increases. It is a No Block, No Miner and No Fee DLT technology that has the inherent functionality of Blockchain while being lightweight and scalable. The unverified transactions in the DAG are called 'Tips' [4]. The tips are selected based on a 'Markov Chain Monte Carlo (MCMC)' algorithm. The rate of approval of incoming transactions is defined by a Poisson point process where a predefined (λ) high controls the transaction approval simulation [4].

A coordinator node is responsible for selecting the unverified transactions and attaching them as tips to newly added transactions. The transactions are uploaded by clients onto Tangle through a coordinator node which performs Tip selection process for the incoming transaction to validate previous two transactions. Validating a Tip involves verifying balances of the respective transaction from a Tip by performing minimal PoW which does not require much computational capability as it does in Blockchain [12].

Each transaction in Tangle is associated with a cumulative weight (CW) which is the number of transactions approved by the subsequent nodes either directly or indirectly [23]. If a node in Tangle has a predefined initial weight of 1 then its CW will be the sum of its initial weight and the CW of all subsequent nodes in the DAG which have either directly or indirectly approved it.

The MCMC method performs a random walk from the genesis node which is the initial node of Tangle and propagates throughout the network until it reaches the node whose transaction has not been referenced and validated by the subsequent nodes. A minimal amount of PoW is done to counter spamming attacks in Tangle. The flow of device registration and authentication mechanisms in PUFchain 3.0 are shown in Figs. 2, and 3.

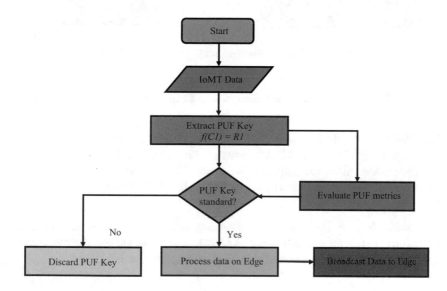

Fig. 2. Procedural flow of enrollment process in PUFchain 3.0

4.2   MAM Overview

MAM is one of the communication protocols for sending and receiving the encrypted information in Tangle through a channel by signing the message using the Merkle Hash Tree (MHT) signature algorithm. The message can be accessed by the receiver using the address of the channel. Whenever a new message of any length and size is uploaded on Tangle a channel is created and the receivers can immediately access the data using the root of the MHT [7, 10]. The transaction in MAM consists of the actual message and the MHT signature of the source [25]. MAM works mainly in three modes: Public,

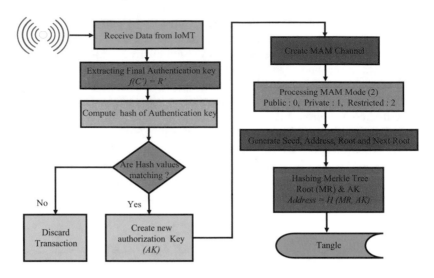

Fig. 3. Procedural flow of authentication process in PUFchain 3.0

Private and Restricted. The working flow of MAM in restricted mode is illustrated in Fig. 4.

Public Mode: In Public mode, the IoT device which is the source collects the data and uploads it onto Tangle. A MAM channel with an address is generated for secure exchange of information. The address of the channel will be the root of the Merkle Tree. The subsequent transaction has to be submitted to the MAM channel using this fetched root.

Private Mode: For applications requiring privacy and confidentiality, as in the case of health record management, the root of the Merkle tree is hashed and the obtained hash is used as the address of the channel to publish and access the data.

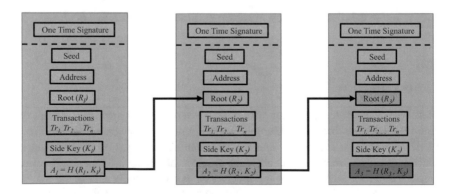

Fig. 4. Masked authentication messaging modes in restricted mode

Restricted Mode: The restricted mode of MAM works by using a channel *Authorization key* or *Side key* along with the Merkle root. The address of the channel for the next transaction is generated by computing the hash of the Merkle root and side key. The message subscriber's access to MAM channel is based on this combined hash value which is confidential and acts as a security layer for machine to machine communications using Tangle.

5   PUFchain 3.0: A Hardware Assisted Robust Authentication Mechanism Using Tangle

The main object of PUFchain 3.0 is to explore the potential of Tangle for hardware assisted security in SC to address the issues with existing device authentication mechanisms which require a non volatile memory to store the secret keys used for authentication. This system also proposes an approach where the conventional network communication protocols which are vulnerable to various types of spoofing attacks could be removed and the IoMT device embedded with a PUF module could connect to an edge server and access the MAM channel only after successful authentication.

Once the IoMT broadcasts the data, the edge server receives the data which contain its fingerprint and performs the authentication by extracting the PUF key and comparing it with the obtained one. If the authentication is successful, the PUF key of the device can be used as the side key for the MAM channel. The edge server creates the MAM channel and uploads the data onto the MAM channel whose address is generated using the side key and the root of the Merkle tree.

Once the transaction is uploaded onto Tangle, a new root is created which will be specific for that channel and a particular client can upload the data in subsequent transactions using the new fetched root.

Each transaction in MAM has a reference address to the next one. The reference address will change based on the working MAM mode. The side key could be changed at any point of time if the secrecy of the side key is anticipated to be compromised [2,7]. The whole transaction in PUFchain 3.0 works in MAM restricted mode where the MAM channel could be accessed using an authentication key based on PUF along with the hash of the root of Merkle Tree [2,6].

5.1   PUF Overview

PUFs can be defined as fingerprint generating functions for electronic devices. PUFs are developed based on intrinsic manufacturing variations during chip fabrication. The stability of these parameters for ICs changes based on the location, temperature and the materials used. PUFs have been classified as *Strong* or *Weak* depending on the configuration. Arbiter PUF, Ring Oscillator PUF and Butterfly PUF are most widely used PUFs due to their power and speed optimized designs. The Arbiter PUF design is delay based, developed to create a PUF key using the micro manufacturing variations associated with wiring between the electronic components in an IC [15].

5.2   Working of Proposed PUFchain 3.0

Device Registration Phase:
In the registration phase, the IoMT device embedded with the PUF module is tested with different challenge response pairs (CRP) and figures of merit of the PUF are evaluated. Table 1 presents the notation used in the proposed PUFchain 3.0. Strong and reliable PUF keys were selected and a random challenge input is tested on the PUF module embedded with the IoMT, and the corresponding PUF key is considered as its fingerprint. The micro controller connected to the client broadcasts the PUF data to Edge server (ES). The working flow of the Enrollment process in PUFchain 3.0 is illustrated in Algorithms 1, 2, and Fig. 5.

Step 1: Initially a PUF key for the challenge input C_{IN1} is extracted. The obtained PUF Key $R1$ from the PUF module of IoMT device PUF_{MID} is evaluated to compute PUF metrics. If 100% reliability is achieved, then P_{MID} is assigned as fingerprint of end IoMT device and broadcast to ES.

Step 2: As soon as it receives the broadcasted PUF key P_{MID} from the IoMT device, the ES extracts a PUF key by giving a challenge input C_{IN2} for the PUF module PUF_{MED} attached on its side and extracts P_{MED}.

Step 3: An exclusive OR (XOR) operation is performed on both the received and extracted PUF keys P_{MID}, P_{MED}. The XOR ed output P_{XOR} is broadcast back to the IoMT as a challenge input C_{IN3} on the client side. The IoMT device receives the input and performs key extraction. The obtained key R_{OUT2} is broadcast back as a challenge input C to the ES.

Step 4: The ES finally computes the SHA-256 Hash (H) of the obtained final PUF key R_{KOUT} for the corresponding input from IoMT. The obtained final hash value H_D is stored in a secure database.

Algorithm 1: 1st level Enrollment Process of PUFchain 3.0

Input: PUF key extraction from PUF module connected to IoMT client
Output: Reliable secure fingerprint for IoMT device to establish secure communication
         with Edge Server
1 Random C_{IN} generation for testing the PUF module.
2 Test the PUF module and perform PUF key extraction
   `// ` $PUF_{MID} \rightarrow f(C_{IN}) = R_{OUT}$
3 Perform PUF metric evaluation.
   `// Calculate Uniqueness, Reliability, Inter-HD & Intra-HD`
4 **if** *PUF keys R_{OUT} are standard* **then**
5 | $P_{MID} \rightarrow R_{OUT}$
   | `// PUF Key is assigned as pseudo identity of the Client`
6 Edge Gateway(EG) connected to IoMT stores the corresponding Key in secure database
   `// ` $P_{MID} \rightarrow$ EG

Table 1. Notations

Notation	Description
PUF_{MID}	PUF module on IoMT Side
PUF_{MED}	PUF module on Edge Server side
C_{IN}	Random Challenge Inputs
C_{IN1}	1st Challenge Input
C_{IN2}	2nd Challenge Input
R_{OUT}	Response Output from PUF module while testing
R_{KOUT}	Response Output from PUF module on ES side
$R_{KOUT'}$	Response Output from PUF module on ES side during authentication
R_{OUT2}	Response Output from PUF module on IoMT side during Enrollment
$R_{OUT2'}$	Response Output from PUF module on IoMT side during authentication
P_{XOR}	XOR ed output during enrollment
$P_{XOR'}$	XOR ed output during authentication
$P_{MID'}$	Pseudo identity of IoMT device (PUF Key) during authentication
$P_{MED'}$	Pseudo identity of Edge Server (PUF Key) during authentication
R_{KOUT}	Final Authentication key during enrollment
$R_{KOUT'}$	Final Authentication key during authentication
$\oplus$	XOR
A_K	Side Key
R_K	Merkle root
H	SHA-256 Hash Function
H_D	Hash output value during Registration
H_A	Hash output value during Authentication
A_M	New fetched root

Device Authentication Phase:

Once the IoMT is authenticated, the ES uploads the entire transaction process details in Tangle. The working flow of the authentication process and transaction update in the MAM channel are presented in Algorithm 3 and Fig. 6.

Step 1: Cryptographic identity of IoMT is verified by performing the PUF key extraction on both End device and ES side from their associated PUF modules.

Step 2: Challenge inputs (C_{IN1}, C_{IN2}) obtained during enrollment are retrieved from the database and given to two PUF modules.

Step 3: The obtained PUF keys ($P_{MID'}$, $P_{MED'}$) are evaluated and XOR ed. The output $C_{IN3'}$ is given as input to PUF on IoMT.

Step 4: The obtained $R_{OUT2'}$ is again tested on the PUF at ES and obtained final key $R_{KOUT'}$ is hashed. Attained hash value H_A is compared with the retrieved H_D.

Step 5: Once the device authentication is considered as successful by the ES, it creates a MAM channel to upload the transaction and fetch the address and broadcast it to the authenticated client to upload its data.

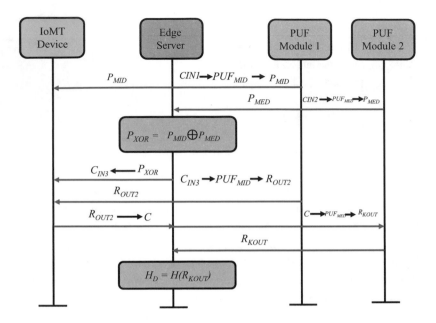

Fig. 5. Processing flow of device enrollment in PUFchain 3.0

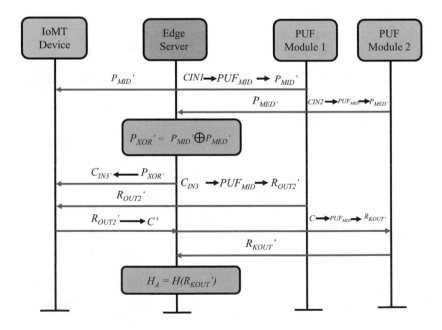

Fig. 6. Processing Flow of Device Authentication in PUFchain 3.0

Algorithm 2: 2nd Level Enrollment process of PUFchain 3.0

---

1 Edge Server (ES) receives PUF key from IoMT Client
   `// Selects a challenge input from` C_{IN}
   `//` $C_{IN} \rightarrow C_{IN2}$
   `//` $P_{MID} \rightarrow$ `ES`
2 ES Performs PUF key extraction from PUF module
   `//` $C_{IN2} \rightarrow R_{OUTED}$
3 ES performs PUF metric evaluation
4 **if** *Reliability of* R_{OUTED} *==100%* **then**
5 $\quad$ $R_{OUTED} \rightarrow PUF_{ED}$
6 $\quad$ f$(C_{IN2}) \rightarrow PUF_{ED}$
7 $\quad$ $PUF_{ED} \rightarrow P_{MED}$
8 Perform XOR Operation
   `//` $P_{XOR} \rightarrow P_{MID} \oplus P_{MED}$
9 ES sends XOR ed output as 2nd Challenge input to IoMT
   `//` $\text{ES} \rightarrow P_{XOR} \rightarrow \text{IoMT}$
10 IoMT gives corresponding XOR ed value as challenge input to its associated PUF module
   `//` $\text{IoMT} \rightarrow P_{XOR} \rightarrow PUF_{MID}$
11 IoMT extracts response output for XOR ed Challenge Input
   `//` $PUF_{MID} \rightarrow \text{f}(C_{IN2}) \rightarrow R_{OUT2}$
12 IoMT sends PUF key as input to Edge Server
13 Edge performs PUF key extraction for the obtained input
   `//` $PUF_{MED} \rightarrow \text{f}(R_{OUT2}) \rightarrow R_{KOUT}$
14 SHA-256 hash function is used to compute hash on the obtained final authentication key
   `//` $\text{Hash} \rightarrow \text{H}(R_{KOUT}) \rightarrow H_D$
15 Store the Hash value along with initial challenge inputs in a SDB
   `//` $H_D, C_{IN1}, C_{IN2} \rightarrow \text{SDB}$

Step 6: The working mode of MAM is specified as '2' which is the restricted mode. An authorization key or side key A_K is created.

Step 7: The authorization key A_K for the MAM channel in the proposed security protocol is predefined as "MYKEY"

Step 8: Once the MAM channel is created, an API link is obtained and broadcast for the working nodes in H-CPS to view the MAM channel.

Step 9: Finally, hashing is performed on the root of the transaction R_K and A_K of the MAM channel to fetch the address (A_M) for the subsequent transaction. The new side key is defined as P_{MID} of IoMT.

Step 10: The subsequent transaction address (A_M) is broadcast back to the authenticated IoMT end device to upload.

The working mode of MAM is specified as "Restricted (2)". The secret key for the MAM is a predefined one which could be changed at any time depending on the security requirements.

Algorithm 3: Authentication process of PUFchain 3.0

---

1 ES extracts challenge inputs from Secure Database
   // SDB$\rightarrow C_{IN1}, C_{IN2}$
2 IoMT and ES perform key extractions
   // $C_{IN1} \rightarrow PUF_{MID} \rightarrow P_{MID'}$
   // $C_{IN2} \rightarrow PUF_{MED} \rightarrow P_{MED'}$
3 Perform XOR operation and corresponding PUF key extractions
   // $P_{XOR'} \rightarrow PUF_{MID'} \oplus \rightarrow P_{MED'}$
4 Obtain final authentication key
   // $PUF_{MED} \rightarrow R_{KOUT'}$
5 Compute hash on obtained final authentication key
   // Hash$\rightarrow$H$(R_{KOUT'}) \rightarrow H_A$
6 **if** $H_A == H_D$ **then**
7 | Device Authentication is successful
8 | Create MAM channel
9 | Assign authorization key
   | // MAM Channel$\rightarrow A_K$
   | // MAM Mode $\rightarrow$Restricted (2)
10 | Upload Pseudo Identity of IoMT and ES
   | // $P_{MID} \rightarrow$ Streams v0 (Channel)
11 | Fetch Next root
   | // MAM Channel $\rightarrow$New Root(N_R)
12 | Perform hash on side key and root
   | // $A_M \rightarrow$H(A_K, R_K)
13 | Broadcast New fetched root and new side key P_{MID}
14 **else**
15 | Discard the transaction
16 | Go to Step 1 for the new Transaction

---

6 Implementation and Validation

The proposed PUFchain 3.0 security is implemented using the Chrysalis version of IOTA Tangle. STREAMS is a new feature of Tangle which introduces new security features to improve the working ecosystem of Tangle by including cryptographic features [7]. The MAM channel used for this implementation has been STREAMS v0 channel. The working code MAM in Tangle is given in [1]. The time taken to upload a transaction into Tangle will be the total time taken for *Tip Selection, Transaction validation*. This is much shorter than the time taken to perform block addition in PoW which is 10 min [18]. The sample outputs of PUFchain 3.0 are given in Fig. 7.

The Single Board Computers (SBC) are connected to PUF modules built on two Xilinx FPGAs for PUF key extraction as, shown in Fig. 8.

An Arbiter PUF is embedded on two Xilinx FPGA boards which are connected to Raspberry pi boards through pmod ports. Baud rate of 9600 is used to extract PUF keys

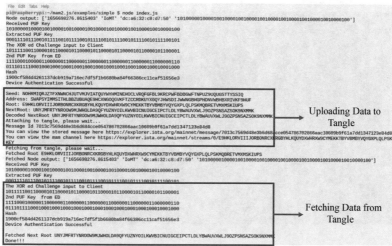

(a) Authentication and Transaction validation outputs

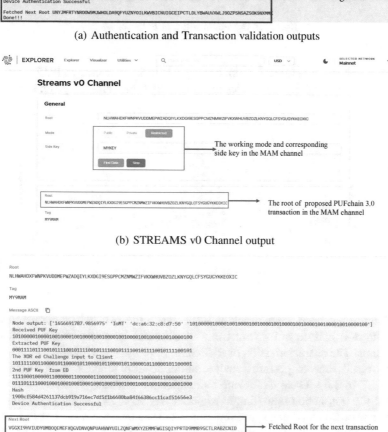

(b) STREAMS v0 Channel output

(c) Fetching Outputs from MAM channel

Fig. 7. Validation of PUFchain 3.0 in Tangle API

Fig. 8. Experimental setup of PUFchain 3.0

from the Raspberry pis. Overall uniqueness of PUF keys from two PUF modules has been approximately 50%. The metrics of Arbiter PUF modules are given in Figs. 9 and 10.

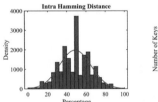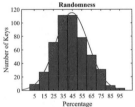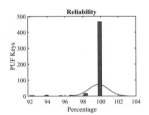

Fig. 9. Figure of Merits of 1st PUF module

Reliability has been approximately 100% when the two PUF modules have been tested with 500 PUF keys for four times at different instances of time and varying temperatures. The characterization of PUFchain 3.0 is given in Table 2.

The overall time to perform device authentication process in PUFchain 3.0 is between 2.7 to 3.6 s. Once the device authentication is done, the average time taken to upload the transaction onto Tangle Mainnet has been 28 s while the mean time to fetch the transaction has been approximately 1 s. The tabulated results of PUFchain 3.0 are given in Table 3 and comparative analysis of PUFchain 3.0 with the state of the art research is given in Table 4.

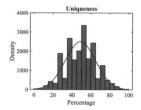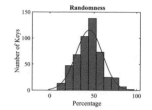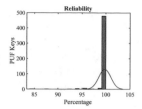

Fig. 10. Figure of Merits of 2nd PUF module

Table 2. Characterization of PUFchain 3.0

Parameters	Results
Application	Smart Healthcare
DLT	IOTA Tangle
Communication Protocol	MAM
PUF Module	Arbiter PUF
Programming	JavaScript, Verilog, Python
Working Mode	Restricted
IOTA Network	Mainnet
Number of PUFs	2
PUF	xc7a35tcpg236-1
Edge Server	Single Board Computer

Table 3. Metrics evaluation of PUFchain 3.0

PUFchain 3.0 Serial No.	Time taken to fetch MAM transaction (sec)	Time to perform Device Authentication (sec)	Time to taken to upload transaction in Tangle network (sec)
1	1.073	3.66	17.31
2	1.266	3.66	19.91
3	1.288	3.66	13.60
4	0.914	3.28	6.18
5	1.288	3.18	58.40
6	1.057	3.72	55.61
7	1.213	3.32	28.54
8	1.12	3.04	32.0
9	1.235	2.96	19.9
10	1.099	2.72	31

Table 4. Comparison with state of the art research

Research Works	Security Protocol	DLT	Area	Approach	Security Primitive
Chaudhary et al. [8]	Auto-PUFchain	IPFS	IC Traceability	Smart Contracts	HAS
Al-Joboury and Al-Hemiary [3]	PoQDB	Blockchain and Cobweb	IoT	MQTT	Data Security
Wang et.al [26]	Blockchain and PUF-Based based Authentication Protocol	Blockchain	Smart Healthcare	Smart Contracts	HAS
Hellani et al. [13]	Tangle the Blockchain	Blockchain and Tangle	IoT	Smart Contracts	Data Security
Bathalapalli et al. [5]	PUFchain 2.0	Blockchain	Smart Healthcare	Proof-of-PUF Enabled Authentication	HAS
PUFchain 3.0 (Current Paper)	**PUFchain 3.0**	IOTA Tangle	Smart Healthcare	MAM	HAS

7   Conclusions

Smart Healthcare is converging various technological solutions to enhance the quality of healthcare systems around the world. Various security solutions are being proposed to address the security vulnerabilities and realize the true potential of the IoMT, which constitutes an important part in H-CPS. This paper proposed and validated a sustainable security approach for device authentication and data confidentiality by utilizing PUF and IOTA Tangle. IOTA Tangle is becoming an alternative for Blockchain in IoT applications which are resource constrained decentralized systems due to its capability in offering a robust security for data as the Blockchain while being *'Miner and Transaction Free'*. By integrating PUF with Tangle, the device integrity can be ensured since each device fingerprint is stored in a DLT. A robust security protocol for device authentication has been implemented and stored in Tangle using MAM in restricted mode. The time taken to upload and retrieve the transaction in PUFchain 3.0 has been well within 1 min which is almost 10× times faster than the PoW consensus mechanism in Blockchain.

Exploring the possibility for a scalable Blockchain based consensus mechanism using PUF and IOTA Tangle to achieve the objective of SbD could be a direction for future research.

References

1. IOTA Foundation. iotaledger. mam.js (2021). https://github.com/iotaledger/mam.js
2. Abdullah, S., Arshad, J., Khan, M.M., Alazab, M., Salah, K.: PRISED tangle: a privacy-aware framework for smart healthcare data sharing using IOTA tangle. Complex Intell. Syst. (2022). https://doi.org/10.1007/s40747-021-00610-8
3. Al-Joboury, I.M., Al-Hemiary, E.H.: A permissioned consensus algorithm based DAGs-to-blockchain in hierarchical architecture for decentralized internet of things. In: Proceedings International Symposium on Networks, Computers and Communications (ISNCC), pp. 1–6 (2021). https://doi.org/10.1109/ISNCC52172.2021.9615865
4. Alshaikhli, M., Elfouly, T., Elharrouss, O., Mohamed, A., Ottakath, N.: Evolution of internet of things from blockchain to IOTA: a survey. IEEE Access 10, 844–866 (2022). https://doi.org/10.1109/ACCESS.2021.3138353
5. Bathalapalli, V.K.V.V., Mohanty, S.P., Kougianos, E., Baniya, B.K., Rout, B.: PUFchain 2.0: hardware-assisted robust blockchain for sustainable simultaneous device and data security in smart healthcare. SN Comput. Sci. 3(5), 1–19 (2022). https://doi.org/10.1007/s42979-022-01238-2
6. Bhandary, M., Parmar, M., Ambawade, D.: A blockchain solution based on directed acyclic graph for IoT data security using IoTA tangle. In: Proceedings 5th International Conference on Communication and Electronics Systems (ICCES). IEEE (2020). https://doi.org/10.1109/icces48766.2020.9137858
7. Carelli, A., Palmieri, A., Vilei, A., Castanier, F., Vesco, A.: Enabling secure data exchange through the IOTA tangle for IoT constrained devices. Sensors 22(4), 1384 (2022). https://doi.org/10.3390/s22041384
8. Chaudhary, C.K., Chatterjee, U., Mukhopadhayay, D.: Auto-PUFChain: an automated inter-action tool for PUFs and blockchain in electronic supply chain. In: Proceedings Asian Hardware Oriented Security and Trust Symposium (AsianHOST), pp. 1–4 (2021). https://doi.org/10.1109/AsianHOST53231.2021.9699720
9. Dey, K., Kule, M., Rahaman, H.: PUF based hardware security: a review. In: Proceedings International Symposium on Devices, Circuits and Systems (ISDCS), pp. 1–6 (2021). https://doi.org/10.1109/ISDCS52006.2021.9397896
10. Gangwani, P., Perez-Pons, A., Bhardwaj, T., Upadhyay, H., Joshi, S., Lagos, L.: Securing environmental IoT data using masked authentication messaging protocol in a DAG-based blockchain: IOTA tangle. Future Internet 13(12), 312 (2021). https://doi.org/10.3390/fi13120312
11. Ghubaish, A., Salman, T., Zolanvari, M., Unal, D., Al-Ali, A., Jain, R.: Recent advances in the internet-of-medical-things (IoMT) systems security. IEEE Internet Things J. 8(11), 8707–8718 (2021). https://doi.org/10.1109/jiot.2020.3045653
12. Guo, F., Xiao, X., Hecker, A., Dustdar, S.: Characterizing IOTA tangle with empirical data. In: Proceedings IEEE Global Communications Conference GLOBECOM. IEEE (2020). https://doi.org/10.1109/globecom42002.2020.9322220
13. Hellani, H., Sliman, L., Samhat, A.E., Exposito, E.: Tangle the blockchain: towards connecting blockchain and DAG. In: Proceedings of the IEEE 30th International Conference on Enabling Technologies: Infrastructure for Collaborative Enterprises (WETICE), pp. 63–68 (2021). https://doi.org/10.1109/WETICE53228.2021.00023

14. Hori, Y., Yoshida, T., Katashita, T., Satoh, A.: Quantitative and statistical performance evaluation of arbiter physical unclonable functions on FPGAs. In: Proceedings of the International Conference on Reconfigurable Computing and FPGAs, pp. 298–303. RECONFIG
2010, IEEE Computer Society (2010). https://doi.org/10.1109/ReConFig.2010.24
15. Joshi, S., Mohanty, S.P., Kougianos, E.: Everything you wanted to know about PUFs. IEEE
Potentials **36**(6), 38–46 (2017). https://doi.org/10.1109/MPOT.2015.2490261
16. Koutras, D., Stergiopoulos, G., Dasaklis, T., Kotzanikolaou, P., Glynos, D., Douligeris, C.:
Security in IoMT communications: a survey. Sensors **20**(17), 4828 (2020). https://doi.org/
10.3390/s20174828, https://www.mdpi.com/1424-8220/20/17/4828
17. Lee, Y.S., Lee, H.J., Alasaarela, E.: Mutual authentication in wireless body sensor networks
(WBSN) based on physical unclonable function (PUF). In: Proceedings of the 9th International Wireless Communications and Mobile Computing Conference (IWCMC), pp. 1314–
1318 (2013). https://doi.org/10.1109/IWCMC.2013.6583746
18. Mohanty, S.P., Yanambaka, V.P., Kougianos, E., Puthal, D.: PUFchain: Hardware-Assisted
Blockchain for Sustainable Simultaneous Device and Data Security in the Internet of Everything (IoE) (2019). 10.48550/ARXIV.1909.06496
19. Pelekoudas-Oikonomou, F., et al.: Blockchain-based security mechanisms for IoMT edge
networks in IoMT-based healthcare monitoring systems. Sensors **22**(7), 2449 (2022). https://
doi.org/10.3390/s22072449
20. Pescador, F., Mohanty, S.P.: Guest editorial security-by-design for electronic systems. IEEE
Trans. Consum. Electron. **68**(1), 2–4 (2022). https://doi.org/10.1109/TCE.2022.3147005
21. Marshal, R., Gobinath, K., Rao, V.V.: Proactive measures to mitigate cyber security challenges in IoT based smart healthcare networks. In: Proceedings of the IEEE International
IOT, Electronics and Mechatronics Conference (IEMTRONICS). IEEE (2021). https://doi.
org/10.1109/iemtronics52119.2021.9422615
22. Razdan, S., Sharma, S.: Internet of medical things (IoMT): overview, emerging technologies,
and case studies. IETE Tech. Rev. (2021). https://doi.org/10.1080/02564602.2021.1927863
23. Shabandri, B., Maheshwari, P.: Enhancing IoT security and privacy using distributed ledgers
with IOTA and the tangle. In: Proceedings of the 6th International Conference on Signal
Processing and Integrated Networks (SPIN), pp. 1069–1075 (2019). https://doi.org/10.1109/
SPIN.2019.8711591
24. Shi, S., Luo, M., Wen, Y., Wang, L., He, D.: A blockchain-based user authentication scheme
with access control for telehealth systems. Secur. Commun. Netw. **2022**, 1–18 (2022). https://
doi.org/10.1155/2022/6735003
25. Silvano, W.F., De Michele, D., Trauth, D., Marcelino, R.: IoT sensors integrated with the distributed protocol IOTA/Tangle: Bosch XDK110 use case. In: Proceedings of the X Brazilian
Symposium on Computing Systems Engineering (SBESC), pp. 1–8 (2020). https://doi.org/
10.1109/SBESC51047.2020.9277865
26. Wang, W., et al.: Blockchain and PUF-based lightweight authentication protocol for wireless
medical sensor networks. IEEE Internet Things J. **9**(11), 8883–8891 (2022). https://doi.org/
10.1109/JIOT.2021.3117762
27. Zheng, X., Sun, S., Mukkamala, R.R., Vatrapu, R., Meré, J.B.O.: Accelerating health data
sharing: a solution based on the internet of things and distributed ledger technologies. J. Med.
Internet Res. **21** (2019)

On the Optimization of LoRaWAN Gateway Placement in Wide Area Monitoring Systems

Bruno Mendes[1]([⊠]) [iD], Noélia Correia[1,2] [iD], and Dário Passos[1] [iD]

[1] CEOT, University of Algarve, Faro, Portugal
{bemendes,ncorreia,dmpassos}@ualg.pt
[2] FCT, Campus de Gambelas, 8005-189 Faro, Portugal

Abstract. LoRaWAN-based wide area monitoring systems may use non-stationary LoRaWAN gateway devices to collect sensor data. In these cases, the most suitable locations for gateways must be found, while taking into account the scarcity of radio resources and energy consumption. In this paper an optimization model is proposed that aims to address this problem. The model ensures that power drain on the most critical devices is minimised fairly, considering an amount of packets to be delivered, and can be used to plan changes of gateway locations periodically, so that the network lifetime is extended. Results show that the optimization model and proposed pipeline are adequate for the planning of wide area monitoring where in the long-run different devices will be communicating in parallel, with the same gateway or different gateways, and sharing the spectrum. The approach can also be used to anticipate any gateway rearrangement need to ensure the extension of the lifetime of the network.

Keywords: Internet of Things · LoRaWAN · Energy saving

1 Introduction

The Internet of Things (IoT) refers to the interconnection of smart devices, and low power wide area network (LPWAN) technologies are now considered a promising platform for the creation of large scale IoT applications (e.g., smart cities, smart agriculture), enabling low bit rate wireless connections covering long distances with minimum power consumption [10,15]. One of these technology is LoRaWAN that operates in the unlicensed frequency band, so that end users are free to build LoRa-based architectures similar to house-owned WiFi routers. This freedom will certainly contribute to the emergence of new IoT applications.

The large-scale deployment of LPWAN for IoT brings many challenges because radio resources are scarce and their management becomes very challenging in practical networks. Therefore, procedures for an efficient and dynamic

© IFIP International Federation for Information Processing 2022
Published by Springer Nature Switzerland AG 2022
L. M. Camarinha-Matos et al. (Eds.): IFIPIoT 2022, IFIP AICT 665, pp. 41–51, 2022.
https://doi.org/10.1007/978-3-031-18872-5_3

management of resources become necessary. In the case of LoRaWAN networks, an adaptive data rate (ADR) mechanism is available that dynamically assigns transmission parameters to the end nodes [8]. In general, the lifespan of the battery and throughput depends on the time on air (ToA), which defines the time required for a packet to travel between an end-device and the gateway, and transmission power (TP). The transmission duty cycle (TDC), defined as the maximum time during which an end-device can access the channel per hour, is also a key constraint in such networks [2]. Such limitation applies also to gateways, and ends up limiting the number of updating packets a gateway can disseminate per hour. This means that a gateway can be prevented from updating all end devices, and global network optimizers should take this limitation into account. A gateway updating packet consumes 2–3 s.

LoRa-based wide area monitoring systems have been proposed in many fields (e.g., tree farms [3,16]). In such deployments, coverage can be ensured by mobile LoRaWAN gateway devices that collect data from sensors located at longer distances, as in [7]. In these cases, an additional problem that needs to be solved is to find the most suitable locations for gateways, and determine when and how to move them for efficient data collection, given the energy consumption at the devices. Here in this article, the LoRa gateway placement problem is addressed and the goal is to assign gateways to places in a way that energy depletion at critical devices is fairly minimized. Although the developed optimization model is able to solve any instance of the problem, our final goal is to move to a real deployment (an orchard, more specifically). Therefore, all information required by the optimization model (in order to make its decisions) was extracted from a simulation developed in OMNet Flora, where the implemented environment conditions and device energy models are similar to the real deployment ones. This way gateway placement (and adequate number of gateways) can be decided before going into the field.

More clearly, the contributions of this article include:

- Mathematical optimization model of the LoRa gateway placement problem, having as goal the fair minimization of energy depletion at critical devices.
- Validation of the optimization model using realistic information extracted from a deployment simulation model developed in OMNet Flora.

The remainder of this article is organized as follows. Section 2 discusses work related with LoRa placement and applications similar to ours. Section 3 introduces some required definitions and formulates the gateway placement problem. Section 4 discusses the steps involved in obtaining the results, and performs an analysis of these. Section 5 draws conclusions and presents future work.

2   Related Work

Mobile LoRaWAN gateways are considered in applications like agriculture, wildlife monitoring and livestock applications where data has to be collected and/or productivity improved, as in [7,9]. In these works in particular, a single mobile gateway is considered and the authors show that it can be a more cost effective choice than using multiple static gateways. These studies do not address the gateway placement planning issue, and do not consider multiple gateways.

Regarding the data collection problem, in [18] it is assumed that gateways are not always available, so devices need to perform local data buffering. The problem of multiple devices having to deliver a larger number of packets, upon gateway availability, is addressed. To avoid bursts of collisions and expedite data collection, a time-slotted transmission scheduling mechanism is proposed. In [17], an offline heuristic approach is proposed to find time-slotted schedules. Information like the number of devices and their spreading factor (SF) is assumed to be known. In contrast to the just mentioned works, an online approach is proposed in [1] where partial knowledge is assumed. This allows the algorithm to adapt to dynamic changes, such as topology changes. This is achieved at the expense of higher energy consumption and longer data collection time than the offline approach. In [4,19], the problem of collecting data using a single SF is addressed. The goal of the SF optimization problem is to maximize the success probability given an amount of data per node and a maximum data collection time window.

The gateway placement problem in LoRa networks was initially addressed in [12], where it is shown to be NP-Hard. The goal is to maximize the average energy efficiency of the network by placing as few gateways as possible. However, this approach does not consider the energy depletion at critical devices, and solutions lead to reduced network lifetime. A LoRaWAN gateway placement model for dynamic IoT scenarios is proposed in [11]. The approach is to group IoT devices when placing gateways, so that each gateway can serve a group of devices. The assessment of the most critical device among such devices, and therefore network lifetime extention is not addressed.

In this work the placement of gateways is done so that the energy depletion at the most critical devices (one per resulting gateway coverage) is fairly minimized. To the best of the authors' knowledge and bibliographic search this is being addressed for the first time.

3   Problem Statement

3.1   Definitions and Notation

Definition 1 (LoRa Bit Rate). *LoRa modulation uses chirp spread spectrum signals to modulate data. The spreading factor determines the number of chirps contained in each symbol, given by 2^{SF}. Therefore, $\frac{BW}{2^{SF}}$, where BW is the bandwidth, gives the symbol rate. Since the number of raw bits that can be encoded by a symbol is SF, and given a coding rate CR, the useful bit rate for a given SF will be $R_{SF} = SF \times \frac{BW}{2^{SF}} \times CR$.*

The bandwidth (BW) in LoRa can be 125 kHz, 250 kHz or 500 kHz.

Definition 2 (Transmission Duty Cycle - TDC). *Ratio of the cumulated sum of transmission times per observation period. The maximum duty cycle ends up being the maximum percentage of time during which an end device can occupy a channel, per hour.*

Definition 3 (Packet Reception Ratio - PRR). *Probability of correct package reception, at a gateway $g \in \mathcal{G}$, assuming an average signal to noise ratio (SNR) for a particular distance between a device $d \in \mathcal{D}$ and the gateway, and assuming a certain SF for transmission.*

Besides the PRR, a no collision probability is also considered by many authors, as in [14]. The traditional ALOHA is usually the underlying medium access protocol.

Definition 4 (Feasible Spreading Factors). *A spreading factor belongs to the set of feasible spreading factors of device $d \in \mathcal{D}$ for communication with location l, denoted by $\mathcal{S}_d^l$, if and only if it can be used for d to communicate with location $l \in \bigcup_{\{g \in \mathcal{G}\}} \mathcal{L}^g$.*

Definition 5 (Most Critical Device). *Assuming $\mathcal{L}^g$ to be the set of possible locations for a gateway $g \in \mathcal{G}$, the most critical device in the coverage area of $g \in \mathcal{G}$, when placed in location $l \in \mathcal{L}^g$, is given by $\Delta_g^l = \arg\max_{d \in \mathcal{C}_g^l} \{B_d^l\}$, where B_d^l is the relative battery consumption of device $d \in \mathcal{D}$ when sending a packet to location l, and $\mathcal{C}_g^l = \{d \in \mathcal{D} : R_{d,s^*}^l \times PRR_{d,s^*}^l \times N_{d,s^*}^l \geq R_{d,s'^*}^{l'} \times PRR_{d,s'^*}^{l'} \times N_{d,s'^*}^{l'}, \forall l' \neq l\}$ is the set of devices that are expected to adjust their SF to s^* (optimal SF) for communication with gateway g at location l.*

The R_{d,s^*}^l, PRR_{d,s^*}^l and N_{d,s^*}^l are the bit rate, PRR and the no-collision probability when device d is communicating to location l using SF s^*, the optimal SF assigned by the ADR mechanism.

Definition 6 (LoRa Gateway Placement Problem - LGP Problem). *Given a set of end node devices $\mathcal{D}$ and a set of gateways $\mathcal{G}$, find the places for gateways that lead to a **fair minimization of energy depletion** in critical devices (considering a set of packets to be sent) while also ensuring that: i) all devices are covered and; ii) device transmission does not violate the TDC. More formally, let us assume that $\chi^U = \{\chi_1, \chi_2, ..., \chi_{|\chi^U|}\}$ is the universe set of all feasible gateway-place assignments. Let us also consider a cost function $f : \chi^U \to \Re^+$ defined by:*

$$f(\chi_i) = \arg\max_{<g,l> \in \chi_i} \{ \frac{P_{\Delta_g^l} \times L_{\Delta_g^l}}{R_{\Delta_g^l,s^*}^l \times PRR_{\Delta_g^l,s^*}^l \times N_{\Delta_g^l,s^*}^l} \times B_d^l \} \qquad (1)$$

where P_d is the number of packets per TDC to be sent by device d, L_d is the average packet length, and the device being considered is the most critical one. Then the most energetically fair gateway placement is given by:

$$\chi_i^* = \arg\min_{\chi_i \in \chi^U}\{f(\chi_i)\} \tag{2}$$

A gateway-place assignment is considered to be feasible if all devices are covered and no device transmission violates the TDC.

That is, from all possible gateway-place assignments, the one that provides the lowest upper bound on depletions at critical devices is the one that should be selected.

3.2 LGP Problem Formulation

Let us assume the following known information:

$\mathcal{D}$ Set of LoRa communicating devices, where $d \in \mathcal{D}$ denotes a specific device.

$\mathcal{G}$ Set of available LoRa gateways, where $g \in \mathcal{G}$ denotes a specific gateway.

B_d^l Relative battery consumption of device $d \in \mathcal{D}$, when communicating with a gateway at location $l \in \bigcup_{\{g \in \mathcal{G}\}} \mathcal{L}^g$, considering the time required for the transmission of all packets; $0 \leq B_d^l \leq 1$.

$\mathcal{S}$ Set of SF-CR configurations, where $s \in \mathcal{S}$ denotes a specific configuration.

$\mathcal{L}^g$ Set of possible locations for gateway $g \in \mathcal{G}$.

C_l Set of covered devices when location $l \in \bigcup_{\{g \in \mathcal{G}\}} \mathcal{L}^g$ is in use.

$\mathcal{S}_d^l$ Set of SFs that can be used for device $d \in \mathcal{D}$ to communicate with a gateway in location $l \in \bigcup_{\{g \in \mathcal{G}\}} \mathcal{L}^g$, $\mathcal{S}_d^l \subseteq \mathcal{S}$.

Let us also consider the following variables:

σ_d^l One if device $d \in \mathcal{D}$ is communicating with location $l \in \bigcup_{\{g \in \mathcal{G}\}} \mathcal{L}^g$; zero otherwise.

$\varphi_d^{g,l}$ One if $d \in \mathcal{D}$ is the most critical device, from all devices covered by gateway $g \in \mathcal{G}$ placed at location $l \in \mathcal{L}^g$; zero otherwise.

$\phi^{g,l}$ One if gateway $g \in \mathcal{G}$ is to be placed at location $l \in \mathcal{L}^g$; zero otherwise.

Π Most difficult transmission conditions among all critical devices (upper bound).

The LGP problem can be solved using the following objective function:

– Objective function:

$$\text{Minimize } \Pi \tag{3}$$

The following set of constraints must be fulfilled:

– Allocation of gateways to places and covering of all devices:

$$\sum_{\{l \in \mathcal{L}^g\}} \phi^{g,l} = 1, \forall g \in \mathcal{G} \tag{4}$$

$$\sum_{\{g \in \mathcal{G}\}} \sum_{\{l \in \mathcal{L}^g : d \in C_l\}} \sigma_d^l = 1, \forall d \in \mathcal{D} \tag{5}$$

$$\sigma_d^l \leq \sum_{\{g \in \mathcal{G} : l \in \mathcal{L}^g\}} \phi^{g,l}, \forall d \in \mathcal{D}, \forall l \in \bigcup_{\{g \in \mathcal{G}\}} \mathcal{L}^g : d \in C_l \tag{6}$$

$$(R_{d,s*}^l \times PRR_{d,s*}^l \times N_{d,s*}^l) \times \sigma_d^l \geq$$
$$\geq (R_{d,s'*}^{l'} \times PRR_{d,s'*}^{l'} \times N_{d,s'*}^{l'}) - \Theta \times (1 - \sigma_d^l),$$
$$\forall d \in \mathcal{D}, \forall l, l' \in \bigcup_{\{g \in \mathcal{G}\}} \mathcal{L}^g : d \in C_l \wedge d \in C_{l'} \tag{7}$$

where Θ is a big value, required for constraints to hold true regardless of the gateway location a device is communicating with. Constraints (4) place gateways at one of the allowed locations, Constraints (5) ensure that all devices are covered. Constraints (6) ensures that communication with a location occurs only if there is a gateway placed in there. Constraints (7) ensure that devices communicate with the gateway location providing the best conditions.

– Most critical device depletion:

$$\sum_{\{d \in \mathcal{D} : d \in C_l\}} \varphi_d^{g,l} = \phi^{g,l}, \forall g \in \mathcal{G}, \forall l \in \mathcal{L}^g \tag{8}$$

$$\varphi_d^{g,l} \leq \sigma_d^l, \forall g \in \mathcal{G}, \forall l \in \mathcal{L}^g, \forall d \in \mathcal{D} \tag{9}$$

$$B_d^l \times \varphi_d^{g,l} \geq B_{d'}^l \times \sigma_{d'}^l - \Theta \times (1 - \varphi_d^{g,l}),$$
$$, \forall g \in \mathcal{G}, l \in \mathcal{L}^g, \forall d, d' \in C_l \tag{10}$$

where Θ is a big value, required for constraints to hold true regardless of a node being considered critical or not, which must hold in mathematical optimization models. Constraints (8) and (9) determine the critical device per gateway cover, while Constraints (10) ensure that it is the one with higher relative energy consumption.

$$\Pi \geq \varphi_d^{g,l} \times \frac{P_d \times L_d}{R_{d,s*}^l \times PRR_{d,s*}^l \times N_{d,s*}^l} \times B_d^l,$$
$$\forall g \in \mathcal{G}, l \in \mathcal{L}^g, \forall d \in \mathcal{D} \tag{11}$$

Constraints (11) determine the most difficult transmission conditions among all critical devices.

– Non-negativity assignment to variables:

$$\varphi_d^{g,l}, \phi^{g,l}, \sigma_d^l \in \{0,1\}; \Pi \in \Re^+. \tag{12}$$

This optimization model can be solved using packages like CPLEX or Gurobi, [5,6], which find the optimal solution given an instance of the problem. Other approaches, such as genetic algorithms and meta-heuristic algorithms, do not guarantee that the optimal solution is obtained, although they are faster to execute. Since the LGP can be planned offline, and since there is no strict time frame for completion, an optimisation model ensuring an optimal solution is preferred.

4   Analysis of Results

The architecture implemented follows the one proposed by the LoRa Alliance. The network has a star-of-stars topology where gateways work as intermediary points between devices and the central network server, allowing for bidirectional communication between these end points. The real deployment is an orchard (Fig. 1) with the following characteristics:

– Orange grove of 45.6-hectares of square-shaped field with 25 sensing devices;
– Orange trees are equally spaced, each having off-the-shelf temperature and luminosity sensors, mounted inside the tree's canopy, to evaluate de impact of local conditions on fruit development;
– Each device is 150 m horizontally and 190 m vertically away from each other

The simulation model developed in OMNet Flora, for the just mentioned real deployment, consideres:

– 2 gateways and 5 different feasible locations for both gateways.
– Oulu path loss model, using $n = 2.32$, $B = 128.95$, $\sigma = 7.8$ and antenna gain of -4.15dB, similarly to [13].
– ADR algorithm for SF optimization;
– Energy model provided by Flora, following values in Table 1.

The first step is to use the simulation model to collect R_{d,s^*}^l, PRR_{d,s^*}^l and N_{d,s^*}^l, which depend on path loss conditions, and B_d^l, resulting from the energy model in use, $\forall l \in \bigcup_{\{g \in \mathcal{G}\}} \mathcal{L}^g$ and $\forall d \in \mathcal{D}$. This is input information to the optimization model. Such characterization of transmission conditions and energy consumption, from every device towards every possible gateway location, is done considering the transmission of 10000 packets per device.

The next stage is to determine the optimal gateway placement given by the mathematical optimization model, and then run the simulation considering the placement of gateways found by the optimization model. Results are compared against other placements. Table 2 summarizes the obtained results, where the placement resulting from the optimization model (and impact of that choice) is

Table 1. Flora Energy Consumption Model.

Mode	Power Consumption (W)
Off	0
Sleep	0.001
Switching	0.002
Receiver, idle	0.002
Receiver, busy	0.005
Receiver, receiving	0.01
Receiver, receiving preamble	0.01
Receiver, receiving header	0.01
Receiver, receiving data	0.01
Transmitter, idle	0.002
Transmitter, transmitting	0.1
Transmitter, transmitting preamble	0.1
Transmitter, transmitting header	0.1
Transmitter, transmitting data	0.1

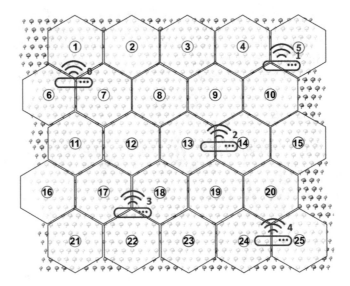

Fig. 1. Schematic representation of the gateways and end node locations.

displayed in bold. Results were similar for a coverage cutoff of 0% (all devices covered by all gateway locations, when in use) and 10% (a device not able to transmit at least 10% of its packets, towards a given gateway location, is considered uncovered).

Table 2. Energy Consumption per Packet (2 GWs).

Gateways positions	Energy Consumption Packet Data Rate			
	Average	Standard Deviation	Lowest	Largest
0 1	0,41	0,23	0,073	0,86
0 2	0,25	0,12	0,07	0,62
0 3	**0,28**	**0,13**	**0,08**	**0,53**
0 4	0,29	0,13	0,08	0,56
1 2	0,29	0,16	0,07	0,70
1 3	0,27	0,14	0,07	0,53
1 4	0,39	0,20	0,07	0,73
2 3	0,28	0,17	0,07	0,66
2 4	0,36	0,21	0,07	0,87
3 4	0,40	0,25	0,08	0,96

Devices end up transmitting a different amount of packets, and for this reason we cannot look at energy consumption in an isolated way. For this reason the results regarding energy consumption per packet are the ones included in Table 2. Results show that the optimization model ends up being capable of finding the best places for gateways, when compared with other possible locations. This is because it was able to select one of the gateway positioning combinations presenting the lowest value in the "Largest" column, meaning that the worst energy consumption per packet is minimized. This solution is one of the fairest solutions because minimizing such upper bound (worst energy consumption) ends up balancing energy consumption among devices, extending network lifetime. The average energy consumption per packet is also one of the lowest, ensuring energy saving in general.

These results allows us to conclude that basing the decision on the most critical nodes, one per coveraged range, and make placements that lead to the minimization of the most difficult transmission conditions among critical devices, is adequate for such kind of deployment where in the long-run different devices will be communicating in parallel, with the same gateway or different gateways, and sharing the spectrum. Any attempt to minimise the sum of device's energy consumption, or maximize the overall throughput, would not be appropriate in this context.

5   Conclusions and Future Work

In this article the LoRa gateway placement problem is addressed and an optimization model is developed that assigns gateways to places in a way that energy depletion at critical devices is fairly minimized. Results show that the optimization model and proposed pipeline are adequate for the planning of LoRaWANs, in particular for wide area monitoring systems requiring multiple gateways, which is a step that should precede any deployment. Planning is done offline, for any real scenario, and applied when appropriate, allowing prior validation of gateways placement. Such pipeline can also be used to anticipate any gateway rearrangement need to ensure the extension of the lifetime of the network, being only required to change the input information. Future work will address the scheduling of gateway rearrangements. More specifically, given an existing deployment, determining when it becomes necessary to carry out a new gateway rearrangement and how to do it without service disruption is an issue that needs to be addressed.

Acknowledgment. This work was supported by FCT (Foundation for Science and Technology) from Portugal within CEOT's (Center for Electronic, Optoelectronic and Telecommunications) UIDB/00631/2020 CEOT BASE and UIDP/00631/2020 CEOT PROGRAMÁTICO projects.

References

1. Abdelfadeel, K.Q., Zorbas, D., Cionca, V., Pesch, D.: Free - fine-grained scheduling for reliable and energy efficient data collection in LoRaWAN (2018). 10.48550/ARXIV.1812.05744, https://arxiv.org/abs/1812.05744
2. Adelantado, F., Vilajosana, X., Tuset-Peiro, P., Martinez, B., Melià-Seguí, J., Watteyne, T.: Understanding the limits of LoRaWAN. IEEE Commun. Mag. **55**, 34–40 (2017). https://doi.org/10.1109/MCOM.2017.1600613
3. B. Mendes, D. Passos, N.C.: Coverage characterization of LoRaWAN sensor networks for citrus orchard monitoring. In: International Young Engineers Forum on Electrical and Computer Engineering (2022)
4. Carvalho, R., Al-Tam, F., Correia, N.: Q-learning ADR agent for LoRaWAN optimization. In: 2021 IEEE International Conference on Industry 4.0, Artificial Intelligence, and Communications Technology (IAICT), pp. 104–108 (2021). https://doi.org/10.1109/IAICT52856.2021.9532518
5. Cplex, I.I.: V12. 1: User's manual for CPLEX. Int. Bus. Mach. Corporation **46**(53), 157 (2009)
6. Gurobi Optimization, LLC: Gurobi Optimizer Reference Manual (2022). https://www.gurobi.com
7. Gutiérrez, S., Martínez, I., Varona, J., Cardona, M., Ricardo, E.: Smart mobile LoRa agriculture system based on internet of things. In: 2019 IEEE 39th Central America and Panama Convention (CONCAPAN XXXIX), pp. 1–6 (2019). https://doi.org/10.1109/CONCAPANXXXIX47272.2019.8977109
8. Hauser, V., Hégr, T.: Proposal of adaptive data rate algorithm for LoRaWAN-based infrastructure. In: 2017 IEEE 5th International Conference on Future Internet of Things and Cloud (FiCloud), pp. 85–90 (2017). https://doi.org/10.1109/FiCloud.2017.47
9. Ikhsan, M.G., Saputro, M.Y.A., Arji, D.A., Harwahyu, R., Sari, R.F.: Mobile LoRa gateway for smart livestock monitoring system. In: 2018 IEEE International Conference on Internet of Things and Intelligence System (IOTAIS), pp. 46–51 (2018). https://doi.org/10.1109/IOTAIS.2018.8600842

10. Li, Y., Yang, J., Wang, J.: Dylora: towards energy efficient dynamic LoRa transmission control. In: IEEE INFOCOM 2020 - IEEE Conference on Computer Communications, pp. 2312–2320 (2020). https://doi.org/10.1109/INFOCOM41043.2020.9155407

11. Matni, N., Moraes, J., Oliveira, H.M., Rosário, D., Cerqueira, E.: LoRaWAN gateway placement model for dynamic internet of things scenarios. Sensors **20**, 4336 (2020). https://doi.org/10.3390/s20154336

12. Ousat, B., Ghaderi, M.: Lora network planning: gateway placement and device configuration. In: 2019 IEEE International Congress on Internet of Things (ICIOT), pp. 25–32 (2019). https://doi.org/10.1109/ICIOT.2019.00017

13. Petajajarvi, J., Mikhaylov, K., Roivainen, A., Hanninen, T., Pettissalo, M.: On the coverage of LPWANS: range evaluation and channel attenuation model for LoRa technology. In: 2015 14th International Conference on ITS Telecommunications (ITST), pp. 55–59 (2015). https://doi.org/10.1109/ITST.2015.7377400

14. Sandoval, R., Garcia-Sanchez, A.J., Garcia-Haro, J.: Optimizing and updating LoRa communication parameters: a machine learning approach. IEEE Trans. Netw. Serv. Manage. **16**(3), 884–895(2019). https://doi.org/10.1109/TNSM.2019.2927759

15. Song, Y., Lin, J., Tang, M., Dong, S.: An internet of energy things based on wireless LPWAN. Engineering **3**(4), 460–466 (2017). https://doi.org/10.1016/J.ENG.2017.04.011

16. Yim, D., et al.: An experimental LoRa performance evaluation in tree farm. In: 2018 IEEE Sensors Applications Symposium (SAS), pp. 1–6 (2018). https://doi.org/10.1109/SAS.2018.8336764

17. Zorbas, D., Abdelfadeel, K.Q., Cionca, V., Pesch, D., O'Flynn, B.: Offline scheduling algorithms for time-slotted LoRa-based bulk data transmission. In: 2019 IEEE 5th World Forum on Internet of Things (WF-IoT), pp. 949–954 (2019). https://doi.org/10.1109/WF-IoT.2019.8767277

18. Zorbas, D., Caillouet, C., Abdelfadeel Hassan, K., Pesch, D.: Optimal data collection time in LoRa networks-a time-slotted approach. Sensors **21**(4) (2021). https://doi.org/10.3390/s21041193,https://www.mdpi.com/1424-8220/21/4/1193

19. Zorbas, D., Maillé, P., O'Flynn, B., Douligeris, C.: Fast and reliable lora-based data transmissions. In: 2019 IEEE Symposium on Computers and Communications (ISCC). pp. 1–6 (2019). https://doi.org/10.1109/ISCC47284.2019.8969766

Agri-Aid: An Automated and Continuous Farmer Health Monitoring System Using IoMT

Laavanya Rachakonda[✉][ID]

Department of Computer Science, University of North Carolina Wilmington,
Wilmington, NC, USA
rachakondal@uncw.edu

Abstract. Along with smart infrastructures, smart institutions and smart services, having smart and healthy people is also a key component of smart villages. There are number of applications and tools that are designed to monitor the growth of the crop but there are little to none to monitor the health of the farmers. Healthcare is not a luxury and it should be accessible to everyone. With that said, Agri-Aid is an automated system that continuously monitors the physiological, vital, environmental and location based features which have a direct or indirect relationship on farmer's health. This device will analyze the features and will let the user understand and allow them to make small changes in the process of farming. When in the case of severe threat to life, the Agri-Aid will connect to doctors automatically for immediate care. Agri-Aid is designed in the IoMT framework and an accuracy of approximately 98% is observed.

Keywords: Smart healthcare · Healthcare Cyber-Physical System (H-CPS) · Internet of Medical Things (IoMT) · Farmer health · Farmer fatigue · Heat strokes · Pesticide exposure · Visually impaired · Hearing impairment · IoT-Edge Computing

1 Introduction

In any given economy, agriculture plays a very critical role. It is the foundation of the successful system for an entire life of an economy. Along with the food production and raw supplies, agriculture enhances the economic growth by creating various job opportunities. In 2020 in the United States, among 19.7 million jobs related to agriculture and food sectors, 2.6 million jobs were accounted for farmers i.e., 1.4% of 10.3% of total employment [43]. The total number of farms in the world is approximately 570 million and there are roughly 500 million people whose livelihood is derived from farming [22].

While approximately 44% of the farmers are poisoned by pesticides every year, heat stroke is considered as the leading cause of death among farmers [6]. According to Center for Disease Control and Prevention, the death rate for farmers is 20% higher than the rest of the civilians in US alone [27].

While the technological industry is set on pace to exceed $5.3 trillion in 2022 [26] and the wearable technology market is projected to reach $380.5 billion by 2028

© IFIP International Federation for Information Processing 2022
Published by Springer Nature Switzerland AG 2022
L. M. Camarinha-Matos et al. (Eds.): IFIPIoT 2022, IFIP AICT 665, pp. 52–67, 2022.
https://doi.org/10.1007/978-3-031-18872-5_4

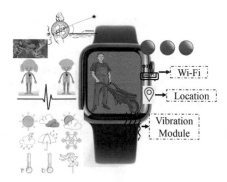

Fig. 1. Device prototype of the proposed Agri-Aid system.

Fig. 2. Proposed Agri-Aid system in the edge computing paradigm.

[11], there have not been many advancements in agricultural sector especially targeting farmer health.

A comparison study reveals that farming can have an effect on the health status of the farmers [10]. Thus, Agri-Aid, a fully automated continuous monitoring IoMT based device is proposed to monitor the vital, weather and geographical parameters of the farmers to detect and predict fatigue, health hazards and exposures to pesticides among them. The device prototype of the proposed Agri-Aid is represented in the Fig. 1.

Agri-Aid is a state-of-the-art Edge computing device in IoMT framework. IoT can be defined as a network of things where each thing in the network is connected and is the capable of transferring information with a unique IP address upon need [35]. When the same fundamentals are applied to medical things and healthcare domains, IoT is termed as Internet of Medical Things (IoMT) [33]. IoMT framework can be observed in Smart Healthcare [32,36], Smart Transportation, Smart cities, etc., [34]

A distributed computing paradigm otherwise known as edge computing has been used here in Agri-Aid as shown in Fig. 2. Such computing paradigm allows the data processing and analyses to be done at the source or at the user end. Real time data processing, bandwidth utilization reduction, lower network traffic, increase in the efficiency, security and privacy of the devices with the reduction in the costs are few among the other advantages of adapting Edge computing [15].

The organization of the paper is as follows: Sect. 2 discusses the motivation behind this research. Section 3 provides the state-of-the-art literature. Section 4 describes how Agri-Aid bridges the gap from the state-of-the-art research. Section 5 discusses the wide range of features both vital and environmental and their significant impact on the farmer health. Section 6 provides a flow of the concept followed by the feature extraction from the discussed parameters. Section 7 describes the working flow of the proposed Agri-Aid system. Section 8 comprises of the ML implementation of the modal and edge implementation of the same. A brief comparison followed by conclusions and future directions are provided in Sect. 9.

2 Motivation Behind the Proposed Agri-Aid System

Study indicates that only a small portion between 7% to 11% of the hired farmers have health insurance provided by the employer [44]. Healthcare services are expensive and not everyone can afford it. Reaching for help and accessing the desired help can be major issues depending upon the location of the farm. Most of the farmers face death because of the lack of knowledge on the side effects of exposure to pesticides or heat strokes. Thus the need for a system to not only monitor the vital signals of the farmers but also to educate about the possible health hazards has become important.

3 Related Prior Research

With the focus being on crop growth and the productivity of agriculture in general, farmer health monitoring and tracking is very much neglected. There are many state-of-the-art literature's and market ready devices for crop growth monitoring but there are no products and little to none literature that focused on unified farmer health monitoring.

With longer exposure of pesticides, regular health checkups especially vision and cardiopulmonary care are very important. There are studies which observe the impact on vitals focusing on pesticide poisoning and have conducted studies with the farmers exposed to certain chemicals to farmers who were not exposed to the same chemicals [8, 25].

The official statistical data on pesticide poisoning in the country is considered under-estimated as only 2% of the cases are reported to the formal health centers [1]. Better quality pesticides may reduce the impact on farmers. Study indicates that the farmers are willing to pay 28% more than what they are currently paying towards pesticides for better health [13].

Health awareness campaigns for the farmers showed the improvements in the symptoms for chronic pesticide poisoning in farmers [41].

The mood and physical activity of the person can determine the mental health of a person. With the early diagnosis of the mental health, the rate of suicides in farmers can be reduced [24].

Older farmer health monitoring plays a very important role as a study shows that in a fatality data of 7064 deaths, over half of the deaths are accounted as older farmers between 1992 and 2004 [28].

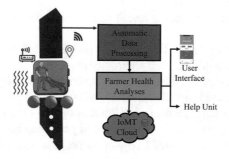

Fig. 3. Broad perspective of the proposed Agri-Aid system.

A study shows that even though most of the farmers are not well educated and have very little knowledge on the technology, with promoting protective eye-wear and training, farmers have experienced effectiveness and comfort with their regular chores [12].

Few questionnaire based approaches have been proposed to analyze the health of the farmers. An automatic risk detection system is proposed which takes the answers from the farmers to certain questions based on the farming practices and generates the risk percentage of the pesticide exposure [23].

There are few worker health monitoring mechanisms that are presented by monitoring the gait parameters, respiration parameters and heat stress of the farmer [3,7]. However, these mechanisms lack an easy access, lack of considering various parameters that effect the health of the farmer.

3.1 Major Issues with the Existing Solutions

Some of the major issues with the existing solutions are discussed below:

- For the farmer health or worker health monitoring, no unified detection is performed as various other physiological, weather and geographical parameters are not considered.
- Real time data processing is never provided.
- Farmers are required to self diagnose the situation and are required to ask for help instead of accessing the help.
- No wearable devices are proposed, thus not taking the complete advantage of the technological capabilities.
- Affordability, reachability and accessibility to the farmers has been neglected.

With this, having Agri-Aid, a wearable or a system to continuously monitor the health of the farmer can be helpful. The broad perspective of Agri-Aid is represented in Fig. 3.

4 Novel Contributions and Issues Addressed Through Agri-Aid

The novel contributions and the issues that are addressed through Agri-Aid are listed below.

- For the farmer health or worker health monitoring, complete unified detection is performed.
- Precautionary methods and notifications are provided to farmers to eliminate excessive exposure to pesticide induced environments.
- Precautionary and timely notifications are provided depending upon the various features that are considered (detail discussion in Sect. 6).
- Real time data analyses is performed at the user end by incorporating Edge computing thus eliminating the delay in the process of providing help.
- The response system is designed in a way to provide care for visually impaired or hearing impaired farmers.
- Along with the regular vital analyses, special analyses is performed for older working adults and for farmers with disabilities.
- A wearable is proposed which allows the farmers to educate, understand and improve their lifestyles.

5   Various Parameters Considered for Farmer Health in Agri-Aid

There are wide range of parameters and life style habits that have an impact on farmer health [30]. Some of the considered features are classified into three categories in Agri-Aid. They are:

5.1   Vital and Physiological Parameters

Eyes and Vision Issues. With prolonged exposure to these pesticides, chronic eye irritations may be developed [38]. This in long term can diminish visual activity. For farmers who are exposed to these pesticides had a probability of 0.53 to get diagnosed with chronic eye issues [30].

Skin Issues. Depending on the method of farming practice, skin contamination varies. Hands and forearms are highly contaminated leading to skin thickening and accentuated markings in the long term [48]. The probability of farmers who are exposed to herbicides and other harmful pesticides to get skin issues was 0.50 [30].

Respiratory Effects. Long term exposure to harmful chemicals can cause respiratory tract issues like cough, cold, rales, tenderness and decreased chest expansion, etc.,. Smoking increases the probability of having respiratory tract infections by 50% [29, 38].

Cardiovascular Issues. Blood hardening is the common issue observed in farmers who practice spraying the pesticides which causes high blood pressure [38].

Gastrointestinal Issues. Pesticides are usually entered into the gastrointestinal tract through mouth. Prolonged intake can cause nausea, vomiting and diarrhea [38].

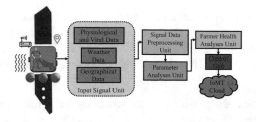

Fig. 4. Architectural flow of the proposed Agri-Aid system.

Neurological Issues. Prolonged exposure to pesticides and pesticide residue environments can lead to nerve numbness [38]. Excessive intake of pesticide residue by any means can also cause motor weakness.

5.2 Weather and Geographical Parameters

High temperatures, heavy UV radiation, wind speeds, wind directions, location, position and angel of the sun, sudden rains, air humidity, air quality, pollen percentage are few of the many factors that can affect the health of the farmer [4].

6 Architectural Flow and Feature Extraction for Farmer Health in Agri-Aid

The architectural flow of the proposed Agri-Aid is represented in Fig. 4.

In this system, features from the mentioned parameters (Sect. 5) are extracted.

6.1 Physiological and Vital Sensor Data Unit

The features which are extracted as sensor signal data from the vital and physiological parameters as mentioned in Sect. 5.1 are discussed in this section. As heat strokes are the major reasons for deaths in farmers as discussed in Sect. 1, the direct and indirect relationship with the physiological and vital signal data to heat strokes is also considered.

Body Temperature. Prolonged exposure to sun and pesticide induced environments can cause irritations and rise in human body temperature. The temperature quickly raises to 106° F or higher within 10 to 15 min. In general, the normal body temperature is considered in the ranges of 97° F to 99° F while temperature higher than 100° F is considered as fever [9].

Humidity. In extreme heat exposure, there will be no sweat discharge. Body becomes hot and dry to touch [16]. The ideal and normal range for humidity in the human body is between 30 to 50% and anything greater than 60% is considered unhealthy [37].

Respiration Rate. Due to extreme heat, as the temperature of the body increases and causes dehydration, the nasal passage, bronchial tubes and lungs may dry out which leads to shortness of breathe. The normal and healthy respiration rate per minute is considered in the range 12 to 16 and anything lower than 12 is considered harmful [42].

Heart Rate. For every degree rise in the human body temperature, the heart beats about 10 beats faster per minute. So when the body is experiencing heat stroke or prolonged exposure of heat, the heart rate significantly rises. A normal resting heart rate is in the range from 60 to 100 beats per minute. When working in farm, farmers should expect an average healthy range from 80 to 157 beats per minutes for ages across 35 to 60 [45].

Loss of Consciousness (Coma). When farmers are exposed to prolonged sun exposure and chemicals from pesticides, the physiological signals inside the human body alter leading to falls, which causes loss of consciousness. So in order to monitor the state of consciousness, the following parameters are considered along with the above discussed data. A detailed explanation of the below discussed signal data is available in [36].

- **Gait** Gait is the pattern a person walks in [40]. With the motor weakness and heat, the coordination of the human body maybe disturbed causing a lag between the movement of legs which can result in falling [31].
- **Twisting** Falls may occur when a balance loss happens when a person's body orients in a different direction than the position of the feet [47]. Accelerometer and gyroscope are used to monitor gait and twisting.
- **Blood Sugar Levels** Sugar levels below 70mg/dL increases the chances of falls by increasing the weakness and older adults may feel anxious, shaky, tiredness and may suffer strokes [14].
- **Blood Oxygen Saturation Levels** If the oxygen saturation levels are lowered due to heat, then farmers may experience breathing issues, asthma, low heart rate and unconsciousness. SpO_2 levels ranging from 95% to 100% are healthy normal in adults [17].

6.2   Weather and Environmental Signal Data Unit

The relative humidity of the surroundings is monitored. The growth and residues of pesticides and chemicals including bacteria and viruses along with the exposure to respiratory tract infections is observed high when the relative humidity is less than 40% and greater than 60% [2]. The ideal outdoor temperature is $75 - 85°$ F, the side effects from the pesticides and exposure to heat starts gradually increasing from $90 - 105°$ F and when the temperature is in the range of 105–130° F, the individuals are advised to stay indoors for protection [46]. If the location of the farm is elevated when compared to the sea level, the sun's radiation, direct light and UV exposure increases [18]. The solar radiation and intensity is observed higher closer to equator [19]. The ideal wind speed ranges from 1.2 to 4mph while 4–6mph is considered a little risky and higher than 6mph is considered danger to spray pesticides [5].

6.3 Geographical Signal Data

The GPS location of the farm and farmer are considered. With this a detailed analyses on the location with respect to altitude, natural calamities, the type of crop that is usually grown, livestock type and population, nearby factories and industries is obtained. A prediction of the productivity of the farm is derived to monitor the mental health of the farmer.

6.4 Parameter Analysis Unit

The detailed representation of the mentioned parameters is shown in Table 1.

Table 1. Parameter range descriptions for farmer health in Agri-Aid.

Wind Speed	Out Temp	HRV	Sugar Levels	SpO$_2$ Levels	Acc	RH	Time	Dust Flow	Air	Body Temp	Body Humidity	Resp Rate	Result
1.2–4 mph	70–85°F	60–90 bpm	70–80 mg/dL	>90	<±3g on Y axes	<40 and >60	8-10AM & 4-7PM	low	No	96–97°F	20–30%	12–16 bpm	No danger
4–6 mph	90–105°F	90–95 bpm	50–70 mg/dL	90–95	>±3g on Y axes	<40 and >60	10-12PM & 2-4PM	med	No	97–98°F	30–40%	12–16 bpm	No danger, plan to take a break
6–9 mph	105–130°F	95–105 bpm	30–70 mg/dL	80–90	>±3g on Y axes	<40 and >60	12–2 PM	high	Yes	98–102°F	40–55%	10–12 bpm	Possible weakness and illness
>9mph	>130°F	>105 bpm	<30 mg/dL or >160 mg/dL	<80	>±3g on Y axes	<40 and >60	12–2 PM	high	Yes	>103°F	>60%	<10 bpm	Heat stroke and illness

From the above gathered signal data, heat index temperature and wet bulb globe temperature score are calculated. These metrics are very important as they also help in analyzing the environmental conditions of the location.

Heat Index. The heat index is a temperature that is obtained by combining temperature and relative humidity in the shaded areas. This value may be much less when compared to the outdoor temperatures as it is predicting the temperatures in shaded areas. The formula to calculate the heat index is denoted in the Eq. 1 [39].

$$HeatIndex(HI) = c1 + c2T + c3R + c4TRH +$$
$$c5T^2 + c6RH^2 + c7T^2RH + c8TRH^2 + c9T^2RH^2 \tag{1}$$

where, T is the ambient temperature in °F, RH is the relative humidity and c1 through c9 are constants; c1 = -42.379, c2 = -2.04901523, c3 = -10.14333127, c4 = -0.22475541, c5 = -71.3783, c6 = -0.05481717, c7 = -0.00122874, c8 = 0.00085282, c9 = -0.00000199.

Wet Bulb Global Temperature. $WBGT$ is a measure of heat stress that is calculated in direct sunlight. This $WBGT$ can be given more credibility than HI as this is calculated under direct sunlight. The formula that is used to calculate $WBGT$ is represented in Eq. 2 [21].

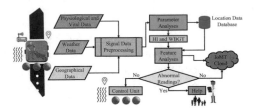

Fig. 5. Working flow of the proposed design in Agri-Aid system.

$$WBGT = 0.7T_w + 0.2T_g + 0.1\,T \tag{2}$$

here, T is the outdoor temperature in °C, Tg is the global thermometer temperature in °C and Tw is the wet bulb temperature in °C. The formula to calculate Tw is given in Eq. 3.

$$Tw = T * arctan[v1 * (RH + v2)^{(1/2)}] + arctan(T + RH)$$
$$- arctan(RH - v3) + v4 * (RH)^{(3/2)} * arctan(v5 * RH) - v6 \tag{3}$$

where T is the temperature in °C, RH is relative humidity and v1 through v6 are constants; v1 = 0.151977, v2= 8.313659, v3=1.676331, v4=0.00391838 , v5=0.023101, v6=4.686035.

6.5 Farmer Health Analyses and Control Unit

Depending on the feature analyses from the above mentioned parameters, the health and wellness of the farmers is analyzed. The inhalation of pesticides, exposure to the pesticide residue environments and exposure to direct sunlight are the main scenarios that are monitored through Agri-Aid system. If the analyzed scenarios produce dangerous outcomes the call for help is automatically made. In healthy outcomes, there are continuous reminders sent to the person to consume water and seek shelter or to rest for a while. If the outcomes do not indicate heat stroke but indicate a possible fall which may be lead to the state of unconsciousness, control mechanisms are provided. The system is provided with a buzzer, LED and a vibration module so that the farmer will get the message even in loud disturbing environments. Continuous monitoring of the vitals will not only help analyze and keep track of the well-being of the farmers but any abnormality in the patterns can be used to detect and predict underlying diseases.

7 Design Flow of the Proposed Agri-Aid for Farmer Health Analyses

The design flow of the proposed Agri-Aid system has been represented in the Fig. 5.

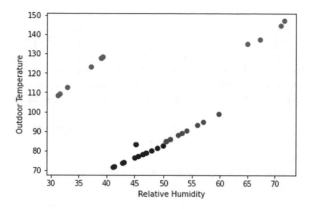

Fig. 6. Scattered plot of some of the features deployed in Agri-Aid system.

The data from the input unit is processed and analyzed. After the required features are extracted, the featured data is compared using the parameter ranges mentioned in Table 1. The design flow of the Agri-Aid System is also represented through an Algorithm 1.

8   Implementation and Validation for Farmer Health Analyses in Agri-Aid

8.1   Signal Data Acquisition

For the geolocational of the farm, a dataset which has the latitudes and longitude information of every country in the world along with the 50 states in the United States is obtained. This data was useful to analyze the solar radiation and the air quality which also includes the wind speed and direction. Alongside, a total of 3500 data samples with respect to the climatic changes were also obtained from open source websites. For the training and testing implemented in Agri-Aid, the parameter ranges from Table 1 is also considered.

8.2   Machine Learning Model for Training and Testing in Agri-Aid System

For the machine learning model, a total number of 9000 samples were used. Out of these, 8000 are used for training while 1000 are used for testing the model. The model had 4 labels- Caution, Extreme Caution, Danger and Extreme Danger and 13 features as mentioned in the Sect. 5. The scattered plot of few features considered in Agri-Aid are shown in Fig. 6.

A classification model has been deployed in Agri-Aid system with a linear stack of layers with 13 layers in the input layer, four dense layers with 25 neurons in each and 4 nodes in the output layer. Rectified linear and sigmoid functions are used as activation functions. 501 epochs with 35 batch size and 0.01 learning rate were considered.

Algorithm 1 Working Principle for Farmer Health Diagnosis in Agri-Aid.

1: Declare and initialize the input variables w for wind speed, ot for outdoor temperature, rh for relative humidity, h for HRV, sl for sugar levels, s for SpO$_2$, t for time, bt for body temperature, bh for body humidity and rr for respiration rate to zero.

2: Declare and initialize the output variables b for buzzer, v for vibrator and l for location to zero.

3: Declare string variables result of diagnosis r, d for dust flow, aq for air quality (VOC), m for measures of control and a for accelerometer to zero.

4: **while** $h \neq 0$ **do**

5:     Start monitoring and gathering physiological, weather and geographical signal data which are w, ot, rh, t, bt, bh, rr, a, aq, d, h, sl, s and l.

6:     Declare and initialize hi for heat index and tw for wet bulb temperature and $wbgt$ for wet bulb globe temperature and set them to zero.

7:     Based on the Equations 2, 3 and 1, calculate tw, $wbgt$ and hi respectively.

8:     **if** $1.2 > w < 4 \wedge 70 > ot < 85 \wedge 60 > h < 90 \wedge 70 > sl < 80 \wedge s > 90 \wedge a <$ 'Threshold' $\wedge$ $40 < rh$ and $rh > 60 \wedge 8 > t < 10 \wedge 16 > h < 19 \wedge 96 > bt < 97 \wedge 20 > bh < 30 \wedge 12 > rr < 16 \wedge$ $d =$ 'low' $\wedge aq =$ 'no' $\vee 80 > hi < 90 \vee 80 > wbgt < 85$ **then**

9:         $r =$ 'Working in direct sunlight can stress your body after 45 minutes. Take minimum 15 minute breaks each hour if continued working.'.

10:         $b = 1 \wedge v = 1 \wedge l = 1$.

11:     **else if** $4 > w < 6 \wedge 90 > ot < 105 \wedge 90 > h < 95 \wedge 50 > sl < 70 \wedge 90 < s > 95 \wedge a >$ 'Threshold' $\wedge 40 < rh$ and $rh > 60 \wedge 10 > t < 12 \wedge 14 > h < 16 \wedge 97 > bt < 98 \wedge 30 > bh < 40 \wedge 12 > rr < 16$ $\wedge d =$ 'med' $\wedge aq =$ 'no' $\vee 90 > hi < 103 \vee 85 > wbgt < 88$ **then**

12:         $r =$ 'Take extreme cautions. Person may experience stress after 30 minutes. Take minimum 30 minutes of break each hour if continued working'.

13:         $m =$ 'Time for a water break!'.

14:         $b = 2 \wedge v = 2 \wedge l = 1$.

15:     **else if** $6 > w < 9 \wedge 105 > ot < 130 \wedge 95 > h < 105 \wedge 30 > sl < 70 \wedge 80 < s > 90 \wedge a >$ 'Threshold' $\wedge 40 < rh$ and $rh > 60 \wedge 12 > t < 14 \wedge 98 > bt < 102 \wedge 40 > bh < 55 \wedge 10 > rr < 12 \wedge d =$ 'high' $\wedge aq =$ 'yes' $\vee 103 > hi < 124 \vee 88 > wbgt < 90$ **then**

16:         $r =$ 'Possible heat stroke. Person may experience body weakness within 20 minutes. Take minimum 40 minutes of break each hour if continued working'.

17:         $m =$ 'Help is alerted. Possible heat stroke!'.

18:         $b = 3 \wedge v = 3 \wedge l = 1$.

19:     **else if** $w > 9 \wedge ot > 130 \wedge h > 105 \wedge sl < 30 \vee sl > 160 \wedge s < 80 \wedge a >$ 'Threshold' $\wedge$ $40 < rh$ and $rh > 60 \wedge 12 > t < 14 \wedge bt > 103 \wedge bh > 60 \wedge rr < 10 \wedge d =$ 'high' $\wedge aq =$ 'yes' $\vee hi > 125 \vee wbgt > 90$ **then**

20:         $r =$ 'Definite heat stroke. Person may loose consciousness within 15 minutes. Seek shelter immediately'.

21:         $m =$ 'Help is on the way. Go indoors and sit'.

22:         $b = 3 \wedge v = 3 \wedge l = 1$.

23:     **else**

24:         $r =$ 'Happy farming!'.

25:         $m =$ 'Happy farming!'.

26:     **end if**

27: **end while**

28: Repeat the steps from 4 through 27.

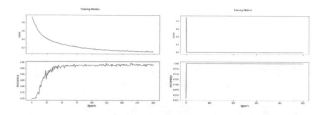

Fig. 7. Loss and accuracy plots of the model for farmer heath as proposed in Agri-Aid system.

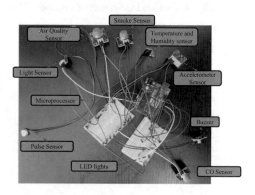

Fig. 8. Real time edge implementation of the proposed Agri-Aid system.

The training epochs deployed in Agri-Aid system is as shown:

Epoch 000: Loss: 0.444, Accuracy: 83.310%
Epoch 050: Loss: 0.000, Accuracy: 87.000%
Epoch 100: Loss: 0.000, Accuracy: 91.000%
Epoch 150: Loss: 0.000, Accuracy: 93.000%
Epoch 200: Loss: 0.000, Accuracy: 97.000%
Epoch 250: Loss: 0.000, Accuracy: 97.000%
Epoch 300: Loss: 0.000, Accuracy: 98.000%
Epoch 350: Loss: 0.000, Accuracy: 100.000%
Epoch 400: Loss: 0.000, Accuracy: 100.000%

A sample of 6 predictions and their confidences are shown:

Example 0 prediction: Danger (100.0%)
Example 1 prediction: Caution (100.0%)
Example 2 prediction: Extreme Danger (100.0%)
Example 3 prediction: Extreme Danger (100.0%)
Example 4 prediction: Extreme Caution (98.4%)
Example 5 prediction: Extreme Danger (99.1%)

The loss and accuracy of the training process during the initial stages towards the end is represented in the Fig. 7.

For the real time edge computing, multiple sensors along with the microprocessor is considered. The edge computing setup in Agri-Aid is represented in Fig. 8.

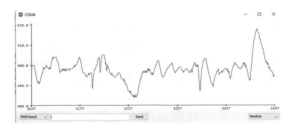

Fig. 9. Serial plot of the exposure to heat in farmers as proposed in Agri-Aid System.

Table 2. Comparison with the state-of-the-art research.

Name	Prototype	Method	Parameters	Stroke Prediction?	Pesticide exposure monitoring?	Accuracy
Jaime, et al. [20]	None	Questionnaire	location, type of crop	None	Partially, Yes	NA.
Baghdadi, et al. [3]	Yes	Microprocessor, placed at ankle	Gait - lifting nd delivering	No	Yes	NA.
Burali, et al. [7]	No	Spirometry	respiration rate, cough, nasal allergies	No	Yes	NA.
Agri-Aid (current paper)	Yes, a wrist watch	Vital, physiological, weather, location based data monitoring	13 features	Yes	Yes	98.67%

The exposure to direct sunlight during the working hours is represented using the serial plotter in Fig. 9.

A brief comparison with existing research is discussed in Table 2.

9   Conclusions and Future Research

9.1   Conclusions

Farmer health is one of the most neglected domains in smart agriculture sector. The crops that are raised by the farmers are given higher priority than the health of the farmers. For any village to be smart, all the components should be smart. People, most importantly farmers comprise most of the population in rural areas. Having prolonged exposures to pesticides, pesticide residue environments and working in the direct sunlight for majority of the day can be very harmful to their health. With the limited scope of help they get, I believe having an automated system to monitor their health can be very helpful. The proposed Agri-Aid watch is not too complicated as anyone with moderate education will be able to handle the device. The response mechanisms are designed keeping in mind the disabilities farmers may have.

9.2   Future Research

Including more robust and personalized response mechanisms is one among the many other future directions of this system. Considering various multi-modal data with security and privacy aspects can also help as education, knowledge and self-care are provided to very hardworking and deserving farmers.

References

1. Ajayi, O., A.F., Sileshi, G.: Human health and occupational exposure to pesticides among smallholder farmers in cotton zones of côte d'Ivoire. Health **3**, 631–637 (2011). https://doi.org/10.4236/health.2011.310107
2. Aliabadi, A.A., Rogak, S.N., Bartlett, K.H., Green, S.I.: Preventing airborne disease transmission: review of methods for ventilation design in health care facilities. Adv. Prev. Med. **2011**, 1–21 (2011)
3. Baghdadi, A., Cavuoto, L.A., Jones-Farmer, A., Rigdon, S.E., Esfahani, E.T., Megahed, F.M.: Monitoring worker fatigue using wearable devices: a case study to detect changes in gait parameters. J. Qual. Technol. **53**(1), 47–71 (2021). https://doi.org/10.1080/00224065.2019.1640097
4. Berry, H.L., Hogan, A., Owen, J., Rickwood, D., Fragar, L.: Climate change and farmers' mental health: risks and responses. Asia Pac. J. Pub. Health **23**(2), 119–132 (2011)
5. Blanco, M.N., Fenske, R.A., Kasner, E.J., Yost, M.G., Seto, E., Austin, E.: Real-time particle monitoring of pesticide drift from an axial fan airblast orchard sprayer. J. Expo. Sci. Environ. Epidemiol. **29**(3), 397–405 (2019). https://doi.org/10.1038/s41370-018-0090-5
6. Boedeker, W., Watts, M., Clausing, P., Marquez, E.: The global distribution of acute unintentional pesticide poisoning: estimations based on a systematic review. BMC Pub. Health **20**(1), 1875–1894 (2020). https://doi.org/10.1186/s12889-020-09939-0
7. Buralli, R.J., et al.: Respiratory condition of family farmers exposed to pesticides in the state of Rio de Janeiro, Brazil. Int. J. Environ. Res. Pub. Health **15**(6), 1–14 (2018). https://doi.org/10.3390/ijerph15061203
8. Crissman, C.C., Cole, D.C., Carpio, F.: Pesticide use and farm worker health in Ecuadorian potato production. Am. J. Agric. Econ. **76**(3), 593–597 (1994). https://www.jstor.org/stable/1243670
9. Del Bene, V.E.: Clinical Methods: The History, Physical, and Laboratory Examinations. 3rd edition. Butterworths, Boston (1990). https://www.ncbi.nlm.nih.gov/books/NBK331/
10. Demos, K., Sazakli, E., Jelastopulu, E., Charokopos, N., Ellul, J., Leotsinidis, M.: Does farming have an effect on health status? a comparison study in west Greece. Int. J. Environ. Res. Pub. Health **26**(10), 776–92 (2013). https://doi.org/10.3390/ijerph10030776
11. Facts, Factors: Insights on Global Wearable Technology Market Size & Share to Surpass USD 380.5 Billion by 2028, Exhibit a CAGR of 18.5 Analysis, Trends, Value, Growth, Opportunities, Segmentation, Outlook & Forecast Report by Facts & Factors (2022). https://www.globenewswire.com
12. Forst, L., et al.: Effectiveness of community health workers for promoting use of safety eyewear by Latino farm workers. Am. J. Ind. Med. **46**(6), 607–613 (2004). https://doi.org/10.1002/ajim.20103
13. Garming, H., Waibel, H.: Pesticides and farmer health in Nicaragua: a willingness-to-pay approach to evaluation. Eur. J. Health Econ. **10**, 125–133 (2009). https://doi.org/10.1007/s10198-008-0110-9
14. Gregg, E.W., et al.: Diabetes and incidence of functional disability in older women. Diabetes Care **25**(1), 61–7 (2002)
15. Hamdan, S., Ayyash, M., Almajali, S.: Edge-computing architectures for internet of things applications: a survey. Sensors (Basel) **20**(22), 6411–6463 (2020)
16. Hifumi, T., Kondo, Y., Shimizu, K., Miyake, Y.: Heat Stroke. J. Intensive Care **6**(30), 1–8 (2018). https://doi.org/10.1186/s40560-018-0298-4
17. Hjalmarsen, A., Hykkerud, D.L.: Severe nocturnal hypoxaemia in geriatric inpatients. Age Ageing **37**(5), 526–529 (2008)

18. Iqbal, M.: Chapter 1 - sun-earth astronomical relationships. In: Iqbal, M. (ed.) An Introduction to Solar Radiation, pp. 1–28. Academic Press (1983). https://doi.org/10.1016/B978-0-12-373750-2.50006-9, https://www.sciencedirect.com/science/article/pii/B9780123737502500069

19. Iqbal, M.: Chapter 6 - solar spectral radiation under cloudless skies. In: Iqbal, M. (ed.) An Introduction to Solar Radiation, pp. 107–168. Academic Press (1983). https://doi.org/10.1016/B978-0-12-373750-2.50011-2, https://www.sciencedirect.com/science/article/pii/B9780123737502500112

20. Jaime Caro, D.L., et al.: Monitoring application for farmer pesticide use. In: 10th International Conference on Information, Intelligence, Systems and Applications (IISA), pp. 1–3 (2019). https://doi.org/10.1109/IISA.2019.8900734

21. Kong, Q., Huber, M.: Explicit calculations of wet-bulb globe temperature compared with approximations and why it matters for labor productivity. Earth's Future **10**(3), 23–34 (2022). https://doi.org/10.1029/2021EF002334

22. Lowder, S.K., Skoet, J., Raney, T.: The number, size, and distribution of farms, smallholder farms, and family farms worldwide. World Dev. **87**, 16–29 (2016). https://doi.org/10.1016/j.worlddev.2015.10.041

23. Lydia, M.S., Aulia, I., Mahyuni, E.L., Hizriadi, A.: Automatic risk detection system for farmer's health monitoring based on behavior of pesticide use. J. Phys: Conf. Ser. **1235**, 1–11 (2019). https://doi.org/10.1088/1742-6596/1235/1/012113

24. Malmberg, A., Simkin, S., Hawton, K.: Suicide in farmers. Br. J. Psychiatry **175**(2), 103–105 (1999). https://doi.org/10.1192/bjp.175.2.103

25. Mancini, F., Bruggen, A.H.C.V., Jiggins, J.L.S., Ambatipudi, A.C., Murphy, H.: Acute pesticide poisoning among female and male cotton growers in India. Int. J. Occup. Environ. Health **11**(3), 221–232 (2005). https://doi.org/10.1179/107735205800246064

26. Michael, P.: How Fast is Technology Advancing? [Growth Charts & Statistics] 2022 (2022). https://mediapeanut.com/how-fast-is-technology-growing-statistics-facts/#:~:text=AdvancesinTechhavegrown,growthpatternyearoveryear

27. Ministry, N.F.W.: Health & Safety (2020). https://nfwm.org/farm-workers/farm-worker-issues/health-safety/

28. Myers, J.R., Layne, L.A., Marsh, S.M.: Injuries and fatalities to US farmers and farm workers 55 years and older. Am. J. Ind. Med. **52**(3), 185–194 (2009). https://doi.org/10.1002/ajim.20661, https://onlinelibrary.wiley.com/doi/abs/10.1002/ajim.20661

29. Nemery, B.: The lungs as a target for the toxicity of some organophosphorus compounds. In: Costa, L.G., Galli, C.L., Murphy, S.D. (eds.) Toxicol. Pesticides, pp. 297–303. Springer, Berlin, Heidelberg (1987)

30. Pingali, P.L., Marquez, C.B., Palis, F.G., Rola, A.C.: The impact of pesticides on farmer health: a medical and economic analysis in the Philippines. In: Pingali, P.L., Roger, P.A. (eds.) Impact of Pesticides on Farmer Health and the Rice Environment. Natural Resource Management and Policy, vol. 7, pp. 343–360. Springer, Dordrecht (1995)

31. Pirker, W., Katzenschlager, R.: Gait disorders in adults and the elderly?: a clinical guide. Wien. Klin. Wochenschr. **129**(4), 81–95 (2016)

32. Rachakonda, L., Sharma, A., Mohanty, S.P., Kougianos, E.: Good-eye: a combined computer-vision and physiological-sensor based device for full-proof prediction and detection of fall of adults. In: Casaca, A., Katkoori, S., Ray, S., Strous, L. (eds.) IFIPIoT 2019. IAICT, vol. 574, pp. 273–288. Springer, Cham (2020). https://doi.org/10.1007/978-3-030-43605-6_16

33. Rachakonda, L., Bapatla, A.K., Mohanty, S.P., Kougianos, E.: SaYoPillow: blockchain-integrated privacy-assured IoMT framework for stress management considering sleeping habits. IEEE Trans. Consum. Electron. **67**(1), 20–29 (2021). https://doi.org/10.1109/TCE.2020.3043683

34. Rachakonda, L., Bapatla, A.K., Mohanty, S.P., Kougianos, E.: BACTmobile: a smart blood alcohol concentration tracking mechanism for smart vehicles in healthcare CPS framework. SN Comput. Sci. **3**(3), 236–259 (2022). https://doi.org/10.1007/s42979-022-01142-9

35. Rachakonda, L., Mohanty, S.P., Kougianos, E.: iLog: an intelligent device for automatic food intake monitoring and stress detection in the IoMT. IEEE Trans. Consum. Electron. **66**(2), 115–124 (2020). https://doi.org/10.1109/TCE.2020.2976006

36. Rachakonda, L., Mohanty, S.P., Kougianos, E.: cstick: a calm stick for fall prediction, detection and control in the IoMT framework. In: Camarinha-Matos, L.M., Heijenk, G., Katkoori, S., Strous, L. (eds.) Internet of Things. Technology and Applications, vol. 641, pp. 129–145. Springer, Cham (2022)

37. Raymond, C., Matthews, T., Horton, R.M.: The emergence of heat and humidity too severe for human tolerance. Sci. Adv. **6**(19), eaaw1838 (2020). https://doi.org/10.1126/sciadv. aaw1838, https://www.science.org/doi/abs/10.1126/sciadv.aaw1838

38. Reigart, J.R., Roberts, J.R.: Recognition and Management of Pesticide Poisonings, 6th edn. CreateSpace Independent Publishing Platform, Scotts Valley (2014)

39. Schoen, C.: A new empirical model of the temperature-humidity index. J. Appl. Meteorol. **44**(9), 1413–1420 (2005). https://doi.org/10.1175/JAM2285.1

40. Sharif, S.I., Al-Harbi, A.B., Al-Shihabi, A.M., Al-Daour, D.S., Sharif, R.S.: Falls in the elderly: assessment of prevalence and risk factors. Pharm. Pract. (Granada) **16**(3) (2018)

41. Sosan, M.B., Akingbohungbe, A.E.: Occupational insecticide exposure and perception of safety measures among cacao farmers in southwestern Nigeria. Arch. Environ. Occup. Health **64**(3), 185–193 (2009). https://doi.org/10.1080/19338240903241077

42. Sprung, C.L., Portocarrero, C.J., Fernaine, A.V., Weinberg, P.F.: The metabolic and respiratory alterations of heat stroke. Arch. Intern. Med. **140**(5), 665–669 (1980). https:// doi.org/10.1001/archinte.1980.00330170081028,   https://doi.org/10.1001/archinte.1980. 00330170081028

43. USDA: Agriculture And Its Related Industries Provide 10.3 Percent Of U.S. Employment (2021). https://www.ers.usda.gov/data-products/chart-gallery/gallery/chart-detail/?chartId=58282

44. Villarejo, D.: The health of US hired farm workers. Ann. Rev. Public Health **24**(1), 175–193 (2003). https://doi.org/10.1146/annurev.publhealth.24.100901.140901, https://doi.org/ 10.1146/annurev.publhealth.24.100901.140901, pMID: 12359914

45. Wilson, T.E., Crandall C., G.: Effect of thermal stress on cardiac function. Exerc. Sport. Sci. Rev. **39**(1), 12–17 (Jan 2011). https://doi.org/10.1097/JES.0b013e318201eed6

46. Zanobetti, A., O'Neill, M.S.: Longer-term outdoor temperatures and health effects: a review. Curr. Epidemiol. Rep. **5**(2), 125–139 (2018). https://doi.org/10.1007/s40471-018-0150-3

47. Zecevic, A.A., Salmoni, A.W., Speechley, M., Vandervoort, A.A.: Defining a fall and reasons for falling: comparisons among the views of seniors, health care providers, and the research literature. Gerontologist **46**(3), 367–376 (2006). https://doi.org/10.1093/geront/46.3.367

48. Zweig, G., Gao, R., Witt, J.M., Popendorf, W., Bogen, K.: Dermal exposure to carbaryl by strawberry harvesters. J. Agric. Food Chem. **32**(6), 1232–1236 (1984). https://doi.org/10. 1021/jf00126a006

A Smart Agriculture Framework to Automatically Track the Spread of Plant Diseases Using Mask Region-Based Convolutional Neural Network

Alakananda Mitra[1] , Saraju P. Mohanty[1(✉)] , and Elias Kougianos[2]

[1] Department of Computer Science and Engineering, University of North Texas, Denton, USA
alakanandamitra@my.unt.edu, saraju.mohanty@unt.edu
[2] Department of Electrical Engineering, University of North Texas, Denton, USA
elias.kougianos@unt.edu

Abstract. Plant diseases reduce agricultural production. They negatively affect fruit and crop quality and reduce yield, causing food shortages. A drop in production harms the global agricultural economy. However, early detection and disease severity estimation are key to disease management, containment, and prevention. Damage localization is the first step in estimating the severity of diseases, which is crucial for the optimum application of pesticides. The current approach needs expert advice for disease detection. For a large farm, it is an expensive and slow process. Automatic plant disease detection eliminates the tiresome task of monitoring big farms and detects the disease early enough to avoid plant degradation. In this article, we propose a fully automated method based on deep neural networks for detecting and localizing leaf diseases. The proposed method is based on Mask R-CNN network. Image augmentation has been performed to achieve higher precision from a small dataset. Transfer learning has been used to save time and achieve better performance. Our proposed method of disease detection is faster, as it automatically localizes the disease along with the disease identification from the leaf images. The images can be taken using a smart phone camera or a low altitude unmanned aerial vehicle (UAV) camera. As a case study, we have applied the method to apple leaves.

Keywords: Smart agriculture · Smart villages · Internet of Agro Things (IoAT) · Plant health · Plant disease · Apple leaves · Mask Region-based Convolutional Neural Network (R-CNN) · ML from small dataset

1 Introduction

The presence of plant diseases has a detrimental effect on the amount of food that can be produced through agriculture - it affects the crop quality and reduces the final yield. Each year crop losses total billions of dollars [26]. If plant diseases are not identified and addressed in a timely manner, it results in increased food insecurity [22]. Hence, early detection and disease severity estimation are the two major steps for disease management, containment, and prevention.

© IFIP International Federation for Information Processing 2022
Published by Springer Nature Switzerland AG 2022
L. M. Camarinha-Matos et al. (Eds.): IFIPIoT 2022, IFIP AICT 665, pp. 68–85, 2022.
https://doi.org/10.1007/978-3-031-18872-5_5

Trees are prone to various fungal pathogens that cause diseases. These diseases can affect plants at any stage of growth and manifest in a variety of plant components, from stems to fruits. Symptoms may include discoloration, form change, wilting, galls, and cankers. However, as disease symptoms are predominantly manifested on leaves, most of the research on identifying plant diseases is focused on leaves or fruits [22].

In developing countries, manual observation is still the most common method of detecting plant diseases. It is an arduous and inefficient process that consumes a lot of time. It also requires expert services, but farmers are not always able to afford such expensive services [33]. Wrong identification and improper use of pesticides cause secondary damage to the plants and contaminate the soil as well as the environment. To solve these problems, different techniques based on computer vision and deep learning have been proposed for the automatic and accurate detection of plant diseases.

Plant monitoring is crucial for disease management. The early detection of plant disease and its prevention by 2030 are two key goals of agricultural research [29]. Here, a fully automatic plant disease detection method is proposed and illustrated in Fig. 1. As a case study, apple leaves have been selected. The proposed method will track the spread of the disease by identifying the disease and detecting the damaged areas. The novelties of the work are as followed:

- The method is fully automatic. No expert service is needed for disease detection.
- Very little effort is needed from the users' side. Users only have to take pictures of the damaged leaves.
- Early detection of the disease is possible.
- This process is the first step of disease severity estimation. Estimation of disease severity plays a pivotal role in calculating the optimal quantity of pesticides.

Continuous monitoring results in the early detection of disease. With further experiments, our proposed method can be used to estimate the damage severity. We aim to save time, money, resources, organisms vital for soil and biodiversity, and to store carbon in the soil to combat climate change [4].

The rest of the paper is organized in the following way: Sect. 2 discusses recent work on plant disease detection. Section 3 presents an overview of the method and network architecture. Experimental details are discussed in Sect. 4. Section 5 presents the results and evaluates the performance of the method, along with a comparative study. Finally, the paper concludes with future work direction in Sect. 6.

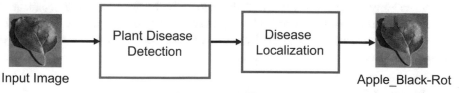

Fig. 1. Scope of the paper

2   Prior Research Work

This section presents state-of-the-art methods based on deep neural networks for plant disease detection. Approaches based on convolutional neural networks (CNNs) are automatic and more efficient. Literature survey reveals that there are mainly two types of studies addressing plant diseases: either classification-based or regions-of-interest (ROI)-based.

2.1 Classification Based Approaches

The majority of classification-based approaches use convolutional neural networks (CNNs). These approaches are automatic and more efficient than the previously used machine learning methods, which rely largely on image processing [34]. Apple leaf disease was correctly identified in [35]. An attention network has been added with EfficientNet-B4 to incorporate both channel and spatial features. Image augmentation has been used over the collected data. High accuracy has been obtained.

Apple leaf disease has also been detected in [11] using a combined structure of DenseNet and XceptionNet as a feature extractor, and finally, classification has been done through a Support Vector Machine (SVM). Early detection of the disease has been the focus of this paper. A high accuracy of 98.82% has been achieved. Five kinds of apple leaf diseases have been detected using SSD with Inception and Rainbow concatenation [19] structure. The proposed model has achieved 78.8% mean average precision (mAP). In [10], an ensemble of pre-trained DenseNet121, EfficientNetB7, and NoisyStudent networks has been used to identify apple leaf diseases with an accuracy of 90%. The model has been deployed as a web application.

Various grape leaf diseases have been detected using a modified Inception structure [24]. A dense connectivity technique has been proposed with the Inception structure for better features. Data enhancement techniques have also been used to increase the dataset size. In the agricultural domain, no large publicly available datasets are found which demands data augmentation in most of the works. A slightly lower accuracy compared to the other papers has been achieved here.

Tomato leaf diseases have been detected using four different CNNs in [9]. InceptionV3 performed much better among the lot with laboratory data compared to field data. A custom shallow CNN has been used for nine different tomato leaf diseases in [8]. A good accuarcy of 91.2% has been achieved after training 1000 epochs. Similarly, a seven layer CNN structure has been used as feature extractor in [18] to detect four of rice leaf diseases. The features have been classified with an SVM classifier with high accuracy. Cross validation ensures the robustness of the model.

The majority of these CNN based methods identify the diseases but no localization of the disease has been performed. However, the severity of the disease can only be known when the damage area of the leaf is calculated. Localization is the first step of damage estimation.

2.2 Region-of-Interests (ROI) Based Approaches

Regions-of-Interest (ROI) deep CNNs are being used in recent plant disease detection works as these structures have the potential to segment the location of the disease. When deep neural networks are used in classification based approaches, no localization of the disease is performed. However, ROI based approaches detect the diseases along with localization. Nine types of tomato plant diseases and pests have been recognized in

[14] using different regions-of-interest (ROI) based structures. Data augmentation has improved mAP maximum 30% in some cases.

A new structure DF-Tiny-YOLO has been presented in [13] for detecting apple leaf diseases. Here, use of smaller CNN kernels reduces feature dimensions and increases network depth without increasing the complexity. Another ROI-based structure, Faster R-CNN, has been used for recognizing rice plant diseases and pests in [20]. Relatively blurry videos have been used as input. A custom CNN is used as the backbone network. Higher accuracy has been achieved compared to existing structures.

There are certain articles where more than one ROI-based structures have been used. In [36], Faster R-CNN and Mask R-CNN both have used for disease identification and detection of the diseased segments. In [30], Mask R-CNN has been used to detect disease infected part of apple leaves whereas the disease has been classified with ensemble subspace discriminant analysis classifier. A hybrid contrast stretching method has been applied. Mask R-CNN has also been used in [7] for detecting strawberry diseases. A systematic approach to data augmentation has been followed, increasing the mAP to 82.43%. A strawberry disease dataset has also been presented here.

These papers indicate that various deep learning networks have achieved good success rates in identifying different plant diseases. However, more information e.g., severity of the disease is needed to control and provide solutions to prevent plant diseases.

3   Proposed Method

3.1   Overview: Proposed Agriculture Cyber Physical System

Plant disease is a serious concern for sustainable farming. Plant diseases are a farmer's worst fear since diseases can wipe out an entire crop and result in significant financial loss. The critical step to preventing plant disease is early detection. In this section, a

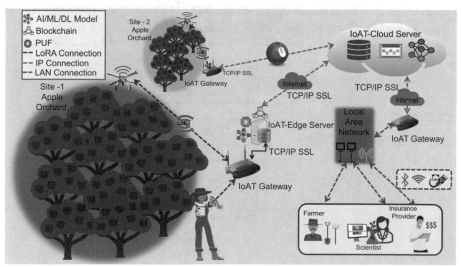

Fig. 2. System overview: A-CPS for plant leaves disease detection. In this A-CPS, UAVs and smart phone cameras are the *things* and farmers, scientists, and insurance providers are the *stakeholders*. Various *networking* and communication options are used at different stages.

smart agriculture [28] framework for automatic tracking of plant diseases is presented. The A-CPS is described in the context of apple leaf disease detection. Figure 2 shows the proposed agriculture cyber physical system (A-CPS) [27] with *things*, *stakeholders*, and *networking*.

The proposed A-CPS is deployed in an edge-cloud setting in an apple orchard. In this A-CPS, farmers, insurance providers, and scientists are the main *stakeholders*. UAVs and smart phone cameras are the *things*. The application has the potential to perform at the edge along with the cloud platform.

Apple leaf images are collected from apple orchards. Low altitude Unmanned Aerial Vehicles (UAVs) or smart phone cameras are used to take the images. They are connected to the Internet-of-Agro-Things (IoAT) gateways through long-range and low-powered LoRA connections. When capturing with an UAV or a phone camera, many leaves will appear in the frame. As a result, before identifying damage to a single leaf, each leaf must be detected using object detection.

IoAT gateways are connected to the *edge server* and *cloud server* through TCP/IP SSL. The images are sent to the cloud server or edge server, if available. Then, the images are processed, diseases are detected, and damage areas are localized using the methodology mentioned in Sect. 3.2. Finally, the result is sent back to the user.

3.2   Methodology for Disease Detection and Localization

In this subsection, the detection method for plant disease is presented in detail. The process workflow is shown in Fig. 3. First, photos of the leaves are taken. Then they

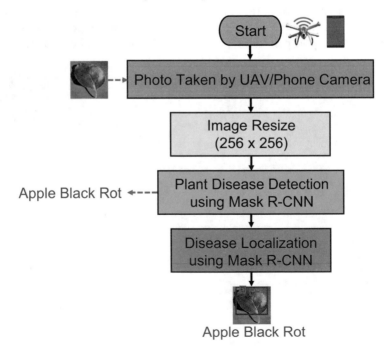

Fig. 3. Process workflow for disease detection and localization system

are resized to 256×256 to be detected using the trained model. A Mask Region-based Convolutional Neural Network (R-CNN) [15] has been used to detect the disease along with disease localization. Hence, the problem is considered as an object detection problem. Object detection is a task in computer vision that involves identifying the presence of one or more items in a given image as well as their location and the category of object that they belong to.

Recently, various deep learning networks have achieved state-of-the-art performance for object detection. Region-based Convolutional Neural Networks (R-CNN) showed promising results. However, an R-CNN is computationally expensive. It takes a long time to train it. A fast R-CNN, on the other hand, is much faster than a slow R-CNN and takes much less time to train. Faster R-CNN is faster than its predecessor since it uses a Region Proposal network rather than ROI pooling. The latest in this series is Mask R-CNN, as shown in Fig. 4.

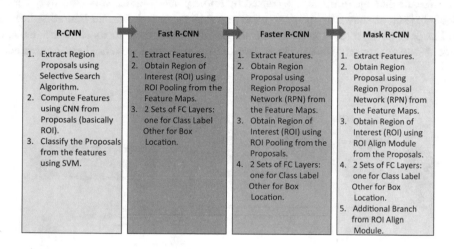

Fig. 4. Evolution of mask R-CNN [32]

In this work, Matterport's implementation [6] of the Mask R-CNN, based on Keras and TensorFlow, has been followed. We have modified the scripts and hyper parameters as per the need of the application. The developmental process workflow is shown in Fig. 5. First, data has been selected and annotated for object detection purposes. Then, the dataset has been split into two parts: *train* and *validate*. Training of the network has been performed with augmented data. Transfer learning has been used. Finally, it was evaluated with the *test* dataset. The procedure is described in Sect. 3.3 and 4.

3.3 Network Architecture for Disease Detection and Localization

Mask R-CNN [15] is a general network for object instance segmentation. Image segmentation is a pixel-based division of objects in an image. It gives information about the shapes and sizes of the detected objects. In this work, Mask R-CNN has been used to

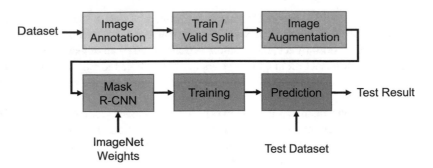

Fig. 5. Workflow for developing the disease detection and localization system

localize the damage of the leaves caused by apple plant diseases. It is built over Faster R-CNN [31], as shown in Fig. 6. Here, along with the class label and bounding box as in Faster R-CNN, a mask is generated for the detected object to localize the damage area. However, for our work, accurate masks for the damage have not been generated.

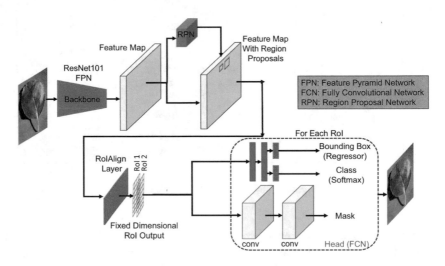

Fig. 6. Mask R-CNN network structure

- Backbone Network: A backbone network is used for feature extraction of the input image. Initially, two different backbone networks, ResNet101 + Feature Pyramid Network (FPN) and ResNet50 + FPN, have been tested, and finally, ResNet-101 [16] and FPN [23] have been selected as the backbone network. The ResNet network, pre-trained on the ImageNet [12] dataset has been used. Extracted features in this stage are used as the input for the next layer.

- Region Proposal Network (RPN): Multiple regions of interest are generated using a lightweight binary classifier in a Region Proposal Network(RPN). A small network slides over the feature maps obtained from the preceding stage. It employs anchor boxes to detect numerous, overlapping, and different-sized objects. These predetermined height-and-width bounding boxes capture object classes' scale and aspect ratio. Final object detection removes background anchor boxes and filters the rest by confidence score from multiple predictions. Detection minimum score is set to 0.9 to include all the damages. Non-Max suppression selects the most confident anchor boxes. Hence, RPN simply tells us whether or not there is something in that area. The model predicts which regions or feature maps contain objects. Anchors are centered at the sliding window and have five scales, one for each feature pyramid level.
- Region of Interest (RoI): Each region proposal has different sizes and shapes. The RoIAlign layer changes the shapes and sizes of all proposals to the same shape and size. It aligns the features with the input. The number of RoI is the same as the number of detected objects. RoI is noted when the Intersection over Union (IoU) of ground truth boxes for the predicted regions are greater than or equal to 0.5.
- Head: The *Head* part takes care of the classification and segmentation. Sets of *fully connected* layers are used for bounding box classification. Classification results are predicted by the first branch of *fully connected layers* and *softmax* activation function, and the *regression* output at the second branch of *fully connected layer* is used to determine the location of the proposed regions in terms of the coordinates of the proposals. For each RoI, the parallel branch built with a *fully convolutional network* (FCN) generates binary masks of size 14×14. During prediction, these masks are scaled up to 28×28.

4 Experimental Validation

In this section, we present the experimental validation of the Mask R-CNN based plant leaf disease detection system with a case study on apple leaves.

4.1 Dataset

The publicly available *PlantVillage* dataset [17] has been used for training and evaluating the method. There are a total of 3171 apple leaf images in the dataset. The leaves are either healthy or infected with diseases. There are three types of apple leaf diseases in the dataset-*Black Rot*, *Apple Scab*, and *Cedar Apple Rust*. They show different symptoms on the leaves.

Small, orange-red dots occur on the leaves' fronts in the early stages of *Apple Rust*. These spots grow to become an orange-yellow patch with red edges. A single leaf can have dozens of disease spots if the infection is severe. 12 weeks after the commencement of sickness, the spot's surface is covered with little bright yellow dots [21].

Apple Scab begins with yellow-green radial or circular patches that become brown to black, with clearly defined edges. Smaller and thicker with curled or twisted leaves are signs of more serious illness. Infected spots will blend into one another, causing large patches to appear on leaves, giving them a burnt look [13,21].

For *Black Rot*, small, purple-black lesions appear on the skin at the beginning of the disease. These develop into spherical spots with a yellow-brown center and brown-purple rims that resemble frog's eyes [13].

1025 infected apple leaf images among 3171 images have been randomly selected to make a balanced dataset of apple leaves. Each type has approximately $300 - 350$ images. The reason behind not choosing all apple leaf images is to limit the time and effort for annotation.

First, 175 random images are kept aside for evaluating the system. The remaining 850 images are divided into training and validation sets with 70:30 ratio. Hence, there are 595 images for training and 255 images for validation. Table 1 describes the details of *training* and *validation* datasets.

Table 1. Dataset details

Types	Number of images		
	Total	Train	Validation
Apple Black Rot	300	210	90
Cedar Apple Rust	250	175	75
Apple Scab	300	210	90
	850	**595**	**255**

4.2   Image Annotation

Annotation of images with ground truth is a critical step of object detector training. Bounding boxes are drawn across the objects in the training datasets. An open source image annotation tool, MakeSense.AI [1] has been used to annotate the data. *Rect* tool has been used for annotating images. Annotation files are stored in .xml format with the two diagonally placed corners' coordinates of the bounding box. During labeling, different colors are used for different classes. Figure 7 shows one sample annotated image of an apple leaf infected with *Apple Black Rot* and Fig. 8 shows some annotated leaf samples.

Fig. 7. Image annotation using image annotation tool MakeSense

4.3 Image Augmentation

For a deep learning model, a large dataset always increases the accuracy of the model. Here, there were only 850 images in our dataset. Data has been augmented on the go to achieve better accuracy. Horizontal flip, vertical flip, affine rotation, affine scaling, and edge detection have been applied to the 850 images. Rotation is set to any random value from $-45°$ to $45°$ and scale value from 0.5 to 1.5.

4.4 Training

The network has been trained on a system with an NVIDIA Tesla P100 GPU and 25 GB of memory. Keras, the deep learning API in Python with TensorFlow at the back-end, scikit-image, pandas, numpy, and imagaug libraries have been used. Transfer learning allowed us to improve the accuracy of the model while simultaneously reducing the amount of time spent on training [25].

While training, the structure of Mask R-CNN is kept unchanged and pre-trained *imagenet* weights of the ResNet networks are loaded. When trained on 20, 000 categories of more than 14M labeled images of the *ImageNet* dataset, the network already knows how to identify the most common aspects of images. Basic features like lines and edges are extracted at the lower layers, whilst more sophisticated and abstract elements, such as those that define classification, are extracted at the intermediate and higher layers.

For training RPN, the number of anchors per image has been kept 256 as in [6] and five square anchor boxes of side [8, 16, 32, 64, 128] have been selected with a width-to-height ratio [0.5, 1, 2]. The number of steps per epoch is kept equal to the number of training images, and the number of validation steps has been chosen as the number of validation images.

The *images per GPU* is set at 1 to fit the memory. The number of available GPUs in our case is 1 which in turn sets the *batch size* at *images per GPU × number of GPU* = 1.

Fig. 8. Annotated apple leaf images from plantvillage dataset [17]. Leaves are infected with three different diseases - Black Rot (top row), Cedar Apple Rust (middle row), and Apple Scab (bottom row).

Stochastic Gradient Descent (SGD) has been chosen as the optimizer, as in [15]. Initial *learning rate* is set at 0.001. Two different backbone networks: ResNet50 + FPN and ResNet101 + FPN have been compared and finally the latter one has been chosen as the feature extractor. Table 2 shows the learning rate schedule for training the network with ResNet101 + FPN as the backbone. Several hyper parameters have been fine tuned for better detection and are stated in Table 3. The rest of the hyper parameters are set at the default values of [6].

Table 2. Learning rate schedule for training with ResNet101 + FPN backbone

Learning Rate (LR)	Trained on	Epochs
0.001	All layers	1–40
0.0001	All layers	41–80
0.00003	All layers	81–120
0.00001	Head	121–160

Table 3. Fine tuned hyper parameters

Hyper parameters	Values
IMAGES_PER_GPU	1
NUM_CLASSES	1+3
STEPS_PER_EPOCH	595
VALIDATION_STEPS	255
LEARNING_RATE	0.001
TRAIN_ROIS_PER_IMAGE	128
RPN_TRAIN_ANCHORS_PER_IMAGE	64
MAX_GT_INSTANCES	200
DETECTION_MAX_INSTANCES	100
IMAGE_MIN_DIM	256
IMAGE_MAX_DIM	256
RPN_ANCHOR_SCALES	$[8, 16, 32, 64, 128]$

5   Performance Evaluation

5.1   Performance Metrics

Mean average precision (mAP) has been used to evaluate the performance of the model. *mAP* takes into account both false positives (FP) and false negatives (FN) and considers the trade-off between *precision* and *recall*. Because of this, *mAP* is a good metric for detection tasks. *Precision* and *recall* are defined in Eq. 1 and 2.

$$Precision = \frac{TP}{TP + FP} \tag{1}$$

$$Recall = \frac{TP}{TP + FN} \tag{2}$$

$$IoU = \frac{Area\ of\ Intersection}{Area\ of\ Union} = \frac{TP}{TP + FP + FN} \tag{3}$$

where, *TP* is the *true positive*, *FP* is the *false positive*, and *FN* is the *false negative*. Equation 3 describes how to calculate the *Intersection over Union (IoU)*. It is a measure of how much the predicted boundary overlaps the ground truth boundary. Depending on the *IoU* threshold value, average precision changes. Usually, *IoU* is varied in the range $0.5 \leq IoU \leq 0.95$.

The *average precision* is defined as the area under the precision and recall curve for the object detector. First, *average precision* AP_i is calculated for each class and then using Eq. 4, *mAP* is calculated.

$$mAP = \frac{1}{N} \sum_{i=1}^{N} AP_i \tag{4}$$

where, N is the total number of classes. Figure 9(a) presents the method for plotting the *Precision-Recall* curve [3] and Fig. 9(b) describes the process of calculating *mAP* [2]. The validation dataset has been used to evaluate the model. 175 unseen images of infected apple leaves from the PlantVillage dataset [17] have also been tested.

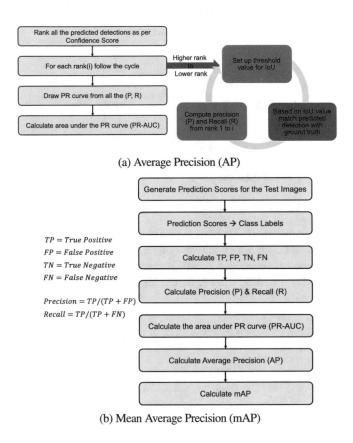

(a) Average Precision (AP)

(b) Mean Average Precision (mAP)

Fig. 9. Workflows for calculating mAP and AP

5.2 Performance Analysis

Figure 10 shows sample predicted apple leaves from the test dataset. The first row shows the images from the PlantVillage dataset [17] and the second row shows the predicted results. It is clear from the predicted results that most of the damage parts have been detected. However, when the number of damage areas is higher, there are still room for improvement. Our model missed some of the damage areas. It is mainly due to the small size of training data. To achieve higher precision, more data is needed for training. More hyper parameter tuning in Table 3 in Sect. 4.4 will contribute to better *mAP*.

Fig. 10. Predicted results by ResNet101 + FPN on test dataset

Table 4 shows the *mAP* for two different scenarios. When ResNet101 + FPN is used as the backbone, a higher *mAP* of 83.8% has been obtained due to the higher number of layers in ResNet101 than in ResNet50. Initially, we started with an 80 : 20 split for training and validation, but ResNet101 started to overfit. To avoid overfitting, image augmentation along with more validation images (train and validation ratio of 70:30) was chosen.

Table 4. Mean Average Precision (mAP) for disease detection network

Backbone network	Image augmentation	Mean Average Precision [mAP(%)] IoU = 0.5
ResNet50 + FPN	Yes	81.9
ResNet101 + FPN	Yes	**83.8**

A few of the predictions were not completely correct. Two examples are shown in Fig. 11. Most of the damaged areas in those two leaves have been correctly predicted, but due to the excessive amount of specular reflection and on the leaf shadow, the top left image has one Apple Scab prediction though it is infected with Black Rot disease. In the top right image, which is infected with Apple Scab, several damage areas are

Fig. 11. Falsely detected results by the detection network. Falsely detected damages are shown with red ovals and missed damage areas are shown with red circles.

missed. One damage area has been predicted as Black Rot. This is also due to heavy specular reflection.

Table 5 compares our work with two of the existing works. Mask R-CNN was used in both works. Additional techniques have been used to achieve higher *mAP*. However, we have concentrated on mostly fine tuning of hyper parameters without along with image augmentation. With more investigation into the effects of different hyper parameters along with image enhancement techniques, the achieved *mAP* can be increased.

Table 5. Comparative analysis with the existing works

Work	Pre-training dataset	Method	Metric	Remarks
[7]	MS-COCO	Mask R-CNN + Systematic approach to Image Augmentation	$mAP = 82.43\%$	For Strawberry diseases
[30]	ImageNet	Image Enhancement + Mask R-CNN + Ensemble Subspace Discriminant	$mAP = 81.8\%$, 86.1%	For Apple leaf diseases. More complex method
Current paper	ImageNet	Mask R-CNN + Image Augmentation	$\mathbf{mAP = 83.8\%}$	Automatic tracking of the spread of disease. Case study apple leaf disease

6   Conclusion and Future Work

Plants, like all other forms of life, are susceptible to contracting many diseases. A plant's ability to develop to its full potential might be hampered by disease [5, 26]. Plant diseases are one of the most significant factors that contribute to crop loss. Plants and trees need to be disease free. Therefore, plant disease diagnosis and damage localization are critical to preventing crop loss. Disease severity is another important factor that needs to be known along with disease detection and damage localization. It decides the amount of pesticide needed. In this paper, we present a Mask R-CNN based method for automatic disease detection and damage localization. These are the prior steps before disease severity estimation. This preliminary research shows promise towards damage severity estimation.

Several improvements can be made in future work. Damage localization can be extended to disease severity estimation. Though apple leaf diseases have only been detected here, the process is valid for any plant/crop whenever the annotated dataset is available. More annotated data will increase the *mAP* of the method. As training data, single leaf images with very distinct backgrounds have been used. But, that is not the case with real-world data where there are different lighting conditions, shadows, specular reflection, and the presence of insects on the leaves. Inclusion of field data into the training images will improve the system. Research on different lighting conditions, shadows, specular reflection, and the presence of insects on the leaves is needed. Some preliminary work on shadow removal has been done in [26]. When taking pictures with UAV or phone cameras, multiple leaves will be present in the frame. Hence, before detecting the damage to a single leaf, each leaf needs to be detected through object detection. Once the damage severity is determined, work might be extended to calculate the optimum pesticide amount.

Acknowledgment. The authors want to thank Madison Huang for helping them label the images of apple leaves from [17].

References

1. Make Sense. https://www.makesense.ai/. Accessed 13 June 2022
2. Mean Average Precision (mAP) Explained: Everything You Need to Know. https://www.v7labs.com/blog/mean-average-precision. Accessed 8 July 2022
3. Mean average precision map for object detection. https://leimao.github.io/blog/Object-Detection-Mean-Average-Precision-mAP/. Acessed 8 July 2022
4. New Study: Agricultural Pesticides Cause Widespread Harm to Soil Health, Threaten Biodiversity. https://biologicaldiversity.org/w/news/press-releases/new-study-agricultural-pesticides-cause-widespread-harm-to-soil-health-threaten-biodiversity-2021-05-04/. Accessed 10 June 2022
5. Plant Disease: Pathogens and Cycles. https://cropwatch.unl.edu/soybean-management/plant-disease. Accessed 02 June 2022
6. Abdulla, W.: Mask R-CNN for object detection and instance segmentation on keras and tensorflow (2017). https://github.com/matterport/Mask_RCNN
7. Afzaal, U., Bhattarai, B., Pandeya, Y.R., Lee, J.: An instance segmentation model for strawberry diseases based on mask R-CNN. Sensors 21(19), 6565 (2021). https://doi.org/10.3390/s21196565, https://www.mdpi.com/1424-8220/21/19/6565
8. Agarwal, M., Singh, A., Arjaria, S., Sinha, A., Gupta, S.: ToLeD: tomato leaf disease detection using convolution neural network. Proc. Comput. Sci. **167**, 293–301 (2020)

9. Ahmad, I., Hamid, M., Yousaf, S., Shah, S.T., Ahmad, M.O.: Optimizing pretrained convolutional neural networks for tomato leaf disease detection. Complexity **2020** (2020)
10. Bansal, P., Kumar, R., Kumar, S.: Disease detection in apple leaves using deep convolutional neural network. Agriculture **11**(7), 617 (2021). https://doi.org/10.3390/agriculture11070617, https://www.mdpi.com/2077-0472/11/7/617
11. Chao, X., Sun, G., Zhao, H., Li, M., He, D.: Identification of apple tree leaf diseases based on deep learning models. Symmetry **12**(7), 1065 (2020). https://doi.org/10.3390/sym12071065, https://www.mdpi.com/2073-8994/12/7/1065
12. Deng, J., Dong, W., Socher, R., Li, L.J., Li, K., Fei-Fei, L.: ImageNet: a large-scale hierarchical image database. In: Proceedings of IEEE Conference on Computer Vision and Pattern Recognition, pp. 248–255. IEEE (2009)
13. Di, J., Li, Q.: A method of detecting apple leaf diseases based on improved convolutional neural network. PLoS One **17**(2), e0262629 (2022)
14. Fuentes, A., Yoon, S., Kim, S.C., Park, D.S.: A robust deep-learning-based detector for real-time tomato plant diseases and pests recognition. Sensors (2017). https://doi.org/10.3390/s17092022
15. He, K., Gkioxari, G., Dollár, P., Girshick, R.B.: Mask R-CNN. CoRR abs/1703.06870 (2017). https://arxiv.org/abs/1703.06870
16. He, K., Zhang, X., Ren, S., Sun, J.: Deep residual learning for image recognition. In: Proceedings of the IEEE Conference on Computer Vision and Pattern Recognition, pp. 770–778 (2016)
17. Hughes, D.P., Salathé, M.: An open access repository of images on plant health to enable the development of mobile disease diagnostics through machine learning and crowdsourcing. CoRR abs/1511.08060 (2015). https://arxiv.org/abs/1511.08060
18. Jiang, F., Lu, Y., Chen, Y., Cai, D., Li, G.: Image recognition of four rice leaf diseases based on deep learning and support vector machine. Comput. Electron. Agric. **179**, 105824 (2020)
19. Jiang, P., Chen, Y., Liu, B., He, D., Liang, C.: Real-time detection of apple leaf diseases using deep learning approach based on improved convolutional neural networks. IEEE Access **7**, 59069–59080 (2019). https://doi.org/10.1109/ACCESS.2019.2914929
20. Li, D., et al.: A recognition method for rice plant diseases and pests video detection based on deep convolutional neural network. Sensors **20**(3), 578 (2020). https://doi.org/10.3390/s20030578, https://www.mdpi.com/1424-8220/20/3/578
21. Li, L., Zhang, S., Wang, B.: Apple leaf disease identification with a small and imbalanced dataset based on lightweight convolutional networks. Sensors **22**(1), 173 (2021)
22. Li, L., Zhang, S., Wang, B.: Plant disease detection and classification by deep learning-a review. IEEE Access **9**, 56683–56698 (2021)
23. Lin, T.Y., Dollár, P., Girshick, R., He, K., Hariharan, B., Belongie, S.: Feature pyramid networks for object detection. In: Proceedings of the IEEE Conference on Computer Vision and Pattern Recognition, pp. 2117–2125 (2017)
24. Liu, B., Ding, Z., Tian, L., He, D., Li, S., Wang, H.: Grape leaf disease identification using improved deep convolutional neural networks. Front. Plant Sci. **11**, 1082 (2020). https://doi.org/10.3389/fpls.2020.01082, https://www.frontiersin.org/article/10.3389/fpls:2020:01082
25. Mitra, A., Mohanty, S.P., Corcoran, P., Kougianos, E.: A machine learning based approach for deepfake detection in social media through key video frame extraction. SN Comput. Sci. **2**(2), 98 (2021). https://doi.org/10.1007/s42979-021-00495-x
26. Mitra, A., Mohanty, S.P., Kougianos, E.: aGROdet: a novel framework for plant disease detection and leaf damage estimation. In: Proceedings of 5th FIP International Internet of Things (IoT) Conference (IFIP-IoT) (2022, accepted)
27. Mitra, A., Singhal, A., Mohanty, S.P., Kougianos, E., Ray, C.: eCrop: a novel framework for automatic crop damage estimation in smart agriculture. SN Comput. Sci. **3**(4), 16p (2022). https://doi.org/10.1007/s42979-022-01216-8

28. Mitra, A., et al: Everything you wanted to know about smart agriculture. CoRR abs/2201.04754 (2022). https://arxiv.org/abs/2201.04754
29. National Academies of Sciences, Engineering and Medicine and Others: Science Breakthroughs to Advance Food and Agricultural Research by 2030. National Academies Press (2019)
30. Rehman, Z.U., et al.: Recognizing apple leaf diseases using a novel parallel real-time processing framework based on MASK RCNN and transfer learning: an application for smart agriculture. IET Image Process. 15(10), 2157–2168 (2021)
31. Ren, S., He, K., Girshick, R., Sun, J.: Faster R-CNN: towards real-time object detection with region proposal networks. Adv. Neural Inf. Process. Syst. 28 (2015)
32. Rosebrock, A.: Mask R-CNN with OpenCV. https://pyimagesearch.com/2018/11/19/mask-r-cnn-with-opencv/. Accessed 10 June 2022
33. Singh, V., Misra, A.: Detection of plant leaf diseases using image segmentation and soft computing techniques. Inf. Process. Agric. 4(1), 41–49 (2017). https://doi.org/10.1016/j.inpa.2016.10.005, https://www.sciencedirect.com/science/article/pii/S2214317316300154
34. Wang, G., Sun, Y., Wang, J.: Automatic image-based plant disease severity estimation using deep learning. Comput. Intell. Neurosci. 2017 (2017)
35. Wang, P., Niu, T., Mao, Y., Zhang, Z., Liu, B., He, D.: Identification of apple leaf diseases by improved deep convolutional neural networks with an attention mechanism. Front. Plant Sci. 12 (2021). https://doi.org/10.3389/fpls.2021.723294, https://www.frontiersin.org/article/10:3389/fpls:2021:723294
36. Wang, Q., Qi, F., Sun, M., Qu, J., Xue, J.: Identification of tomato disease types and detection of infected areas based on deep convolutional neural networks and object detection techniques. Comput. Intell. Neurosci. 2019 (2019)

Security and Safety

Sensor-Based PUF: A Lightweight Random Number Generator for Resource Constrained IoT Devices

Maaike Hillerström[1], Ikram Ullah[2(✉)], and Paul J. M. Havinga[2]

[1] University of Twente, Enschede, The Netherlands
m.a.m.hillerstrom@student.utwente.nl
[2] Pervasive Systems Group, Department of Computer Science,
University of Twente, Enschede, The Netherlands
{i.ullah,p.j.m.havinga}@utwente.nl

Abstract. Internet of Things (IoT) prevalence is surging swiftly over the past years, and by 2050, the number of IoT devices are expected to exceed 50 billion. IoT has been deployed in many application domains such as smart health, smart logistics and smart manufacturing. IoT has significantly improved quality of our day-to-day life. However, IoT faces multiple challenges due to its lack of adequate computational and storage capabilities and consequently it is very strenuous to implement sophisticated cryptographic mechanisms for security, trust and privacy. The number of IoT devices are increasing drastically which potentially leads to additional challenges namely transparency, scalability and central point of failure. Furthermore, the growing number of IoT applications induces the need of decentralized and resource constrained mechanisms. Therefore, in this paper, we propose a decentralized Random Number Generator (RNG) based on sensor Physical Unclonable Functions (PUF) in smart logistics scenario. PUF is a secure and lightweight source of randomness and hence suitable for constrained devices. Data is collected from various sensors and processed to extract cryptographically secure seed. NIST tests are performed to appraise the aptness of the proposed mechanism. Moreover, the seed is fed into an Elliptic Curve Cryptographic (ECC) mechanism to generate pseudo-random numbers and keys which can potentially be used for authentication, encryption and decryption purposes.

Keywords: Internet of Things · Decentralization · Random number generator · NIST · ECC

1 Introduction

In this paper, we propose a lightweight sensor-based PUF random number generator. As per Gartner IoT definition, "IoT is the network of physical objects that contain embedded technology to communicate and sense or interact with their internal states or the external environment" [1]. Physical objects can be any device that can be connected to the Internet such as sensors, smartphones and tablets. Over the years, the freight transportation industry has undergone some significant changes, which introduce new challenges. Transportation companies have more vehicles to manage, their customers have

© IFIP International Federation for Information Processing 2022
Published by Springer Nature Switzerland AG 2022
L. M. Camarinha-Matos et al. (Eds.): IFIPIoT 2022, IFIP AICT 665, pp. 89–105, 2022.
https://doi.org/10.1007/978-3-031-18872-5_6

higher delivery demands, and the transportation network has become more complex [4]. IoT has been playing a significant role to overcome these challenges. For instance, traditional logistics processes are mainly manual, thus error prone and time consuming. IoT has transformed the traditional logistics into smart logistics which is more dynamic, robust and efficient.

IoT devices generate and exchange enormous amount of data and these data are commonly called as "big data" [2]. Various IoT services use "big data" for monitoring, optimization, learning, automation [6] and ultimately impel eminent applications for our day-to-day life. In the pursuance of secure data communication and access, there is growing need for IoT data security. Although, many security schemes are proposed in the literature, however, most of them are developed for mobile devices, which have more power and computational resources than the resource constrained IoT devices and conventional schemes are not scalable. For smart logistics, the limited power, storage and computational resources of the IoT devices must be taken into account when developing IoT security schemes. Another important requirement for smart logistics security mechanisms is implicit security, where human interactions (manual configuration) are not required to set up and configure keys, since in smart logistics sensors are deployed remotely and are large in numbers. This means that the sensors are capable of generating their own cryptographic keys without the necessity of manual configuration or a central party [27]. This we refer to as an implicit and decentralized cryptographic scheme.

Furthermore, random number generators play a very crucial role in cryptographic mechanisms [33,36]. Insecure random number generators can imperil security algorithms and ultimately lead to vulnerabilities [27]. PUFs are a very good candidate for randomization, as they are very secure by relying on uncontrollable manufacturing variations and they are suitable for constrained devices. Due to the manufacturing variations for instance each accelerometer or gyroscope generates different data, even when they share the exact same movements. Therefore, this research focuses on the use of sensor-based PUF to generate random numbers for cryptographic mechanisms in smart logistics. In our proposed algorithms, we extract randomness from data based on the manufacturing variations of the sensors, which can be ultimately used in implicit security mechanisms. Furthermore, a sensor-based PUF uses the already existing sensors in the node without the need of any additional hardware. This would reduce the costs, since no additional sensory circuit is required. We have illustrated that the proposed algorithms are adept to extract randomness from sensor data. The randomness is validated through NIST tests. We have also compared our results with SRAM PUFs [32]. Furthermore, we have used an existing Elliptic Curve Cryptographic (ECC) mechanism [35] as pseudo-random number generator based on the extracted seed.

2   Our Contributions

In this research, various algorithms are proposed to extract secure random seed from sensor-based PUF for decentralized IoT application particularly for smart logistics. NIST tests are performed. And finally, an ECC mechanism is used to generate pseudo-random numbers and cryptographic keys from the extracted seed.

3 Background Knowledge

In this section, we provide a brief introduction of terminologies that are related to randomness in information security.

Entropy. Entropy is "the measure of randomness in data" [28]. In other words, it is "the amount of uncertainty an attacker faces to determine the value of a secret" [29]. A sequence which has n bit entropy has the same randomness of a uniformly distributed n bit sequence [29]. It is a key factor in information theory. As defined in [30], let us suppose a random sequence $\{x_1, ...x_n\}$ with probability $(p_1, ..., p_n)$ then the entropy of a discrete random variable X is given below.

$$H(X) \equiv H(p_1, ..., p_n) = -\sum_{i=1}^{n} p_i logp_i \tag{1}$$

Randomness Extractor. Randomness extraction is the primary phase of key generation [31]. It is a mechanism to transform a minimal entropy source into a shorter but maximal entropy (uniformly distributed). The output of randomness extractor is non-deterministic and thus suitable for cryptographic purposes. Not all sources of randomness in the raw format are random enough. Therefore, randomness extraction is used. Randomness extractor can be represented as below.

$$Ext : \{0, 1\}^q \rightarrow \{0, 1\}^p \quad where\, q > p \tag{2}$$

Fast Fourier Transform (FFT). Fast Fourier Transform (FFT) is one of the most important mathematical operation that is used to represent data in the frequency domain. It is fast mechanism to depict frequency components of the data (spectral analysis). It can be formulated as below.

$$X_k = \sum_{n=0}^{N-1} x_n e^{-2\pi ikn/N} where\, X_k \;\; is \;\; amplitude \;\; and \;\; phase \tag{3}$$

Shuffling Algorithm. Fisher-Yates Shuffle is a simple shuffling algorithm to obtain a random permutation of a finite array. In order to shuffle an array (Arr) with n elements, generate a random number between $(0, .., n-1)$, and swap the $n-1$ element of the array with the element at the index position of the random number, in the next iteration generate a random number between $(0, .., n-2)$ and swap the element at position $n-2$ with the element at the index position of the random number and so on. Pseudo-code of the Fisher-Yates algorithm is given below.

```
for i from n-1 downto 1 do
    j ← random integer such that 0 ≤ j ≤ i
    exchange Arr[j] and Arr[i]
```

Hamming Distance. Hamming distance corresponds to the positions where two binary sequences (X, Y) differ. It is used to compare bit sequences of equal length. Hamming distance tests are performed to compare the output sequences of the randomness extractor for uniform distribution. It can be represented as below.

$$f_{HD}(X, Y) = \sum_{i=0}^{n} x_i \oplus y_i \tag{4}$$

Elliptic Curve. Elliptic Curve Cryptography (ECC) is a public-key cryptography. It is a collection of asymmetric key generation, digital signatures, encryption and decryption mechanisms. Elliptic Curve (EC) is illustrated by an equation below. The curve has two main features: horizontal symmetry and non-vertical lines on the curve can intersect the curve at no more than 3 places. Let E be an elliptic curve over a finite field F and a, b, x and y are elements on the field.

$$E : y^2 = x^3 + ax + b \tag{5}$$

NIST Test Suite. Presently, NIST is a standard state of the art randomness validation suite [32]. The NIST test suite [34] contains multiple statistical tests, designed for cryptographic purposes, that analyses a sequence for its randomness.

4   Related Work

PUFs are based on the natural variabilities that emerge from the manufacturing process, which make it impossible to create an identical device with the same circuit characteristics. These uncontrollable, device specific variations serve as a digital fingerprint to the device and can be used for various security applications such as device-identification, authentication and in encryption key generation. Many different PUF types have been designed in the last decade. The *optical* PUF consists of a transparent optical medium that is explicitly added to the device during manufacturing. The *coating* PUF is an explicit PUF based on a coating layer added on the chip. In case of a *magnetic* PUF [30] on a magnetic strip a ferromagnetic material is added, consisting of particles varying in size, shape and position. *Memory* PUFs are based on the preferred stable state of memory cells. The *threshold voltage (Vt)* PUF is based on the manufacturing variations of transistors. The *carbon nanotube* PUF exploits the manufacturing variations of the transistor. The *power distribution* PUF is based on the unique characteristics of power transfer lines in the power distribution grid in a circuit. The *acoustical* PUF uses acoustical delay lines of a circuit to characterize a system. The *super high information content (SHIC)* PUF uses nano-diodes in a matrix configuration, where each diode has an unique output. A *board* PUF is an explicit PUF consisting of a layer of capacitors implemented on a printed circuit board (PCB). A *delay based* PUF is an implicit PUF based on variations in delay of two identical paths in the chip circuit. In the *arbiter* PUF a comparator determines which path is the fastest and accordingly outputs a '0' or a '1' as PUF response. The *clock* PUF is very similar to the *arbiter* PUF, as it determines the fastest path in the clock network of the circuit. A *Ring-Oscillator (RO)* PUF measures the delay of two identical circuit paths in a different manner as it is based on an oscillating frequency. A *Radio Frequency (RF)* based PUF uses the characteristics of a radio frequency wave to identify a system. The *sensor* PUF uses a sensor or a combination of multiple sensors to produce the PUF output. In Table 1 an overview of the comparison is given. As can be seen from Table 1 most PUFs are explicit and have extrinsic evaluation. This means that for most of these PUFs additional manufacturing steps are needed, which costs valuable time and money. In this research our aim is to propose PUFs mechanisms that are suitable for constrained devices and decentralized application without requiring dedicated hardware or architecture.

Table 1. PUFs comparison table. Implicit PUFs are inherent to the device, explicit PUFs need manufacturing variations explicitly added to the device. Extrinsic evaluation means the output is evaluated outside the PUF device, intrinsic evaluation happens on the PUF device. The Fractional Hamming Distance (FHD) inter is the similarity between the output from two different PUFs to the same input. The FHD intra is the similarity between the output from one input given to the same PUF twice. In modeling attacks, the PUF can be cloned when input-output pairs are known.

PUF	Reference	Parameter	Implicity	Evaluation	FHD inter (%)	FHD intra (%)	Tamper evident	Modeling attack
Optical	[7,8]	Light intensity	Explicit	Extrinsic	49.79	25.25	Yes	Not possible
Phosphor	[9,10]	UV light intensity	Explicit	Extrinsic	?	?	Yes	?
Coating	[7,11]	Capacitance	Explicit	Extrinsic	~50	<5	Yes	Possible
Magnetic	[10,12]	Magnetic field	Implicit	Extrinsic	?	?	Yes	?
SRAM	[7,13]	Transistor power-up state	Implicit	Intrinsic	49.97	3.57	?	Possible
Threshold Voltage	[10,14]	Transistor voltage	Implicit	Intrinsic	50	1.30	?	?
Carbon nanotube	[10,15]	Transistor current	Explicit	Extrinsic	49.67	1.90	?	Not possible
Power distribution	[7,16]	Resistance	Explicit	Extrinsic	?	?	Yes	?
Acoustical	[7,17]	Frequency spectrum	Implicit	Extrinsic	?	?	Yes	Possible
SHIC	[10,18]	Voltage/ current	Explicit	Extrinsic	?	?	?	Not possible
Board	[10,19]	Capacitance	Explicit	Extrinsic	47.21	3.63	Yes	Not possible
Arbiter	[7,20]	Signal delays	Implicit	Extrinsic	23	5	?	Possible
Clock	[10,21]	Clock signal	Implicit	Extrinsic	50.30	5.07	Yes	?
Ring-oscillator	[7,22]	Frequency	Implicit	Extrinsic	46	0.48	?	Possible
Radio frequency	[7,23]	Radio frequency scattering	Explicit	Extrinsic	?	?	Yes	?
MEMS	[10,24]	Accelerometer values	Explicit	Extrinsic	42.64	92.17	?	?
Sensor PUF	[25]	Characteristics photo diodes	Explicit	Extrinsic	?	?	No	?
Sensor PUF	[26]	Accelerometer values	Implicit	Extrinsic	?	?	No	?

5   Randomness Extraction

Sensor data in the raw format is mostly biased, correlated and not random enough to be used for key derivation. Therefore, randomness extraction mechanisms are used to transform weakly random (raw) sensor data into uniformly distributed sequence. We propose various algorithms aiming to extract uniformly distributed random seed from sensor-PUF data. As described earlier, the methods to obtain random sequences are designed for constrained devices. To randomize the sensor data, we have come up with four algorithms (Algorithm 1, 2, 3, 4).

Algorithm 0. Raw sensor data and combinations of various sensor data is tested for randomness without applying any randomness extraction mechanism.

Algorithm 1. This algorithm aims to randomize the sensor data by multiplying it with a set of three decimal digits of the constants e or π. For both constant up to trillion digits are known, therefore this algorithm does not have reuse the digits in a considerable time. Even if the algorithm would randomize a data stream of one million data points, the constants e or π would last at least, without reusing digits, 10 million and 16 million times, respectively. Five million digits of both constants e or π are loaded and for both constants their decimals are grouped per three decimals. Next, the data is multiplied with the constant's decimal values, from either e or π. Each data point is multiplied with one group of three digits. For example, multiplication of Acc_x, Acc_y, Acc_z with constant e is as follows: $Acc_{x1} \times e_{1-3}$, $Acc_{y1} \times e_{4-6}$, $Acc_{z1} \times e_{7-9}$, $Acc_{x2} \times e_{10-12}$, $Acc_{y2} \times e_{13-15}$, $Acc_{z2} \times e_{16-18}$, etc. After the multiplication the absolute value of the result is taken and the result is converted to binary and tested with the NIST test suite. The pseudo-code is shown in Algorithm 1.

Algorithm 1: Random Sequence generation by multiplication with π

Input: SensorData
Output: RandomSeed
for *i in range(3000, length(SensorData)-3000)* **do**
  └ ProcessedData ← SensorData
PiDecimals ← DecimalsPi
for *i in range(length(PiDecimals) - 3)* **do**
  │ GroupedPiDecimals ← ((PiDecimals(i) × 100) + (PiDecimals(i + 1) × 10) +
  │ PiDecimals(i + 2))
  └ i = i + 3
for *i in range(length(ProcessedData))* **do**
  │ ProcessedData.YPR ← ExtractDecimals(ProcessedData.YPR)
  └ ProcessedData.Heading ← ExtractDecimals(ProcessedData.Heading)

for *i in range(length(ProcessedData))* **do**
  └ MultipliedData ← ProcessedData(i) x GroupedPiDecimals(i)

for *i in range(length(MultipliedData))* **do**
  └ AbsMultipliedData ← abs(MultipliedData)
RandomSeed ← AbsMultipliedData

Algorithm 2. In this algorithm, a bitwise XOR operation on various combinations of data samples is performed. Each data point is converted to a binary value to perform the bitwise XOR operation. Next, the XOR operation takes place in various combinations. In Table 3 the different XOR combinations are given. The bitwise XOR has been performed in the denoted order in the column combinations. For instance, $Acc_x \oplus Gyro_y \oplus Mag_z$ means that first the Acc_x data is XORed with the $Gyro_y$ data and the result is XORed with Mag_z. The pseudo-code is shown in Algorithm 2.

Algorithm 2: Random Sequence generation with XORing of sensor data

---

Input: SensorData
Output: RandomSeed
for *i in range(3000, length(SensorData)-3000)* **do**
  └ ProcessedData ← SensorData
for *i in range(length(ProcessedData))* **do**
  └ AbsDataToProcess ← abs(ProcessedData)
for *i in range(length(ProcessedData))* **do**
  │ ProcessedData.Yaw ← ExtractDecimal(ProcessedData.Yaw)
  │ ProcessedData.Pitch ← ExtractDecimal(ProcessedData.Pitch)
  │ ProcessedData.Roll ← ExtractDecimal(ProcessedData.Roll)
  └ ProcessedData.Heading ← ExtractDecimal(ProcessedData.Heading)
for *i in range(length(AbsDataToProcess))* **do**
  └ BinaryData ← Convert2Binary(AbsDataToProcess)
for *i in range(length(BinaryData))* **do**
  │ $Result_1$ ← XOR($BinaryData_1 \oplus BinaryData_2$)
  └ $Result_2$ ← XOR($Result_1 \oplus BinaryData_3$)
RandomSeed ← $Result_2$

Algorithm 3. The third algorithm is an extension of Algorithm 2. First, the Fast Fourier Transform (FFT) is applied to the data, after which the XOR operation from Algorithm 2 is performed. The FFT of each data stream is calculated separately. This means that no sensors are combined and that the multiple data streams (x, y, z) from one sensor are kept separated as well. The FFT is calculated on the data as one sequence. The result of a FFT consists of a real and an imaginary part. In this algorithm, only the real part is used and the imaginary part is discarded. Besides this, only the decimal number of the real part is used and the integer part is discarded as well. The next step is to convert every data stream to binary values, to be able to perform the bitwise logical XOR operation. Similar to Algorithm 2, the XOR operation is applied to various data combinations as shown in Table 3. The pseudo-code is shown in Algorithm 3.

Algorithm 4. Among all the algorithms mentioned previously, Algorithm 4 is an optimal and secure randomness extraction mechanism. This algorithm is an extension of Algorithm 3. In this algorithm, shuffling is applied to the output data stream of Algorithm 3. Fisher-Yates algorithm is used to perform shuffling and extract random permutations of various bits sizes (i.e. 100000, 512000). Fisher-Yates algorithm is being used since it is unbiased (every permutation is equally likely), linear in time and is fast. The pseudo-code is shown in Algorithm 4.

Algorithm 3: Random Sequence generation with XORing of FFT processed sensor data

---

Input: SensorData
Output: RandomSeed
for i *in range(3000, length(SensorData)-3000)* **do**
  └ ProcessedData ← SensorData
for i *in range(length(ProcessedData))* **do**
  └ AbsDataToProcess ← abs(ProcessedData)
for i *in range(length(ProcessedData))* **do**
  │ ProcessedData.YPR ← ExtractDecimal(ProcessedData.YPR)
  └ ProcessedData.Heading ← ExtractDecimal(ProcessedData.Heading)
for i *in range(length(ProcessedData))* **do**
  │ FFTDataRealImj ← FFT(ProcessedData)
  │ FFTDataReal ← abs(real(FFTDataRealImj))
  └ FFTData ← ExtractDecimal(FFTDataReal)
for i *in range(length(FFTData))* **do**
  └ FFTBinary ← Convert2Binary(FFTData)
for i *in range(length(FFTBinary))* **do**
  │ $FFTXOR_1$ ← XOR($FFTBinary_1$ ⊕ $FFTBinary_2$)
  └ $FFTXOR_f$ ← XOR ($FFTXOR_1$ ⊕ $FFTBinary_3$)
RandomSeed ← $FFTXOR_f$

Algorithm 4: Extraction of Random Seed

Input: SensorData
Output: RandomSeed
for i *in range(3000, length(SensorData)-3000)* **do**
  └ ProcessedData ← SensorData
for i *in range(length(ProcessedData))* **do**
  │ FFTDataRealImj ← FFT(ProcessedData)
  │ FFTDataReal ← abs(real(FFTDataRealImj))
  └ FFTData ← ExtractDecimal(FFTDataReal)
for i *in range(length(FFTData))* **do**
  └ FFTBinary ← Convert2Binary(FFTData)
for i *in range(length(FFTBinary))* **do**
  │ $FFTXOR_1$ ← XOR($FFTBinary_1$ ⊕ $FFTBinary_2$)
  └ $FFTXOR_f$ ← XOR ($FFTXOR_1$ ⊕ $FFTBinary_3$)
DataSize ← length ($FFTXOR_f$)
RandomPerm ← FisherYates(DataSize, 100000)
for i *in range(length(RandomPerm))* **do**
  │ DataPoint ← RandomPerm (i)
  └ RandomSeed ← $FFTXOR_f$(DataPoint)

---

6   Sensor-Based PUF Data Acquisition

This section aims to construct and implement a method with which datasets of sensor data are obtained. The sensing platform is integrated into pallets, and contain several types of sensors, among which an IMU. We have used a 9DoF Inertial Measurement Unit (IMU) as shown in Fig. 1 to gather the movement data. It uses an accelerometer, gyroscope and magnetometer to determine with an on-board processor the linear and angular motion of the object it is attached to. It also uses the on-board processor to calculate the quaternions, yaw, pitch, roll and heading of the device. In this research, we have used both individual sensor data and combining multiple sensors data, namely: accelerometer (x, y, z) $axis$, gyroscope (x, y, z) $axis$, magnetometer (x, y, z) $axis$, quaternions (w, x, y, z) $axis$, yaw, pitch, roll and heading. The purpose behind combining multiple sensors data (i.e. accelerometer + gyroscope + magnetometer) is to analyse the impact of combination on randomness. The data is obtained by driving in a car, in trips ranging from 50 KM to 150 KM. The dataset contains subsets from different car trips, each with the same IMU configurations and positioning of the IMU in the car console. The data is sampled at 100 Hz. The first and last 30 s of data of each trip are removed. This is because during this time the car is assumed to be stationary, making it very unlikely random data would be created by the sensors. At a sampling rate of 100 Hz, 30 s of data amounts to 3000 samples. The absolute value of all data is taken. For some analyses, the data on the different axes of sensors with multiple axes are combined in one data stream per axis. For example, the accelerometer generates data on 3 axes; (x, y, z) $axis$ are combined in one accelerometer data stream. Before combining the yaw, pitch roll (YPR) data into one stream, the decimal values are extracted, to be used for the tests. The integer values are discarded, since visual inspection showed that these are not random values. Also, the decimal values of the heading data are used. Furthermore, for some analyses, the data from multiple sensors are combined into a single stream per axis (i.e. $Acc_{x1} + Gyro_{x1} + Mag_{x1}$).

Fig. 1. Inertial Measurement Unit (IMU) is used to gather the movement data.

7 Results and Discussion

This section discusses the results of the randomness tests performed with the NIST test suite. For the NIST tests, the standard configuration is used, meaning all statistical tests are run. The data is input as ASCIIâĂŹs 0s and 1s and is tested in one sequence. The algorithms are tested on various data sets and varying data points. The size of input bits tested with NIST are ranging from 130000 bits till 1100000. The average size of input bits is approximately 800000. The results of the tests are consistent.

Results of Algorithm 0. The results of Algorithm 0 is shown in Table 2. None of the tested data from sensors and combinations of sensors are random. All tested configurations failed almost all the NIST tests. Therefore we conclude that the gathered data in the its raw form is not random and thus as such not suitable for cryptographic usage.

Results of Algorithm 1. Table 2 shows that Algorithm 1 is not successful in randomizing the data. All tested sequences are not random and failed most of the tests. This is the case for both multiplication by e or π, as well as multiplication the full dataset or only half the dataset. For seven out of eighteen tests the 'rank' and 'linear complexity' tests passed, for both e or π, with the Yaw, Pitch, Roll (decimals) combination for π as exception. This combination did not pass the 'rank' test. The results show that even less tests are passed after manipulation by Algorithm 2, compared to Algorithm 0. Based on our analyses, multiplying sensor data by some constant does not make it random. For Algorithm 1, randomness results almost remained the same when multiplied by e or π. The results shown in the Table 2 is for e.

Results of Algorithm 2. Table 3 shows that results of Algorithm 2 are improved significantly compared to Algorithm 1. For Algorithm 2, based on XORing datapoints, most individual tests are passed and with that most tested sequences (combinations) are determined random. For some sequences the 'random excursions' and 'random excursions variants' tests are executed. In all cases this test is performed, the test passed.

Results of Algorithm 3. For the tests of Algorithm 3 the same sequences are used as for Algorithm 2, this time only the mantissa of Yaw, Pitch & Roll and Heading are used. The algorithm is tested both on the full dataset and half of the dataset. A large percentage of the tested sequences turned out to be random and passed the tests. When the fourier transform is performed on small data points, the sequence Mag_x, Mag_y, Mag_z and the sequence Yaw, Pitch, Roll, Heading are three out of four times not random. For all the sequences where all data points are used to calculate the fourier transform, the results are random. Table 3 shows the results of Algorithm 3.

Results of Algorithm 4. Table 4 NIST results of Algorithm 4 for a random permutation of bits size 100000. The results illustrate that Algorithm 4 has effectively passed all the NIST tests. Which shows that Algorithm 4 is capable of extracting secure and random seed. Furthermore, from a random sequence of bits size 500000 generated by Algorithm 4, 20 different sequences of bits sizes 5000 are extracted and pairwise hamming distance is calculated. Figure 2 shows the pairwise comparison of the 20 different permutations. The results shows that each sequence is completely different from the other sequences. Which clearly demonstrate that the sequences are uniformly distributed; the probability of occurrence of each sequence is almost equal. Algorithm 4 NIST results are compared with SRAM PUFs [32] for the same NIST settings and size of input bits

(512000). Table 5 shows comparison of Algorithm 4 with SRAM PUFs [32]. The results demonstrate the dominance of Algorithm 4 in randomization by passing all NIST tests and assures its feasibility for cryptographic applications.

Table 2. Results of randomness for Algorithm 0 and 1. The percentages depict percentage of sub tests passed. ✓ represents the NIST test is passed, while ✗ represents the NIST test is failed. Blue color depicts Algorithm 0 and green color depicts Algorithm 1. For Algorithm 1, combination of various sensor data is not performed. A – means either the test is not performed or NIST test suite gives no result. On average, the number of input bits to NIST test suite are 800000.

Data stream	Frequency	Block Frequency	Cumulative Sums	Runs	Longest Run	Rank	FFT	Non Overlapping	Overlapping	Universal	Approx Entropy	Random Excursions	Rand Excu Variant	Serial	Linear Complexity
Acc	✗✗	✗✗	✗✗	✗✗	✗✗	✓✗	✗✗	4% 0%	✗✗	✗✗	✗✗	– –	– –	✗✗	✓✗
Gyro	✗✗	✗✗	✗✗	✗✗	✗✗	✓✓	✗✗	5% 5%	✗✗	✗✗	✗✗	– –	– –	✗✗	✓✓
Mag	✗–	✗–	✗–	✗–	✗–	✓–	✗–	0% –	✗–	✗–	✗–	– –	– –	✗–	✓–
Quaternions	✗✗	✗✗	✗✗	✗✗	✗✗	✓✗	✗✗	6% 0%	✗✗	✗✗	✗✗	– –	– –	✗✗	✓✗
YPR	✗✗	✗✗	✗✗	✗✗	✗✗	✗✓	✗✗	0% 13%	✗✗	✗✗	✗✗	– –	– –	✗✗	✓✓
Heading	✗✗	✗✗	✗✗	✗✗	✗✗	✓✗	✗✗	7% 0%	✗✗	✗✗	✗✗	– –	– –	✗✗	✓✗
Acc+Gyro+Mag	✗–	✗–	✗–	✗–	✗–	✓–	✗–	1% –	✗–	✗–	✗–	– –	– –	✗–	✓–
Gyro+Mag	✗–	✗–	✗–	✗–	✗–	✓–	✗–	0% –	✗–	✗–	✗–	– –	– –	✗–	✓–
Mag+Quaternions	✗–	✗–	✗–	✗✗	✗✗	✓–	✗–	2% –	✗–	✗–	✗–	– –	– –	✗–	✓ –

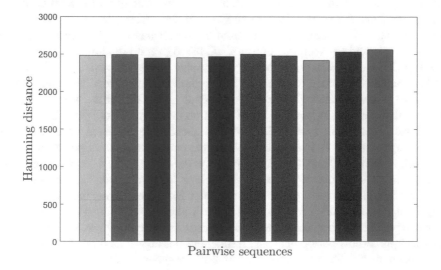

Fig. 2. Pairwise hamming distance between 20 sequences of bits size 5000 each.

8 Complexity

The unique features of the proposed randomness extraction algorithms are that we have used very simple and faster operations (functions) in order to be suitable for decentralized and implicit cryptographic schemes. For the Fisher-Yates algorithms, the time complexity is $O(N)$ where N is the size of the input array (sequence). For FFT, the time complexity is $O(NlogN)$ where N is the data size. The time complexity for XOR operation is $O(N)$, where N is the size of the binary sequences.

9 Pseudo-random Number Generator

Extracting secure seed from sensor-based PUF data might not always be desirable or feasible, so alternatively, we can use a pseudo-random number generator (PRNG) to generate long runs of pseudo-random numbers from the seed. PRNG feeds the seed into a deterministic algorithm to generate pseudo-random sequences in short time and the sequences are statistically pretty close to random. A standard PRNG has three characteristics: deterministic, efficient and periodic. The output of PRNG should be identical to uniformly distributed random variables [33]. Furthermore, PRNG generate uncorrelated sequences and has long period before repeating the cycle. We use an exiting ECC based random number generator [35] to generate pseudo-random numbers and the aim is to demonstrate the use case of the extracted sensor-based PUF seed for key derivation purposes. In comparison with other public key cryptography (RSA), ECC requires smaller key size but proffer similar security. A 256-bit ECC key provides approximately same security as 3072-bit RSA key [36]. Thus it is computationally efficient. Furthermore, ECC is scalable thus suitable for distributed IoT applications. Besides that, ECC is used in Bitcoin to generate public and private keys. The employed ECC mechanism [35] is premised on the addition of points on an EC over finite field. ECC requires random numbers to generate random curves [35] and secret parameters. We propose to use the extracted random sequences from the sensor-based PUF as seed to generate random curves and EC secret parameters. EC based pseudo-random generator as proposed in [35], can be integrated in a cryptographic system, is shown in Fig. 3 and it works as follow. Primarily, a finite field F, an elliptic curve E, a point on the curve P, and a seed k_1 are selected. The size of k_1 depends on the size of the finite field F. We presume that the seed k_1 and the initial point on the curve P can be generated from the our extracted sensor-based PUF random sequences. k_1 which is a seed in the first cycle is input into the $k_n P$ module. The module performs the multiplication between k_n which is an integer and P which is point on the curve and subsequently generates a $k_n P$ point. A sequence of pseudo-random bits x_n are obtained. The new seed k_{n+1} is formed by adding the x-coordinate of the point and the cycle number. As the authors [35] claim, the mechanism can be implemented without an additional hardware or software component which makes it suitable for constrained IoT devices. Furthermore, the statistical properties, period analysis, results and possible structural variations in the block diagram of EC based pseudo-random number generator are available at [35].

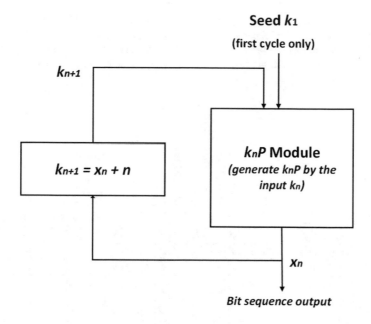

Fig. 3. Block diagram of ECC based pseudo-random number generator [35].

Table 3. Results of randomness for Algorithm 2 and 3. The percentages depict percentage of sub tests passed. ✓ represents the NIST test is passed, while ✗ represents the NIST test is failed. Blue color depicts Algorithm 2 and green color depicts Algorithm 3. A – means either the test is not performed or NIST test suite gives no result. On average, the number of input bits to NIST test suite are 800000.

Data stream	Frequency	Block Frequency	Cumulative Sums	Runs	Longest Run	Rank	FFT	Non Overlapping	Overlapping	Universal	Approx Entropy	Random Excursions	Rand Excu Variant	Serial	Linear Complexity
$Acc_x \oplus Gyro_y \oplus Mag_z$	✓✓	✓✓	✓✓	✗✓	✓✓	✓✓	✓✓	56% 97%	✗✓	✓✓	✗✓	– 100%	– 100%	50%✓	✓✓
$Q_w \oplus Q_x \oplus Q_y \oplus Q_z$	✓✓	✓✓	✓✓	✓✓	✓✓	✓✓	✓✓	99% 99%	✓✓	✓✓	✓✓	– 100%	– 100%	✓✓	✓✓
$Yaw \oplus Pitch \oplus Roll$	✓–	✓–	✓–	✗–	✗–	✓–	✓–	64% –	✓–	✓–	✗–	100% –	100% –	✗–	✓–
$Yaw \oplus Pitch \oplus Roll \oplus Heading$	✓✓	✓✓	✓✓	✓✓	✓✓	✓✓	✓✓	100% 100%	✓✓	✓✓	✓✗	100% –	100% –	✓✓	✓✓
$Q_w \oplus Yaw \oplus Heading$	✓✓	✓✓	✓✓	✓✓	✓✓	✓✓	✓✓	97% 100%	✓✓	✓✓	✓✓	– 100%	– 100%	✓✓	✓✓
$Q_w \oplus Yaw \oplus Heading \oplus Acc_x \oplus Gyro_y \oplus Mag_z$	✓✓	✓✓	✓✓	✓✓	✓✓	✓✓	✓✓	99% 99%	✓✓	✓✓	✓✓	88% 100%	100% 100%	✓✓	✓✓
$Acc_x \oplus Acc_y \oplus Acc_z$	✗✓	✗✓	✗✓	✗✓	✗✓	✓✓	✗✓	25% 100%	✗✓	✗✓	✗✓	– 100%	– 100%	✗✓	✓✓
$Gyro_x \oplus Gyro_y \oplus Gyro_z$	✓✓	✓✓	✓✓	✓✗	✓✗	✓✓	✓✓	100% 95%	✗✗	✓✓	✓✗	100% 100%	100% 100%	✓✓	✓✓
$Mag_x \oplus Mag_y \oplus Mag_z$	✓✓	✓✗	✓✓	✗✗	✓✗	✓✓	✓✓	51% 99%	✓✓	✗✓	✗✗	100% 88%	100% 100%	50%✗	✓✓

Table 4. Results of randomness for Algorithm 4. The number of input bits to NIST test suite are 100000. The percentages depict percentage of sub tests passed. ✓ represents the NIST test is passed, while ✗ represents the NIST test is failed. A – means either the test is not performed or NIST test suite gives no result because the test is not applicable, since there are an insufficient number of cycles.

Data stream	Frequency	Block Frequency	Cumulative Sums	Runs	Longest Run	Rank	FFT	Non Overlapping	Overlapping	Universal	Approx Entropy	Random Excursions	Rand Excu Variant	Serial	Linear Complexity
$Acc_x \oplus Gyro_y \oplus Mag_z$	✓	✓	✓	✓	✓	✓	✓	100%	✓	–	✓	87.5%	100%	✓	✓
$Q_w \oplus Q_x \oplus Q_y \oplus Q_z$	✓	✓	✓	✓	✓	✓	✓	100%	✓	–	✓	–	–	✓	✓
$Yaw \oplus Pitch \oplus Roll \oplus Heading$	✓	✓	✓	✓	✓	✓	✓	100%	✓	–	✓	–	–	✓	✓
$Q_w \oplus Yaw \oplus Heading$	✓	✓	✓	✓	✓	✓	✓	100%	✓	–	–	–	–	✓	✓
$Q_w \oplus Yaw \oplus Heading \oplus Acc_x \oplus Gyro_y \oplus Mag_z$	✓	✓	✓	✓	✓	✓	✓	100%	✓	–	✓	–	–	✓	✓
$Acc_x \oplus Acc_y \oplus Acc_z$	✓	✓	✓	✓	✓	✓	✓	98.6%	✓	–	✓	–	–	✓	✓
$Gyro_x \oplus Gyro_y \oplus Gyro_z$	✓	✓	✓	✓	✓	✓	✓	100%	✓	–	✓	–	–	✓	✓
$Mag_x \oplus Mag_y \oplus Mag_z$	✓	✓	✓	✓	✓	✓	✓	98.6%	✓	–	✓	100%	100%	✓	✓

Table 5. NIST test results of Algorithm 4 are compared with True random number generator based on SRAM PUFs [32]. The results of both the mechanisms are based on same NIST settings and input bits size of 512000.

Test	SRAM PUFs [32]	Our proposed Algorithm 4
Frequency	✓	✓
Cumulative sum	✓	✓
Runs	✓	✓
FFT	✓	✓
Longest run	✓	✓
Block frequency	✓	✓
Approximate entropy	✓	✓
Rank	✓	✓
Serial	✓	✓
Universal	✓	✓
Random excursions	n.a.	✓
Random exc. variant	n.a.	✓
Linear complexity	n.a.	✓
Overlapping template	n.a.	✓
Non-overlap. temp.	n.a.	98.6%

10   Conclusion

Secure access and sharing of data is very important in smart logistics. Random number generators play an important role in security mechanisms. However, generating random numbers is not necessarily straight forward or easy, especially for IoT devices and in IoT circumstances generating random numbers is more challenging. A sensor-based PUF that utilizes the sensors on an IoT device is a potential solution, as physical variations among the sensors could provide a good source of randomness. We proposed various lightweight randomness extraction mechanisms while taking into account the limited power, storage and computational resources of the IoT devices in smart logistics. Based on our analysis, sensor data in the raw form is not random, multiplying sensor data by some constant does not make the data random, XOR operation can somehow improve the randomness, and incorporation of XOR, FFT and random permutation significantly improve randomness and security of the seed. We can conclude that sensor data if processed accordingly can adequately be used to extract cryptographically secure random numbers.

Acknowledgment. This work has been partially supported by the EFRO, OP Oost program in the context of Countdown project.

References

1. Gartner Glossary. www.gartner.com/en/information-technology/glossary/internet-of-things. Accessed 11 Mar 2021
2. Hajjaji, Y., Boulila, W., Farah, I.R., Romdhani, I., Hussain, A.: Big data and IoT-based applications in smart environments: a systematic review. Comput. Sci. Rev. **39**, 100318 (2021). https://doi.org/10.1016/j.cosrev.2020.100318. ISSN 1574-0137
3. Eason, G., Noble, B., Sneddon, I.N.: On certain integrals of Lipschitz-Hankel type involving products of Bessel functions. Phil. Trans. Roy. Soc. London **A247**, 529–551 (1955)
4. Lee, S., Kang, Y., Prabhu, V.V.: Smart logistics: distributed control of green crowdsourced parcel services. Int. J. Prod. Res. **54**(23), 6956–6968 (2016)
5. UNECE. Terminology on combined transport. United Nations Economic Commission for Europe, New York and Geneva (2001)
6. Ullah, I., Meratnia, N., Havinga, P.: iMAC: implicit message authentication code for IoT devices. In: 2020 IEEE 6th World Forum on Internet of Things (WF-IoT), New Orleans, LA, USA, pp. 1–6 (2020). https://doi.org/10.1109/WF-IoT48130.2020.9221331
7. Maes, R., Verbauwhede, I.: Physically unclonable functions: a study on the state of the art and future research directions. In: Sadeghi, A.R., Naccache, D. (eds.) Towards Hardware-Intrinsic Security. Information Security and Cryptography, pp. 3–37. Springer, Heidelberg (2010). https://doi.org/10.1007/978-3-642-14452-3_1
8. Pappu, R., Recht, B., Taylor, J., Gershenfeld, N.: Physical one-way functions. Science **297**(5589), 2026–2030 (2002)
9. Chong, C.N., Jiang, D., Zhang, J., Guo, L.: Anti-counterfeiting with a random pattern. In: 2008 Second International Conference on Emerging Security Information, Systems and Technologies, pp. 146–153. IEEE (2008)
10. McGrath, T., Bagci, I.E., Wang, Z.M., Roedig, U., Young, R.J.: A PUF taxonomy. Appl. Phys. Rev. **6**(1), 011303 (2019)

11. Tuyls, P., Schrijen, G.-J., Škorić, B., van Geloven, J., Verhaegh, N., Wolters, R.: Read-proof hardware from protective coatings. In: Goubin, L., Matsui, M. (eds.) CHES 2006. LNCS, vol. 4249, pp. 369–383. Springer, Heidelberg (2006). https://doi.org/10.1007/11894063_29
12. Indeck, R.S., Muller, M.W.: Method and apparatus for fingerprinting magnetic media. US Patent 5,365,586, 15 November 1994
13. Guajardo, J., Kumar, S.S., Schrijen, G.-J., Tuyls, P.: FPGA intrinsic PUFs and their use for IP protection. In: Paillier, P., Verbauwhede, I. (eds.) CHES 2007. LNCS, vol. 4727, pp. 63–80. Springer, Heidelberg (2007). https://doi.org/10.1007/978-3-540-74735-2_5
14. Lofstrom, K., Daasch, W.R., Taylor, D.: IC identification circuit using device mismatch. In: 2000 IEEE International Solid-State Circuits Conference. Digest of Technical Papers (Cat. No. 00CH37056), pp. 372–373. IEEE (2000)
15. Konigsmark, S.T.C., Hwang, L.K., Chen, D., Wong, M.D.F.: CNPUF: a carbon nanotube-based physically unclonable function for secure low-energy hardware design. In: 2014 19th Asia and South Pacific Design Automation Conference (ASP-DAC), pp. 73–78. IEEE (2014)
16. Helinski, R., Acharyya, D., Plusquellic, J.: A physical unclonable function defined using power distribution system equivalent resistance variations. In: 2009 46th ACM/IEEE Design Automation Conference, pp. 676–681. IEEE (2009)
17. Vrijaldenhoven, S., et al.: Acoustical physical uncloneable functions. Philips Internal Publication PR-TN-2004-300300 (2005)
18. Rührmair, U., Jaeger, C., Hilgers, C., Algasinger, M., Csaba, G., Stutzmann, M.: Security applications of diodes with unique current-voltage characteristics. In: Sion, R. (ed.) FC 2010. LNCS, vol. 6052, pp. 328–335. Springer, Heidelberg (2010). https://doi.org/10.1007/978-3-642-14577-3_26
19. Wei, L., Song, C., Liu, Y., Zhang, J., Yuan, F., Xu, Q.: BoardPUF: physical unclonable functions for printed circuit board authentication. In: Proceedings of the IEEE/ACM International Conference on Computer-Aided Design, pp. 152–158. IEEE Press (2015)
20. Lee, J.W., Lim, D., Gassend, B., Suh, G.E., Van Dijk, M., Devadas, S.: A technique to build a secret key in integrated circuits for identification and authentication applications. In: 2004 Symposium on VLSI Circuits. Digest of Technical Papers (IEEE Cat. No. 04CH37525), pp. 176–179. IEEE (2004)
21. Yao, Y., Kim, M.B., Li, J., Markov, I.L., Koushanfar, F.: ClockPUF: physical unclonable functions based on clock networks. In: Proceedings of the Conference on Design, Automation and Test in Europe, pp. 422–427. EDA Consortium (2013)
22. Gassend, B., Clarke, D., Van Dijk, M., Devadas, S.: Silicon physical random functions. In: Proceedings of the 9th ACM Conference on Computer and Communications Security, pp. 148–160. ACM (2002)
23. DeJean, G., Kirovski, D.: RF-DNA: radio-frequency certificates of authenticity. In: Paillier, P., Verbauwhede, I. (eds.) CHES 2007. LNCS, vol. 4727, pp. 346–363. Springer, Heidelberg (2007). https://doi.org/10.1007/978-3-540-74735-2_24
24. Aysu, A., Ghalaty, N.F., Franklin, Z., Yali, M.P., Schaumont, P.: Digital fingerprints for low-cost platforms using mems sensors. In: Proceedings of the Workshop on Embedded Systems Security, p. 2. ACM (2013)
25. Rosenfeld, K., Gavas, E., Karri, R.: Sensor physical unclonable functions. In: 2010 IEEE International Symposium on Hardware-Oriented Security and Trust (HOST), pp. 112–117. IEEE (2010)
26. Fukushima, K., Hidano, S., Kiyomoto, S.: Sensor-based wearable PUF. In: Secrypt, pp. 207–214 (2016)
27. Ullah, I., Meratnia, N., Havinga, P.: Entropy as a service: a lightweight random number generator for decentralized IoT applications. In: 2020 IEEE International Conference on Pervasive Computing and Communications Workshops (PerCom Workshops), Austin, TX, USA, pp. 1–6 (2020). https://doi.org/10.1109/PerComWorkshops48775.2020.9156205

28. Johnston, A.M.: Comments on cryptographic entropy measurement. Juniper Networks. amj@juniper.net, 30 October 2019. https://eprint.iacr.org/2019/1263.pdf
29. Grassi, P.A., Garcia, M.E., Fenton, J.L.: NIST special publication 800–63-3. Digital Identity Guidelines. https://nvlpubs.nist.gov/nistpubs/SpecialPublications/NIST.SP.800-63-3.pdf
30. Simion, E.: Entropy and randomness: from analogic to quantum world. IEEE Access **8**, 74553–74561 (2020). https://doi.org/10.1109/ACCESS.2020.2988658
31. Fouque, P.-A., Pointcheval, D., Zimmer, S.: HMAC is a randomness extractor and applications to TLS. In: Proceedings of the 2008 ACM symposium on Information, computer and communications security (ASIACCS 2008), pp. 21–32. Association for Computing Machinery, New York (2008). https://doi.org/10.1145/1368310.1368317
32. Leest, V.V.D., Sluis, E.V.D., Schrijen, G.J., Tuyls, P., Handschuh, H.: Efficient implementation of true random number generator based on SRAM PUFs. Intrinsic-ID, Eindhoven (2012). https://www.intrinsic-id.com/wp-content/uploads/2017/05/True-Random-Number.pdf
33. Röck, A.: Pseudorandom number generators for cryptographic applications. Diplomarbeit zur Erlangung des Magistergrades an der Naturwissenschaftlichen Fakultat der Paris-Lodron-Universitat Salzburg Salzburg, March 2005
34. Rukhin, A.L., et al.: NIST Special Publication 800-22: a statistical test suite for random and pseudorandom number generators for cryptographic applications. NIST, April 2010
35. Lee, L.-P., Wong, K.-W.: A random number generator based on elliptic curve operations. Comput. Math. Appl. **47**(2–3), 217–226 (2004). https://doi.org/10.1016/S0898-1221(04)90018-1. ISSN 0898-1221
36. Suárez-Albela, M., Fernández-Caramés, T.M., Fraga-Lamas, P., Castedo, L.: A practical performance comparison of ECC and RSA for resource-constrained IoT devices. In: 2018 Global Internet of Things Summit (GIoTS), Bilbao, Spain, pp.1–6 (2018). https://doi.org/10.1109/GIOTS.2018.8534575

A Logic Programming Approach to Incorporate Access Control in the Internet of Things

Ilse Bohé[✉], Michiel Willocx, Jorn Lapon, and Vincent Naessens

DistriNet - KU Leuven, Technology Campus, Ghent, Belgium
{ilse.bohe,michiel.willocx,jorn.lapon,vincent.naessens}@kuleuven.be

Abstract. In the present digital world, we depend on information technology more than ever. Our economy, health, well-being and even our lives depend on it. Information security is a basic requirement, with access control playing a key role in limiting potential risks. However, the digital environment is no longer limited to data, access to the IoT space must also be handled properly.

Logic has shown to be very useful in access control. It has been used to formally explain and verify access control policies. Here, logic is employed as a reasoning service in support of other systems. However, a general access control mechanism for logic programs is not available.

This paper presents a structural approach that brings Access Control to Logic Programming. It allows to constrain access to the knowledge base, supporting the use of impure predicates, preventing unauthorized side effects (i.e. controlling IoT devices) taking place.

Keywords: Access control · Logic programming · Impure logic · IoT

1 Introduction

The technological revolution has given rise to impactful technologies. Sharing and processing information is a key factor for improvement. Unfortunately, the many examples of data breaches [3,6] and the loss of privacy represent a permanent threat. Several access control strategies have been developed to help in securing this data. Although access control may seem conceptually straightforward, its integration is often complex and error-prone. Over the years, research on access control that harnesses logic is substantial: it has been used to formally verify security properties; to explain, express and enforce access control policies, etc. While knowledge bases may house huge amounts of data and knowledge, research on the use of access control within knowledge representation and reasoning systems is very limited. As former research shows, logic easily lends itself in expressing and enforcing access control policies. However, no structural approach is available to enforce access control inside logic programs.

This work examines how common access control mechanisms can be enforced in logic programs such as programs written in Prolog, Datalog, Logica [9] and

© IFIP International Federation for Information Processing 2022
Published by Springer Nature Switzerland AG 2022
L. M. Camarinha-Matos et al. (Eds.): IFIPIoT 2022, IFIP AICT 665, pp. 106–124, 2022.
https://doi.org/10.1007/978-3-031-18872-5_7

Yedalog [5]. A straightforward approach would be to verify access control policies and remove predicates that do not comply with the policy during consultation of the program. This mimics standard access control to resources as a whole (e.g. a file). In logic programs, however, access control can be much more versatile. Not only access to data or entities can be controlled, but also access to knowledge (i.e. the reasoning itself). Resulting in complex access control logic. Intuitively, when access is denied, the knowledge should appear as nonexistent, and the user only has a limited view on the knowledge base. In other words, queries requiring inaccessible knowledge for its reasoning, do not return results. Otherwise, they must produce the same results as if no access control were used. In that sense, impure predicates require special care. Impure predicates result in side effects, when the predicate is resolved [17]. For instance, consider the `open(Lock)` predicate that opens the smart door lock, `Lock`. It is impossible to revert the side effects upon backtracking. In the light of access control, it is therefore very important that side effects only occur when allowed.

Contributions. This paper presents a solution that evaluates access control policies during resolution in logic programs, taking special care for impure predicates, (e.g., actions in the IoT space). It provides a high expressiveness and fine-grained control of the program and makes it a widely applicable approach. A *deny as soon as possible* strategy is used, but decisions are postponed until they can be decided with certainty. Moreover, as enforcement occurs during inference, the approach easily extends to the dynamic case such as a reactive system (i.e., one that responds to external inputs). In this approach, access rules are defined as part of the program logic. In other words, the rules can take advantage of the program's knowledge base. Hence, expressing access control strategies, such as resource based, role based and relationship based access control, is straightforward. To validate and demonstrate the approach, an implementation is provided as a Prolog meta-interpreter, named ACoP. It can easily be integrated in existing Prolog programs with minimal effort. Overhead is limited to defining the access rules, also in Prolog.

The remainder of this paper is structured as follows. Section 2 points to related work in the field of access control. Section 3 explains the design of the proposed solution. More details on the Prolog implementation of ACoP can be found in Sect. 4 together with an evaluation of the implementation. Section 5 discusses the work and the paper ends with conclusions.

2   Previous and Related Work

A Logic Programming IoT Reasoning Middleware. The work builds on a previously proposed reasoning middleware for the IoT [2]. The middleware hosts a modular, module-based, logic reasoner, developed in Prolog. Each module has its own functionality, including access control. In this work we look at how the existing access control module can be extended to support multiple access control strategies, without increasing the overhead for the developer.

Access Control. For many years, logic programming has been used to support access control [1,12,15]. Also more recent work takes advantage of formal logic to realize and verify access control models. There are several established access control models, ranging from easy to implement strategies, such as consulting an access control matrix, over rule based access control (RBAC), to more complex strategies such as organizational based access control (OrBAC) [18] and relationship based access control (ReBAC) [8]. Huynh et al. defined an alternative strategy that uses priority, modality and specificity to handle conflicts [10]. The multi-layered access control model was implemented in both ProB and Alloy. ProB is a model checking tool for the B programming language, helping the developer by detecting errors in B specifications [13]. Similarly, Alloy is a language for describing structural properties [11]. Both languages are thus suited for writing complex access rules policies, free of conflicts. The work of Kolovski et al., provide a formalization of XACML, using description logic which is the basis for the Web Ontology Language (OWL) [12]. Now, XACML is a widely used and standardized access-control policy language.

In the related work described above, the use of logic programming is limited to either the specification, the design and/or verification of access control policies. The logic programs are merely used as a tool or in the backend of a bigger non-logic-based system. On the contrary, the proposed solution can be used inside logic programs to enforce access control. Provided translation, however, rules written in B, Alloy or XACML can be used by ACoP.

Sartoli et al. use Answer Set Programming (ASP) to implement adaptive access control policies, allowing access control on incomplete policies and imperfect data [16]. This approach is interesting as it can handle exceptional cases and supports dynamic environments where former believes may conflict with new observations. While the policies are specified and handled in ASP, the focus is also in providing support as backend solution towards external systems.

Bruckner et al. present a policy system that allows to compile access control policies in the application logic [4]. An automatically created domain specific language is therefore cross-compiled into the host language. Although the system puts no restrictions on the host language, it is unclear if it transfers to logic programming languages as well.

To the best of our knowledge, ACoP is the first to provide a solution to apply access control to logic programs. Hence, the focus of this paper is on how access control can be enforced on the reasoning of logic programs. It not only allows to control access to data or entities, but also to control access to knowledge (e.g., rules).

Support for Logic Programming Languages. Several logic programming languages exist. The proposed solution is validated by a Prolog implementation, and can be integrated into existing Prolog programs. Nevertheless, the approach may be extended to other logic programming languages as well. Examples are Datalog [14], a subset of Prolog, or the more recent Logica [9], a modern logic programming language for data manipulation. However, while in Prolog the meta-interpreter and policies can be fully written in the language itself, writing a meta-interpreter for Datalog and Logica may require more effort and the possibilities to define access control rules will be more restricted.

3   General Approach

Access control is the act of ensuring that a user only has access to what she is entitled to. It is usually defined in three levels, using an access control policy, a security model and a security mechanism [15]. The *policy* expresses the rules according to which control must be regulated. The *security model* provides a formal model of the policy and its working, and the *security mechanism* defines the low level functionality that implements the controls as formally stated in the model. Logic programs naturally support logic-based formulations of access control policies, providing clean foundations and a high expressiveness. In fact, it merges both access control policy and security model, into a single formal specification of the policy. In the remainder, we make no distinction between both, and will use the access control policy to denote both.

In this work, access control policies are defined at the predicate level, by specifying whether access to the predicate is allowed or denied. To ensure completeness (i.e., in case no authorization is specified), a default policy is used. Whether an open (i.e., default access) or a closed policy (i.e., default access denied) is used, is configured at design time by the policy administrator.

Figure 1 shows the structure of a target logic program, protected by the ACoP system. Queries sent to the ACoP system are resolved by the access control module implementing the security mechanism. The burden of adding access control to a logic program is very limited. Introducing access control to a target program requires no changes to the program itself. It only requires the definition of the access control policies and the configuration of the the access control module.

In the following sections, the policies and the access control module will be defined.

3.1   Access Control Strategy and Policies

The applied access control strategy in ACoP is the following: *deny access as soon as possible*. Therefore, access is already verified before the predicate is being resolved, i.e., preliminary access control. If, based on the defined access control policies, it determines that access is denied, resolution will stop. If it cannot yet determine whether access is denied, an attempt will be made to resolve the predicate. Once the predicate is resolved, access is verified again with the now resolved predicate.

Inaccessible data appears as nonexistent. Thus, the user only has a limited view of the entire knowledge base. Queries to inaccessible data do not return any answers, while queries for accessible data should produce the same results as when no access control is used. Note that this may result in a change of semantics: When no results are retrieved, it may either indicate that no answers to the query exist, or that the user has insufficient rights to access the information.

In general, access control policies use a combination of an *Object*, being the resource to which access is requested, and a *Condition*, defining the constraints that need to hold before access is granted. Based on the type of conditions that can be specified, different access control models exist (e.g., attribute-based, role-based, rule-based, discretionary or mandatory access control). For instance, conditions may relate to the subject, the current context, the allowed operations, etc.

In ACoP, objects are represented by predicates, with no restrictions on how conditions are defined. In other words, any access control model can be supported. The object of an access policy is either allowed or denied, depending on customised conditions. Basically, allow and deny access policies, are defined as follows:

```
allow(Pred(...)) :- <conditions>.
deny(Pred(...)) :- <conditions>.
```

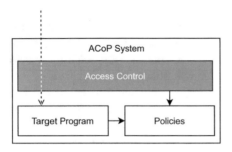

Fig. 1. Structure of the ACoP access control system

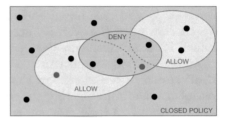

Fig. 2. Venndiagram depicting allowed or denied predicates (•) for a closed policy

Positive and Negative Policies. The permission of an access policy is either positive (`allow`) or negative (`deny`), granting and refusing access to the predicate respectively. `Pred` is the target predicate (defined or used in the Program) to which the permission applies, i.e. the access rule's object. The predicate may contain a number of atoms as arguments to constrain the applicability of the permissions, others may be left open (i.e., remain variable).

Optional `conditions` define under what circumstances the permission applies. These conditions may contain custom logic, or refer to predicates defined by the target program. Sometimes, permission is not based on the validity of a predicate in a target program, but on whether access to that predicate is granted. Therefore, the predicate `access/1` is introduced. This predicate allows to verify if access is granted to a predicate in the target program.

Multiple permission rules may be defined on the same predicate, both allow or deny, and with different conditions or arguments. The access control module will correctly resolve the potentially conflicting policies, based on the configured access control strategy.

By supporting both allow and deny policies, ACoP allows for more fine-grained rules, in contrast to whether only one type of permission can be specified. In Listing 1.1, the specification of some example access control policies is given for a manufacturing environment. The predicate `user/1` requests the identifier

```
% policy 1
allow(machine(M)) :- user(U), line_manager(U,P), location(M,P).
% policy 2
allow(start_machine(M)) :- access(machine(X)).
% policy 3
deny(start_machine(M)) :- night_time.
```

Listing 1.1. Example access control policies in a manufacturing environment.

of the entity issuing the request to access the object of the policy. The policies are the following. In general, a machine M is accessible to the manager of the production line in which the machine is located (policy 1). Starting a machine M is permitted when access to the machine itself is allowed (policy 2). However, starting a machine during night time is prohibited (policy 3). Hence, policy 3 further restricts policy 2.

Completeness. For *completeness*, it is required to resolve authorization when no permissions are defined. Therefore, ACoP can be configured for either an *Open* or a *Closed* policy. In an open policy strategy, access is granted by default, while in a closed strategy, access is denied. In traditional access control systems, closed policies are custom as a fail-safe alternative when no permission is defined. However, in logic programs, it could make sense to use an open policy. For instance, in a reactive system controlling a robot, all reasoning is by default allowed, except for the impure predicates that are used to control the robot.

Conflict Resolution. To ensure consistency, proper conflict resolution is required. The meaning and resolution of permissions depends on the strategy in use. In a closed policy, one should define allow policies to provide access to predicates. In other words, accessible predicates must be 'allow listed'. To support a more fine grained allow listing, deny policies may overrule accessible predicates. As shown in Figure 2, a deny policy may partially overrule one or more allow policies at once. The opposite reasoning applies for an open policy. Deny policies restrict access to predicates (deny listing). Analogous to the closed case, allow policies may overrule the deny policies, and make access less stringent. This also defines how conflicts are resolved. When access is granted by default, this is also what takes precedence in case of a conflict. Contrarily, when access is denied, denial takes precedence.

Controlled Reasoning. In traditional systems, access control only applies to resources. In contrast, in logic programs, access control can be extended towards its logic rules. When no explicit permissions were found for a certain predicate, ACoP can be configured to infer permissions based on logic rules defining the predicate. In the following, this will be denoted as *body resolution*. This is achieved by scanning the knowledge base for clauses that define the predicate P. Permissions for P are inferred from the predicates defining P (i.e., the body). Permissions for the defining predicates may also be derived from their definition, making access control a recursive process.

Compound Statements. Access on a compound statement depends on the accessibility of the predicates in the statement. Therefore, a conjunction of predicates is allowed when each predicate is accessible, while in a disjunction at least one of the predicates must be accessible. This also reflects what would happen in the 'absence' of certain knowledge.

Impure Logic and the IoT Environment. A straightforward approach to integrate access control into logic programming would be to check for each resolved predicate used during inference, whether it is allowed to be accessed, and only proceed if it is. Otherwise, it fails and proceeds by backtracking. This approach would work in pure logic, but fails as soon as *impure predicates* are involved. The problem with impure predicates is that during resolution of the predicate, side effects can take place which cannot be undone during backtracking.

Since access control is particularly relevant for applications in the IoT space, e.g., sending instructions to a robot, controlling an actuator in a house, etc., it is important to cover this case. Applying access control should be transparent and handle a query as if the knowledge were absent. Access to an impure predicate must therefore be checked before side effects can take place. Hence the preliminary access control and the default strategy to deny access as soon as possible.

3.2   Terminology and Working Example

Before elaborating the process step by step,the terms *subsumption, unification* and *resolution* that are often used in the context of logic programming are explained in more detail. A working example in the field of smart manufacturing, used in Sect. 3.3, is presented.

Subsumption. A predicate A subsumes a predicate B if the predicate A can be made equivalent to B by only instantiating variables in A. For example `location(M,P)` subsumes `location(m1, P)` as the former can be made equivalent to the latter by only instantiating variable M to m1. The predicate `location(M,p1)` does not subsume `location(m1,P)` because, in order to make the predicates equivalent, also variables in the second predicate must be instantiated.

Unification. A predicate A is unifiable with a predicate B if A can be made equivalent to B by instantiating variables in A and/or B. Similarly a predicate A is unified to predicate B if all variables are instantiated to make A equivalent to B. The predicate `location(M,p1)` is unifiable with `location(m1,P)` by instantiating the variable M to m1 and variable P to p1. After unification both predicates are equal (i.e. `location(m1,p1)`).

Resolution. During resolution of a predicate, a logic program recursively searches for terms in the knowledge base that unify with the predicate. After resolution the predicate is resolved. If no unifications can be found, resolution fails. For impure predicates, this is also the moment that side effects occur.

Working Example. Listing 1.2 presents the working example. It consists of machines located in production lines controlled by a line manager. The impure

```
user(alice).
production_line(l1).      machine(m1).      location(m1, l1).
production_line(l2).      machine(m2).      location(m2, l1).
line_manager(bob, l2).    machine(m3).      location(m3, l2).
line_manager(alice, l1).

start_production_line(P) :- production_line(P), location(M,P),
    ↪  start_machine(M).
machine_state(M,S) :- machine(M), request_state(M, S).
% ACCESS CONTROL POLICY 1
allow(location(_,_)).
% ACCESS CONTROL POLICY 2
allow(machine(M)) :- user(U), line_manager(U,P), location(M,P).
% ACCESS CONTROL POLICY 3
allow(start_machine(M)) :- access(machine(M)).
% ACCESS CONTROL POLICY 4
allow(machine_state(M,_)) :- user(U), line_manager(U,L), location(M,L).
```

Listing 1.2. Working Example.

predicates in this example are **start_machine/1**, which sends a request to start a machine, and **request_state/2** to request the current state (on/off) of a machine.

3.3 ACoP Mechanism

To integrate the above access control strategy, ACoP defines a security mechanism, able to enforce permissions on predicates. The rules are applied dynam-

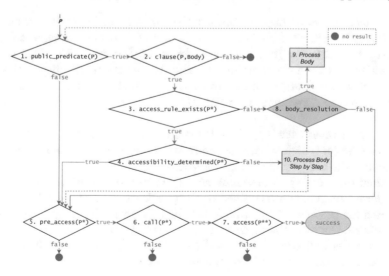

Fig. 3. Simplified flowchart of the ACoP mechanism

ically during logic inference of a query. It intervenes the normal execution by verifying access during resolution. Figure 3 visualizes the logic used to resolve a single predicate based on its access control policies. The same scheme is used for both the open and closed policy strategy, and with or without body resolution. Each step for resolving a predicate P while enforcing access control is explained below. In order to elucidate the procedure, some steps are demonstrated using the example in Listing 2.

1. `public_predicate(P)`. The first step filters impure and private built-in predicates from public facts and rules present in the knowledge base. For impure and private predicates, examining clauses (step 2) will be unsuccessful, furthermore, body resolution is not meaningful. Thus, for these predicates, control is passed to step 5. For public facts or user defined rules, control is passed to step 2.

   Example 1. The predicate `start_machine(m1)` is an impure predicate and will be forwarded directly to step 5.
   The predicates `machine(M)`, `machine_state(M,S)` and `start_production_line(P)` can be mapped to public facts or rules in the knowledge base, and are forwarded to step 2.

2. `clause(P, Body)`. The second step searches for clauses (i.e. facts and rules) in the knowledge base matching the predicate P. When a clause is found, P is unified with the head of that clause (denoted as P'). In case of rules, Body is unified with the body of the rule. For facts, Body is unified with the atom `true`. Hence, Body is not yet resolved and potential side effects do not take place. Alternative clauses are handled on backtracking. If no clause can be found, resolution stops.

   Example 2. Searching for clauses that match `machine(M)`, results in P being unified to `machine(m1)` (i.e. P'), and after backtracking `machine(m2)` and `machine(m3)`. In all cases Body is unified to `true`. The predicate `machine_state(M,S)` is unified to `machine_state(M,S)`, hence the predicate does not change. Body, however, is unified with the compound term `(machine(M), request_state(M,S))`.

3. `access_rule_exists(P')`. The third step checks whether or not an access rule exists for which the target predicate is unifiable with predicate P'. This depends on the predicate name and the arguments of the predicate under evaluation (i.e. P'). A matching access control policy exists if the predicate under evaluation can be unified to the predicate in the policy. If at least one match for predicate P' can be found, further action is taken in step 4. If no access rules match the predicate, access cannot be decided by the provided access rules and control is passed to step 8. The predicate will then either be resolved based on body resolution or determined by the default policy.

Example 3. Policy 2 of the working example matches predicate `machine(m1)`, as the policy's target predicate, `machine(M)` can be made equivalent to the predicate `machine(m1)`.

For `start_production_line(l1)`, however, no matching access rule can be found. In that case, the predicate, together with its matching `Body`, is forwarded to step 8.

4. `accessibility_determined(P')`. This step checks whether or not access to `P'` can already be determined based on the defined access rules. It checks whether the target predicate of each matching access rule (determined in step 3) subsumes the predicate `P'`. In addition, ACoP verifies that no variables are present in both the head and body of the access rule. Those variable terms must be instantiated before access can be properly determined. In case accessibility is determined, step 5 grants or denies access to the predicate. If accessibility is not yet determined (i.e., an access rule matches but does not yet subsume `P'`), the body of the rule will be examined until access is determined in step 10.

Example 4. Accessibility for `machine(m1)` can be determined, as the target predicate of policy 2 (i.e. `machine(M)`) can subsume `machine(M)` and all arguments are sufficiently instantiated to determine access. Access to query all machine states (i.e. `machine_state(M, S)`) cannot be determined yet. Although the target predicate of policy 4 (i.e. `machine_state(M,_)`) subsumes `machine_state(M, S)`, the variable M must be instantiated before access can be determined.

5. `pre_access(P')`. This step preliminary verifies access to the predicate before resolution. This check only fails if it is sure that access to the predicate is denied. Otherwise, the predicate is handed to step 6. Note that the default access control strategy, either open or closed, is taken into account if no access rules match. In case of pure logic, preliminary access control is only useful to stop prematurely, omitting this step would not affect the obtained results. In impure logic, however, this step prevents impure predicates to be executed if not allowed, as the occurred side effects can not be rolled back on backtracking.

6. `resolve(P')`. In this step, the predicate `P'` is resolved. In case of a rule or fact, this means that `Body` defined in step 2 is resolved. In case of an impure or private predicate, the predicate itself is resolved and possible side effects take place. As in execution without access control, when resolving the predicate fails, resolution fails. Otherwise, `P'` is resolved (denoted as `P''`) and is further handled in step 7.

7. `access(P'')`. Similar to step 5, permission to access `P''` is verified. This second iteration is required since additional arguments in the predicate might be instantiated, and certain policies may become applicable. Note that the default access control strategy is also taken into account here. If access is still allowed, the resolution of the predicate ends successfully, else it fails.

8. `body_resolution`. When no explicit permissions are defined for the predicate, this step consults the configuration and checks whether `body_resolution` is active. If that's the case, it proceeds to step 9. Otherwise the predicate is passed to step 5, that takes the default strategy into account to decide upon access to the predicate.

9. *Process Body.* In this block, access to the predicate P' is decided based on the body of the found in step 2. It does this with body resolution, by repeating the entire process for each predicate in Body, taking into account access control in compound statements as described in Sect. 3.1.

   Example 5. The predicate `start_production_line(11)` with body (`production_line(11)`, `location(M,11)`, `start_machine(M)`) ends up in this step. The entire process is thus repeated for the compound term (`production_line(11)`, `location(M,11)`, `start_machine(M)`). As a result all machines in production line will unlock, with the condition that the user has the authority to do so.

10. *Process Body Step by Step.* When a matching access rule exists for the predicate (step 3), but access cannot yet be determined (step 4), the terms in Body are resolved step by step. Processing the body step by step causes variables to be instantiated leading to one of the events below, causing the processing to stop.
    (a) *Access to the predicate P' becomes determined.* Enough terms in Body are resolved such that variables in P' become instantiated and allow to determine the accessibility to the predicate based on the defined access rules. In other words, there exists an access rule's predicate that subsumes predicate P'. Accessibility will then be decided in step 5.
    (b) *The access rules no longer apply.* It is possible that by resolving terms in Body, the arguments are instantiated such that there are no more access rules for which the target predicate matches with predicate P'. Access to predicate P' can then still be decided using body resolution (step 8 and 9).
    (c) *The body is entirely executed.* If after resolving the entire body, the matching access rules are still not subsumable, and thus will never be. Access must be decided using body resolution if applicable (step 8 and 9).

Special care must be taken when Body contains impure predicates, because side effects cannot be reversed. Therefore, an additional access control check is performed on the original predicate before resolving impure predicates during the step by step processing of the body. Impure predicates are thus only executed if access is granted. It is important to keep observing the original predicate to check when one of the above events occurs, as well as to keep track of the terms that have already been resolved. As a term in the body of a rule might be defined by a rule itself, processing the body step by step is a recursive process. After processing the body, already resolved terms must be taken into account such that already executed impure predicates, and corresponding side effects, are not executed twice.

Example 6. The predicate `machine_state(M,S)` with body (`machine(M)`, `request_state(M, S)`) is handled here. To begin, the first term of the compound body (i.e. `machine(M)`) is resolved, resulting in the variable M being instantiated to `m1`. Consequently the original predicate is instantiated to `machine_state(m1,S)`. Now it is necessary to check again whether access to the predicate can be determined (step 4). As the predicate is sufficiently instantiated, and policy 4 subsumes the predicate, access can be decided. The predicate is forwarded to step 5, where the access is determined. As the current user is line manager of the production line where machine `m1` is part of, access is granted and the predicate can be resolved (step 6). The state of the machine is requested and returned to the user.

To generalise the case of access control from a single predicate to compound statements (used in both user queries and logic rules), ACoP applies the rules discussed for compound statements in Sect. 3.1. However, in a conjunction, the resolution of predicates that come later may instantiate variables. As a result, certain access rules may become applicable later. Therefore, an additional access control check is performed on the predicates earlier in the chain to ensure that access is still granted.

4   A Prolog Implementation of ACoP

To validate the security mechanism discussed in Sect. 3, an implementation is available for SWI-Prolog. Access control is enforced by a Prolog meta-interpreter that can be plugged in and configured in any Prolog program. The implementation can be found at https://github.com/ku-leuven-msec/ACoP. In this section, we will take a closer look at some of the implementation details.

4.1   Implementing the Access Control Logic

The meta-interpreter takes advantage of query expansion to replace normal query resolution with inference that includes the ACoP's access control logic. This allows an almost plug-and-play use of access control in an existing program. Access control is transparent to the user and queries send to the reasoner automatically resolve with access control in place.

In the previous section, the steps required to implement the security mechanism have been discussed. The implementation of the most important constructs in Prolog are now discussed in more detail.

public_predicate. As described in Sect. 3.3, the first step is to separate public predicates from private and impure predicates. This is done using the *predicate_property/2* predicate which provides the properties of a given predicate. In the proposed implementation, predicates with the *built_in* or *foreign* property are defined as private, resp. impure predicates. While the former specifies built-in predicates for which no body can be retrieved, the latter defines predicates that have its implementation defined in the C-language. The execution of such predicates often result in side effects (i.e. impure predicates).

Access. The implementation to determine access builds upon the basic predicate subsumes_chk/2 which checks if a predicate can be subsumed by another given predicate.

To determine access to a predicate, two additional rules are defined. The match_allow/1 and match_deny/1 predicates, as shown in Listing 1.3, verify whether there is a definition for a positive, resp. negative permission that matches the predicate P. A policy matches a predicate only if the predicate in the policy (Pol) is more generic or equivalent to P (i.e., using subsumes_chk/2). The access predicate for both the open and closed policy strategy is presented.

```
% Matching allow, resp. deny policies.
match_allow(P) :- copy_term(P,Pol), allow(Pol), subsumes_chk(Pol,P).
match_deny(P) :- copy_term(P,Pol), deny(Pol), subsumes_chk(Pol,P).
% Open policy
access(P) :- (match_allow(P); \+match_deny(P))), !.
% Closed policy
access(P) :- (match_allow(P), \+match_deny(P))), !.
```

Listing 1.3. Checking if access to a predicate is allowed based on current knowledge.

In the *open policy* case, it looks for a matching allow or the absence of a matching deny rule. Hence, access is allowed if there is *a matching allow or no matching deny*. It fails only if there is no matching allow and a matching deny policy.

In the *closed policy* case, reasoning is slightly different, and requires *a matching allow policy and no deny* to be successful. If there is no allow rule or there is a deny rule that applies to the predicate P, access is denied. When a predicate matches multiple policies, backtracking is not desired, therefore, the cut-operator prevents alternative resolutions for granting access.

Process Body Step by Step. When processing the body of a rule step by step, as described in Sect. 3 the current state is tracked. The state keeps track of the terms that have already been resolved and the terms that have not yet been resolved, in order to prevent duplicate resolution of impure predicates. Therefore the predicate state is introduced and defined as follows:

state(Predicate, Resolved, ToResolve).

Predicate is the head of the rule and also the predicate under evaluation, Resolved is a list of the resolved terms and ToResolve is a list of the terms that are not yet resolved. As a term in the body of a rule might be defined by a rule itself, processing the body step by step is a recursive process and the Resolved-list can also contain states of terms. The original predicate for which access must be defined is being monitored after every step, either until access can be decided, the existing access rules are no longer applicable, or the body is completely resolved. The final state is handled depending on how the processing ended. If access is determined and allowed, all terms in `ToResolve` are being resolved. If the existing rules are no longer relevant or the body is entirely processed, body resolution can still be used to decide access. In case body resolution is applicable, it is first checked whether access to the previously resolved terms is allowed. If access is allowed, all terms in `ToResolve` are processed taking into account the access policy.

4.2 Evaluation

Figure 4 shows the execution time for the query `?- machine(M)`, in function of the machines per production line. The smart manufactory as described in Listing 1.1 and consists of 3 managers each controlling 5 production lines. Adding access control clearly has implications to the performance of the logic program. The current implementation is built to support different scenarios, but does not yet include major optimizations. Nevertheless, it is clear that the way access control policies are defined only has a linear impact on the performance of the program.

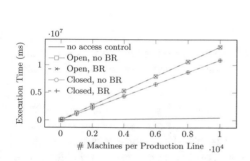

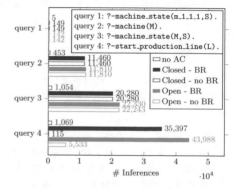

Fig. 4. Execution time for a variable number of predicates

Fig. 5. Amount of inferences for different queries in different setups

Figure 5 shows the amount of inferences for different queries in the previously presented manufactory setting with ten machines per production line. Several conclusions can be made based on the four performed queries.

- For queries on predicates for which access rules exist (i.e. query 1, 2 and 3), there is no difference in a setup with or without body resolution. Since matching access rules can be found, body resolution must not be performed. Thus, the execution time is independent from whether body resolution is enabled or not.
- The more specific a query is, the smaller the overhead caused by access control. This is because the amount of variables to instantiate is lower (i.e. query 1 versus query 3).

- The amount of inferences for an open policy are different than for a closed policy. This is both a result of how access control is handled and how the policies are defined. For the open policy, ACoP can already stop resolution if at least one matching allow rule can be found. For the closed policy, however, not only an allow rule must be found but all deny rules must be verified to be sure access is allowed. Access control could therefore be determined more quickly in the case of an open policy, which is the case for query 1. For this example, however, the open policy rules are very basic and equal to the closed policy rules complemented with a deny rule without conditions on `machine/1`, `start_machine/1` and `machine_state/2`. This results in an increased overhead for the open policy and becomes more apparent when more steps in the ACoP process have to be taken (i.e. queries 2, 3 and 4).
- The amount of inferences for query 4 depends on the body resolution setting. There is no matching access control rule for this query. In case body resolution is disabled, ACoP can quickly decide whether or not to resolve the predicate, with little impact on the query. When body resolution is enabled, access must be controlled for each predicate in the body of the rule, which quickly increases the number of steps. Note that for this query the closed policy without body resolution is the only case for which access control is denied, resulting in a lower number of inferences than when access control is disabled.

5   Discussion

While access control to resources is well-studied, applying this to predicates and rules is not straightforward. Below, we discuss a number of aspects that need careful treatment.

Filtering on 'Outputs' - When an access control policy on an impure predicate filters on 'output' arguments (i.e., arguments that only get instantiated after resolution), it implies that the predicate is resolved (i.e. side effect take place) before it is denied access. A warning during consultation time could inform the developer of such cases, to make adjustments to the policies, if necessary. Note that the reasoner must know the output argument, which can be accomplished by annotating the output arguments during development time.

access(...) - The `access` predicate may be used in the body of a rule to verify whether access to another predicate is allowed. This may possibly lead to infinite loops. Hence, special care must be taken when this predicate is used. Especially when body resolution is active.

Insufficient Instantiation - Often, access control policies filter on the values of arguments. In complex cases, one of the arguments of the predicate under control may be used to compare with some value. An example is shown in Listing 1.4. Although this seems intuitively correct, the query results in an error. Since access control is also verified before resolving the predicate, the arguments of the predicate may still be variable (both for pure and impure predicates). Using variables,

```
age(X,A) :- info(X,birthdate,date(Y)), calculate_age(Y,A).
allow(age(_,A)) :- A>18.
?- age(X,Y).
```

Listing 1.4. Example of an insufficient instantiation error.

while non-variables are expected may result in unexpected behavior. Since it cannot be derived from the predicates whether arguments are allowed to be variable, it is not possible to verify this automatically.

To handle this, either the arguments used in the filter must be instantiated properly, or the developer needs to take additional measures when defining the rules. For instance, `nonvar/1` can be used to check whether a term is already instantiated, before performing arithmetic operations. Another solution to solve such problems is by giving the possibility to ignore the argument during preliminary access control. For instance, by annotating such arguments.

Support and Conflict Resolution - As discussed in Sect. 3.1, conflict resolution is determined by the default policy. In a closed policy, deny rules take precedence, while in an open policy, allow rules take precedence, even in the presence of body resolution. This makes it possible to write access rules that will not be considered, but give the developer an unjustified feeling of control. Adding support to track and warn users of aforementioned cases could prevent the misleading feeling of security.

Data Privacy - Although access control may help in preventing access to specific information, it does not prevent that rules may still leak information. Finding solutions to prevent such leakage is left for future work.

Supporting Access Control Strategies. Since ACoP does not constraint the conditions in policies, it naturally supports various access control strategies. While for Identity Based Access Control (IBAC), a policy may verify the identity of the current user or her membership in an access control list, Role Based Access Control (RBAC) may go one step further and check the user for required roles. Similarly, supporting Relationship Based Access Control (ReBAC), often used in the context of social networking systems, simply requires a check whether the current user has a certain relation to the owner of some asset. Some examples may be found in Appendix A.

6 Conclusions

This paper presented ACoP, an access control mechanism that enforces access control in existing logic programs. Access control is fine grained on the level of predicates, supporting multiple established access control strategies. The solution takes into account the use of impure predicates and applies a *deny as soon as possible* strategy to prevent prohibited side effects from taking place. The presented Prolog meta-interpreter shows that the integration does not entail excessive overhead.

Appendices

A   Example Support for Access Control Strategies

ACoP can easily be used to enable various access control strategies. Several examples of how possible strategies can be implemented can be found in this section.

Identity Based Access Control. One of the most basic access control strategies is Identity Based Access Control (IBAC). Access to a resource is determined based on the identity of the individual trying to access the resource. An IBAC strategy for accessing files can be achieved using ACoP with the using the rule,

```
allow(file(<filename>) :- current_user(<user_identifier>).
```

in a closed policy. For example can access to *file1.txt* be granted for both *Alice* and *Bob* in the following way:

```
allow(file(file1.txt) :- current_user(alice).
allow(file(file1.txt) :- current_user(bob).
```

In IBAC, an access control list (ACL) is often used to bundle all identifiers together. To support use of an ACL, the ACoP access rule can be defined as follows, assuming that `acl(L)` unifies L with a list of the identifiers that may access he resource:

```
allow(file(file1.txt) :- current_user(U), acl(L), member(U,L).
```

Role Based Access Control. Role based access control (RBAC) was first introduced by Ferraiolo et al. in 1992 [7]. It is since a widely used strategy in large companies and as the name states based on roles assigned to users of the system. An example for the role based access control strategy, is a blogpost website, where dependent on the role, a user can take several actions. The limited set of possible roles and actions that can be taken on the blogpost website can be found in Table 1.

Table 1. Blogpost website: roles and actions

	Visitor	Subscriber	Admin
Add/Remove user			✓
Publish posts			✓
Comment on posts		✓	✓
Read posts	✓	✓	✓

To enable RBAC using ACoP, the users of the system must be defined together with their role. The closed policy used for the blogpost website will then be:

```
user_role(alice, admin).
user_role(bob, subscriber).
user_role(_, visitor).
```

Defining the actions that can be taken by each role can easily be done as follows:

```
allow(add_user(_)) :- current_user(U), user_role(U,admin).
allow(publish_post(_)) :- current_user(U),user_role(U,admin).
allow(post_comment(_,_)) :- current_user(U),
    ↪  (user_role(U,admin);user_role(U,subscriber)).
allow(read(P)).
```

Relationship Based Access Control. Relationship based access control (ReBAC) was first introduced by Gates in 2007 [8]. Access control policies to resources are defined based on relationships between users, and are mainly used in the context of social networking systems. Figure 6 gives an example of a social networking system with friend relations and personal information and photo resources.

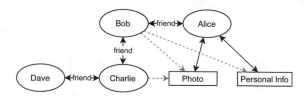

Fig. 6. Social network system with friend relations

The access control policy is the following. A user has access to a users personal information, if they have a friend relation. A user has access to a users photos, if the person is a friend of the owner (i.e. has a friend relationship), or if they have a friend relation with a friend of the owner. To enable the ReBAC policy, using the ACoP system, users must be defined together with the resources they own as well as the relationships between the users. The policy can then be described as follows, using a closed policy:

```
allow(personal_info(I)) :-  owner(O,I), current_user(U), friend(U,O,
    ↪  friend).
allow(photo(P)) :- owner(O,P), current_user(U), (relation(U,O,
    ↪  friend); (relation(U,F,friend),relation(F,O, friend))).
```

Note that the relation/3 predicate could also be simplified and defined using a friend/2 predicate.

References

1. Abadi, M.: Logic in access control. In: 2003 Proceedings of 18th Annual IEEE Symposium of Logic in Computer Science, pp. 228–233. IEEE (2003)
2. Bohé, I., Willocx, M., Lapon, J., Naessens, V.: Towards low-effort development of advanced IoT applications. In: Proceedings of the 8th International Workshop on Middleware and Applications for the Internet of Things, pp. 1–7 (2021)
3. Böhme, R., et al.: A fundamental approach to cyber risk analysis. Variance **12**(2), 161–185 (2019)
4. Bruckner., F., et al.: A framework for creating policy-agnostic programming languages. In: Proceedings of the 9th International Conference on Data Science, Technology and Applications - DATA, pp. 31–42. INSTICC, SciTePress (2020)
5. Chin, B., et al.: Yedalog: exploring knowledge at scale. In: 1st Summit on Advances in Programming Languages (SNAPL 2015), Dagstuhl, Germany, pp. 63–78 (2015)
6. Edwards, B., et al.: Hype and heavy tails: a closer look at data breaches. J. Cybersecur. **2**(1), 3–14 (2016)
7. Ferraiolo, D., Kuhn, D.: Natl institute of standards and tech., dept. of commerce, Maryland, role-based access control. In: Proceedings of 15th National Computer Security Conference (1992)
8. Gates, C.: Access control requirements for web 2.0 security and privacy. IEEE Web **2**, 12–15 (2007)
9. Google Open Source: Logica (2021). https://opensource.google/projects/logica. Accessed 05 May 2021
10. Huynh, N., Frappier, M., Pooda, H., Mammar, A., Laleau, R.: SGAC: a patient-centered access control method. In: 2016 IEEE Tenth International Conference on Research Challenges in Information Science (RCIS), pp. 1–12 (2016). https://doi.org/10.1109/RCIS.2016.7549286D
11. Jackson, D.: Alloy: a lightweight object modelling notation. ACM Trans. Softw. Eng. Methodol. **11**(2), 256–290 (2002)
12. Kolovski, V., et al.: Analyzing web access control policies. In: Proceedings of the 16th international conference on World Wide Web, pp. 677–686 (2007)
13. Leuschel, M., Butler, M.: ProB: a model checker for B. In: Araki, K., Gnesi, S., Mandrioli, D. (eds.) FME 2003. LNCS, vol. 2805, pp. 855–874. Springer, Heidelberg (2003). https://doi.org/10.1007/978-3-540-45236-2_46
14. Maier, D., et al.: Computing with Logic: Logic Programming with Prolog. Benjamin-Cummings Publishing Co., Inc, USA (1988)
15. Samarati, P., de Vimercati, S.C.: Access control: policies, models, and mechanisms. In: Focardi, R., Gorrieri, R. (eds.) FOSAD 2000. LNCS, vol. 2171, pp. 137–196. Springer, Heidelberg (2001). https://doi.org/10.1007/3-540-45608-2_3
16. Sartoli, S., et al.: Modeling adaptive access control policies using answer set programming. J. Inf. Secur. Appl. **44**, 49–63 (2019)
17. Sterling, L., et al.: The Art of Prolog: Advanced Programming Techniques. MIT Press, Cambridge (1994)
18. De Capitani di Vimercati, S.: Access control policies, models, and mechanisms. In: van Tilborg, H.C.A., Jajodia, S. (eds.) Encyclopedia of Cryptography and Security, pp. 13–14. Springer, Boston (2011). https://doi.org/10.1007/978-1-4419-5906-5_806

Comprehensive Open-Source SCA Course Modules for Hands-On IoT Security Education

Mateus Augusto Fernandes Amador$^{(\boxtimes)}$ (ID), Brooks Olney (ID),
Srinivas Katkoori (ID), and Robert Karam (ID)

University of South Florida, Tampa, FL 33620, USA
{mateusf1,brooksolney,katkoori,rkaram}@usf.edu

Abstract. With the rapid growth of the Internet of Things (IoT) and increasing reliance on network-connected devices, IoT security, which integrates components of hardware and cybersecurity, is more important than ever. Hence, we must improve and expand training opportunities for students in IoT security. Experiential learning is an essential component of education for engineering and cybersecurity in particular. In this work, we describe three comprehensive hands-on IoT security experiments built using off-the-shelf development boards which can provide a low-cost and accessible experiential learning opportunity for students in this area.

Keywords: Internet of Things (IoT) · Security · Side-Channel Analysis (SCA) · Education · Experiential learning

1 Introduction

The Internet of Things (IoT) is an ongoing technology transition with the goal of connecting the unconnected. IoT application domains are varied and diverse, including transportation, healthcare, consumer electronics, public services, defense, and more [7,14,15,23]. These devices are regularly exposed to potential attacks with significant economical losses and public safety risks [1,18]. Due to the cyberphysical nature of IoT devices, their security necessarily integrates components of hardware and cybersecurity [5,25]. In particular, hardware security has often been lacking in devices and overlooked by researchers in contrast to software security [24].

To ensure that current and future IoT devices are secure from malicious attacks, we must focus not only on changing development methodologies and prioritizing security as a design metric, but also on addressing deficiencies in training the next generation of IoT engineers [2,21]. In particular, providing students with interactive practical experiences to efficiently motivate and instill

This material is based upon work supported by the National Science Foundation under Grant No. DGE-1954259. Contact: rkaram@usf.edu.

long-term knowledge about IoT security [11]. To this end, we have developed and contextualized several security course modules focusing on IoT security that can be integrated into upper-level courses to provide students with *hands-on, experiential learning* for IoT security topics.

In this paper, we describe three of these course modules which focus on a wide range of side-channel analysis (SCA) attacks to identify vulnerabilities in IoT devices. In particular, one performs a password checker, another performs a symmetric key encryption (SKE), and another performs a public key encryption (PKE). Students learn the motivation behind these cryptosystems, go through the mathematics of one particular example for each (i.e., simple loop password checker, AES, and RSA respectively), and gain an understanding for how naïve implementations may be vulnerable to various SCA attacks. They then attempt the attacks themselves (password or key recovery), integrate countermeasures with the implementations, and show the efficacy of the countermeasures. These modules, and others in the course, run on inexpensive, commercial/off-the-shelf hardware, and use only open-source tools and languages in an effort to minimize the barrier to entry/integration into existing courses at other universities.

The rest of the paper is organized as follows: Sect. 2 provides a background on experiential learning, SCA Attacks, IoT security, and the basics for the course modules that students learn. Section 3 describes each of the course modules, student tasks, and expected learning outcomes. Section 4 provides key takeaways from a pilot offering of the course in Fall 2021. Finally, Sect. 5 concludes with future directions for the research.

2   Background

In this section, we provide a brief overview of experiential learning, which is central to the curriculum design, and summarize the relevant IoT security topics explored by students in these course modules.

2.1   Experiential Learning and Hardware Security

Broadly, experiential learning is the process of "learning by doing". Integrating experiential learning methods into course modules can benefit engineering education by helping students connect theories and knowledge learned during lectures to real world situations through hands-on experiences [8,11,16]. Therefore, the theory is *contextualized* in IoT. Most models of experiential learning are based on Kolb's Experiential Learning Theory (ELT) [8], which operates by creating knowledge through experience [26]. ELT can be modeled using Kolb's Experiential Learning Cycle, which has the following stages: 1) active experimentation, concrete experience, reflective observation, and abstract conceptualization, after which the steps are repeated until students attain the desired learning outcome.

These practices allow students to gain experience from real-world examples and develop many skills, including critical thinking, research, meta-cognitive thinking, epistemic cognition, scientific inquiry, engineering innovation and problem solving [8, 26]. Because hardware security vulnerabilities and their exploits are inherently complex – requiring background knowledge in areas such as cryptography, statistics, and electrical circuits – experiential learning is well suited to training students in IoT security [11]. A mostly theory-based course covering IoT security is well suited to discussing topics such as supply chain security, testing and verification, and intellectual property piracy. Students can mount attacks using pre-recorded data, but without access to the original hardware, they cannot *actively experiment* with different implementations and countermeasures, reacquire data, form hypotheses, or reflect on their concrete experiences after the experiment. Putting the experiment itself in context – in this case, IoT – is also important to motivate students and connect the experiment to the real world. In summary, access to a hardware platform is essential to perform these experiments.

2.2   Side-Channel Analysis (SCA) Attacks

As computer hardware devices perform various computations, their physical properties can be measured and used to identify what *functions* are being performed and even the contents of the underlying *data* [22]. These physical properties are referred to as side-channel leakages, and come in many forms. For example, as transistors switch on and off, the effects can be seen on the power consumption on the chip, as well as in the electromagnetic and thermal emanations measured externally.

Simple Power Analysis (SPA) Attacks. An SPA attack involves visual inspection of the power waveforms measured from the device during operation. This can be accomplished by looking at peaks within the waveform at specific locations. For example, a basic "if statement" may produce a higher spike when its condition evaluates as `true`. Moreover, the time it takes to perform certain operations can be used as a way to determine what the inputs are to the algorithm [13].

Differential Power Analysis (DPA) Attacks. A DPA attack can exploit *data-dependent leakages*, where the power consumption of a crucial operation is dependent on the data inputs [12]. Essentially, the idea of DPA is that small differences in power consumption can be measured for the same operation performed across different inputs – one where a targeted bit in the result is a 1, and the other a 0. This difference can be exploited to deduce the secret key during operation.

Template-Matching Attack. To process more complex power traces, a sum of absolute differences (SAD) template-matching approach may be used. If an algorithm is repeating the same instructions, the power is expected to match very

---

Algorithm 1. Naïve Password Checker v1.0

    Input: *input_pw*: string with password given by the user to check
    Output: Indicate access granted or not based on the *input_pw*
1 *secret_pw* ← "RealPassword";   /* Real password stored in the system */
2 *wrong_pw* ← False;
3 **for** i ← 0 **to** Size(*secret_pw*)–1 **do**
4   **if** *secret_pw*[i] != *input_pw*[i] **then**
5   *wrong_pw* ← True;
6   **break**;

7
8 **if** *wrong_pw* **then**
9   Print("INCORRECT PASSWORD!");
10 **else**
11   Print("ACCESS GRANTED!");

---

closely between iterations (assuming that there are no countermeasures in place). The attacker begins by defining a *template* signal with the region of interest in the power trace. Then, sweep this template along every point in the signal under attack, subtracting the two, taking the absolute value, and adding the result. If the two regions match very closely, then its SAD output is close to 0. Otherwise, the output will be higher [6]. In contrast to SPA, SAD template-matching allows one to identify similarities between power traces within a moving window instead of a sample-wise comparison (i.e., one power sample at a time).

2.3 IoT Security

Generally, an IoT system consists of edge sensors that send data to a central unit for processing. The central unit uses software applications to process the collected data for intelligent decision making. As an edge node cannot be physically protected or continuously monitored, it can be easily attacked [10]. For this reason, edge sensors often rely on password checkers for user credentials and access verification, SKE cryptosystems (e.g., AES) for secure communication and data transfer, and PKE cryptosystems (e.g., RSA) for secure connections and distribution of SKE keys. The attacker can gain access to the edge node and interfere with the legitimate operation. For example, they can modify the transmitted data. Typically, the transmitted data is encrypted. In these course modules, students observe first-hand how vulnerable unprotected systems are.

Password Checkers: Periodically, edge nodes may be accessed by users and/or administrators. However, a naïve password checker implementation may be exploited by an attacker through SCA. For example, a simple power analysis (SPA), such as timing analysis, can be used to break a basic loop design in which the input and secret password are compared character-by-character, and

---

Algorithm 2. Naïve Password Checker v2.0 (w/Random Delay)

Input: *input_pw*: string with password given by the user to check
Output: Indicate access granted or not based on the *input_pw*
1 *secret_pw* ← "RealPassword";   /* Real password stored in the system */
2 *wrong_pw* ← False;
3 **for** i ← 0 **to** Size(*secret_pw*)–1 **do**
4 | **if** *secret_pw*[i] != *input_pw*[i] **then**
5 | | *wrong_pw* ← True;
6 | |_ **break**;

7
8 **if** *wrong_pw* **then**
9 | /* Countermeasure Attempt: insert a random delay   */
10 | *wait* ← Rand() %12345;
11 | **for** *delay* ← 0 **to** *wait* **do**
12 | |_ ; /* Do Nothing */
13 |_ Print("INCORRECT PASSWORD!");
14 **else**
15 |_ Print("ACCESS GRANTED!");

---

then break as soon as it finds an incorrect character (Algorithm 1). The attacker can simply brute force each character at a time instead of the whole password at once. This reduces the complexity from $O(n^m)$ to $O(n*m)$, where n is the number of possible valid characters that the password may have and m is the number of characters in the secret password. Therefore, the designer should implement the respective countermeasures to prevent similar security vulnerabilities.

However, identifying the appropriate countermeasure requires an understanding of the trade-offs and threat model, including the access and capabilities of the attacker. The countermeasure needs to be simple enough to not produce high power, performance, and resources overheads, but not too unsophisticated that it does not protect the system as desired. For instance, a random delay could be inserted before letting the user know the password in an attempt to confuse the attacker (Algorithm 2). However, the attacker can still identify relevant power spikes (e.g., at the break statement) before the random delay begins. Thus, designers need to be more vigilant to truly protect their system.

SKE and AES: Once the users have been verified safely and allowed access to their systems, they may need to communicate and transfer confidential information between them. However, since this access is typically facilitated through public infrastructure, we need to encrypt the data to prevent data theft or manipulation. Hence, a symmetric key encryption (SKE) such as AES is used to protect the content transferred. Just as before, for a given threat model, making certain assumptions about the knowledge and capabilities of the attacker, the implementation of the encryption may be broken, leading to key recovery [9,20].

Algorithm 3. Square-and-Multiply (SAM)

Input: b: base
Input: m: modulo
Input: exp_bin: exponent represented as an array of n bits
Output: r: result from the modular exponentiation

1 $r \leftarrow b$;
2 $i = n - 1$;
3 **while** $i > 0$ **do**
4 | $r \leftarrow (r * r) \bmod m$;
5 | **if** $exp\_bin[--i] == 1$ **then**
6 | |_ $r \leftarrow (r * b) \bmod m$;

7 **return** r;

Attacks such as differential or correlation power analysis (DPA or CPA) have been successfully used against implementations of AES and other SKEs [3,17]. For example, this issue may be present in the AES algorithm during the substitution bytes (S-box) step, as we will demonstrate later in Sect. 3.3.

PKE and RSA: On the other hand, even if the SKE implementation has been adequately hardened, these depend on a secret key that both edge nodes need beforehand through a secure channel. However, these systems or users may be too far away for them to transfer the key offline. Moreover, an SKE system becomes less and less secure as more users require access (and the secret key). Therefore, we also need to encrypt and communicate keys through efficient, reliable, and secure mechanisms. Otherwise, an eavesdropper can decrypt the ciphertext generated by the SKE, defeating any countermeasure implemented. Currently, most IoTs uses PKEs to safely authenticate, generate, and distribute the secret key for the respective SKE.

An example of PKE that students can learn is RSA. Mathematically, the security of RSA is derived from the computational difficulty of factoring the product of two large prime numbers. In a naïve implementation, an attacker can exploit the fact that certain operations depend on the present value of a key bit and can be observed from side channels [4]. Encrypting a plaintext p requires first representing it as an integer, then computing the ciphertext as $c = p^e \bmod m$, where e is a public key exponent, and n is a public key modulo. To decrypt, the plaintext is computed as $p = c^d \bmod m$, where $d = e^{-1} \bmod \phi(m)$ and is kept secret. The value of $\phi(m)$ (Euler's totient function) depends on two large prime factors of m, which is difficult to extract.

Alternatively, the secret key d may be detected using power SCA. Since the RSA decryption involves modular exponentiation, which is commonly performed using the square-and-multiply (SAM) algorithm (Algorithm 3) for resource-constrained microcontrollers. This algorithm takes as arguments the base b, modulus N, and exponent in binary exp_bin – which for each bit of the exponent, performs one or two operations. To begin with, the base b is copied into a temporary variable r. If the current key bit is 0, $r = (r * r) \bmod N$, and the loop iterates to the next key bit. If the current key bit is 1, the same function $r = (r * r) \bmod N$ is performed, but then it is multiplied once more by the original base value, $r = (r * b) \bmod N$. Hence, the number of operations inside the loop depends on the current key bit. The attacker can exploit this factor to effectively read the secret key d from the power trace.

3   Description of Course Modules

In this section, we explain the general setups for the experiments and a description for each of the course modules provided to the students, including their tasks and expected learning outcomes.

3.1   Hardware and Software Setup

The students are provided with a ChipWhisperer (CW) Nano [19]. This board is small (about $60 \times 30 \times 3\,\mathrm{mm}$) and powered by a micro-USB cable. The CW Nano has two onboard processors, one that is controlled through a Python API and Jupyter Notebooks, and a second *victim* microcontroller programmed in C.

The CW software is open-source and deployed as a virtual machine (VM) image, which greatly simplifies deployment on students' systems. The Python-controlled CW acquisition board can be used as a kind of USB oscilloscope which records the power consumed by the *victim* in real-time while it executes various functions. The *victim* can be controlled using a serial protocol, which allows students to write, flash, and execute different firmware on the *victim*. Simultaneously, they can record, observe, analyze, and plot the results in real time from within the Jupyter Notebook environment.

3.2   Password Checker Module

Module Description: In this course module, teams of students attack two implementations of example naïve password checkers (Algorithms 1 and 2). Students are given a training password to test, practice, and become familiar with ChipWhisperer and password checkers. Once the students gain sufficient experience and implement a plausible attack, they will repeat the procedure with a secret password. Students learn to perform SPA, perform power timing analysis attacks on relevant spikes, and improve countermeasures.

Student Tasks: Students must complete the following tasks in this module:

1. Implement the training Password Checkers v1.0 and v2.0 (Algorithms 1 and 2) in C and flash the compiled binary file to the *victim*.
2. Send sample input passwords (*input_pw*) to the *victim* with a varying number of correct characters and collect power traces.
3. Plot and analyze the average power trace (P_{avg}) as in Fig. 1(a).

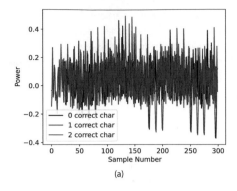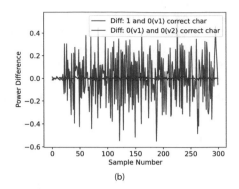

(a)   (b)

Fig. 1. Password Checker Module: Plots of example (a) average power traces for password inputs with 0, 1, 2 correct characters; and (b) power difference between 0 vs 0 correct (red) and 0 vs 1 correct (blue) characters.

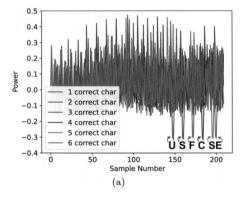

```
Char Found: U
Char Found: S
Char Found: F
Char Found: C
Char Found: S
Char Found: E
Password: USFCSE
Confirm USFCSE: ACCESS GRANTED
```

(a)   (b)

Fig. 2. Password Checker Module: (a) Plot of example average power traces for respective correct character found during the SPA attack. (b) Example confirmation and attack output when finding the password for the training Naïve Password Checkers v1.0 and v2.0.

4. Plot and analyze the power difference (P_{diff}) for the input passwords *input_pw* with a varying number of correct characters as in Fig. 1(b).
5. Identify a relevant spike in P_{diff} where it could indicate the end of the loop or break statement.
6. Implement an SPA attack to find a single correct character. If given a password starting with i correct characters, then the algorithm should return the $i+1$ correct character and plot the respective power trace as in Fig. 2(a).
7. Iterate the single-character SPA attack to find all the characters in the real secret password.
8. Verify the recovered password (Fig. 2(b)).
9. Repeat these procedures for a secret password (*secret_pw*) stored in a given binary firmware to flash to the *victim*.

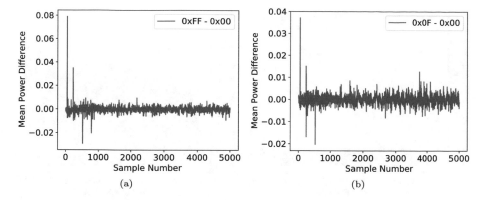

Fig. 3. AES module (Part A): plots of example mean power difference at byte 0 between AES inputs (a) 0xFF vs 0x00; and (b) 0x0F vs 0x00.

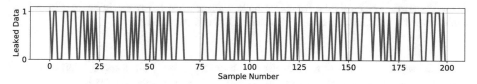

Fig. 4. AES module (Part B): LSB output data from random sample inputs into an AES S-Box model.

10. Once successful, implement in C a working countermeasure on the password checker v1.0 (Algorithm 1) that will defeat the SPA attack implemented in previous steps. Flash the compiled binary file to the *victim* and test the implemented SPA attack. Verify that the countermeasure thwarts the attack.

11. Report the findings, discuss the results, and draw meaningful conclusions.

Expected Learning Outcomes: By the end of the experiment, students will become familiar with basic SCA, SPA, timing attacks, and respective countermeasures in password checkers. They will gain a better understanding on the related topics and importance through their experiences they gathered through this module. This module should give them strong foundations for the following modules on AES and RSA (Sects. 3.3 and 3.4).

3.3   AES Module

Module Description: In this course module, students build on their knowledge of SPA and experiment with more sophisticated SCA attacks on an implementation of AES. In particular, the students investigate the usage of DPA and CPA on the AES S-box to gain an understanding of how the attacks work. The

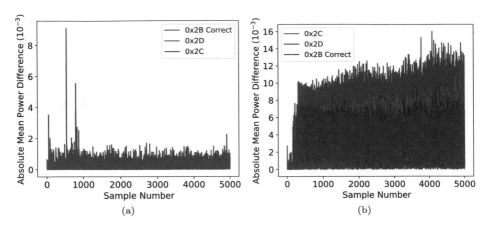

Fig. 5. AES module (Part C): plots of example absolute mean power difference between 0/1 AES S-Box LSB outputs for different key guesses on (a) the original AES; and (b) the AES with additional internal random delay countermeasure.

students work through three Jupyter Notebooks (A-C) that have been modified from existing experiments provided in the CW software suite [19].

Student Tasks: Students must complete the following tasks in this module:

1. Program the CW with the AES implementation from the provided library.
2. Work through notebook A to capture many traces at a time for two inputs - 0xFF and 0x00.
3. Divide the traces into two groups, one for each input
4. Average the traces in each group to filter out noise from the measurements.
5. Compute the differential between the two traces, plot using matplotlib and inspect the peak as in Fig. 3(a).
6. Repeat the same process but with inputs that have a HW difference of 4 (e.g., 0x0F and 0x00) and plot as in Fig. 3(b).
7. Work through notebook B to conceptualize the process of recovering a byte of the AES key.
8. Complete the steps to build the foundation of the DPA attack on AES.
9. Plot the LSB of the results from random sample inputs to the AES S-Box as in Fig. 4.
10. Work through notebook C to apply the attack from B to an actual hardware implementation of AES.
11. Automate the attack over the entire AES key, plot a few example CPA outputs as illustrated in Fig. 5(a), and compare the recovered results from the hardware to the actual key as shown in Table 1.
12. Modify the provided implementation of the AES in C code to include a random delay as a countermeasure to the attack.

13. Repeat the attack above, plot a few example CPA outputs as shown in Fig. 5(b), and compare the recovered key with the actual key, the attack should be thwarted by the countermeasure as given in Table 2.
14. Report the findings, discuss the results, and draw meaningful conclusions.

Table 1. AES module (Part C): example of key recovered output and actual key values for the original AES.

Key	Hex bytes	Accuracy
Recovery key	[2B, 7E, 15, 16, 28, AE, D2, A6, AB, F7, 15, 88, 09, CF, 4F, 3C]	16/16 bytes
Actual key	[2B, 7E, 15, 16, 28, AE, D2, A6, AB, F7, 15, 88, 09, CF, 4F, 3C]	(100%)

Table 2. AES module (Part C): example of key recovered output and actual key values for the AES with additional internal random delay countermeasure.

Key	Hex bytes	Accuracy
Recovery key	[B3, A2, 90, 79, 46, EF, 9B, 23, FA, 5A, 59, B7, 7C, 4D, A4, D2]	0/16 bytes
Actual key	[2B, 7E, 15, 16, 28, AE, D2, A6, AB, F7, 15, 88, 09, CF, 4F, 3C]	(0%)

Expected Learning Outcomes: Through this experiment, the students gain an understanding of the basics of the AES algorithm, and the S-box in particular. They observe the leakage of the S-box, and learn to exploit it by using classic DPA. Finally, they use this knowledge to mount the attack and reveal the whole key.

3.4   RSA Module

Module Description: In this course module, teams of students attack an implementation of the square-and-multiply (SAM) algorithm – a key component of RSA that enables modular exponentiation – on a resource-constrained microcontroller development board. Students are encouraged to apply critical thinking to identify vulnerabilities in the design to extract the secret key through SCA attacks. The module has a tutorial that introduces the topic and basic attack setup, enabling students to familiarize themselves with the attack. In particular, students learn about improving Signal-to-Noise Ratio (SNR), template-matching attacks such as the sum of absolute differences (SAD), and their countermeasures.

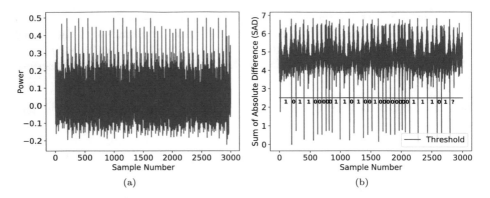

Fig. 6. RSA module: plots of example (a) average power trace and (b) SAD algorithm output.

Table 3. RSA module: example key recovered output and actual key values from Fig. 6(b).

Key	Hex	Binary	Accuracy
Recovery key	6C1A403A	01101100000110100100000000011101?	31/32 bits
Actual key	6C1A403B	01101100000110100100000000011011	(96.9%)

Student Tasks: Students must complete the following tasks in this module:

1. Implement SAM in C and flash the compiled binary file to the *victim*.
2. Send sample exponent keys to the *victim* and collect power traces.
3. Plot and analyze the average power trace (P_{avg}) as in Fig. 6(a).
4. Identify a suitable portion of P_{avg} to serve as the template T for SAD.
5. Implement SAD to compare T against P_{avg} and plot results as in Fig. 6(b).
6. Determine a threshold for the SAM results to discern matches (values under the threshold) as in Fig. 6(b) and collect this in a binary match vector M_{bin}.
7. Examine the spacing between each match and determine when the *victim* is processing 1 or 0 key-bit, a larger space indicates a 1 key-bit (Fig. 6(b)).
8. Read off the key values from the plot and automate this process using M_{bin}.
9. Compare the recovered and actual keys (Table 3). Note that the SAD attack is unable to get the LSB because there is no next match to compare to.
10. Report the findings, discuss the results, and draw meaningful conclusions.

Expected Learning Outcomes: By the end of the experiment, the students will become familiar with complex SCA, template-matching attacks using SAD on a SAM algorithm. The student will learn how the SAM algorithm works and its potential security vulnerabilities on RSA for IoT devices. This module will close many gaps in the students' understanding on SCA and the importance of hardware security design on IoT through hands-on experiences.

4   Results

Feedback from students in the Fall 2021 course was generally positive, based on interactions with students during the semester. Some critical feedback of the course stemmed from a lack of relevant and accessible resources for Python development. Many of the students felt it was difficult to translate the high level topics and requirements of the modules to producible Python code. To improve upon this, we have developed more supplementary material to teach students relevant techniques in Python for analyzing raw binary, using data processing tools such as Numpy and Matplotlib, interfacing with hardware, and reading official documentation.

The students also fulfilled the expected learning outcomes outlined in the prior section. The password checker module taught the students about the basics of SCA and how different results from functions can cause measurable spikes in power. The AES module reinforced their understanding of these concepts by first having them compare the power consumption of AES with different inputs. Then, the module guided them through preliminary steps for the attack to teach them the unfamiliar concepts of DPA. After these two module, the students were much more familiar with the CW platform and had a strong basis to work from for the following RSA module. In the RSA module, the students were provided with less resources to start from than in the previous labs, so they had to rely on the lessons and concepts learned earlier. Most students were able to derive the correct RSA key, and analyses in their reports demonstrated a link between their conceptual understanding of the attack and the successful outcomes of their experiments. This was a common theme across all the experiments.

5   Conclusion

In this paper, we presented a comprehensive set of course modules that provide students with hands-on, experiential learning with IoT security experiments. It uses off-the-shelf, low-cost development boards and open-source tools to make integration into existing university courses feasible. These modules teach students about SCA attacks to identify and exploit vulnerabilities in IoT devices for simple password checkers through SPA timing attacks, key recovery for AES encryption using DPA, and in RSA during the SAM algorithm using SAD template-matching attacks. Students learn the motivation behind SKE and PKE, the mathematics of SAM and RSA, and gain an understanding of how naïve implementations may be vulnerable to SCA attacks. Through this, students gain real-world experience and develop critical thinking, research, and engineering problem solving skills. Furthermore, we will consider future incremental improvements and other practical projects based on feedback from students.

References

1. Abdullah, A., Hamad, R., Abdulrahman, M., Moala, H., Elkhediri, S.: CyberSecurity: a review of internet of things (IoT) security issues, challenges and techniques. In: 2019 2nd International Conference on Computer Applications & Information Security (ICCAIS), pp. 1–6. IEEE (2019). https://doi.org/10.1109/CAIS.2019.8769560

2. Al-Emran, M., Malik, S.I., Al-Kabi, M.N.: A survey of internet of things (IoT) in education: opportunities and challenges. In: Hassanien, A.E., Bhatnagar, R., Khalifa, N.E.M., Taha, M.H.N. (eds.) Toward Social Internet of Things (SIoT): Enabling Technologies, Architectures and Applications. SCI, vol. 846, pp. 197–209. Springer, Cham (2020). https://doi.org/10.1007/978-3-030-24513-9_12

3. Albiol, P., Manich, S., Arumí, D., Rodríguez-Montañés, R., Gómez-Pau, A.: Low cost AES protection against DPA using rolling codes. In: 2021 XXXVI Conference on Design of Circuits and Integrated Systems (DCIS), pp. 1–6 (2021). https://doi.org/10.1109/DCIS53048.2021.9666192

4. Aljuffri, A., Reinbrecht, C., Hamdioui, S., Taouil, M.: Multi-bit blinding: a countermeasure for RSA against side channel attacks. In: IEEE 39th VLSI Test Symposium (VTS), pp. 1–6 (2021). https://doi.org/10.1109/VTS50974.2021.9441035

5. Arias, O., Wurm, J., Hoang, K., Jin, Y.: Privacy and security in internet of things and wearable devices. IEEE Trans. Multi-Scale Comput. Syst. 1(2), 99–109 (2015). https://doi.org/10.1109/TMSCS.2015.2498605

6. Atallah, M.: Faster image template matching in the sum of the absolute value of differences measure. IEEE Trans. Image Process. 10(4), 659–663 (2001). https://doi.org/10.1109/83.913600

7. Baker, S.B., Xiang, W., Atkinson, I.: Internet of things for smart healthcare: technologies, challenges, and opportunities. IEEE Access 5, 26521–26544 (2017). https://doi.org/10.1109/ACCESS.2017.2775180

8. Desai, P., Bhandiwad, A., Shettar, A.S.: Impact of experiential learning on students' success in undergraduate engineering. In: 2018 IEEE 18th Conference on Advanced Learning Technologies (ICALT), pp. 46–50 (2018). https://doi.org/10.1109/ICALT.2018.00018

9. Dinesh Kumar, S., Thapliyal, H., Mohammad, A.: FinSAL: FinFET-based secure adiabatic logic for energy-efficient and DPA resistant IoT devices. IEEE Trans. Comput. Aided Des. Integr. Circ. Syst. 37(1), 110–122 (2018). https://doi.org/10.1109/TCAD.2017.2685588

10. Hassija, V., Chamola, V., Saxena, V., Jain, D., Goyal, P., Sikdar, B.: A survey on IoT security: application areas, security threats, and solution architectures. IEEE Access 7, 82721–82743 (2019). https://doi.org/10.1109/ACCESS.2019.2924045

11. Kaneko, K., Ban, Y., Okamura, K.: A study on effective instructional design for IoT security education focusing on experiential learning. Int. J. Learn. Technol. Learn. Environ. 2(1), 1–18 (2019)

12. Kocher, P., Jaffe, J., Jun, B.: Differential power analysis. In: Wiener, M. (ed.) CRYPTO 1999. LNCS, vol. 1666, pp. 388–397. Springer, Heidelberg (1999). https://doi.org/10.1007/3-540-48405-1_25

13. Kocher, P.C.: Timing attacks on implementations of Diffie-Hellman, RSA, DSS, and other systems. In: Koblitz, N. (ed.) CRYPTO 1996. LNCS, vol. 1109, pp. 104–113. Springer, Heidelberg (1996). https://doi.org/10.1007/3-540-68697-5_9

14. Lin, J., Yu, W., Zhang, N., Yang, X., Zhang, H., Zhao, W.: A survey on internet of things: architecture, enabling technologies, security and privacy, and applications.

IEEE Internet Things J. **4**(5), 1125–1142 (2017). https://doi.org/10.1109/JIOT.
2017.2683200

15. Lv, Z., Qiao, L., Kumar Singh, A., Wang, Q.: AI-empowered IoT security for smart cities. ACM Trans. Internet Technol. **21**(4), 1–21 (2021). https://doi.org/10.1145/3406115

16. Mantwill, F., Multhauf, V.: Application of agile experiential learning based on reverse engineering as support in product development. In: Krause, D., Heyden, E. (eds.) Design Methodology for Future Products, pp. 65–81. Springer, Cham (2022). https://doi.org/10.1007/978-3-030-78368-6_4

17. Mazumdar, B., Mukhopadhyay, D.: Construction of rotation symmetric S-boxes with high nonlinearity and improved DPA resistivity. IEEE Trans. Comput. **66**(1), 59–72 (2017). https://doi.org/10.1109/TC.2016.2569410

18. Mohamad Noor, M.B., Hassan, W.H.: Current research on internet of things (IoT) security: a survey. Comput. Netw. **148**, 283–294 (2019). https://doi.org/10.1016/j.comnet.2018.11.025

19. O'Flynn, C., Chen, Z.D.: ChipWhisperer: an open-source platform for hardware embedded security research. In: Prouff, E. (ed.) COSADE 2014. LNCS, vol. 8622, pp. 243–260. Springer, Cham (2014). https://doi.org/10.1007/978-3-319-10175-0_17

20. Ramesh, C., et al.: FPGA side channel attacks without physical access. In: 2018 IEEE 26th Annual International Symposium on Field-Programmable Custom Computing Machines (FCCM), pp. 45–52 (2018). https://doi.org/10.1109/FCCM.2018.00016

21. Ramlowat, D.D., Pattanayak, B.K.: Exploring the internet of things (IoT) in education: a review. In: Satapathy, S.C., Bhateja, V., Somanah, R., Yang, X.-S., Senkerik, R. (eds.) Information Systems Design and Intelligent Applications. AISC, vol. 863, pp. 245–255. Springer, Singapore (2019). https://doi.org/10.1007/978-981-13-3338-5_23

22. Rostami, M., Koushanfar, F., Karri, R.: A primer on hardware security: models, methods, and metrics. Proc. IEEE **102**(8), 1283–1295 (2014). https://doi.org/10.1109/JPROC.2014.2335155

23. Sarker, I.H., Khan, A.I., Abushark, Y.B., Alsolami, F.: Internet of things (IoT) security intelligence: a comprehensive overview, machine learning solutions and research directions. Mob. Netw. Appl. 1–17 (2022). https://doi.org/10.1007/s11036-022-01937-3

24. Sidhu, S., Mohd, B.J., Hayajneh, T.: Hardware security in IoT devices with emphasis on hardware trojans. J. Sens. Actuat. Netw. **8**(3), 42 (2019). https://doi.org/10.3390/jsan8030042

25. Xu, T., Wendt, J.B., Potkonjak, M.: Security of IoT systems: design challenges and opportunities. In: 2014 IEEE/ACM International Conference on Computer-Aided Design (ICCAD), p. 417–423 (2014). https://doi.org/10.1109/ICCAD.2014.7001385

26. Kolb, D.A.: Experiential Learning: Experience as the Source of Learning and Development. Pearson Education (2014). ISBN: 9780133892505

Improving Network Load Using a Cloud-Edge MAS-Based Architecture for Industrial Safety Applications

Gibson Barbosa[1] , Djamel Sadok[1] , and Luis Ribeiro[2]([⊠])

[1] Networking and Telecommunications Research Group (GPRT),
Federal University of Pernambuco, Recife, Brazil
{gibson.nunes,jamel}@gprt.ufpe.br
[2] Division of Product Realization, Department of Management and Engineering,
Linköping University, 581 83 Linköping, Sweden
luis.ribeiro@liu.se

Abstract. Internet of Things, in particular, the concept of Industrial Internet of Things (IIoT), is one of the key technological pillars of the Fourth Industrial Revolution, also known as Industry 4.0. In this context, one of the areas of interest is safety, whereby multiple intelligent sensors may be permanently connected to a central system to autonomously or semi-autonomously identify safety hazards. Vision systems are a popular sensor in the safety domain as they can simultaneously monitor many different safety concerns. However, the continuous video stream transmission and the increasing number of intelligent devices in IIoT networks introduce additional pressure on the network. There is a risk that the network resources may become overloaded. This paper proposes and discusses a reference architecture for identifying safety risks. The architecture allows multiple sensors to be plugged into the system. The input of the different sensors is then dynamically weighed as the risk situation evolves. The architecture explores sensor-level intelligence (at the edge layer) to mitigate the network overloading problem. Edge agents quickly assess the risk, deciding whether or not to forward their signals to a local cloud agent for further processing. The cloud agent can then selectively request more information from other edge agents. The architecture is tested in a use case for operators' safety in the assembly of aircraft components and uses intelligent vision systems as safety devices. In the selected use case, the accuracy of the system and its impact on the network load are assessed.

Keywords: Multi-agent systems · IoT · Industry 4.0

1 Introduction

The Industry 4.0 [18] is the fourth step in different evolutionary milestones that revolutionized the industrial activities. The Internet of Things (IoT) is a key

Published by Springer Nature Switzerland AG 2022
L. M. Camarinha-Matos et al. (Eds.): IFIPIoT 2022, IFIP AICT 665, pp. 140–157, 2022.
https://doi.org/10.1007/978-3-031-18872-5_9

enabling concept of Industry 4.0 and a set of technologies that permits sensors, machines, or everything with some processing capability to be connected to a network. However, connectivity alone does not solve any industrial problem, and Industrial IoT frameworks and architectures must provide the flexibility to address many different use cases. One such case is safety [21]. Multi-sensor environments provide an interesting framework for evaluating safety risks in complex scenarios.

A way to do that is using vision systems that can be used to identify safety events. However, the use of more complex devices, such as vision systems, in industrial networks comes at the cost of network load. Because of that, some works like [3,5] and [23] propose strategies that bring the image processing algorithms closer to the cameras on the edge of the network. This alternative is called Edge Computing [8,20]. With that, processing can be distributed to devices at the edge of the network, which reduces the need to transmit heavy raw data. However, such systems are dedicated to improving the streaming of image processing. In many contexts, it is interesting to be able to combine data from different sensors in a coherent way.

This work proposes a reference architecture that considers a Multi-Agent System (MAS) structure for information exchange between agents in low-end Edge devices and high-end Servers. Each agent represents a processing unit in the Edge computing layer that can process locally or pass along the data to a server in a cloud for further heavy-duty and high accuracy processing. This proposal is thought to reduce the overload in IIoT networks avoiding unnecessary data being transmitted to the centralized server. A safety-related use case is used to show-case the proposed architecture, and the architecture contributes in the following directions (1) a MAS-based reference architecture for IIoT edge-cloud computing, (2) a system to detect collision risks in industrial environments, (3) a multi-camera dataset that describes a human interaction activity in the industry and (4) Evaluation of the utilization of edge devices to retransmit camera stream in a WiFi network.

This work is organized as follow. Section 2 presents the works related to this proposal. Section 3 describes proposed architecture. Section 4 details the use case and prototype implementation. Section 5 discusses the experiments and results. Finally, Sect. 6 summarizes the main findings of the work.

2   Related Works

Human safety using IoT networks is a relatively unexplored domain. The work in [22] applies an IIoT in the mining industry. It monitors and analyzes previous and real-time atmospheric and ground stability information. The system alerts people at risk using alert lights and controls the fan ventilation in the mine using the MQTT protocol. In [15] an IIoT-based industrial monitoring system is proposed. Their IIoT structure has sensor nodes that transmit data to the gateway node, responsible for forwarding the information to a monitoring software in a cloud server using MQTT and AWS.

Some works propose systems that use IoT devices to transmit frames in the network. For example, [6] proposes a raspberry Pi Based video streaming service that can transmit to multiple mobile devices. This system streams to android applications using a JSON structure to transport images. The system successfully supports transmitting video streams for different devices, but the device processing power impacts transfer time and the Quality of Service (QoS). The work [10] applies edge devices to Real-time traffic flow data analysis in an intelligent transport system. It is used for heterogeneous and congested traffic conditions evaluation. The Mez system [7] employs an on-demand video frame transmission from IoT camera nodes to an edge server. The application in the edge server can specify network latency upper bound and accuracy lower bound that the application can tolerate for the transmission of the frames. The boundaries for latency and accuracy are achieved by modifying the video frames, analyzing quality parameters, like resolution, color space, blurring, or reducing the size, with the possibility of artifact removal and Frame differencing. The SlugCam proposed in [1] uses camera agents that transfer information based on pre-implemented computer vision algorithms. It is a solar-powered camera agent that communicates in a wireless network. The user defines the algorithms to extract needed information from images.

Different frameworks also are proposed for the IIoT context. The framework in [17] intends to offer efficient and resilient communication over critical disaster circumstances. It looks to use timely detect abnormal events, locate the event site and workforce, generate alerts to workers and emergency service providers, and guide humans to safe places. They consider a four-layer IIoT network: data acquisition, host computing system, cloud computing, and application. The framework proposed by [13] uses ontologies to automate reasoning and decision-making. The user, who does not need to be an expert in ontologies, can insert safety actions into the processing workflow, which uses the new knowledge in the decisions to mitigate the possible hazards. The system is demonstrated in an application to recommend the best protection equipment in a risky situation.

There are many contact points between these previous works and the work discussed in this paper. However, the present work seeks to evaluate the impact of local processing in network load and discusses an architecture that can potentially scale to a large number of sensors that are selectively enabled over a network to improve the detection accuracy of events of interest. The architecture is also not restricted to specific use cases and offers a modular and re-configurable structure that allows users to quickly customize a system to change conditions or the addition and removal of new sensors and actuation devices.

3   Architecture

Figure 1 presents an overview of the architecture. The architecture assumes that sensors have their computational infrastructure or can be connected to an edge computing device. The architecture also assumes a network infrastructure that makes computational resources with high computational capabilities available in a conventional cloud/edge setup.

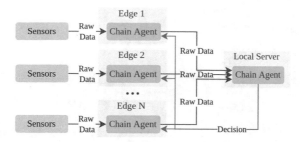

Fig. 1. High-level visualization of the architecture for multiple edge devices.

The Chain agent in Fig. 1 is the main active entity in the architecture. Chain agents can be located at edge or cloud levels and are responsible for processing relevant system information. Edge chain agents pre-process and evaluate raw data collected directly from one or several sensors and decide whether said data must be forwarded up the chain for a more accurate evaluation. Later, the Cloud chain agent will perform a more thorough data analysis and make a decision on the system. Such decisions may include: acting upon the system, asking additional Edge agents for data, and informing Edge agents that decisions have been taken and their data is no longer needed.

The general idea is that the edge agents will act as the system's first responders providing a continuous, local and quick evaluation of a developing system situation. Therefore, the edge layer is a filter that limits potentially unnecessary network traffic.

Even if the use case, later detailed, explores risk identification in an industrial environment, the architecture itself applies to many other scenarios where network utilization needs to be balanced in the presence of sensors that require high network bandwidth. In this context, chain agents, their processing and actions are configured through description files and use specific interaction interfaces enabling the creation of more complex decision chains. Holonic aggregation of chain agents is therefore possible as depicted in Fig. 2 providing additional flexibility in other domains.

The communication between the chain agents uses a publish/subscribe pattern whereby the agents lower in the hierarchy subscribe to the topics of agents higher up. MQTT (Message Queuing Telemetry Transport) is the protocol used with the current implementation of the architecture using the Mosquitto server [11].

The internal architecture of chain agents is depicted in Fig. 3 and is composed of the following modules: Interfaces, Rx Window, Ensemble, Decision, and Attention. As earlier mentioned, the behavior of the agent and particularly of its modules is configured by the description file.

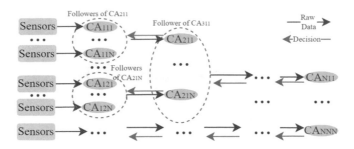

Fig. 2. Architecture multilevel chaining.

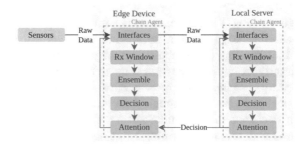

Fig. 3. Reference architecture internal modules interaction.

Interfaces, as the name suggests, are software integration mechanisms for the inclusion of new sensors and actuators in the system. The integration code for the new sensor, or actuator, must implement a specific software interface defined by the platform. Through such an interface, the raw data from the sensor becomes harmonized with the information processing and execution semantics of the agent. In the case of actuators, system actuation information is converted to native commands. Interfaces need to be created only once for each new sensor or actuator integrated into the architecture. The interface module then channels the data internally to other modules, forwards it further up the chain, or actuates on the system. Interfaces, even for the same device, may expose/make available several variables of interest for the system.

The *Rx window module* is responsible for processing the data generated by different sensors and reaching the chain agent through the different interfaces. Different sensors will have different data throughput rates. For example, in a sensor outputting data with a frequency 10 Hz, the Rx window module guarantees that 10 Hz that data from the sensor is processed. As mentioned, this module manages all the available interfaces. By defining the size of the data reception window, it is possible to control the frequency at which data is forwarded and analyzed by the subsequent modules in the chain agents' internal architecture. The reception window is configurable, and hence the user can decide, given the sensor available in the system, how much time the system should wait to compile data from the different sensors. Due to different throughput rates, different sensors will buffer a distinct number of data points in the same reception window.

The *Ensemble module* is responsible for summarizing all the information received in a given data reception window. The presence of multiple sensors with different data throughput rates may give rise to conflicting information. The purpose of this module is, therefore, to try to decide on what is, most likely, the status of the system, given the data received on each reception window. Internally the module takes a two-step approach. First, it decides on the information coming from each interface. Different interfaces may have buffered a different amount of data points for the same window. With a decision on the value for each interface, then the module attempts to fuse the information from all the different interfaces. The fused information is then forwarded to the decision block for further processing. Many different strategies can be considered for fusing information. In the present case, to demonstrate the feasibility of the architecture, a set of simple mechanisms are considered. In the first step, the current implementation considers values as literals and uses majority voting for fusing the data. On the second step, a unanimous vote in a specif direction is required. For example, in the use case later explained, the edge chain agent can only claim that there is no risk if all the interfaces unanimously vote for no risk; otherwise, the second stage evaluation defaults to the presence of risk. The ensemble fuses the information based on the variables made available by the interfaces. If different interfaces provide data related to the same variable, the ensemble guarantees that the different sources are fused. Therefore, the ensemble's output is the fused value for all the variables exposed by the interfaces.

The *Decision module* receives the response from the *Ensemble* and applies user-defined decision rules. Such rules are specified in the description file. The outcome of the decision module is a set of user-specified actions. These local actions can only be applied to the system if a higher-order chain agent does not create an overriding decision. The decision from higher-order layers invalidated the local decision. The attention module manages which action ends up taking effect in the system.

As mentioned, many of the actions of the chain agents can be configured by the user through the usage of Description Files. An excerpt of a description file, which will be later detailed, can be found in Listing 1.1. Such files are JSON documents where the following parameters need to be defined.:

- **id**: represents the agent identification.
- **leader**: the id of an agent upper in the hierarchy if there is one; otherwise takes the value "none".
- **rxperiod**: the value of the reception window for the Rx Window module, which needs to be regulated as a function of the throughput rate of the sensor present in the system and the desired reactivity of the edge chain agents.
- **mqtt**: the network information of the MQTT server supporting system communication.
- **interfaces**: the names of the classes containing the software integration interfaces to be used by the chain agents for determining the value of the different variables of interest.

- **perceptions**: represents the variables' names the interfaces have to use to send information to the chain agents. It is a structure where each key is the name of the variable, and the value for that key is an array of strings that represents the values that an interface can send when using that variable.
- **actions**: represents the variables' names the interfaces have to use to receive information from the architecture. It is a structure where each key is the name of the variable, and the value for that key is an array of strings representing the values that an interface has to implement to receive data.
- **rules**: represents the decision rules that will be triggered by the system. It is a list of structures with the "if" and "then" tags. The "if" and "then" assumes a structure with one or more components. The components of the "if" need to have the names of the variables defined in perceptions as keys. The value for that key has to be one of the values defined for that variable. In the "then" tag, it has to assume one of the variables defined in the actions and put the value that this variable assumes when the "if" conditions are triggered. The value has to be in the defined values for that action variable.

In the forthcoming sections, a concrete application case of the proposed architecture is discussed in the context of an industrial safety application.

4 Use Case

4.1 Demonstration Scenario

The instantiation of the architecture was demonstrated in a mock-up scenario that simulates assembly operation in an aircraft cargo door. Due to the nature of some operations, only one person may be in the vicinity of the cargo door, a safety risk arises otherwise. In the current scenario, whenever a second person is detected in the vicinity of the cargo door, the system exhibits a message and a sound noticing that. However, more appropriate real-world actions would include activating emergency stops in motorized tools in operation, alerting the operators, raising alarms, etc.

The current system is monitored by four security cameras connected to a network and placed around the cargo door (Fig. 4). Standstill pictures from the live stream of the four cameras can be seen in (Fig. 5). In this case, the four cameras correspond to four inputs in the system and four sources of information for the same set of variables. The previous creates a scenario of information redundancy common in safety applications. Even if the scenario explored relates to a safety application, the authors would like to stress that the system, as is, does not meet any criteria for real-world usage (i.e., is not a safety system), and it serves only the purpose of demonstrating the architecture which also has a much broader potential applicability than just the one considered.

In the scenario considered, one operator is working on the cargo door when a second operator invades the scene and comes in contact with the first. The system will work with the live stream from the cameras, but for the purpose of analysis and comparison of results, the scenario was also recorded into a 30 s dataset. In the first 16 s, Person 2 goes around the aircraft cargo door. Then, it collides with Person 1 for 10 s. Finally, Person 2 walks away for 4 s. Each camera perspective is recorded for the dataset at 10 fps and a 320×320 pixels resolution.

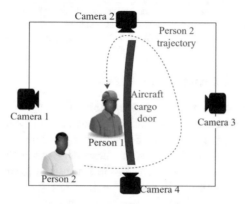

Fig. 4. Scenario.

Fig. 5. Scenario visualization from different cameras' perspectives.

The technical infrastructure is summarized in Table 1. There are four Edge devices (raspberry pis), a WiFi router, and a Local server machine. Each camera is directly connected to an Edge device by cable using the Ethernet interface. The Edge communicates with the Server via a WiFi network (802.11n).

Table 1. Specification of the devices in the scenario.

Device	Model	Specification
Camera	Foscam R2M	Resolution: 1920 × 1080 (2.0 MP), Frame rate: 25 fps (1080P)
WiFi Router	D-Link GO-RT-N300	Standard: 802.11b/g/n Speed: 300 Mbps 2.4 GHz
Edge	Raspberry Pi 3 B+	Processor: Quad Core 1.2 GHz Broadcom BCM2837 RAM: 1 Gb, SO: Raspberry Pi OS 32 bit
Server	HP Workstation Z2 G5	Processor: Intel(R) Xeon(R) W-1250 CPU @ 3.30 GHz RAM: 16 GB SSD, SO: Ubuntu 20.04.3 LTS GPU: NVIDIA Quadro RTX 4000 8 GB

4.2   Interfaces and Description Files

Specific interfaces were defined for this scenario (Fig. 6). As mentioned, integration interfaces guarantee the harmonization of raw sensor/actuator data with the execution semantics of the system. At the edge device, the chain agent has the interface *H-H Collision Edge* which allows the system to receive data from the cameras and detect collisions. The second interface (*Transfer Frame*), working in tandem with the first, allows redirecting the video frames up the chain for further processing. The Cloud chain agent in the server also has a collision detection interface (*H-H Collision Server*) with a more accurate collision detection algorithm in comparison to the edge device and an interface to raise alarms (*Print State*) when a collision between two operators is detected.

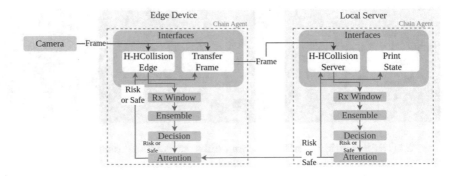

Fig. 6. Reference architecture with the interfaces for the specific application.

The Description File for this system is presented below in the Listing 1.1. The id of this edge device is "edge1". His leader, up the chain, has the id "server1". It considers a window time to receive data of 0.1 s. The MQTT server is running in a machine with IP: "192.168.0.6" and port: "1883". It executes the interfaces "HHCollisionEdge" and "TransferFrame". There is only one possible perception variable, that is called "collision", this variable can assume two literal values, "true" or "false". Also, there is only one possible action variable, that is called "risk", that can be "true" or "false". For the last, there is two rules. The first rule says that if a collision is true ("if": {"collision": "true"}), then there is a risk ("then": {"risk": "true"}). The second rule says that if a collision is false ("if": {"collision": "false"}), then there is not a risk ("then": {"risk": "false"})

Listing 1.1. Description File for edge agent.

```
1  {"id": "edge1",
2   "leader": "server1",
3   "rxperiod": "0.1",
4   "mqtt":{"ip":  "192.168.0.6", "port": "1883"},
5   "interfaces": ["HHCollisionEdge", "TransferFrame"],
6   "perceptions": {"collision": ["true", "false"]},
7   "actions": {"risk": ["true", "false"]},
8   "rules":[
9     {"if": {"collision": "true"}, "then": {"risk": "true"}},
10    {"if": {"collision": "false"},"then": {"risk": "false"}}]  }
```

The implementation of the interfaces is discussed now. The Transfer Frame that is in the Edge device begins to transmit the frames to the server when the decision received is {"risk":"true"}. It uses the OpenCV library [4] to read the frames and applies the ImageZMQ library [2] to transmit OpenCV frames to the server. Otherwise, it does nothing. The Print State interface, in the Local Server, is a visual feedback to print in the screen the safety state in the environment, so it prints Risk when receives {"risk":"true"}, else it prints Safe.

The H-H Collision is in the edge device and the Local Server. The difference between this interface in these devices is only the applied model for object detection and how it reads the frames. In the Edge devices, it uses a simpler model that requires low memory and processing power to return responses, that is, the Mobilenet v2 [19]. To read the frames in the Edge device, it uses the OpenCV library. For the Local Server, it uses the YOLOv3 base version [16] that requires more memory and processing, but it is more precise than the Mobilenet v2. To read the images, the Server uses the ImageZMQ library.

Figure 7 illustrates the process to make the collision detection. First, an object detection model is applied, which returns an array with the boxes for all the objects identified in the frame. From the identified objects, the boxes with humans are selected. With all the human boxes, the algorithm now evaluates the collision. For that, it evaluates the overlap between each two by two combinations of human boxes. The calculus of the overlap is based on the Intersection over Union (IoU) metric. However, instead of the Union of boxes, it applies the smallest human box in the image as a reference because a smaller box completely covered by a bigger box has to return the maximum level of possible contact. This represents a short person in front of a taller person. The use of IoU would only return the proportion of the smaller box related to the bigger one. Therefore, the overlap is calculated using the Intersection over Smaller (IoS), Eq. 1 refers to the adopted IoS metric:

$$IoS(x,y) = \frac{H_x \cap H_y}{\min{(H_x, H_y)}} \tag{1}$$

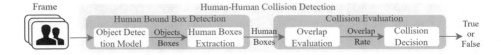

Fig. 7. Human-Human Collision detection module.

H_x and H_y are the boxes of the humans x and y, respectively, where $x \neq y$.

With the IoS for each pair of humans in the scene, the Overlap Evaluation step returns the largest IoS among all the pairs evaluated. This represents the Overlap Rate (OR) for that frame. It is calculated following the Eq. 2.

$$OR = \max_{\forall x,y \in P, x \neq y} IoS(x,y) \tag{2}$$

where P is the set of all People identified in the frame.

For the last, the collision decision considers a pre-established threshold. If the OR is equal or is above this threshold, it returns that the collision is True for that frame. Whereas if the OR is below the threshold, it is False for collision. In the application, we consider a threshold of 5% to be considered a collision.

4.3   Technical Execution Flow

The execution starts with the camera sending a frame to the Edge device. The H-H Collision Edge module process this frame and identifies if there is a collision. It outputs the result to the Rx Window that receives all the detections for the pre-defined window period. Then it passes on all received data to the ensemble. The ensemble converts it into one single perception, with the variable "collision", then forwards it. The Decision step receives the collision information and applies the rules defined in the description file. If there is a collision, it returns that there is a Risk; else, it is Safe. Considering that the server did not send any message, the attention only passes along the Edge decision to his interfaces. If the decision is Safe, the H-H collision Edge continues processing more frames. However, if the response is risk, the H-H collision Edge stops the processing, and the Transfer Frame starts the processing, sending all the received frames to the server.

When the server receives the frames from the edge device, it does the same process reported in the previous paragraph. However, with one difference, the attention output is also passed on to the Edge device and the Print State interface, which prints in the local server if there is risk or not.

The attention module in the Edge now uses the Server decision to be passed along to the local interfaces when the server sends the decision of Risk or Safe to the Edge. If the server had sent risk, the Transfer Frame interface keeps sending the frames, and the H-H collision Edge keeps stopped. However, if the server reports that it is Safe, Transfer Frame stops, and the H-H collision Edge restarts to process.

5   Experiments and Results

This section discusses the results obtained while considering the use case in Sect. 4 and the dataset generated and mentioned therein. The analysis focuses on the impact of the solution on the network traffic with and without the edge devices, as well as the accuracy for the architecture application on the selected use case.

5.1   Network Impact

The equipment defined in Table 1 was setup in different ways according to Fig. 8 to validate the extent to which the edge/cloud architecture proposed impacts the performance of the network. The difference among the configurations is mainly how the devices (camera or Edge device) are connected to the router. In the first case, the camera is directly connected to the router using an Ethernet link (IEEE 802.3 Local Area Network). The second configuration uses a wireless camera communicating in the multi-antenna high data rate 802.11n standard. Finally, the third configuration connects the camera to the Edge device Ethernet interface. In turn, the edge device wirelessly connects to the server. TCP is the underlying transport protocol to exchange flows among the devices.

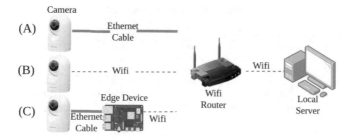

Fig. 8. Configurations for the communication devices used for the network experiment.

The following evaluation metrics are considered: Acknowledgement Round Trip Time (ARTT), packet loss, and the number of exchanged packets. The ARTT is calculated as the time the cameras or edge devices take to respond with an acknowledgment (Ack) for packages sent by the local server. As the cameras do not implement a network interface that can be easily monitored, all packet level measurements are carried out at the server's network interface. The lost packets metric refers to the level of packets that are dropped during their transmission. We also compute the number of packets successfully received by the server. The higher this is, the more packet processing overhead the CPU requires to handle such traffic. The following parameters are considered to evaluate network impact: frame resolution 640×640 pixels at 15 fps for a 10 min transmission period. The number of cameras in the experiment is increased from 1 to 4.

A video transmission resolution of 640 × 480 pixels and a frame rate corresponding to 15 FPS were adopted. These represent upper bounds that allow the processing of frames by edge devices in the experiments. An experiment lasts 10 min, at the end of which a network trace is captured using the tcpdump [9,14] network packet analyzer running at the server machine. This duration is estimated as sufficient to extract meaningful insights and identify possible transmission patterns. Running longer experiments has shown no advantages and generates unnecessarily big packet capture files. The number of cameras is gradually increased from 1 to 4 cameras. Observe that in the case of configuration C (Fig. 8), increasing the number of cameras also increases the number of the Edge devices, as each camera is directly connected to an edge device.

Table 2 collects the results generated by the suggested experiments. It shows that the inclusion of Raspberry Pi as an edge device considerably impacts the ARTT. Observe that ARTT deteriorates even further when increasing the number of these devices. Setups A and B (i.e., without the use of Raspberry devices) exhibit no significant difference for this metric. Every time a new device is included, there is a corresponding increase of at least 0.288 ms that is observed in the case of experiment configuration C. Also, the higher standard deviation obtained by the edge device-based configuration shows that introducing additional devices introduces new outliers and increases delay.

Table 2. Network results.

Qty	Co nf	ARTT/packet (ms)	Packet qty	Packet loss	% loss	Qty	Co nf	ARTT/packet (ms)	Packet qty	Packet loss	% loss
1	A	0.03 ± 0.18	63746	0	0.00%	3	A	0.03 ± 0.24	217571	0	0.00%
	B	0.04 ± 0.21	69088	258	0.37%		B	0.03 ± 0.20	194207	384	0.20%
	C	0.08 ± 2.82	296604	398	0.13%		C	0.65 ± 12.01	513148	1565	0.30%
2	A	0.03 ± 0.02	142637	0	0.00%	4	A	0.03 ± 0.19	294433	0	0.00%
	B	0.03 ± 0.21	125440	400	0.32%		B	0.04 ± 0.49	270021	568	0.21%
	C	0.36 ± 8.70	392886	1091	0.28%		C	1.09 ± 17.88	602576	2589	0.43%

The number of packets increases by approximately 75000 for Configurations A and B, while it increases by around 10000 in the case of Configuration C. This last one achieves a more significant amount of packets from a single camera. Although the increase in the number of transmitted packets is linear, more packets are needed for the first connection. The wired connection is loss-free, independently of the number of used cameras. On the other hand, the WiFi configuration suffers some level of packet loss. For example, the configuration with the Edge device suffered a maximum packet loss of 0.43% when using four devices. Note that this packet loss level does not significantly affect the transmission quality [12].

The obtained results showed that the use of the Raspberry Pi led to a degradation in the network transmission flow compared to other configurations. Nonetheless, it does not result in a significant loss of information for the intended application. Hence considering our application context, the most significant benefit of adopting such devices is their ability to process the video streams locally and relieve the network from their transmission. Our application takes advantage of this result. Most of the time, there is no risk of accidents being detected, and therefore all processing will be local while saving network resources. In the rare event of a safety risk being detected, transmission occurs from these devices.

Additional advantages of using an edge device, such as a Raspberry PI, include the fact that an edge device may select different system configurations. Unlike the used cameras, it may alter frame size and the compression rate parameters. Finally, transmission efficiency may be improved using devices with more processing power and optimizing the installed software libraries, especially those related to the TCP/IP stack.

5.2   Accuracy Analysis

This experiment evaluates the impact on the general accuracy when using the proposed architecture. The dataset presented in Sect. 4.1 is used in this experiment. The accuracy is measured based on the right identification of a Risk or Safe situation in each dataset frame. The experiment compares the results produced when using the Proposed Architecture (PA), with other models: YOLO v3 (YV3), Mobilenet v2 (MN), and Mobilenet v2→YOLO v3 (MN→YV3). The YV3, MN, and MN→YV3 are applied directly to each dataset frame in a single machine (server device described in Table 1). The MN→YV3 first applies the MN in the frame; if this model detects risk, then the YV3 is applied to the frames of different perspectives, with a unanimity ensemble as described in Sect. 3. The MN→YV3 is near our approach, although it runs on a single computer and has no network between models' execution. The PA is used by applying Configuration C from Fig. 8 for the network communication.

Different cameras are used in this evaluation, considering the positions illustrated in Fig. 4. There is an evaluation for each camera individually, cameras 1, 2, 3, and 4. We also evaluate multi-camera scenarios, one with the four cameras at once (labeled as configuration 1-2-3-4) and the other with the cameras 2, 3, and 4 (labeled as configuration 2-3-4). On all cameras, each frame's resolution is 320×320 pixels, a 10 fps frame rate is considered, and different combinations of models are tested.

The results are evaluated in terms of the metrics: accuracy (ACC), sensitivity (SEN), and specificity (SPE). They are calculated as in the Eq. 3, based on the classification metrics: True Positives (TP), True Negatives (TN), False Positives (FP), and False Negatives (FN).

Also, it is evaluated the mean time per frame and Frames Per Second (FPS) that the models YV3, MN, and MN→YV3 require to process in a single machine. The MN→YV3, in this case, considers only the MN detection of frames from one single camera perspective for then pass along to be processed by the YV3. Three different machines are considered: the Edge device, the Server device with GPU, and the Server device without GPU. It was executed for the 300 frames of the dataset.

$$ACC = \frac{TP + TN}{TP + TN + FP + FN} \quad SEN = \frac{TP}{TP + FN} \quad SPE = \frac{TN}{TN + FP} \quad (3)$$

Table 3 has the time, and FPS obtained for the execution of different models and processing machines. When using the YV3 model, the Edge device has one frame processed every 4.5 s, which does not allow us to run this model in the Edge device for a real-time application. That is why this device uses the MN, which can process 6.3 frames each second. The MN could be applied in the Server to a higher fps. However, for our application is more critical that there we have a more accurate model in the Server, that is the case of YV3.

Table 3. FPS for different models and processing machines.

Model	Edge	Server CPU	Server GPU
YV3	0.223 ± 0.008	9.233 ± 0.423	38.028 ± 2.717
MN	6.306 ± 0.671	102.270 ± 5.327	159.042 ± 9.842
MN→YV3	0.211 ± 0.006	8.432 ± 0.337	32.484 ± 2.098

As the Server CPU process in 9.2 fps with YV3 and Edge with MN is 6.3 fps, The application of at least two Edge devices processing in parallel surpasses the processing of YV3 in a Server without GPU. When the Server has GPU is necessary to have at least 7 Edge devices. However, the network transmission is the limiting in this case, so when processing in the Edge devices, the level of network load evaluated in the Table 2 (configuration C) is avoided most of the time when there is no risk. The FPS of the MN→YV3 is lower than the other models for all devices due to having to process first the MN and then the YV3.

Table 4 presents the results for accuracy experiments. The PA model is the only one with the Standard Deviation once each execution can result in different results due to the network. The others are deterministic models that run on a single computer.

Table 4. Accuracy results.

C	Model	ACC	SEN	SPE	C	Model	ACC	SEN	SPE
1	YV3	0.96	1.00	0.94	3	YV3	0.68	0.00	1.00
	MN	0.98	0.95	1.00		MN	0.67	0.00	1.00
	MN→YV3	0.97	0.98	0.97		MN→YV3	0.67	0.00	1.00
	PA	0.97 ± 0.01	1 ± 0.01	0.96 ± 0.01		PA	0.68 ± 0	0 ± 0	1 ± 0
2	YV3	0.92	1.00	0.89	4	YV3	0.55	0.05	0.79
	MN	0.67	0.02	0.98		MN	0.63	0.03	0.92
	MN→YV3	0.89	0.71	0.97		MN→YV3	0.60	0.02	0.87
	PA	0.93 ± 0.04	0.85 ± 0.13	0.96 ± 0.03		PA	0.62 ± 0.03	0 ± 0	0.92 ± 0.05
2	YV3	0.82	1	0.734	1	YV3	0.80	1.00	0.70
3	MN	0.617	0.052	0.887	2	MN	0.91	0.95	0.89
4	MN→YV3	0.79	0.711	0.828	3	MN→YV3	0.86	0.98	0.81
	PA	0.82 ± 0.07	0.76 ± 0.17	0.85 ± 0.06	4	PA	0.86 ± 0.05	0.99 ± 0.02	0.8 ± 0.07

When using only a single camera, the camera 1 perspective has the best ACC of all models, followed by camera 2, camera 3, and the last is camera 4. This is justified, given that camera 1 is positioned tacking the humans side by side, camera 2 and camera 4 have humans occlusion since one human is in front of the other, but for camera 2 this is more favorable once it is a little more inclined to a position that has a better vision of the different human's complete body. Camera 3 clearly does not take the humans interaction, only the passage of the Person 2, which does not represent a collision, so this justifies the low SEN = 0 and SPE = 1 for all models, given that it always returns the safe state once it can not see the collision, due to the occlusion caused by the cargo door.

When comparing experiments with multiple cameras (1-2-3-4 and 2-3-4) to experiments with single cameras (1, 2, 3, and 4), the ACC results with single Cameras 1 and 2 surpass those with multi-cameras, being around 11% more accurate for the PA model. However, when using single cameras, they have to trust in their position and be positioned in the best place, while the multi-camera can consider different perspectives and make a unified decision. This makes the multi-camera a good result. Because for example, suppose that the collision occurs in front of camera 3 instead of camera 1. The camera 1 ACC would drop, but the multi-camera model still can keep the ACC as it considers the response of camera 3 too. The configuration 2-3-4 is interesting; once it disregards the camera in the best position, that is camera 1. Moreover, even without it, keep accuracy near the one with 1-2-3-4, except for the MN model.

At first sight, the MN model has the best ACC for most configurations (1, 4, and 1-2-3-4). This is an unexpected result because this model is more restricted, prioritizing processing speed over accuracy. However, the fact is that for Camera 1 all the models have similar results with at most 2% of difference. For camera 4 the MN takes advantage once it most of the time returns the safe state. This improves his SPE, while YV3 commits more mistakes in this case. The models MN→YV3 and CA take advantage of it because they have a previous detection using MN, then apply YV3, so the ACC and SPE are near the MN.

The PA follows the MN→YV3 ACC for all configurations, staying in the standard deviation range. This shows that including the PA does not impact the general ACC of the system.

6   Conclusion

This work presented and discussed the construction of a reference architecture for safety risk identification. The proposal is based on an edge/cloud computing structure to parallelize sensor processing in an industrial environment and avoid centralizing the information transmission and processing to a local server. One of the primary intentions of the proposed architecture was to alleviate network load and eventually assess whether more mission-critical applications could coexist and share network resources with other devices. The evaluated scenario showed that, compared to conventional solutions where images are continuously streamed to a cloud infrastructure, the proposed architecture generates more traffic during transmission. However, it does not continuously transmit, using network resources only when needed. Part of the increased traffic can be justified by the lesser efficient protocols used in the current implementation of the architecture and on the choice of edge devices. Still, given that safety occurrences are relatively rare, one can argue that the overall reduction in network load is attainable and concrete.

However, such reduction is not useful if the accuracy becomes compromised. In this respect, the paper has also evaluated the accuracy of different risk detection models. Edge devices must necessarily use simpler detection algorithms due to their limited computational power. The results suggest that it is possible to find a balanced compromise that makes the edge/cloud solution proposed useful. Indeed the higher computational power of cloud resources, particularly using GPU processing, enables very high processing rates. However, these come at the cost of network load. The positioning of the sensors matters naturally, but the results also show the benefits of the sensorial fusion offered by the platform.

Overall, the results suggest that the proposed platform offers an interesting and re-configurable distributed solution for multi-sensor industrial applications.

Acknowledgments. This work was realized with the support of the Conselho Nacional de Desenvolvimento Científico e Tecnológico - Brasil (CNPq); Centro de Pesquisa e Inovação Sueco-Brasileiro (CISB); SaaB; and Division of Product Realization, PROD, Department of Management and Engineering at Linköping University. Under the agreement of CNPq/CISB/Saab scholarships.

References

1. Abas, K., Obraczka, K., Miller, L.: Solar-powered, wireless smart camera network: an IoT solution for outdoor video monitoring. Comput. Commun. **118**, 217–233 (2018)
2. Bass, J.: ImageZMQ: Transporting OpenCV Images (2020). https://github.com/jeffbass/imagezmq
3. Berardini, D., Mancini, A., Zingaretti, P., Moccia, S.: Edge artificial intelligence: a multi-camera video surveillance application. In: International Design Engineering Technical Conferences and Computers and Information in Engineering Conference, vol. 85437, p. V007T07A006. American Society of Mechanical Engineers (2021)
4. Bradski, G., Kaehler, A.: Opencv. Dr. Dobb's J. Softw. Tools **3**, 2 (2000)
5. Chen, J., Li, K., Deng, Q., Li, K., Philip, S.Y.: Distributed deep learning model for intelligent video surveillance systems with edge computing. IEEE Trans. Ind. Inform. (2019)
6. Filteau, J., Lee, S.J., Jung, A.: Real-time streaming application for IoT using Raspberry Pi and handheld devices. In: 2018 IEEE Global Conference on Internet of Things (GCIoT), pp. 1–5. IEEE (2018)
7. George, A., Ravindran, A., Mendieta, M., Tabkhi, H.: Mez: a messaging system for latency-sensitive multi-camera machine vision at the IoT edge. arXiv preprint arXiv:2009.13549 (2020)
8. Hu, Y.C., Patel, M., Sabella, D., Sprecher, N., Young, V.: Mobile edge computing-a key technology towards 5G. ETSI White Paper **11**(11), 1–16 (2015)

9. Jacobson, V.: TCPDUMP (1989). ftp://ftp.ee.lbl.gov
10. Khan, A., Khattak, K.S., Khan, Z.H., Gulliver, T., Imran, W., Minallah, N.: Internet-of-video things based real-time traffic flow characterization. EAI Endorsed Trans. Scalable Inf. Syst. **8**(33), e9 (2021)
11. Light, R.A.: Mosquitto: server and client implementation of the MQTT protocol. J. Open Source Softw. **2**(13), 265 (2017)
12. Mansfield, K.C., Jr., Antonakos, J.L.: Computer Networking for LANS to WANS: Hardware, Software and Security. Cengage Learning (2009)
13. Mayer, S., Hodges, J., Yu, D., Kritzler, M., Michahelles, F.: An open semantic framework for the industrial internet of things. IEEE Intell. Syst. **32**(1), 96–101 (2017)
14. McCanne, S., Jacobson, V.: The BSD packet filter: a new architecture for user-level packet capture. In: USENIX Winter, vol. 46 (1993)
15. Prasad, G.S.C., Pillai, A.S.: Role of industrial IoT in critical environmental conditions. In: 2018 Second International Conference on Intelligent Computing and Control Systems (ICICCS), pp. 1369–1372. IEEE (2018)
16. Redmon, J., Farhadi, A.: YOLOV3: an incremental improvement. arXiv preprint arXiv:1804.02767 (2018)
17. Reegu, F., Khan, W.Z., Daud, S.M., Arshad, Q., Armi, N.: A reliable public safety framework for industrial internet of things (IIoT). In: 2020 International Conference on Radar, Antenna, Microwave, Electronics, and Telecommunications (ICRAMET), pp. 189–193. IEEE (2020)
18. Rüßmann, M., et al.: Industry 4.0: the future of productivity and growth in manufacturing industries. Boston Consulting Group **9**(1), 54–89 (2015)
19. Sandler, M., Howard, A., Zhu, M., Zhmoginov, A., Chen, L.C.: MobileNetV2: inverted residuals and linear bottlenecks. In: Proceedings of the IEEE Conference on Computer Vision and Pattern Recognition, pp. 4510–4520 (2018)
20. Varghese, B., Wang, N., Barbhuiya, S., Kilpatrick, P., Nikolopoulos, D.S.: Challenges and opportunities in edge computing. In: 2016 IEEE International Conference on Smart Cloud (SmartCloud), pp. 20–26. IEEE (2016)
21. Wu, F., Wu, T., Yuce, M.R.: An internet-of-things (IoT) network system for connected safety and health monitoring applications. Sensors **19**(1), 21 (2018)
22. Zhou, C., Damiano, N., Whisner, B., Reyes, M.: Industrial internet of things: (IIoT) applications in underground coal mines. Min. Eng. **69**(12), 50 (2017)
23. Zhou, Z., Liao, H., Gu, B., Huq, K.M.S., Mumtaz, S., Rodriguez, J.: Robust mobile crowd sensing: when deep learning meets edge computing. IEEE Netw. **32**(4), 54–60 (2018)

An Ontology-Based Solution
for Monitoring IoT Cybersecurity

Said Daoudagh[1]([✉]) [iD], Eda Marchetti[1] [iD], Antonello Calabrò[1] [iD],
Filipa Ferrada[2,3] [iD], Ana Inês Oliveira[2,3] [iD], José Barata[2,3] [iD],
Ricardo Peres[2,3] [iD], and Francisco Marques[2] [iD]

[1] ISTI-CNR, Pisa, Italy
{said.daoudagh,eda.marchetti,antonello.calabro}@isti.cnr.it
[2] Uninova Institute, Centre of Technology and Systems (CTS), Caparica, Portugal
{faf,aio,jab,ricardo.peres,fam}@uninova.pt
[3] NOVA School of Science and Technology, FCT-NOVA, Caparica, Portugal

Abstract. *Context:* Systems of Systems (SoSs) are becoming an emerging architecture, and they are used in several daily life contexts. *Objective:* The aim is to define a reference environment conceived for monitoring and assessing the behavior from the cybersecurity point of view of SoS when a new IoT device is added. *Method:* In this paper, we propose the Domain bAsEd Monitoring ONtology (DAEMON), an ontology that formally models knowledge about monitoring and System of Systems (SoS) domains. We also conceived a reference supporting architecture, and we provided the first proof-of-concept by implementing different components. *Results and Conclusion:* For the feasibility purpose, we have validated our proof-of-concept in the context of the EU BIECO project by considering a Robot Navigation use-case scenario.

Keywords: Cyber security · Internet of Things (IoT) · Monitoring · Ontology · System of Systems (SoS)

1 Introduction

Nowadays, most ICT systems and applications rely on the integration and interaction with other (third parties) components or devices because it is a valid means for increasing productivity and reducing, at the same time, the overall development costs. However, even if effective, this practice can expose the ICT systems to high risks regarding security, privacy, and safety. Additionally, in most cases, there are difficult and costly procedures for verifying if these solutions have vulnerabilities or if they have been built, taking into account the best security and privacy practices. However, detecting vulnerabilities accurately in ICT components and understanding how they can propagate over the supply chain is extremely important for the ICT ecosystems. To find a suitable and

Published by Springer Nature Switzerland AG 2022
L. M. Camarinha-Matos et al. (Eds.): IFIPIoT 2022, IFIP AICT 665, pp. 158–176, 2022.
https://doi.org/10.1007/978-3-031-18872-5_10

effective compromise, one commonly adopted solution for vulnerability detection is using a monitoring system, i.e., a means for the online analysis of functional and non-functional properties. Usually, this system relies on the collection of events produced by the systems, devices, or components during the execution and uses complex event patterns for assessing a specific property. Indeed, the patterns are associated with observable normal (or abnormal) behavior and can be exploited to raise alarms or implement countermeasures promptly. Nevertheless, even if notably efficient and effective, a monitoring system's design, implementation, and management can be an effort and time-consuming activity. In this paper, according to the definition provided in [18] that considers the IoT system as "the latest example of the System of Systems (SoS), demanding for both innovative and evolutionary approaches to tame its multifaceted aspects" we focus mainly on the System of Systems (SoS). Monitoring SoS involves all the stages of the software development process and different stakeholders, such as SoS domain experts, device developers, or monitoring experts. The complexity of the monitoring activity could increase when new devices (or components) are dynamically included in the SoS environments [35].

To overcome this issue, in [14] some of the authors of this paper presented an initial solution. It focused on the definition of a common framework for collecting together, in a manageable and user-friendly way, the knowledge coming from different sources: SoS domain experts, standards, guidelines, monitoring, and developers experts. The purpose was to join concepts and definitions about the SoS and monitoring into a unique manageable ontology-based representation [14]. In this paper, we leverage this recent proposal by:

1. extensively modifying the initial core ontology (i.e., MONTOLOGY) and deriving a new one called Domain bAsEd Monitoring ONtology (DAEMON). In particular, we introduce modules that make the ontology more manageable and comprehensive, and we add new concepts to the modules to better represent the monitoring of a SoS knowledge;
2. we customize the proposed reference architecture by revising the components' interaction and roles and introducing new ones for better managing the new elements;
3. we validate the proposed customization using a real case study provided within an ongoing European project. In particular, we consider the Multi-Robot Navigation use case scenario and its specific set of functional and non-functional properties.

Outline. Section 2 discusses the related works concerning the ontologies, cybersecurity specification and vulnerabilities in the context of SoSs, and Monitoring systems. We introduce DAEMON ontology in Sect. 3 by describing its main modules, concepts and the relationship between them. Section 4 describes DAEMON's reference architecture and how the components interact. We illustrate, in Sect. 5, the validation of both DAEMON and its reference architecture through a Multi-Robot Navigation use-case scenario within an ongoing EU Project. Section 6 concludes the paper by also highlighting our current and future works.

2   Related Works

Ontology-Based System of Systems (SoS). In recent years, much research has been conducted on modeling System of Systems (SoS). Dridi et al. [16] classified SoS modeling into seven main classes: Model-Driven Architecture, Model-Driven, Services-Oriented Architecture, Ontology, Architecture Description Language, Bigraph, and Hybrid. To properly model SoS, one cannot separate their inherent engineering processes, which involve planning, analyzing, organizing, and integrating constituent/component systems (CS), i.e., the System of Systems Engineering (SoSE). In this context, ontology-based approaches for modeling SoS are needed to establish domain concepts and link the SoS processes consistently using common language and semantics, which are essential in the planning and analysis processes [16,20,25,31,40]. Ontologies can be used to deal with the interoperability and scalability of SoS, supporting the creation of new domain ontologies as well as the reusability of existing ones. A top-level ontology/upper ontology, such as BFO, DOLCE, among others [3,5,29,34], is a highly general representation of categories and relations common to all domains. In addition, efforts have been made to create meta-models for representing SoS/-SoSE ontologies: Dridi et al. [16] use a model or set of models to document and communicate from the system requirements level down to the software implementation level, Nilsson et al. [31] proposed an ontology for SoS that uses Object Process Methodology (OPM) ISO 19450 to facilitate collaboration among organizations with focus on safety aspects, Baek et al. [4] developed a conceptual meta-model for representing SoS ontology and Langford et al. [25] created a framework that embraces ontology of systems and SoS to expose the true nature of emergence. On the other side, ontologies might be domain-specific intended to describe individual systems or domains of interest. In response to this, some work has been done to develop ontologies for SoS/SoSE in different domains [20,27].

In light of this, Internet-of-Things (IoT) systems can be engineered from the perspective of SoS. IoT applications involve the integrated operation of many subsystems, or constituent systems (CS) that are physically and functionally heterogeneous maintaining their advanced cyber-physical functionalities. Similarly, it is important to develop ontologies to share semantic information between IoT subsystems. In response to this challenge, in recent years several proposals for ontology have emerged from the semantics and IoT research communities aiming at describing concepts and relationships between different entities. In 2009, Scioscia and Ruta proposed to use the technologies of semantic web with IoT and developed the semantic web of things (SWoT) [37]. The W3C Semantic Sensor Network Incubator Group has developed the SSN ontology[1], to describe the sensors, observations, and related concepts in the sensor network. Gyrard et al. proposed the M3 Ontology [21] framework that assists users in reusing the domain knowledge and interpreting sensor measurements to build IoT applications. The oneM2M base ontology [33], developed within the oneM2M global open standard for M2M communications and the IoT, is a top-level ontology

---

[1] The W3C SSN is available at: https://www.w3.org/TR/vocab-ssn/.

specifying the minimal ontology that is required such that other ontologies can be mapped into oneM2M as the example of Smart Appliances Reference Ontology (SAREF) [15]. More recently, Bermudez-Edo et al. proposed the IoT-Lite ontology [8] which is a light ontology that represents the resources, entities and services of the IoT. It is an instantiation of the W3C SSN Ontology and is also a base ontology that can be extended to represent IoT concepts in a more detailed way in different domains. A comprehensive ontology catalog is available online and maintained by LOV4IoT (Linked Open Vocabularies for IoT) [26], aiming at encouraging the reuse of domain knowledge already designed and available on the WWW.

The DAEMON ontology, proposed in this paper, aims at representing the monitoring of SoS knowledge. It leverages the previous MONTOLOGY by extending and introducing new concepts useful for a better knowledge representation, such as the rule hierarchy and skill (see Sect. 3). DAEMON is specifically conceived for being the connection between SoS and the monitoring ontologies, that in the best of our knowledge is still not yet offered. Nevertheless, SoS ontologies like IoT-Lite or oneM2M Base Ontology can be integrated and reused in our proposal. DAEMON intention is not to substitute but use integrate exiting knowledge. Therefore, the SoS module (see Sect. 3) aims at representing the point of integration where the different ontologies concepts can be used and integrated into DAEMON.

Cybersecurity Specification and Vulnerability. In literature, several comprehensive sets of functional and non-functional (including security, safety and privacy) requirements that can be used for guiding research, technology development, and design are currently available. These sets can be found in recent European Projects documentations, such as [1,38], or standards and specifications such as [17,39], or available backlog list containing structured security and privacy user stories [7]. These available heterogeneous sources, while very useful from a cybersecurity and vulnerability specification point of view, are generally kept generic and domain-specific agnostic. The proposal presented in this paper intends to provide a methodology for collecting and organizing together the generic and specific knowledge about a target application domain into a unique reference ontology. The aim is to focus only on the most suitable functional and non-functional properties of each specific context to better focus the monitoring and assessing activity on the expected behavior of IoT/SoS/Ecosystem/Components. In Sect. 5, a specific example in the robotic domain is provided.

Monitoring Systems. Monitoring systems have been applied in several domains such as: traffic [41], automotive [19], avionic [22], healthcare [36], industry [10]. In almost all the application contexts, the existing monitoring proposals aim to: i) providing a powerful, concise and unambiguous specification language for the validation properties specification [24]; ii) defining mechanisms for the conformity assessment of the system against the selected properties [13].

Recently, the massive and extensive usage of the internet promotes the adoption of monitoring approaches able to mitigate the risk of cyber-attacks. Among them the most promising solutions are: *Security Information and Event Manage-*

ment (SIEM), *eXtended Detection and Response* (XDR), or *Endpoint Detection and Response (EDR)*. *SIEM* systems gather, aggregate and normalize information from various events related to potential security violation occurred within the system [11] whereas, XDR and EDR can boost the SIEM analysis providing a set of information and tools that will enhance the analysis executable through the SIEM. Usually, the collected data are stored in *Data Lake* [23] useful for advanced forensic analysis.

This work aims to leverage the existing proposals and provide a collaborative, easy-to-use, and effective solution for applying the monitoring activity inside target domains. In particular, we provide facilities for easily: (1) identifying the most suitable functional and non-functional properties that can be used during the monitoring activity to detect failures and vulnerabilities promptly; (2) instantiating the selected properties into monitoring rules able to capture, infer and analyze complex events; (3) allowing the detection of critical problems, failures, and security vulnerabilities; (4) validating the trust and security level of the run-time behavior of SoS and its devices or components; (5) rising warnings and enabling (non-blocking) system reconfiguration to assure a trustworthy execution.

3   DAEMON Ontology

The aim of Domain bAsEd Monitoring ONtology (DAEMON) is to help the different SoS stakeholders gather functional and non-functional properties related to the different part of SoS, and consequently enabling the definition of concrete monitoring rules each related to a specific property. As a result, we can define a reference set of meaningful rules to be monitored during the SoS execution so as to automatically demonstrate the compliance (non-compliance) with the selected properties.

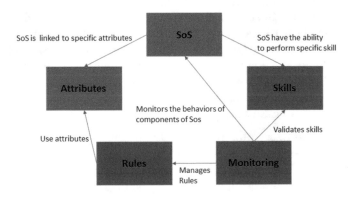

Fig. 1. DAEMON ontology modules.

The starting point of DAEMON ontology is the MONitoring onTOLOGY (MONTOLOGY) ontology [14], which models the SoS and monitoring main concepts and defines the relationships between them. MONTOLOGY is a core component of MENTORS (i.e., a monitoring environment for SoS) [14] and it is composed of two main modules: System of Systems (SoS) Module (containing eight concepts) and Monitoring Module (which contains five concepts), with a total of 13 (thirteen) concepts.

Therefore, the basic idea of DAEMON is to extend MONTOLOGY by adding new concepts, and to reorganize the content into a more manageable and modular way, so as to enable interoperability and facilitate both the extensibility and maintainability. More precisely, as reported in Fig. 1, we divide DAEMON in five modules: (1) SoS (Fig. 2); (2) Attributes (Fig. 3); (3) Skills (Fig. 4); (4) Rules (Fig. 5); and (5) Monitoring (Fig. 8).

The remainder of this section provides more details about how we derived DAEMON by reusing the most relevant parts of MONTOLOGY and how we reconstructed the new content in a more comprehensive set of modules. For the aim of readability, in the following figures, we report the new concepts/classes introduced in DAEMON by coloring the shape outline in red.

SoS Module. The SoS module aims at representing the most relevant concepts related to the System of Systems (SoS) domain and the relationship between them. Differently from MONTOLOGY, we model the *SystemOfSytems* as a composition of *System*, and it is influenced by a specific *Environment* in which it operates and it is executed. Therefore, a *System* is a collection of *Devices* that represent the object of the monitoring activities. As in MONTOLOGY, each *Device* is composed of a specific set of *Components*.

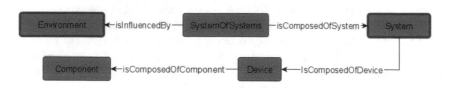

Fig. 2. System of Systems (SoS) module.

Attributes Module. An *Attribute* is a functional and non-functional property related to a specific SoS concept. Examples of attributes could be (1) the communication latency between the components; (2) the average amount of the messages is under a certain level, so as to avoid or detect DoS attacks; or (3) the number of the allowed/authorized connections.

Therefore, this module contains all the concepts related to the observable properties of the concepts in the SoS module. As in Fig. 3, we extend this module with the two specific concepts; *QualititaveAttribute*, and *ObservableAttribute*, which is a quantitative attribute used for defining both the *Measure* and *Metric* used for defining monitoring rules[2]. We also expand the *Attribute* hier-

---

[2] Note that, in MONTOLOGY *Measure* and *Metric* are directly connected with the *Attribute* class.

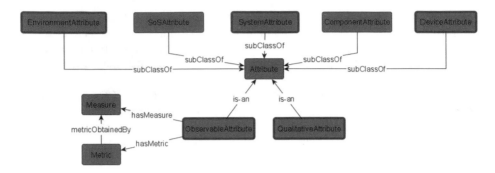

Fig. 3. Attributes module.

archy by adding three sub-classes: *EnvironmentAttribute*, *SystemAttribute* and *DeviceAttribute*. The purpose is to have specific attributes for each of the SoS's concepts/classes, so as to enable the monitoring of their behavior throughout specific monitoring rules.

Skills Module. The skills module allows modeling the skills related to the different concepts in SoS module. A *Skill* represents an ability of an agent (active or passive) to perform a specific action, such as the ability of connection or the ability of movement. The original concept of *Skill* modelled in MONTOLOGY has been extended into two different ways. Firstly, we create a skill hierarchy by leveraging the original concept *Skill* as super-class of the hierarchy, and we add two specific sub-classes (*BasicSkill* and *ComplexSkill*) that are connected with each other through the relation *isComposedBy*. As in the Figure, a *ComplexSkill* can be composed both through a set of *BasicSkill*, or/and iteratively throughout a set of *ComplexSkill*. Secondly, we introduce the concept of *ObservableSkill*, i.e., the observed ability related to the SoS concept that can be validated through the monitoring facilities. Differently from MONTOLOGY, we connect the *Requirement* class directly to *ObservableSkill* through the *isRelatedToSkill* association. Therefore, each *ObservableSkill*, specified as a set of *Requirements*, can be verified through a specific *Rule*.

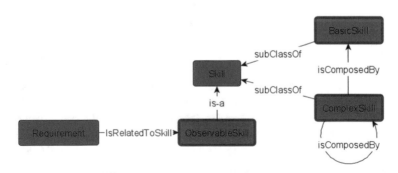

Fig. 4. Skills module.

Rule Module. This module contains all the concepts related to rule at different level of specification. A rule is a set of instructions related to analysis of the occurrences of one or more events in a stream or a cloud of events. Usually, rules are structured as a set of if-then-else sequences. In particular, DAEMON leverages the concept of rule by providing a well-formed hierarchy with the following sub-classes (see Fig. 5): AbstractRule, WellDefinedRule, and InstantiatedRule.

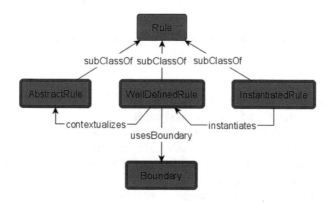

Fig. 5. Rule module.

AbstractRule points out a rule that is generic, not yet instantiated within the execution context and it has been simply gathered from the navigation of the ontology. *WellDefinedRule* refers to a rule ready for being translated to the destination language of the Complex Event Processor and related to the monitoring of a specific device. It is also expressed in terms a set of boundaries (see *Boundary* concept in Fig. 5) that contains specific values that express the applicability ranges of the rule. The last case is related to the *InstantiatedRule*, which is a rule written using the language understandable by the monitoring engine.

To better clarify the complexity of the process involved in obtaining a processable rule, in Fig. 6 we report a graphical representation of the evolution of the rule: from an abstract to an instantiated one.

Fig. 6. Rules transformation process.

In particular, an abstract rule is a very generic natural language description of the objective of the auditing activity that is easily understandable by non-expert users. For instance, the maximum number of established simultaneous connections between two components. The abstract rule is then refined into the well-defined rule, that is a semi-structured and implementable rule, where

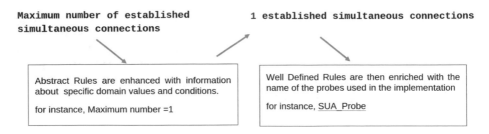

Fig. 7. From abstract to well-defined rule enrichment process.

the users need to add few specific details about the context. For instance, the maximum number of established simultaneous connections. In Fig. 7, we report an example of abstract and well-defined rules.

Finally, the well-defined rule, enriched with the name of the probes used by the user, will be automatically translated into an instantiated rule according to the monitoring language used. This will be used by the run-time monitor during the auditing framework execution.

A typical structure of an instantiated rule can be summarized as follows:

```
1  declare    // Optional
2  rule "rule name"
3      // Attributes
4      when
5          // Conditions
6      then
7          // Actions
```

It contain one or more rules that define at a minimum the rule conditions (when) and actions (then).

Monitoring Module. Monitoring Module aims at modeling monitoring concepts and relationships between them. The core class of the Monitoring module is the *Monitor*, which observes rules organized in *Calendar*, i.e., an ordered set of rules. Each *Calendar* is able to validate a specific *ObservableSkill* at run-time defined in the Skills module. The *Monitor* has a specific *EntryPoint* that is used to communicate with the *Probe*.

A *Probe* is a piece of software code, that can be injected into the observed/-monitored component, device, or system, and is capable of sending *Events* according to a specific format. The probes can send events at regular intervals or every time a specific situation occurs. The sent events contain information related to the occurrence of actions on the observed SoS entity.

The term *Event* defines the change of a state within a system. This change of state is generated when a function is invoked within the system under auditing. The injected *Probe* will pack this atomic action into an event and notify it to the *Monitor* for executing the processing action on the event stream. For being correctly managed by a concrete monitor, the event should contain several pieces of information needed for analyzing a snapshot of what is happening within the System Under Test.

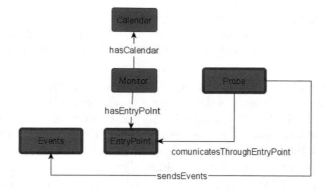

Fig. 8. Monitoring module.

4   Reference Architecture

In this section, we present the reference architecture of the DAEMON methodology introduced in the previous section. This architecture revises the proposal of [14] by introducing new components, interaction and actors. The new proposal is schematized in the Fig. 9 and described as in the following:

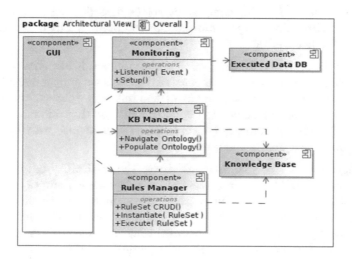

Fig. 9. DAEMON reference architecture.

GUI. This component provides the graphical user interface and the DAEMON facilities to different stakeholders such as: *Business Manager*, who is in charge of the selection and refinement of the functional and non-functional properties and the management of the possible notification of violations; the *Rules-Maker* who is in charge of providing an implementation of the well-defined rules into the target monitoring language; *Ontology Expert* who is the responsible of the ontology management that includes its conceptualization, implementation and maintenance; and the *Developer Expert* in charge of instrumenting the code with probes.

Monitoring. This component is the core of the analysis of the system execution. It relies on an event-driven publish-subscribe architecture. Different monitoring tools can be used for implementing this component as mentioned in Sect. 2. One of the main sub-component is the Complex Event Processor (CEP) [2], that is in charge of inferring simple and complex pattern according to well-defined rules selected by the DAEMON stakeholder. Through the operation called *Setup*, reported in Fig. 9, the monitor component can be prepared for rule execution and events listening. During the execution, through the operation *Listening(Event)*, reported in Fig. 9, the monitoring component is able to start the evaluation of the different instantiated rules. Indeed, the monitoring activity of the life-cycle of each instantiated rule can be into three different stages:

- inactive, i.e., if first event of the rule condition is not received yet;
- active, i.e., if first event has been received and the monitoring is listening further ones;
- satisfied, i.e., when the rule condition is satisfied and the action associated to the rule is executed. In this case the rule passes again to the inactive stage.

Executed Data DB. This component stores data derived from system execution and analysis done by the *Monitoring* component. The data can be used later on for further analysis.

Knowledge Base (KB) Manager. This component is in charge of the DAEMON ontology management by means of the following operations: *Navigate Ontology* that allows the management of the ontology through the *GUI*, and, the selection of the desired ruleset; *Populate Ontology* that allows the definition of individuals for each ontology concept. These can be also used by the *Rules Manager* for further analysis and refinements.

Knowledge Base. This component stores the DAEMON specification and its individuals. DAEMON is represented as a Resource Definition Framework (RDF) [28] graph, it is saved in a triple store. In particular this component contains the sets of abstract, well-defined and instantiated rules and it is invoked by **Rule Manager** for updating or instantiating the single rule or a ruleset. The component provides facility for performing suitable queries.

Rules Manager. Rules Manager is the component that takes care of the management of the rules created, updated and used by the user during the usage of the system. This component supervises the evolution of the rules from *Abstract* to *Well-Defined* and finally to *Instantiated* as depicted in Fig. 6. The main operations are: *RuleSet CRUD*, that defines the creation, reading, updating or deleting of a RuleSet; *Instantiate (RuleSet)*, that allows the instantiation of the well-defined rules into instantiated ones; *Execute(RuleSet)*, that loads a RuleSet of instantiated rules into the *Monitoring* component.

Considering the DAEMON architecture usage, usually the *Ontology Manager* by means of the *Populate Ontology* operation can populate DAEMON with individuals and assertions about the SoS or the device. The *Business Manager* can use the operation *Navigate ontology* to explore the already existing knowledge and to perform specific queries about suitable rules to be monitored. The selected rules are then instantiated into the CEP through the *Instantiate RuleSet* operation, so that the *Monitoring* component could check during the SoS execution, if they are satisfied. This component is also in charge of storing the monitoring data for subsequent analysis performed by the *Business Manager*.

5   BIECO Use Case: Multi-robot Navigation

With the main aim of ensuring trust within ICT supply chains, a holistic security framework is proposed by the EU BIECO Project[3] The framework comprises a set of tools and methodologies for vulnerability assessment, auditing, risk analysis, determining the best mitigation strategies, ensuring resilience and certifying the security and privacy properties of the ICT components and the complete supply chain. The BIECO framework is then validated by four different use case scenarios for distinct sectors, namely: the ICT Gateway (smart grid/energy), the AI Investments platform (financial), the Smart Microfactory (industry), and the Autonomous Navigation. For the work presented in this paper, we will focus on the last use case, specifically a multi-robot autonomous navigation system.

5.1   Use Case Scenario: Multi-robot Navigation

The use case scenario is a *CoppeliaSim* simulation with multi-robot navigation scenario for intralogistics, where software monitoring the behavior of the autonomous mobile robot in runtime, tries to detect situations in which safety concerns might be encountered.

The environment in which the multi-robot operates is a simulation of the shopfloor that includes a representation of the costmap layers used for navigation applying Robot Operating system (ROS) and its visualization tool (Rviz). Besides the navigation plans, the navigation costmap also includes a set of obstacles that can be found in the environment as illustrated in Fig. 10. Therefore, under normal conditions all robots should follow the given trajectory and avoid each other and additional obstacles.

Despite the numerous components of the architectural structure of the autonomous navigation use case, namely in terms of hardware, navigation, and supervision, we will focus on the interactions that the autonomous navigation robot components might have for navigation, namely for the local planner module in the navigation environment, where:

- The navigator component controls the execution of navigation goals based on the task sent by the task manager, acting like an orchestrator, and

---

[3] EU H2020 BIECO project Grant Agreement No. 952702, https://www.bieco.org/.

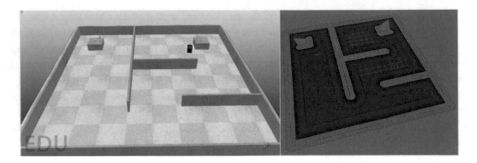

Fig. 10. Simulation of the shop-floor for the controlled environment implemented in CoppeliaSim (left). Visualization in RViz of the costmap layers for autonomous navigation, including obstacles and the navigation plans (right).

- The local planner component that, given a global plan to follow and a costmap including goals, final position and direct sensory input obstacle information, produces motion commands to send to a mobile base (locomotion controller).

Aligned with the DAEMON Ontology described in Sect. 3, this use case can be represented as being influenced by the environment where it operates and including several systems present in the shop floor, being one of them the autonomous navigation multi-robot system. This system includes several devices, such as: *Robot_ Unit_ 1*, *Robot_ Unit_ 2*, *Station_ 1*, *Station_ 2*, *Task_ Manager*, *etc.*, as shown in Fig. 11. Supported by DAEMON, each device is therefore composed of a set of components, as is the case of the *Robot_ Unit_ 1* device, that is composed of for example *Local_ Planner_ 1*, *Global_ Planner_ 1*, *ROS_ Bridge*, *Navigator_ 1*, *etc.*

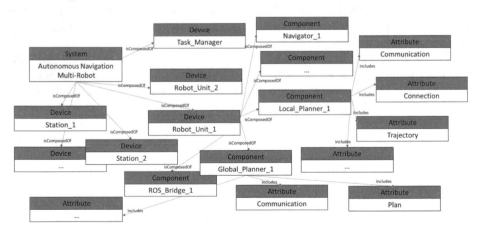

Fig. 11. System use-case in DAEMON (a small example).

For the functional and non-functional properties of the components, each device includes several attributes, as also depicted in Fig. 11.

The mapping of the use case with DAEMON proceeds to the other modules, as is the case of attribute *trajectory* of the *Local_Planner_1* that is composed of *linear_velocity* and *angular_velocity* as the *observable attribute* metric, being measured in *euler_angles* and *length*.

Considering the case where the insertion of malicious code into one of the components of the autonomous navigation occurs, it would severely impair the system causing not only security concerns but also probably safety issues. As the mobile robots are operating in a shopfloor shared with human workers a possible malicious code insertion in their navigation system could lead to collisions and injuries.

Moreover, among several cyber-threats that can be considered in such scenario, we would like to highlight the following with catastrophic severity:

- Malicious code installed or being installed to replace the genuine software component;
- Accidental code errors that can be introduced during software development or maintenance activities;
- Viruses or worms can penetrate the ICT network from the internet and corrupt data in the system;
- Data Injection where the attacker modifies sensible data published by the system.

With the main aim at monitoring and collecting data from the environment, the *Local_Planner* and *Global_Planner* of the autonomous navigation robots have been instrumented with probes to listen to the events related to their execution. Considering the provided feedback on events, the DAEMON execution includes two different conceptual steps: the navigation and the analysis. The navigation includes the selection of the proper rules and boundaries so that it can ensure the safety and trustworthy behavior in the context of addition or update of a new module within the local planner of the Multi-Robot Navigation environment. At this stage, the refinement of the initial auditing rules will take place. After the instrumentation of the system under auditing with the probes, the analysis phase can start, as described in the following subsection.

5.2   Analysis Stage

As mentioned in Sect. 2, different monitoring facilities can be used for instantiating the monitoring component. The implementation considered in this paper relies on the Drools[4] as rule language and Apache Artemis[5] as messages broker. During the Analysis stage, the set of well-defined rules are leveraged into executable monitoring rules through *Instantiate(RuleSet)* operation. Considering the well-defined rule shown in Fig. 7, the result of the instantiation is shown in the Listing 1.1.

---

[4] https://www.drools.org/.
[5] https://activemq.apache.org/.

As in the listing, the rule is divided into two parts: the former (lines 16–21) checks if a connection is established between *Local_Planner* and *Global_Planner*; the latter (lines 23–28) checks if any additional connection is established in the meanwhile. In particular, within the *aEvent*, that is waiting for an occurrence of an event of type *ConcernBaseEvent* (line 16), sent by *SUAProbe* (line 18) to the *Monitoring* (line 19) with an attribute *Name* set to *Connection* (line 17) and payload *Data* set to *established* (line 20). The two parts of the rule (lines 16–21 and lines 23–28 in Listing 1.1) differentiate by the *getConsumed* parameter (lines 21 and 28) that is set to true as soon as the first connection is notified. In case of more than one connection is established, a notification is sent (line 30, Listing 1.1).

```
1   package it.cnr.isti.labsedc.concern.event;
2   import it.cnr.isti.labsedc.concern.event.ConcernBaseEvent;
3   import it.cnr.isti.labsedc.concern.notification.Manager;
4
5   dialect "java"
6   declare ConcernBaseEvent
7        @role( event )
8        @timestamp( timestamp )
9   end
10
11  rule "check that only one connection is active"
12  no-loop
13  salience 200
14  dialect "java"
15      when
16          $aEvent : ConcernBaseEvent(
17          this.getName == "Connection",
18          this.getSenderID == "SUA_Probe",
19          this.getDestinationID == "Monitoring",
20          this.getData == "established",
21          this.getConsumed == true);
22
23          $bEvent : ConcernBaseEvent(
24          this.getName == "Connection",
25          this.getSenderID == "SUA_Probe",
26          this.getDestinationID == "Monitoring",
27          this.getData == "established",
28          this.getConsumed == false);
29      then
30          Manager.print("Connection amount violation on Local Planner");
31          retract($aEvent);
32          retract($bEvent);
33  end
```

Listing 1.1. Instantiated Rule Example.

The instantiate rule is then injected into the CEP of the Monitoring Component so that the monitoring activity can start. This includes running the *Local planner* and *Global Planner* within the Multi-Robot Navigation environment and the listening of events related to their execution sent by the relative probes. In the execution of the presented Use Case, a malicious code attack has been simulated. For this purpose, the malicious code injection is performed through the UI provided with the controlled environment. Due to this malicious behavior, the number of connections between the *Local planner* and *Global planner* increases over the threshold that has been set to 1. On the monitoring side this causes the violation of the *check that only one connection is active* rule shown in Listing 1.1. In this case a notification is generated and sent by the Monitoring component (line 30, Listing 1.1). This untrusted behavior detected can be alternatively managed by the monitoring providing a dynamic reconfiguration suggestion to the Controlled Environment or putting in place an instant countermeasure returning the system to a safe and trusted condition.

6   Conclusion and Future Work

In this paper, we introduced DAEMON, an ontology that models SoS and monitoring concepts uniquely and comprehensively to help SoS stakeholders monitor the behavior of SoS at runtime. DAEMON is supported by a reference architecture that enables: i) lowering down costs of developing and setting up the monitoring environment, i.e., allowing the use of available monitor engines (e.g., GLIMPSE [6,9]); ii) improving quality control by smart and effective rules specification and encoding; iii) increasing flexibility and productivity and making the monitor designers agnostic of the domain-specific challenges (see for instance [32]); and iv) increasing the interoperability by using standardized and domain- independent specification technologies (e.g., OWL [30] for the Ontology description, and RuleML [12] or Drools[6] for instantiating rules).

We have validated our proposal through the Multi-Robot Navigation use-case scenario within the EU BIECO project, demonstrating the feasibility of both DAEMON and its reference architecture. Inside the BIECO project, we are finalizing a customized implementation of the DAEMON architecture. As a future work, we plan to use the BIECO release to evaluate the effectiveness, and the overhead of the DAEMON application. In particular, we are currently working on validating our proposal within the ICT Gateway (smart grid/energy) and the Smart Microfactory (industrial environment) use case scenarios. This will provide important data for the DAEMON performance not only in terms of processing and communication overhead, but also of development and usage effort. Additionally, comparison against related solutions will be also provided as well as the contextualization of DAEMON in other technological domains such as IoT for smart cities.

Acknowledgements. This work was partially supported by the EU H2020 BIECO project Grant Agreement No. 952702, by the CyberSec4Europe H2020 Grant Agreement No. 830929, and by the Portuguese "Fundação para a Ciência e Tecnologia" "Strategic program UIDB/00066/2020" (UNINOVA-CTS project).

---

[6] https://www.drools.org/.

References

1. Peres, R.S., et al.: The BIECO conceptual framework towards security and trust in ICT ecosystems. In: Testing Software and Systems, Cham, pp. 230–232 (2022)
2. de Almeida, V.P., Bhowmik, S., Lima, G., Endler, M., Rothermel, K.: DSCEP: an infrastructure for decentralized semantic complex event processing. In: 2020 IEEE International Conference on Big Data (Big Data), pp. 391–398. IEEE (2020)
3. Arp, R., Smith, B., Spear, A.D.: Building Ontologies with Basic Formal Ontology. The MIT Press, Cambridge (2015)
4. Baek, Y.M., Song, J., Shin, Y.J., Park, S., Bae, D.H.: A meta-model for representing system-of-systems ontologies, pp. 1–7. ACM (2018)
5. Bajaj, G., Agarwal, R., Singh, P., Georgantas, N., Issarny, V.: A study of existing ontologies in the IoT-domain. arXiv preprint arXiv:1707.00112 (2017)
6. Barsocchi, P., Calabrò, A., Ferro, E., Gennaro, C., Marchetti, E., Vairo, C.: Boosting a low-cost smart home environment with usage and access control rules. Sensors **18**(6), 1886 (2018)
7. Bartolini, C., Daoudagh, S., Lenzini, G., Marchetti, E.: GDPR-based user stories in the access control perspective. In: Piattini, M., Rupino da Cunha, P., García Rodríguez de Guzmán, I., Pérez-Castillo, R. (eds.) QUATIC 2019. CCIS, vol. 1010, pp. 3–17. Springer, Cham (2019). https://doi.org/10.1007/978-3-030-29238-6_1
8. Bermudez-Edo, M., Elsaleh, T., Barnaghi, P., Taylor, K.: IoT-lite: a lightweight semantic model for the internet of things, pp. 90–97. IEEE (2016)
9. Bertolino, A., Calabrò, A., Lonetti, F., Sabetta, A.: GLIMPSE: a generic and flexible monitoring infrastructure. In: Giandomenico, F.D. (ed.) Proceedings of the 13th European Workshop on Dependable Computing, EWDC 2011, Pisa, Italy, 11–12 May 2011, pp. 73–78. ACM (2011)
10. Bhamare, D., Zolanvari, M., Erbad, A., Jain, R., Khan, K., Meskin, N.: Cybersecurity for industrial control systems: a survey. Comput. Secur. **89**, 101677 (2020)
11. Bhatt, S.N., Manadhata, P.K., Zomlot, L.: The operational role of security information and event management systems. IEEE Secur. Priv. **12**(5), 35–41 (2014)
12. Boley, H., Tabet, S., Wagner, G.: Design rationale for RuleML: a markup language for semantic web rules. In: Proceedings of the 1st Semantic Web Working Symposium, Stanford University, California, USA, 30 July–1 August 2001, pp. 381–401 (2001)
13. Burns, M., Griffor, E., Balduccini, M., Vishik, C., Huth, M., Wollman, D.: Reasoning about smart city. In: 2018 IEEE International Conference on Smart Computing (SMARTCOMP), pp. 381–386 (2018)
14. Calabrò, A., Daoudagh, S., Marchetti, E.: MENTORS: monitoring environment for system of systems. In: Mayo, F.J.D., Marchiori, M., Filipe, J. (eds.) Proceedings of the 17th International Conference on Web Information Systems and Technologies, WEBIST 2021, 26–28 October 2021, pp. 291–298. SCITEPRESS (2021)
15. Daniele, L., den Hartog, F., Roes, J.: Created in close interaction with the industry: the smart appliances REFerence (SAREF) ontology. In: Cuel, R., Young, R. (eds.) FOMI 2015. LNBIP, vol. 225, pp. 100–112. Springer, Cham (2015). https://doi.org/10.1007/978-3-319-21545-7_9
16. Dridi, C.E., Benzadri, Z., Belala, F.: System of systems modelling: recent work review and a path forward. In: 2020 International Conference on Advanced Aspects of Software Engineering (ICAASE), pp. 1–8 (2020)
17. Regulation (EU) 2016/679 of the European Parliament and of the Council of 27 April 2016 (General Data Protection Regulation). Official Journal of the European Union L119, pp. 1–88, May 2016

18. Fortino, G., Savaglio, C., Spezzano, G., Zhou, M.: Internet of things as system of systems: a review of methodologies, frameworks, platforms, and tools. IEEE Trans. Syst. Man Cybern. Syst. **51**(1), 223–236 (2020)
19. Fotescu, R.P., Constantinescu, R., Alexandrescu, B., Burciu, L.M.: System for monitoring the parameters of vehicle. In: Advanced Topics in Optoelectronics, Microelectronics and Nanotechnologies X, vol. 11718, pp. 55–61. SPIE (2020)
20. Franzén, L.K., Staack, I., Jouannet, C., Krus, P.: An Ontological Approach to System of Systems Engineering in Product Development (2019)
21. Gyrard, A., Bonnet, C., Boudaoud, K., Serrano, M.: Lov4iot: a second life for ontology-based domain knowledge to build semantic web of things applications. In: 2016 IEEE 4th International Conference on Future Internet of Things and Cloud (FiCloud), pp. 254–261 (2016)
22. Hidayanti, F.: Design and application of monitoring system for electrical energy based-on internet of things. Helix **10**(01), 18–26 (2020)
23. Holubová, I., Vavrek, M., Scherzinger, S.: Evolution management in multi-model databases. Data Knowl. Eng. **136**, 101932 (2021)
24. Khan, S., Nazir, S., García-Magariño, I., Hussain, A.: Deep learning-based urban big data fusion in smart cities: towards traffic monitoring and flow-preserving fusion. Comput. Electr. Eng. **89**, 106906 (2021)
25. Langford, G., Langford, T.: The making of a system of systems: ontology reveals the true nature of emergence, pp. 1–5. IEEE (2017)
26. LOV4IoT: Lov4iot-IoT ontology catalog: reusing domain knowledge expertise. http://ww.lov4iot.appspot.com/?p=lov4iot-iot. Accessed 15 Aug 2022
27. Lynch, K., Ramsey, R., Ball, G., Schmit, M., Collins, K.: Conceptual design acceleration for cyber-physical systems, pp. 1–6. IEEE (2017)
28. Manola, F., Miller, E.: RDF Primer. W3C Recommendation, WWW Consortium (2004). http://www.w3.org/TR/rdf-primer/
29. Mascardi, V., Cordì, V., Rosso, P.: A comparison of upper ontologies. In: WOA, vol. 2007, pp. 55–64. Citeseer (2007)
30. Motik, B., Patel-Schneider, P.F., Parsia, B.: OWL 2 web ontology language structural specification and functional-style syntax (second edition). W3C recommendation, World Wide Web Consortium (2012)
31. Nilsson, R., Dori, D., Jayawant, Y., Petnga, L., Kohen, H., Yokell, M.: Towards an ontology for collaboration in system of systems context. In: INCOSE International Symposium, vol. 30, pp. 666–679 (2020)
32. Barsocchi, P., Calabró, A., Lonetti, F., Marchetti, E., Palumbo, F.: Leveraging smart environments for runtime resources management. In: Winkler, D., Biffl, S., Bergsmann, J. (eds.) SWQD 2018. LNBIP, vol. 302, pp. 171–190. Springer, Cham (2018). https://doi.org/10.1007/978-3-319-71440-0_10
33. oneM2M Partners Type 1: Base ontology (2019). https://www.onem2m.org/images/pdf/TS-0012-Base_Ontology-V3_7_3.pdf
34. Partridge, C., Mitchell, A., Cook, A., Sullivan, J., West, M.: A survey of top-level ontologies - to inform the ontological choices for a foundation data model. University of Cambridge (2020)
35. Rastogi, V., Srivastava, S., Mishra, M., Thukral, R.: Predictive maintenance for SME in industry 4.0. In: 2020 Global Smart Industry Conference (GloSIC), pp. 382–390 (2020)
36. Santos, M.A., Munoz, R., Olivares, R., Rebouças Filho, P.P., Del Ser, J., de Albuquerque, V.H.C.: Online heart monitoring systems on the internet of health things environments: a survey, a reference model and an outlook. Inf. Fusion **53**, 222–239 (2020)

37. Scioscia, F., Ruta, M.: Building a semantic web of things: issues and perspectives in information compression, pp. 589–594. IEEE (2009)
38. Sforzin, A., Bobba, R., et al.: D5.4-Requirements Analysis of Demonstration Cases Phase 2 (2021). https://cybersec4europe.eu/publications/deliverables/
39. Skouloudi, R.C., Malatras, A., Dede, G.: Guidelines for securing the internet of things. European Union Agency for Cybersecurity (2020)
40. Walden, D.D., Roedler, G.J., Forsberg, K.J., Hamelin, D.R., Shortell, T.M.: Systems Engineering Handbook, 4th edn. Wiley, Hoboken (2015)
41. Won, M.: Intelligent traffic monitoring systems for vehicle classification: a survey. IEEE Access **8**, 73340–73358 (2020)

SWIoTA: Anomaly Detection for Distributed Ledger Technology-Based Internet of Things (IOTA) Using Sliding Window (SW) Technique

Sathish A. P. Kumar[1]([✉]), Norman Ahmed[2], and Anastasios Bikos[3]

[1] Cleveland State University, Cleveland, OH, USA
s.kumar13@csuohio.edu
[2] Air Force Research Laboratory, Rome, NY, USA
norman.ahmed@us.af.mil
[3] University of Patras, 265 04 Patra, Achia, Greece
mpikos@ceid.upatras.gr

Abstract. IOTA is a Digital Ledger Technology (DLT) prototype for IoT applications that has attracted a rising popularity in recent years. One issue that acts as obstacle to its widespread adoption are the cybersecurity concerns. Some of the security concerns in IOTA include Denial of Service (DoS) double spending, parasite attacks, and DDoS attacks. In this work, we developed a Machine-Learning (ML) approach to create security threat index that can be utilized to proactively provide defenses to the IOTA decentralized infrastructure as well as individual nodes against potential compromises. Our approach is established on the sliding window customized technique to classify the data generated from the DAG-based nodes for cybersecurity anomaly detection. To validate the approach, we implemented "DoS attacks" threat model in the DLT-based IoT environment using Raspberry Pi devices and experimented our security methods and algorithms in this environment. The preliminary experimental results are promising.

Keywords: Distributed ledger technology · Internet of Things · Tangle · Cybersecurity · Sliding Window technique · Anomaly detection · Machine learning

1 Introduction and Background

The concept of Blockchain technology has got traction recently due to the increasing utilization of decentralized systems and the spreading need for integrity in the data management [3, 20]. The Blockchain [6] technology is based on an innovative data structure that is feasible to be used as a ledger for many applications. Bitcoin and Ethereum [24] are the most popular implementation of the cryptocurrency concept, which run on distributed ledgers. While DLT was originally used for recording financial transactions through bitcoins as well as other cryptocurrencies [6], this technology is being used in several domains such as Internet of Things (IoT) [7, 9–12, 22]. One such recent and

L. M. Camarinha-Matos et al. (Eds.): IFIPIoT 2022, IFIP AICT 665, pp. 177–194, 2022.
https://doi.org/10.1007/978-3-031-18872-5_11

versatile research effort that uses the distributed ledger protocol is Tangle [16]. Tangle is utilized as cryptography on the Internet of Things (IoT) to store P2P transactions. As shown in Fig. 1, Tangle is a Directed Acyclic Graph (DAG) where a vertex, defining a transaction, has two ancestors, serving as the transactions it acknowledges. As per its protocol, a Proof of Work (PoW), or a Proof of Stake (PoS – an alternate solvability of the consensus based on intrinsic properties, such as the number of obtained tokens), has to be fulfilled when adding a transaction to the Tangle. This should hinder an adversary from doing network spamming. However, it is not yet clear the amount of cybersecurity impact from the PoW/PoS instantiation in the Tangle. IoT connects various physical devices that we use on a daily basis and enable them to interact with each other through the Internet. This ensures the intelligence of the devices [4, 5, 8]. IoT is used in a variety of domains such as military, healthcare, logistics, utilities and smart cities [1]. IoT is expected to revolutionize the future innovations especially related to Industry 5.0. Use of IoT is expected to rise on an exponential basis over the coming years. Security is an important issue due to a huge number of devices that are linked to the Internet and the massive attack surface area associated with it [2, 21]. Many of these physical devices from an Internet of Things perspective are easy targets for the intrusion due to the huge attack surface area and moreover they rely on exterior resources and are often left disregarded. Due to the integration of DLT with IoT, cybersecurity and trust management in the consensus scenarios is a very important consideration [13–15, 17–20, 23, 25, 26, 30].

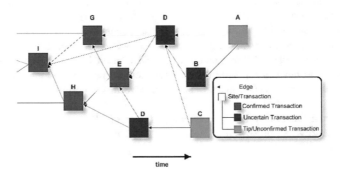

Fig. 1. An example instance of a Tangle

Following are the contributions of this work: a. Prototype a formal sliding window-based approach (SWIoTA) to construct a security threat index for each DAG-based device to achieve anomaly detection, in real time, and b. evaluate the performance of the previous anomaly detection approach using detection with outlier factor and Mahanabolis distance metric.

The rest of the paper is organized as follows. In Sect. 2 we illustrate the security problem and its importance. Methodology is described in Sect. 3. Section 4 describes the experimentation and performance evaluation results. Future work recommendations are described in Sect. 5. Finally, Sect. 6 describes the conclusion.

2   Problem Statement and Rationale

2.1   Problem Statement

While there are several attacks possible in the DLT-based IOT, per literature review one of the important attacks that needs attention is Denial of Service (DoS) attacks. In this work, leveraging our earlier work [4, 31–36], our objective is to implement anomaly detection algorithms to detect attack and to protect the DLT framework-based IoT network from DDoS attacks.

2.2   Rationale for DoS Threat Model

The proposed approach leverages our private Tangle network for IoT as a test platform and integrate the proposed security methods into the existing DLT-based framework for IoT.

While setting up the Private Tangle network, the Hornet nodes and participating clients are assumed to be added using a permission-based approach. As the name suggests, in the private tangle setup, the participating nodes does not connect to public Internet directly. Only participants that are in the local area network are allowed to participate. The IP addresses of the hornet nodes belong to a private network domain. By configuring port forwarding on the gateway, it is possible to allow geographically remote participants, but still each remote participant needs to know the IP/port of the gateway, and it is still permission based. In such a Private Tangle setup, due to the permission-based nature, the administrators could relax the security precautions against the local area network participants. For instance, they might allow any local IP to request remote-proof-of-work. Our setup followed the Private Tangle based network and assumed that local participating/transacting clients are trusted implicitly. We assume that one of the local devices is compromised and started to run an attacker script. The attacker that compromised the local device is utilizing PyOTA client library. With PyOTA python library [29], attacker can send Zero-value-messages to any Hornet node in the Private tangle. Our attack uses Zero-value-messages, but in a threaded manner. From the attack script, we create as many threads as possible and each thread sends a zero-value-message request to the same hornet node. Without threaded approach, PyOTA client would wait for a response before sending the next request. But with threaded request, attacker can send hundreds of requests in a couple of seconds and keep the target Hornet nodes resources tied for significant amount of time.

2.3   The SWIoTA Blockchain Security Contribution

Utilizing the previous underlying assumptions, we formally depict SWIoTA, a dynamic, lightweight, and portable cybersecurity framework which exploits the blockchain concept to perform purely on-line (dynamic & stateless) and distributed anomaly detection on resource constraint devices such as Internet-of-Things (IoT).

Through a centralized coordinator entity (Compass), inside our IoTA network topology, our framework model is being trained and provides detection decisions for each connected node based on their own locally examined resource behaviors. The introduction of the Sliding Window (SW) emerges as a vital fully dynamic component which holds the properties of a moving window with short memory across the time axis of the evolving node resources. Co-deploying the SW with highly accurate Machine Learning operations that are based on output-code classifiers can characterize anomaly behaviors, other than technical losses, with much higher sensitivity. Our unique contribution is the adoption of the SW technique alongside customized classifiers. This deployment seems prominent and energy efficient for lightweight IoT.

3 Methodology

To invoke the multiclass strategy to generate our labelled security threat index, we follow the notation of the design of continuous codes using Quadratic Programming, which is primarily an optimization problem. Output-labelling based methods often consist of representing each class with specific index. During detection, the indexes are arrived based on the learning from the input data. During the prediction time, the classifiers used during the detection time can be used to project new points and the class that is nearest to the points projected will be used for the prediction.

3.1 Error-Correcting Output-Code Multiclass Strategy

For convenience we use the square of the norm of the matrix (instead the norm itself). Our ML classifier H(x) is constructed from a code matrix M and a set of binary classifiers $\bar{h}(x)$. The matrix M is of size $k \times l$ over R where each row of M is corresponding to a class $y \in Y$. Provided an instance x, the classifier H(x) predicts the label y which maximizes the confidence function K(h(x), Mr), H(x) = argmaxr $\in$ y{K(h(x), Mr)}. Since the code is over the real numbers, we can assume here without loss of generality that exactly one class concentrates the maximum value according to the function K. To simplify the equations, we denote by $\tau i = 1yi - \eta i$, the difference between the correct point distribution and the distribution obtained by the optimization problem. Thus, the general dual optimization problem can become therefore:

$$max_\tau \quad \partial(\tau) = -\frac{1}{2}\beta^{-1}\sum_{i,j}K\left(\bar{h}(x_i), \bar{h}(x_j)\right)\left(\bar{\tau}_i \cdot \bar{\tau}_j\right) - \sum_i\left(\bar{\tau}_i \cdot \bar{\beta}_i\right) \tag{1}$$

subject to:

$$\forall i \quad \bar{\tau}_i \leq \bar{1}_{yi}$$

and:

$$\bar{\tau}_i \cdot \bar{1} = 0$$

and our (optimal) classification rule becomes:

$$H(x) = argmax_r\left\{\sum_i \tau_{i,r}K\left(\bar{h}(x), \bar{h}(x_i)\right)\right\} \tag{2}$$

The general equations for designing output codes using the optimization problem described above, also provides, as a special case, our algorithm for building multiclass Support Vector Machines, in order to label the security threat index.

3.2   Classification Problem

Our anomaly detection scheme follows the practice of Output-code multiclass strategy (also referred as "error-correcting output codes") to output the label indexes based on the closeness of those labels. This class strategy allows to approximate a multi-class classification problem with a binary classifier. Each class is converted into a code of "0" s and "1" s. The length of the code is known as the code size. The codes associated with the classes are stored in the codebook. When a new sample arrives, the label's code is extracted from the codebook. Then, each classifier is trained on the corresponding part of the code, which can be either a 0 or a 1. For the prediction part, the classifier outputs a probability. These probabilities are compared to each code in the codebook, and the label that is the closest is selected as the most likely class. Manhattan distance is being utilized to determine that closeness.

Inside our paradigm use case we performed Multiclass Classification with Error-Correcting Output Code-based classifier. For instance, since we need to obtain 10 unique labels, or security threat indexes (from 0–10), we will have a target cardinality length space of 10 classes.

3.3   The Sliding Window (SW) Concept

Our fully ad-hoc Sliding Window technique much resembles the *moving average* calculation process. In statistical analysis, a moving or rolling average is an estimation to analyze data points by interpreting a series of averages, or means, of versatile subsets of the complete data set. Our approach holds additional dynamic properties such as *sliding average* property, *memory property* and *left/right feedback* (at the inputs/outputs of the window). As we can illustrate at Fig. 2, the "moving" window stochastically slides across the time axis (with an empirical static size of 8 value), inputs the resource monitoring metrics and fully-feeds back in recursive cycles all its convoluted results. Notably, although the size of the window is 8, it moves sequentially (with step size of 1 value)

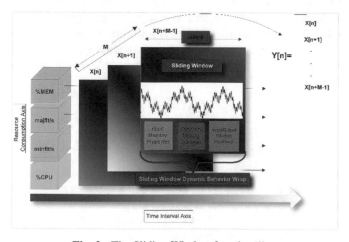

Fig. 2. The Sliding Window functionality.

among the previous axes. Such behavior of our SW can easily approximate a type of dynamic convolution and it can be viewed as an instance of a low-pass filter utilized in signal processing.

3.4 Threat Index Computation Process

PROCESS STEPS:
1 INPUT ARRAY with size: {arbitrary length x 4}
2 DEFINE sliding window {W} with size=8
3 FOR EACH ARRAY ROW (with STEP=1):
4   APPLY sliding window {W}
5   {W} OUTPUTS correlation coefficients of
     ARRAY values
6   GET upper triangular part of step 5 output
7 1D interpolate ALL VALUES from step 6
from +0 to +10
8 INPUT data AND ARRAY samples to ML
Classifier
9 OUTPUT Security Threat Index (label) PER
ARRAY ROW

Listing. 1. Threat Index Computation Pseudocode

We input resource consumption metrics array for each DAG-based node of the ledger. We output the same array but labelled, this time, with a security threat index (as indicated in Listing 1), which indicates the security severity of a presence or not of any security threat. It can be utilized for anomaly detection and security threat attack prevention on the IOTA. We retrieve the correlation coefficients between neighboring values in the ARRAY and get the upper triangular part, using the sliding window custom technique. The benefit of this sliding window concept is that (1) it converges stochastically over the Monte Carlo distribution probability density function of the time axis expansion of the DAG, and (2) it covers inter correlation features extraction from the array data samples that are neighboring enough, thus have same anomaly or idle behavior. Our correlation coefficients formula

$$r = \frac{n(\sum xy) - (\sum x)(\sum y)}{\sqrt{\left[n\sum x^2 - (\sum x)^2\right]\left[n\sum y^2 (\sum y)^2\right]}} \tag{3}$$

In Eq. 3, r is correlation coefficient, x represents values of the x-variable in a sample, y represents values of the y-variable in a sample and n is the number of samples.

Getting the upper triangular parts, as per step 6:The sliding window moves gradually over the timing axis every step -one- to extract inter-correlation values from pre-training data. The aim is to create pre-training indexed features. We collect all correlated values onto a new matrix, as shown in Fig. 3. We then 1D interpolate these values into our

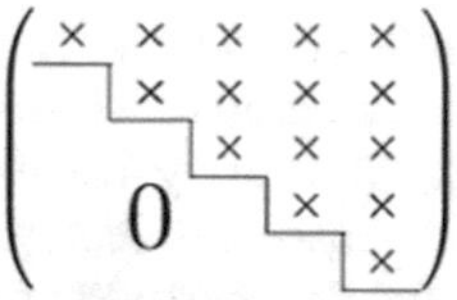

$$\begin{pmatrix} \times & \times & \times & \times & \times \\ & \times & \times & \times & \times \\ & & \times & \times & \times \\ & 0 & & \times & \times \\ & & & & \times \end{pmatrix}$$

Fig. 3. Correlation matrix

numerical index scale from +0 to +10. Finally, we input the interpolated data (such as pre-training features) and training array samples to the Multiclass Classifier (H(x)) and multilabel algorithm ML library. The goal is to perform a multiclass classification task with more than two classes and label the Threat Index per each array row.

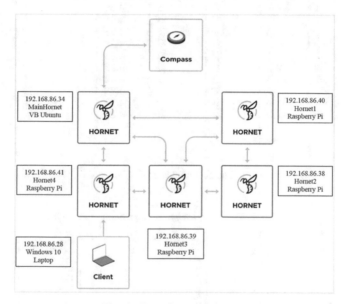

Fig. 4. Experimentation setup

4 Experimentation and Results

In this particular section, we demonstrate our experimental setup, threat model implementation, analysis, data collection and experimental results.

4.1 Private Tangle Setup

It is an IOTA network that we have full control over compared to public network. This Tangle will only connect to the nodes that we provide. Our private network is set up using the open source technology that make up the public IOTA networks. Compass as shown in Fig. 4, is the main coordinator, that we implemented using the open source software. For our experiments needs we used four Raspberry Pis and one virtual machine Ubuntu device. We initiated the experiments by installing the hornet that will include the Compass. As shown in Fig. 4, the compass was deployed on the virtual box with Ubuntu. Then we installed the Hornet for the Raspberry Pi after reassuring that the Hornet that is already installed is not being executed. Figure 4 depicts our main network topology to instantiate our IOTA experiments using the Raspberry Pi's.

4.2 Denial of Service Threat Model Implementation

	%CPU	minflt/s	majflt/s	%MEM	Threat Index
0	1.49	0	0.5	4.33	2
1	1	0	0	4.33	1
2	2	0.5	1	4.33	2
3	1.5	0	0	4.33	2
4	1	0	0	4.33	1
5	2.5	0	0	4.33	3
6	1.49	0	0	4.33	2
7	2	0	1	4.33	2
8	1	0	0	4.33	1
9	1.5	0	0	4.33	2
...	...	...	...	...	...

Fig. 5. Input parameters

Time interval	%CPU	minflt/s	majflt/s	%MEM
0	1.49	0	0.5	4.33
1	1	0	0	4.33
2	2	0.5	1	4.33
3	1.5	0	0	4.33
4	1	0	0	4.33
5	2.5	0	0	4.33
6	1.49	0	0	4.33
7	2	0	1	4.33
8	1	0	0	4.33
9	1.5	0	0	4.33
10	1	0	0	4.33
11	0.5	0	0	4.33
...	...	...	...	...
288	1	0	0	4.45
289	1.5	0	0	4.45
290	1	0	0	4.45
291	0.5	0	0	4.45
292	2.5	0	1.5	4.45
293	1	0	0	4.45
294	6.5	0	0	4.45
295	1	0	0	4.45
296	1.5	0	0	4.45
297	2.5	0	1.5	4.45
298	1	0	0	4.45

Fig. 6. Output threat index

To emulate DoS attack, we selected one Hornet on the network and then launched as many transactions as we can in a short period of time. First, we tried to send transactions, then we modified our code to send multiple transactions in a short period of time. The modified code below will send as many transactions as it can in a given time. It creates multiple threads to send transactions so that it does not have to wait for the reply of each transaction before sending the next one. We will also be collecting time for each transaction, along with it we will also keep track of how many transactions we send out. The duration of the loop can be changed in the code and IP address target could be changed using the code as well. In one second we were able to send 18 transactions. During this setup, we were targeting the hornet on the Virtual Box, which at the time of setup was using 4 CPU cores. This is why the return time on each transaction is exceptionally low. When setting up an actual attack, it is better to target a hornet on one of the Raspberry PIs because it is a slower device. When configured for 14 min, Raspberry Pi will usually take more than 2 min to respond to each transaction.

4.3 Data Collection

We used pidstat command to collect the data. We also captured the heartbeat data for the hornet by using journalctl command. We then used nethogs to collect network traffic data. All these commands wrote to a log file or a text file. Hence, we created a script to extract the data to a more usable format. As shown in Fig. 5, the data that we captured include CPU usage, memory usage, minor faults, and major faults. These explicit parameters were used to generate threat Index, which is explained in the following paragraphs. In terms of aggregating ground-truth labels, or correctly mapping identified security label(s) between benign and non-benign states, it is the mathematical formality of the SW algorithm itself (see Section IV.D) that is able to generate such outputs.

4.4 Anomaly Detection Using Sliding Window Technique

We executed the PIDSTAT command from the IOTA customized environment to retrieve real time /proc/stat resource monitoring status for our scenario's Hornet components. The generated results (filtered) are tabulated below for 300 time slot intervals as shown in Fig. 5. These time intervals typically last for 3 to 4 s. The first column represents the timeline interval for the experimentation. In IOTA and DLT-based ledger framework(s) the time evolution of the Tangle and the Graph is both of paramount importance and a generic feature of the IOTA itself, because as time 't' progresses, even more transactions are logged (confirmed state), whereas others become unconfirmed or invalidated. Inside the scope of our mathematical concept setup we mainly focus, or take into consideration four resource metrics (%CPU, minflt/s, majflt/s and %MEM).

We will try to solve a multi-variate classification problem to generate a single label index, which we name as Threat Index, based on Machine Learning approach. Following the above customized mathematical technique and the Python ML libraries, we obtain the Threat Index per ARRAY ROW. We follow the below steps and incorporate a customized mathematical strategy to label the ARRAY rows with the security threat index (with numerical range from +0 to +10); where *0 to 3 is Low Security Risk, 4 to 6 is Medium Security Risk, and 7 to 10 is High Security Risk.* Following the above customized mathematical technique plus the Python ML libraries we obtain the security threat index as shown in Fig. 6.

Figures 7 and 8 illustrate our experimental results for a custom IOTA deployment scenario using four Hornet devices and the Compass. The horizontal axis corresponds to the time interval during the course of the experiments. The vertical axis represents the newly generated threat index. Figure 7 depicts the idle, or no attack presence state. Specifically, this figure projects what is a typical running experimental state of a Hornet IOTA device node, without any security attack occurrence scenario. We could map this phase as a before and/or after an attack would take place. During the time interval from 920 (Second(s)) till 1100 (Second(s)), we subjected the Tangle network with DoS attack. After DoS attack is carried out, as shown in the Fig. 8, it is clearly noticeable that the security threat index appears to climb at maximum threshold of 10, which flags as an anomaly. As we will evaluate our detection scheme in the next subsection, we concentrate on the accuracy sensitivity metrics to derive the ratio of false positives as well as f-measurement to estimate the correct mapping of security anomaly indexes among correctly identified security anomaly traits.

SWIoTA framework successfully identifies the attack duration segment within its time frame. The rate of correct mappings between technical losses and non-technical losses (anomalies) also seems quite promising, as it is observable in same figure that some early spikes before the attack takes place, or even after the attack correspond to technical incident(s) and not necessarily security incident, thus not being able to raise an alarm.

4.5 Performance Validation Experiments

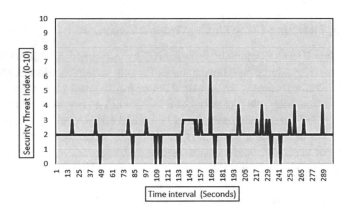

Fig. 7. Idle state

From an evaluation perspective, it is important for the applications to check if a new data point is in the same distribution as existing data point, or if that is an outlier (anomaly). This is especially important if the application is related to anomaly detection to detect abnormal or unusual observations. From an anomaly detection perspective, the outlier data points cannot be part of dense cluster and the classifiers/estimators assumes them to be part of the low- density regions. The objective of the outlier detection is to

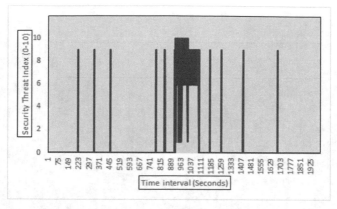

Fig. 8. Attack state (Color figure online)

delineate core of regular observations from the outliers. It is worth noticing that these ML anomaly prediction techniques encompass PCA analysis and are considered the most innovative techniques currently deployed for network traffic threat detection/isolation. The processing of data with huge set of variables is particularly challenging. While there are many methods for dimension reduction, the most popular approach that is being applied is principal component analysis (PCA). We compare the performance analysis of our "sliding window" and ML technique with PCA/LOFs "conventional" approaches [28]. Hereby, we input/utilize to these libraries our same input monitoring data metrics file from the 4 Hornets. As shown in Fig. 8, the regular observations and abnormal observations cluster separately as expected. This validates the threat index detected using our sliding window approach. Namely, the observations inside the green dashed 2D surface belong to the idle (non-Anomaly) threat indexes, or states, whereas *anything outside is considered an Anomaly observation.*

Lastly, we collate & correlate the observation dynamics between our sliding window (SW) technique across the Mob distance in terms of their Hamming Distance (Positive Predictive Value, or PPV).

The Mahalanobis distance metric: One of the popular technique used for evaluating the cluster and classifier analysis is The Mahalanobis distance metric. We implemented this metric to measure of our classifier that distinguishes "normal" vs "anamoly" classes.

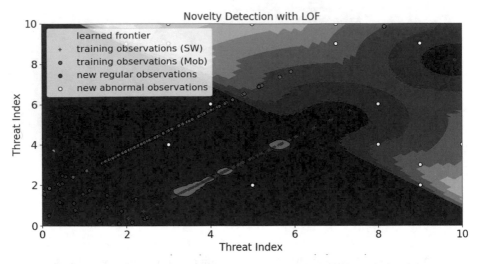

Fig. 9. Novelty detection with Local Outlier Factor (featuring Sliding Window technique vs Mahalanobis distance)

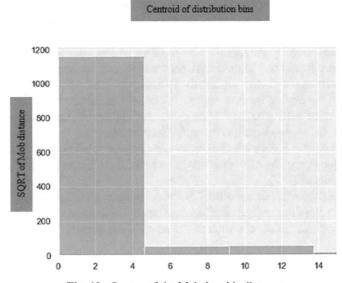

Fig. 10. Square of the Mahalanobis distance

2) Threshold value to detect an anomaly: The square of the Mahalanobis distance to the centroid of the distribution should follow a $\chi 2$ distribution, if the assumption of normally distributed input variables are fulfilled. This is also the basis of assumption behind the above calculation of the "threshold value" for flagging an anomaly. Since we cannot assume the input variables to be normally distributed, it is better to visualize the distribution of the Mahalanobis distance comparing it to threshold values in order to flag anomalies. As shown in Fig. 9, we visualized the square of the Mahalanobis distance, to ensure that it follows a $\chi 2$ distribution. Then we visualized the Mahalanobis distance itself as shown in Fig. 10. Based on the distributions shown in Fig. 11, the computed threshold value comes to 3.8, which is 3 standard deviations from the center of the distribution and is used to flag an anomaly. We can then save the Mahalanobis distance, as well as the threshold value and "anomaly flag" variable for both training and testing data in a data frame. That way any observed distance above the threshold value can be flagged as an anomaly. As shown in Fig. 12, we plot the computed anomaly metric (Mob distance) and confirm when it crosses the anomaly threshold. Based on our proposed approach and the comparison models, it seems illustratively enough we have strong accuracy, threat detection estimation, and predictability as we fall inside the same attack time margin on both figures, Fig. 8 and Fig. 12 during the time index interval between 912 and 1100, when the attack takes place against the IOTA hornets and as shown in Fig. 12, the Mob distance lies above the estimated red line threshold (event indicated as Anomaly), and as shown in Fig. 8, our estimated threat index is again high enough to be classified as a real attack (around 10). Finally, Fig. 13 confirms the latter. Inside the former figure, SW stands for Sliding Window, Mob dist is the practical implementation of Novelty Detection/Local Outlier Factor(s) (using Mahalanobis distance), and Thresh is simply the objective Anomaly indicator for both processes. Any indication above that limit is strictly considered as an Anomaly. The reason we are co-deploying SW vs Mob technique is that we need to exploit a comparison scheme for our methodology, as we will illustrate next.

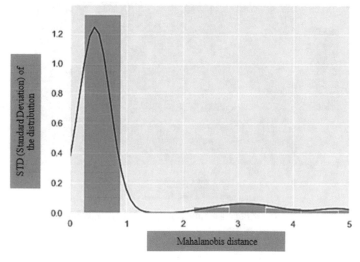

Fig. 11. Mahalanobis distance

From visually observing the two (sub)plots in Fig. 12, the level of coincidence (Hamming distance of Threat Indexes) between two fundamentally versatile procedures is remarkable. Thus, we can derive the accuracy of the sliding window technique seems promising. In fact, how accurate an intrusion detection system, alike our sliding window methodology for cybersecuring the IOTA ledger, could be evaluated? Retrieved from the research literature [27], several accuracy metrics such as False Positive Ratio (FPR), True Negative Ratio (TNR), Detection Rate (DR), F1 score and Misclassification rate can be introduced.

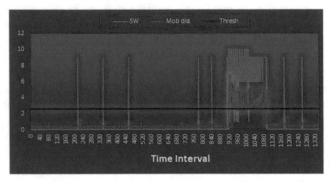

Fig. 12. Comparison plot of our Sliding Window technique vs Mahalanobis distance vs threshold

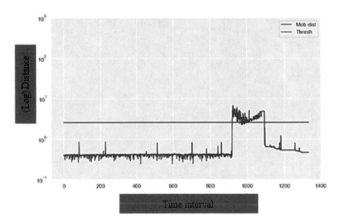

Fig. 13. Plot of Mahalanobis distance vs threshold

Table 1. Performance evaluation results

Window Size	8
True Negatives (TN)	1805
True Positives (TP)	149
False Negatives (FN)	32
False Positives (FP)	7
True Positive Rate (TPR)	0.8232
False Positive Ratio (FPR)	0.0039
Positive Predictive Value (PPV)	0.9551
True Negative Rate (TNR)	0.9961
Negative Predictive Value (NPV)	0.9826
False Negative Rate (FNR)	0.1768
ACC	0.9804
F1 score	0.8843

Table 1 depicts the numerical (Machine Learning) ML-based result metrics for our ad-hoc intrusion detection technique (sliding window). It is, therefore, clearly apprehended that the (Sliding Window) SW technology appears to outrun, since a wellstanding, but totally versatile approach (PCA/Mahalanobis distance), seems equivalent to it in terms of overall precision, or detection accuracy. We depict our numerical finding results in Table 1 following an empirical size for the (sliding) window. We comprehend the crucial importance of early detection for any types of security anomalies within IOTA-based infrastructures; and our technique manages to achieve that aim in a sound and robust manner. In an overall manner, our IOTA intrusion detection system achieves **an accuracy level of 98% (ACC), with an F-measure of 88%**.

A final discussion point for the readers would be why we (pre)select a static window size of 8 for the sliding window ad-hoc approach? Our numerical findings appear to *empirically* explain the case. It seems fair enough that this empirical value outruns far better than less, or much higher values. One potential reason is that we have four resource monitoring metrics (e.g., *CPU usage, memory usage, minor faults, and major faults*), thus the ideal constant declaration for such window size would be double the amount of the metric inputted to the ML-Classifier. Still, we leave the same discussion for future work, in terms of increasing the number or monitoring metrics; should the window size adjust?

5   Future Work Recommendations

In future we plan to refine our approach by studying the impact of additional parameters, using the data generated for Denial of Service (DoS) attacks. In addition, we plan to include additional parameters and distribute weights based on the parameter importance extracted from data mining techniques. Our work only considered zero-value transactions; the experiments can be extended by studying the impact of non-zero value transactions compared to zero value transactions to the IOTA network from a DoS attack perspective. Future work can be improved by introducing a reinforcement learning (RL) rule into the sliding window, to increase anomaly detection accuracy. In the future, we plan to apply regressor to predict threat index, in addition to detecting the threat index. This will lead to a peak performance of threat index accuracy.

6 Conclusion

As per literature review, the integration of DLT to IoT makes the IoT devices more vulnerable and prone to attacks. One of the important attacks that we addressed is DoS attacks. We implemented the threat model and our security algorithms in the practical DLT-based private tangle network. In our research, we demonstrated the potential of our security algorithms and methods to protect the DLT-based IoT system and integrate our methods to the existing lightweight DLT framework for IoT. The proposed approach could be potentially used to securely deploy blockchain framework- based IoT and low powered peer to peer systems in the real-world applications.

References

1. Danzi, P., Kalor, A.E, Stefanovic, C., Popovski, P.: Analysis of the communication traffic for blockchain synchronization of IoT devices. In: 2018 IEEE International Conference on Communications (ICC), pp. 1–7. IEEE Press, New York (2001)
2. Varshney, G., Gupta, H.: A security framework for IoT devices against wireless threats. In: 2017 2nd International Conference on Telecommunication and Networks (TEL-NET), pp. 1–6. IEEE Press, New York (2017)
3. Ghiro, L., Maccari, L., Cigno, R.L: Proof of networking: can blockchains boost the next generation of distributed networks? In: 2018 14th Annual Conference on Wireless On-demand Network Systems and Services (WONS), Isola, pp. 29–32 (2018)
4. Kumar, S.A, Vealey, T., Srivastava, H.: Security in Internet of Things: challenges, solutions, and future directions. In: 49th Hawaii International Conference on System Sciences (HICSS), pp. 5772–5781. IEEE Press, New York (2016)
5. Bikos, A.N., Sklavos, N.: The future of privacy and trust on the Internet of Things (IoT) for healthcare: concepts, challenges, and security threat mitigations. In: Recent Advances in Security, Privacy, and Trust for Internet of Things (IoT) and Cyber-Physical Systems (CPS), pp. 63–90. Chapman and Hall/CRC (2020)
6. Nakamoto, S.: Bitcoin: a peer-to-peer electronic cash system (2008)
7. Christidis, K., Devetsikiotis, M.: Blockchains and smart contracts for the Internet of Things. IEEE Access **4**, 2292–2303 (2016)
8. Atzori, L., Iera, A., Morabito, G.: The Internet of Things: a survey. Comput. Netw. **54**(15), 2787–2805 (2010)
9. Roy, S, Ashaduzzaman, M, Hassan, M and Chowdhury, A. R..: BlockChain for IoT security and management: current prospects, challenges, and future directions. In: 5th International Conference on Networking, Systems and Security (NSysS), pp. 1–9 (2018)
10. Muzammal, S.M., Murugesan, R.K.: A study on leveraging blockchain technology for IoT security enhancement. In: Fourth International Conference on Advances in Computing, Communication & Automation (ICACCA), pp. 1–6 (2018)

11. Yin, S., Bao, J., Zhang, Y., Huang, X.: M2M security technology of cps based on blockchains. Symmetry **9**(9), 193 (2017)
12. Rahulamathavan, Y., Phan, R., Phan, C.W., Rajarajan, M., Misra, S., Kondoz, A.: Privacy-preserving blockchain-based IoT ecosystem using attribute-based encryption. In: 2017 IEEE International Conference on Advanced Networks and Telecommunications Systems (ANTS), pp. 1–6. IEEE Press, New York (2017)
13. Hammi, M.T., Hammi, B., Bellot, P., Serhrouchni, A.: Bubbles of trust: a decentralized blockchain-based authentication system for iot. Comput. Secur. **78**, 126–142 (2018)
14. Liu, B., Yu, X.L., Chen, S., Xu, X., Zhu, L.: Blockchain based data integrity service framework for IoT data. In: 2017 IEEE International Conference on Web Services (ICWS), pp. 468–475. IEEE (2017)
15. Bramas, Q.: The Stability and the Security of the Tangle. hal-01716111v2 (2018)
16. Popov, S.: The Tangle. White paper. https://iota.org/ (2016)
17. Heilman, E., Narula, N., Tanzer, G., Lovejoy, J., Colavita, M., Virza, M., Dryja, T.: Cryptanalysis of Curl-P and Other Attacks on the IOTA Cryptocurrency. IACR Cryptology ePrint Archive: 344 (2019)
18. Roode, D., Gerard, I.U., Havinga, P.J: How to break IOTA heart by replaying? In: 2018 IEEE Globecom Workshops (GC Wkshps), pp. 1–7. IEEE Press, New York (2018)
19. Tennant, L.: Improving the Anonymity of the IOTA Cryptocurrency (2017)
20. Moubarak, J., Chamoun, M., Filiol, E.: On distributed ledgers security and illegal uses. Futur. Gener. Comput. Syst. **113**, 183–195 (2020)
21. Tekeoglu, A., Ahmed, N.:TangoChain: a lightweight distributed ledger for Internet of Things devices in smart cities. In: 2019 IEEE International Smart Cities Conference (ISC2): Blockchain Enabled Sustainable Smart Cities (Bless 2019) Workshop (IEEE ISC2 2019-Bless Workshop) (2019)
22. Fernández-Caramés, T.M., Fraga-Lamas, P.:A review on the use of blockchain for the Internet of Things. IEEE Access **6**, 32 979–33 001 (2018)
23. Lin, I.C., Liao, T.C.: A survey of blockchain security issues and challenges. Netw. Secur. **19**(5), 653–659 (2017)
24. Atzei, N., Bartoletti, M., Cimoli, T.: A survey of attacks on ethereum smart contracts (SoK). In: Maffei, M., Ryan, M. (eds.) POST 2017. LNCS, vol. 10204, pp. 164–186. Springer, Heidelberg (2017). https://doi.org/10.1007/978-3-662-54455-6_8
25. Siegel, D.: Understanding The DAO Attack. https://www.coindesk.com/understanding-dao-hack-journalists/
26. Baldwin, C.: Bitcoin worth 72 million stolen from bitfinex exchange in Hong Kong (2016). http://reut.rs/2gc7iQ9. Accessed 25 Nov 2019
27. Khatibzadeh, L., Bornaee, Z., Bafghi, A.: Applying catastrophe theory for network anomaly detection in cloud computing traffic. Secur. Commun. Netw. **2019**, 1–11 (2019)
28. Robust covariance estimation and Mahalanobis distances relevance. https://scikit-learn.org/stable/auto_examples/covariance/plot_mahalanobis_distances.html
29. Ester, M., Kriegel H., Sander, J., Xu, X : A density-based algorithm for discovering clusters in large spat ial databases with noise. In: Proceedings of the Second International Conference on Knowledge Discovery and Data Mining (KDD-1996), pp 226–231 (1996)
30. Bikos, A.N., Kumar, S.: Securing digital ledger technologies-enabled IoT devices: taxonomy, challenges and solutions. IEEE Access **10**, 46238–46254 (2022)
31. Alampalayam, S.K., Kumar, A., Srinivasan, S.: Statistical based intrusion detection framework using six sigma technique. IJCSNS **7**(10), 333 (2007)
32. Alampalayam, S.P., Kumar, A: Security model for routing attacks in mobile ad hoc networks. In: 2003 IEEE 58th Vehicular Technology Conference, VTC 2003-Fall (IEEE Cat. No. 03CH37484), vol. 3, pp. 2122–2126. IEEE Press, New York (2003)

33. Alampalayam, S.K., Natsheh, E.F: Multivariate fuzzy analysis for mobile ad hoc network threat detection. Int. J. Bus. Data Commun. Netw. (IJBDCN) **4**(3), 1–30 (2008)

34. Srinivasan, S., Alampalayam, S.P.: Intrusion detection algorithm for MANET. Int. J. Inf. Secur. Priv. (IJISP) **5**(3), 36–49 (2011)

35. Gohil, M., Kumar, S. :Evaluation of classification algorithms for distributed denial of service attack detection. In: 2020 IEEE Third International Conference on Artificial Intelligence and Knowledge Engineering (AIKE), pp. 138–141. IEEE Press, New York (2020)

36. Bikos, A.N., Kumar, S.: Reinforcement learning-based anomaly detection for Internet of Things distributed ledger technology. In: 2021 IEEE Symposium on Computers and Communications (ISCC), pp. 1–7. IEEE Press New York (2021)

Smart Home

A Framework for the Integration of IoT Components into the Household Digital Twins for Energy Communities

Kankam O. Adu-Kankam[1,2]([📧]) and Luis M. Camarinha-Matos[1]

[1] School of Science and Technology and UNINOVA - CTS, Nova University of Lisbon, Campus de Caparica, Monte de Caparica, 2829-516 Caparica, Portugal
k.adu@campus.fct.unl.pt, cam@uninova.pt
[2] School of Engineering, University of Energy and Natural Resources (UENR), P. O. Box 214, Sunyani, Ghana

Abstract. The concept of Cognitive Household Digital Twins (CHDTs) was proposed as a mechanism to assist constituent households in Renewable Energy Communities to engage in collaborative actions that are expected to facilitate sustainable energy consumption in these communities. A CHDT represents a digital twin of a unit of physical households in a community. By integrating IoT components at the appliance level of the Physical Twin, a CHDT becomes a "living model" of its physical counterpart by receiving real-time data that reflects the households' energy consumption or appliance use-behaviors. When CHDTs are endowed with some intelligence or cognitive abilities, they become cognizant of the operational state of the physical system using the received data. Based on these data, CHDTs can make autonomous and rational decisions on behalf of the households' owners. Furthermore, through the integrated IoT components, CHDTs can send control signals back to connected appliances to regulate their operations. In this context, a population of CHDTs can engage in collective actions with the aim of promoting sustainable energy consumption in the ecosystem. In this work, we show how the CHDT's architectural framework enables them to collaborate. A multi-method approach that integrates systems dynamics, agent-based, and discrete event modeling techniques is used for the development of a prototype model. Several scenarios are then implemented in this environment to verify the validity of the approach.

Keywords: Digital Twins · IoT · Collaborative Networks · Cognitive Digital Twins · Renewable Energy Communities

1 Introduction

It is widely acknowledged that the Earth's resources are depleting at a very alarming rate. This is partly due to the proportion of overexploitation of resources to meet the insatiable demands that modern-day society places on these resources. In a recent study [1], it was claimed that 40% of global resources are consumed by buildings alone.

© IFIP International Federation for Information Processing 2022
Published by Springer Nature Switzerland AG 2022
L. M. Camarinha-Matos et al. (Eds.): IFIPIoT 2022, IFIP AICT 665, pp. 197–216, 2022.
https://doi.org/10.1007/978-3-031-18872-5_12

Furthermore, these buildings were noted to consume about 40% of global energy as well as 25% of global water [1]. Consistent with these numbers, from the perspective of the European Commission, buildings account for roughly 40% of the EU's energy consumption and 36% of CO_2 emissions in Europe [2]. As a result, buildings have been labelled as Europe's single greatest energy consumer. Other comparable studies, such as [3] have also expressed concerns about the steady rise in energy consumption within buildings. The authors in [4] have attributed these escalating concerns to the rising demand for comfort, resulting from the need for larger amounts of home equipment. Other mentioned reasons include increased purchasing power and improvement in the quality of life of residents. As a result, growing attention is being put on more effective energy management approaches and the use of renewable energy sources.

Although several useful contributions have been made toward the solution of this problem, there is still ample room for novel approaches. In a related study [5], two complimentary concepts, namely the Collaborate Virtual Power Plant Ecosystem (CVPP-E) and Cognitive Household Digital Twin (CHDT) were introduced. In the study, the authors described a CHDT as a digital twin (DT) or replica/model of a real household that could be endowed with some level of intelligence, allowing it to take input from the Physical Twin counterpart to make some basic energy consumption choices on its behalf. It was also suggested that CHDTs could be programmed to have cognitive and autonomous capabilities, allowing them to play complementary roles as decision-making agents in households.

Virtualization of the physical household into DTs as suggested in [5] is intended to help manage the complexities that arise when multiple actors, who are autonomous, heterogenous, and geographically distributed, each with different energy consumption preferences, options, priorities, and expectations, come together to form a community, and more specifically, a Renewable Energy Community. The underlying management technique relies on the notion of collaboration as demonstrated in other studies such as [6, 7]. In this paper, we propose a framework for the CHDTs showing the roles that the integration of IoT components can play in the feasibility of the concept. To guide the work, the following research questions are addressed:

- How can the integration of IoT components in household appliances enable the feasibility and functionality of the Cognitive Household Digital Twin (CHDT) concept?
- How can the integration of IoT components facilitate the cognitive and decision-making capabilities of the CHDTs?

2   Related Works

Some related works in the application of Digital Twin (DT) concepts in the domain of energy are as follows. In [8], a household digital twin, which is a data-driven multi-layer digital twin that aims to mirror households' actual energy consumption is proposed. Another study described in [9] also proposed a forecasting approach where the DT of a physical household could use data from the physical twin to forecast the energy consumption for the next day. Similarly, in [10] a DT-driven technique was adopted for improving the energy efficiency of indoor lighting based on computer vision and dynamic building information modelling (BIM). A case study conducted in [11] proposed a battery energy storage system digital twin that forecasts the state of charge by applying artificial intelligence. Finally, a novel DT-based day-ahead scheduling method is proposed [12]. In this case, a deep neural network is trained to make statistical cost-saving scheduling by learning from both historical forecasting errors and day-ahead forecasts.

3 Theoretical Background

In this section, we provide a brief overview and discussion of the underlying concepts of the CVPP-E and their related CHDTs.

3.1 The Concept of Collaborative Virtual Power Plant Ecosystem (CVPP-E)

A renewable energy community (REC) is based on free and voluntary participation, according to the European Parliament and the Council of the European Union [13]. It is autonomous and managed by the involved stakeholders. Members of RECs can generate renewable energy (e.g., photovoltaic) for local use and store, sell, or share the excess with other members of the community. We focus on the REC notion by creating a digital twin replica of the community. The CVPP-E represents the community environment in our model. This ecosystem is a kind of Virtual Organizations Breeding Environment or business ecosystem [14] in which members approach energy use and exchanges collaboratively. As a result, members participate in collaborative efforts aimed at achieving some goals that may be shared by the entire community.

The CVPP-E idea results from incorporating collaborative concepts and methods from the field of Collaborative Networks (CNs) into the area of Virtual Power Plants (VPP). The result of this synthesis is a type of REC that uses collaborative principles and mechanisms in its operation to ensure sustainable energy consumption and exchange, while also exhibiting VPP characteristics, such as the ability to aggregate excess energy from the community and sell it to the grid. A CVPP-E in the proposed formulation includes: (a) the community manager who promotes collaborative activities and behaviours, (b) multiple actors who may include prosumers and consumers, and finally (c) a common community-owned energy storage system.

3.2 The Notion of Cognitive Household Digital Twin (CHDT)

In the developed prototype, each CVPP-E actor is modelled as a software agent that mimics the actual actor's traits and actions. These software agents are designed to live and interact with one another within a digital REC environment, namely the CVPP-E. A Cognitive Household Digital Twin represents a unit of household in this environment. CHDTs are also modelled to possess some cognitive abilities, allowing them to serve as supplementary decision-making agents on behalf of their physical counterparts. These software agents can make logical and independent judgments on their owners' behalf (owners of the physical households). We thus mimic the population of households in a typical community by aggregating many CHDTs. Using agent-based technology, we simulate each household as having distinct behaviours, resulting in a community with stochastic global behaviour. The CDHTs' decisions are based on their preferences for sustainable energy usage or value systems. CHDTs are expected to be able to engage in collaborative initiatives such as pursuing common goals, sharing common resources, mutually influencing one another, and engaging in collective actions due to their cognitive and decision-making capacities.

The implementation of collaborative characteristics in CHDTs is expected to improve the CVPP-E performance and sustainability. The diversity of households in terms of size, as well as the number of inhabitants dwelling in each one, is critical to the community. To address this point, we divided the constituent households (and hence the corresponding CHDTs) into five groups. This classification and accompanying data were derived from a survey performed in [6]. The following categories are considered: (a) Households with single pensioners, (b) Households with single non-pensioners, (c) Households with multiple pensioners, (d) Households with children, and (e) Households with multiple people but no dependent children. The CVPP-E (community) population size may always be configured to include any number of households from each category.

3.3 Abstraction Levels of CHDTs in Line with Digital Twin Technology

According to [15], DTs can have three levels of abstraction. By relating these abstraction levels to the CHDT concept, the following definitions are proposed:

Household Asset Twins: When two or more components work together, they form what is known as an asset. Asset Twins according to [15] allow the analysis of interactions that occur at the components level. This helps to provide a plethora of asset performance data that can be evaluated and transformed into actionable insights or actions. In the context of the CVPP-E/CHDT concepts, each embedded household appliance can be considered a Household Asset Twin.

CHDT System or CHDT Unit Twin: A unit constitutes a collection of assets that enable one to see how different assets come together to form an entire functioning system. System twins help to provide visibility regarding the interaction of assets and may be used for performance enhancements. In the context of the CVPP-E/CHDT concepts, each unit of a household can be considered a CHDT System Twin or CHDT Unit Twin.

CVPP-E Process Twin: The third abstraction level is called the Process Twins. According to [15], this is a collection of systems that work together to form an entire production facility. In this case, all these systems are synchronized to operate at peak efficiency. This can help to determine the precise timing schemes that ultimately influence the overall effectiveness of the process. The CVPPE in this case can be considered as a type of a Process Twin.

## 4	Architectural Framework of a CHDT

In this section, we discuss the architectural framework for the CHDTs. As shown in Fig. 1, the framework is constituted of four main blocks: (a) the cognitive block, (b) the decision block, (c) the control block, and (d) the influence block. In the following sections, a brief description of each block is provided.

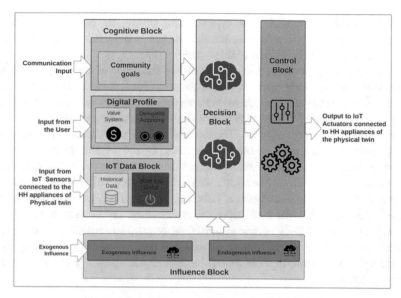

Fig. 1. The architectural framework of the CHDT

4.1 Cognitive Block

CHDTs are not only digital replicas of physical assets but are also expected to have some level of intelligence that enables them to have cognizance (explicit knowledge) of different attributes of their physical counterpart besides the current operational states of the asset. The considered attributes may include the behavioral preferences of the user. The cognitive block is constituted of the following sub-blocks:

Community Goals: As part of its cognitive capabilities, a CHDT would often have cognisance of all the goals that are suggested or proposed by the community manager. Although it may possess knowledge of the community goals, it would only join a coalition or participate in collaboration activities that are compatible with the goals of its physical twin.

Digital Profile: The digital profile of a CHDT is used to represent the preferences of the user. The digital profile of a CHDT is constituted of (a) the value system, and (b) the delegated autonomy of the CHDT.

Value System: The value system represents the preferences, choices and options of the physical twin that has been transferred to the CHDT. In the context of this study, the value system of a CHDT is a list of preferences that represent the values of the owner. This informs the kind of choices and decisions that the CHDT makes. Technically, the value system of individuals may differ from one person to another, therefore, the notion of a value system enables the collective objective of the community to be met without compromising the individual preferences and expectations of each user or actor. In Fig. 2 we illustrate six types of value systems. These are:

(a) 100% renewable sources. For this type of value system, the preference of the owner is to consume energy from only renewable sources. Any other source of energy that is non-renewable is forbidden to this actor.

(b) The mixed energy sources value system. For this type of value system, the user considers the use of energy from mixed sources. These mixed sources may include a mix of renewable and non-renewable sources. It may be possible for the owner to specify the preferred ratio of renewable sources to non-renewable.

(c) The free rider's values system. Technically this is not a value system. It rather represents an instance where the owner fails to define a value system.

(d) Cost savings value system. This represents users whose priority is to save cost and therefore prefer to use certain appliances at times when tariffs are at the lowest.

(e) Revenue or income values system. This may represent owners who want to participate in activities like demand response actions to earn revenue or sell energy from their roof-mounted photovoltaic system (PV system) to earn additional income.

(f) Load management value system represents owners who are willing to have some appliances (interruptible loads) be interrupted for the purpose of grid load management.

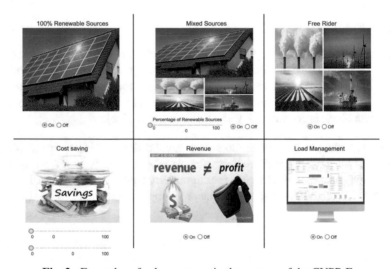

Fig. 2. Examples of value systems in the context of the CVPP-E

Delegated Autonomy: The notion of delegated autonomy is the specific instruction that a household owner assigns to its CHDT to be followed in carrying out or executing its value system. In the implemented prototype, this may include (a) the delegation of deferrable loads (DDL), which means deferring the use of certain appliances until a later time without affecting the quality of service (QoS) to the user. In the prototype model, three appliances are used for DDL. These include (i) a washing machine, (ii) a dishwasher, and (iii) a clothes dryer. DDL can be carried out by either deferring any single appliance out of the three, any two appliances, or all three appliances. (b) Interruption of Interruptible Loads (IIL). Some appliances are considered to have good thermal inertia, which is the capacity of a material to store heat and delay its transmission [16]. For such appliances, their normal use can be interrupted for a period without affecting the QoS of the user. Appliances such as refrigeration, air conditioning, and electric boilers are considered to have such properties. An IIL is a grid management strategy where an energy supplier can shut off or disconnect such appliances at the supplier's discretion or per a contractual agreement. In the context of the proposed CVPP-E, this technique can also be adopted as a strategy for delegated autonomy. Figure 3 below shows how DDL and IIL can be implemented. A user can implement delegated autonomy by selecting the radio button labelled "delegate". By selecting "undelegate", the appliance becomes undelegated. The coordination process between a user and a CHDT can be achieved through three simple steps. These are step 1: The user loads the appliance. Step 2a: For smart appliances, the CHDT automatically detects the presence of a load and is turned on automatically. Step 2b, for non-smart appliances, the user may manually turn the appliance on after loading. Step 3, once the appliance is in the "on" state, a signal will be sent to the CHDT indicating its readiness to be used. The CHDT will then take over the process and operate the appliance based on the pre-defined digital profile of the user.

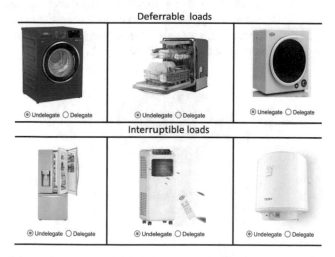

Fig. 3. How delegated autonomy (DDL & IIL) can be implemented in the CVPP-E prototype

IoT Data Block: This block represents the IoT interface between the household appliances and the CHDT. This block is constituted of two sub-blocks:

(a)   the historical data block, which is a database that contains historical data of each appliance's use-behaviour, over time. By integrating AI techniques, the CHDT can glean some behavioural patterns from these historical data for prediction and decision-making purposes, on behalf of the physical twin.

(b) Status data: This block communicates the operational status of an appliance to the CHDT. Such data may include information such as whether the appliance is currently in the "On "or "Off" states. For appliances such as refrigerators and air conditioners, sensorial data such as the operating temperature etc. could be collected. In future studies, data about the thermal comfort of rooms or the living environment in households may also be useful for the CHDTs in their decision-making, particularly concerning the regulation of temperature in the living environment.

In Fig. 4, we illustrate how the integrated IoT components communicate wirelessly with a central router to reach the CHDT that is hosted in the cloud. Control signals can also be sent from the CHDT via the router to the various appliances to enable control instructions to be carried out. A firewall at the interface ensures the security of users.

Generally, DTs are hosted and operated in an environment called Digital Twin Environment. The connection between the physical and virtual objects can be achieved through several communication channels. However, the Institute of Electrical and Electronics Engineers has proposed a standard namely, IEEE 1451 which constitutes a family of smart transducer interface standards, that defines a set of open, common, network-independent communication interfaces for smart transducers (sensors or actuators) to achieve sensor data interoperability between cyber and physical components of CPS. The standard defines a smart transducer as either a sensor and/or actuator that can identify and describe itself, has the data processing capability to present sensor data or accept actuation values, respectively, in measurement units, has network communication capability, and is easy to use, enabling plug-and-play functionality [17].

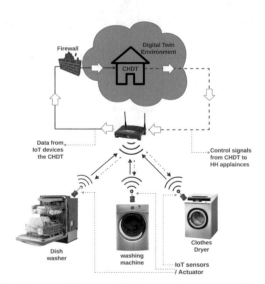

Fig. 4. Communication framework between IoT sensors/actuators and the household appliances

4.2 Control Block

This block connects the CHDT to each of the embedded appliances. The input of the control block accepts output from the decision block and the output of the control block serves as input to actuators that are connected to each of the appliances. At this stage of the study, an open loop control system is considered. This is because the expected control actions at this level may include switching off appliances between the "on" and "off" states. In future studies where complex actions like controlling thermal comfort by monitoring and adjusting room temperature or using CHDTs in demand response techniques such as interruption of loads, other control models may be suitable.

4.3 Influence Block

Knowledge from social network analysis has shown that the decision of participants on social networks can be influenced by network influencers. As claimed by [18], people usually look up to influencers on social media to guide them with their decision-making. There are various strategies for spreading influence in a social system or network. One powerful strategy that has been used to favourably impact individuals in a variety of ways is the power of internet information dissemination [19, 20]. Companies have used this technique, known as the "viral phenomenon" or "viral marketing," to encourage sharing amongst individuals with social connections, because it is recognized that social recommendations may assist improve traffic to business websites, resulting in increased engagement and income. In the developed prototype model, two types of influences are considered. These are:

Exogenous Influence: This represents influences that originate from the external environment of a CHDT. This may constitute an influence from the community manager or other influencer CHDTs within the community. The outcome of some preliminary results obtained by studying endogenous influences within the CVPP-E can be seen in Sect. 5.

Endogenous Influence: The type of influence that originates from inside of a CHDT.

4.4 Decision Block

This block forms the central part of the CHDT. It is the place where all decisions of the CHDT are made. The decision block accepts inputs from (a) the community goal block, (b) the digital profile block, (c) the IoT data block, and (d) the influence block. In Fig. 5, a Business Process Management Notation language is used to illustrate how CHDTs make decisions based on the various inputs.

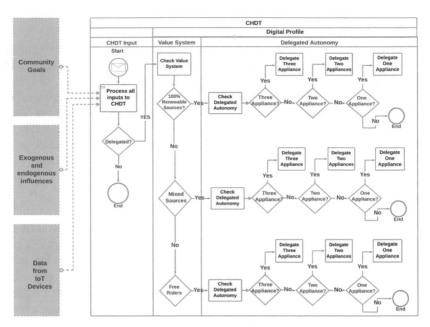

Fig. 5. A BPMN representation of the decision-making process of a CHDT

4.5   Addressing Ethical and Other Relevant Concerns

Addressing Ethical Concerns: The CVPP-E concept is designed to be less intrusive and would not require users to submit sensitive personal data besides their digital profiles, which reside in the users' CHDT memory and will not be shared with any third party inside or external to the community. Furthermore, the notion of influence will not work on CHDTs who have already defined their digital profiles. It is rather intended to influence free rider CHDTs who are part of the community and yet have not defined their digital profiles, and therefore their behaviours are inimical to the collective interest of the community. This is a common phenomenon in communities where some members do not conform to the community norms. A typical example is the notion of the "tragedy of the commons," where some members abuse or overexploit a shared community resource for their personal or parochial gains. Furthermore, since this is a closed community, it will not be possible for external and malicious influences to access the CHDTs.

Addressing Appliance Heterogeneity: In developing the prototype model, appliance heterogeneity for all the appliances was taken into consideration. A key parameter that differentiates these appliances is their power ratings. This, parameter determines how much electricity an appliance may consume per unit time, usually measured in watt-hours (Wh) or kilowatt-hours (Kwh). This parameter may vary from appliance to appliance based on the size, features, and year of manufacture, among other factors. To help cater for the wide variety of appliances, a uniform probability distribution function expressed in the form of *"uniform discrete function (x, y)"* is adopted. Where x is the possible minimum appliance power rating and y is the possible maximum appliance power rating. Using this technique, the model will stochastically assign a value between x and

y to every unit of an appliance in the model. This technique does not only make each appliance assume a different rating but also enables them to behave differently.

Addressing Multiple Value Systems: In the CVPP-E, CHDTS can have multiple value systems. For instance, a prosumer CHDT could have a value system of (a) 100% renewable energy consumption, (b) revenue generation, and (c) cost-saving. However, these value systems should be arranged in a hierarchical order of priority (priority list).

Addressing Collision of Value Systems: This can be addressed in two ways. These are: (a) at the CHDT level. Here, the value system that is higher in the priority list of the CHDT will override the lower priority value system. (b) at the community level, the community may also define some values, such as sustainability values, as a priority in their value system. In such instances, the sustainability values will always override any other values that conflict with them.

5   Scenario for Testing the Control Capabilities of CHDTs

To illustrate the control capabilities of the CHDTs. We consider a scenario where a CHDT sends a series of control signals to switch appliances between the "on" and "off" states. Three appliances, namely a washing machine, dishwasher, and tumble dryer are controlled. Table 1 shows the time at which the control signals are transmitted and the corresponding control action that the signal is expected to achieve. Figure 6 shows the use behaviour of the three appliances without the control signals. In Fig. 7 we illustrate the use behaviour of the three appliances when control signals are received by these appliances. The period between each "on" and "off" cycle is 10 h.

Table 1.   Periodic control signals to test the control capabilities of CHDTs

	Time (hours)									
	20	30	50	60	80	90	110	120	140	150
Control action	Off	On	Off	On	Off	On	Off	On	Off	On

In Fig. 10, we show the outcome of the model without any control signals. The figure shows continuous consumption without any interruptions.

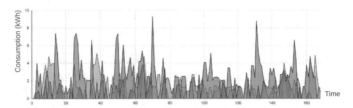

Fig. 6. Profile of three appliances without control signals

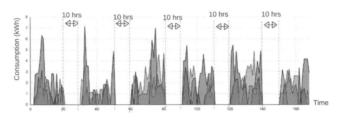

Fig. 7. Profile of three appliances with "On" and "Off "control signals

To further illustrate the decision-making and control capabilities of these CHDTs, we discuss in Sect. 5 some outcomes of previous studies, that were conducted using two different scenarios. However, to better understand these studied cases, it may be relevant to provide some insight into the prototype model that was used for the study. Firstly, the prototype model is constituted of several sub-models that are integrated to function as a single model. This technique allows modeling the different actors and systems that interact to allow the CVPP-E to accomplish its intended functionalities. Some of the sub-models are as follows:

(a) the PV and local storage sub-model (Fig. 8) which is used to model the embedded PV systems for prosumers,
(b) The embedded household appliances model (Fig. 9) is used to model all embedded appliances. Nine appliances were considered in the model
(c) The prosumer model (Fig. 10), which is used to model prosumers, and
(d) The consumer model (Fig. 11) is used to model consumers.

Depending on the intended use, a sub-model in AnyLogic [21] can be created using one of three modelling strategies. For example, all models that display dynamic behaviours, with continually changing parameters, are simulated using System Dynamics modelling techniques. The photovoltaic system (PV system) and local storage sub-model, as well as the embedded household appliances sub-models, are examples of system dynamics models. Multi-agent system approach was also used to model the changing states (active and inactive states) of prosumer and consumer CHDTS. Finally, all aspects of the model that needed the formation of an entity endowed with autonomous qualities were also modelled using agent-based modelling techniques.

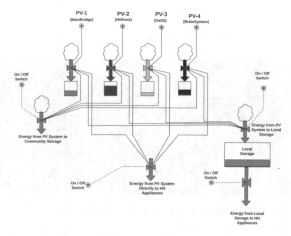

Fig. 8. A model of a four PV system, local storage and the three outputs of the PV system

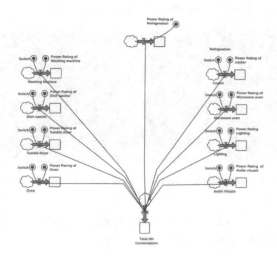

Fig. 9. A System Dynamics model of all nine embedded household appliances

Although the prototype model is constituted of several other sub-models, the shown ones, thus, Figs. 8, 9, 10 and 11 form the core of the prototype. Discussed in the next section are the outcomes of some previous studies.

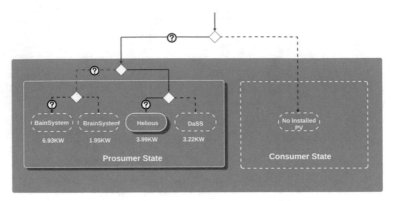

Fig. 10. An agent-based model of an active prosumer CHDT with an active 3.99 kW PV system

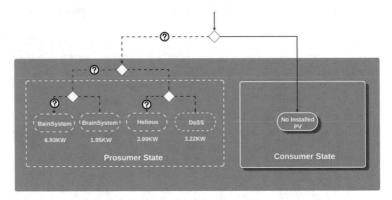

Fig. 11. An agent-based model of an active consumer with no installed PV system

6   Discussion of the Outcome of Preliminary Studies Conducted Using the Developed Prototype

In this section, we present the outcome of some preliminary studies conducted using the prototype model. We illustrate with two examples, thus, (a) modelling delegated autonomy and (b) modelling mutual influences.

6.1   Scenario 1: Modelling Delegated Autonomy

In Tables 1 and 2, we show some selected scenarios that were used to test the CVPP-E prototype at an earlier stage [22]. For instance, the data shown in Table 2 was sourced from [23]. For demonstration purposes, Table 2 shows data for only three out of the nine household appliances that were embedded in each CHDT. These parameters were used to model each of the appliance´s use-behaviours. Furthermore, in Table 3, we considered different scenarios of varying prosumer and consumer populations. For each scenario, we tested different degrees of delegated autonomy. Delegation in this sense means that the CHDT has been given authority by its owner to make some rational decisions on his/her behalf. In this example, the goal is to minimize community consumption within a certain period namely the "vending window" (Fig. 12) so that the saved energy could be vended to the power grid. We tested different delegated autonomy options, i.e., delegating either 1, 2, or 3 of any of the appliances mentioned in Table 2. In Fig. 12 we show the outcome of one scenario, thus, scenario 1 (Table 3). This outcome shows that, within the vending window, the CHDTs carried out the control instruction (delegated autonomy) which is to defer the use of these appliances within the defined period (vending window), thus resulting in zero consumption.

Table 2. Parameters that were used to model the various household appliances [23].

Type of appliance	Annual power (kwh)			Peak periods		Number of wash cycles year
	Min	Average	Max	P1	P2	
Washing machine	15.00	178	700	5am–4pm	5pm–2am	284
Tumble dryer	64.25	497	1600	5am–12pm	6pm–11pm	280
Dishwasher	33.32	315	608	5am–3am	6pm–2am	270

Table 3. The population size of the various HH in the sample scenario

Scenarios		Degree of delegation	Number of delegated appliances	Percentage of CHDT population (%)	
				Delegated	Undelegated
1	High population of delegated CHDTs	Full	3	100	0
2	Low population of delegated CHDTs	Full	3	10	90
3	High population of delegated CHDTs	Full	3	90	10
4	High population of delegated CHDTs	Partial	2	90	10
5	High population of delegated CHDTs	Partial	1	90	10

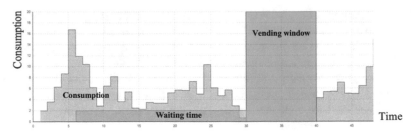

Fig. 12. The outcome of collective action behaviours for scenario 1 (Table 3)

6.2 Scenario 2: Modelling Mutual Influence of CHDTs

In a study conducted in [24], the concept of mutual influence was explored. Under this scenario, the following parameters were assumed: (a) Positive influence: Uniform distribution (0, 2), (b) Negative influence: Uniform distribution (−2, 0), (c) Frequency of transmission: Uniform distribution (0, 3) times per week, (d) Impact: Uniform distribution (0, 5) hours from the moment of receiving the influence, (e) Decision constant (∝) = 50. Details of other relevant parameters such as Duration of Use, Appliance Power Rating, Frequency of Use etc. can be found in [24].

Table 4 below, describes two different cases, constituting of different population sizes, that were considered. In all cases, the influencer CHDTs attempt to influence the "influencee" CHDTs to use the loads mentioned in Table 2 only when the energy available is from renewable sources, thus, directly from PV sources, local storage or community storage and to avoid using energy from the grid. A total population size of 50 CHDTs was used. Two scenarios as shown in Table 4 were considered.

Table 4. Two cases with varying population sizes are used to test collective decision-making.

Cases	Population (%)					
	Influencer population "A"	Influencee population	Positive influencer population	Negative influencer population	Prosumer population	Consumer population
Case-1a	90%	10%	90%	10%	20%	80%
Case 1b	90%	10%	10%	90%	20%	80%

At the end of the model run (728 h), Figs. 13a & b show the characteristics of the modelled influence that was received by two different CHDTs, i.e., CHDT-1 and CHDT-2. The pulses that appear below the X-axis represent negative influences whilst the ones above the X-axis are positive influences.

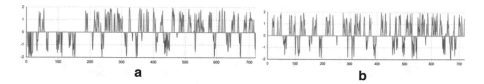

Fig. 13. a. Influences received by CHDT-1. **b.** Influences received by CHDT-2.

In Figs. 14a and b, we show how the aggregation of influences over time can be used to determine the overall behavior of a CHDT. We also illustrate how the overall behavior can be used in decision-making. For instance, Figs. 14a, and b show CHDTs 3&4. Initially CHDT 3 was negatively influenced however the general behavior changed into a positive one after 500 h. This CHDT could not decide because its behavior (thus, the aggregation of influence) over time could not cross the threshold "$\propto$". In Fig. 14b, CHDT 4 was positively influenced right from the beginning of the model until the finish. CHDT 4 was able to make a decision at 300 h.

By comparing the outcome of case-1a and case-1b (Figs. 15a & b), the outcome of the model shows that when the population of positive influencers was high (90% in case-1a against 10% case-1b) the majority of the CHDTs were influenced positively, hence, the majority were able to make a decision to switch consumption from the grid to renewable sources hence consumption from the grid was about 51% as compared to 69% in case-1b) where the number of positive influencers was low (10%). Furthermore, consumption from the community storage, local storage and PV appreciated significantly in case of 1a more than in case 1b. This can also be attributed to the difference in the population of positive influencers.

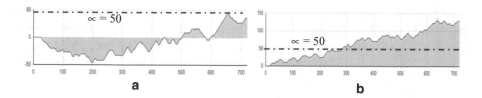

Fig. 14. a. CHDT-3. **b.** CHDT-4.

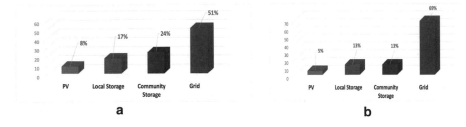

Fig. 15. a. Case-1a. 90% positive influencers. **b.** Case-1b. 10% positive influencers.

7 Conclusion and Future Works

This work showed how the integration of IoT devices could facilitate (a) the collection of data from the household asset twins to the CHDT, and (b) how control signals from the CHDT could be used to regulate the "on" and "off" states of the asset twins. In the study, the abstraction levels of the CHDT in the context of the digital twin were also described. An illustration of the control capabilities of the CHDT was also shown. Furthermore, this study showed a detailed architecture of the CHDT and all the necessary components to enable the functionality of the concept. Additionally, outcomes from two previous studies using the developed prototype model were demonstrated. In all, the work has shown that the CHDT concept is feasible. Furthermore, the study has helped to establish the fact that IoT and digital twin concepts are a key prerequisite for the development of the CHDT concept. The IEEE 1451 family of smart transducer interface standards have also been suggested.

In future studies, other collaborative behaviours such as value co-creation which is an aspect of collaboration where members of a community or an ecosystem jointly create a new product or service that results in the generation of value for the mutual benefit of members. In such circumstances, the contribution of each member towards the created value is highly relevant and can be contentious if not managed adequately. In the context of the CVPP-E, some members, particularly, prosumers may contribute tangible value in the form of renewable energy that is contributed from the locally installed PV systems. On the contrary, consumers may contribute intangible value by denying themselves the use of certain household appliances (aka delegation of deferrable loads) to enable the reduction of energy consumption in the community. This kind of self-imposed denial of service could be considered an intangible contribution toward value co-creation. In future studies, these aspects of tangible and intangible value creation shall be explored further and also in detail.

Acknowledgement. We acknowledge project CESME (Collaborative & Evolvable Smart Manufacturing Ecosystem and the Portuguese FCT program UIDB/00066/2020 for providing partial financial support for this work.

References

1. Aversa, P., Donatelli, A., Piccoli, G., Luprano, V.A.M.: Improved thermal transmittance measurement with HFM technique on building envelopes in the mediterranean area. Sel. Sci. Pap. - J. Civ. Eng. **11**(2), 39–52 (2016). https://doi.org/10.1515/sspjce-2016-0017
2. European Comission: Energy performance of buildings directive. (2019). https://ec.europa.eu/energy/topics/energy-efficiency/energy-efficient-buildings/energy-performance-buildings-directive_en. Accessed 28 Mar 2020
3. Han, Y., et al.: Energy consumption analysis and saving of buildings based on static and dynamic input-output models. Energy **239**, 122240 (2022). https://doi.org/10.1016/j.energy.2021.122240
4. IDEA: Analyses of the energy consumption of the household sector in Spain (2011). www.cros-portal.eu/sites/default/files/SECH_Spain.pdf%5Cn
5. Adu-Kankam, K.O., Camarinha-Matos, L.M.: Towards a hybrid model for the diffusion of innovation in energy communities. In: Camarinha-Matos, L.M., Ferreira, P., Brito, G. (eds.) DoCEIS 2021. IFIP Advances in Information and Communication Technology, vol. 626, pp. 175–188. Springer, Cham (2021). https://doi.org/10.1007/978-3-030-78288-7_17
6. Adu-Kankam, K.O., Camarinha-Matos, L.M.: A collaborative approach to demand side energy management. In: Camarinha-Matos, L.M., Afsarmanesh, H., Ortiz, A. (eds.) Boosting Collaborative Networks 4.0. PRO-VE 2020. IFIP Advances in Information and Communication Technology, vol. 598, pp. 393–405. Springer, Cham (2020). https://doi.org/10.1007/978-3-030-62412-5_32K
7. Adu-Kankam, K.O., Camarinha-Matos, L.M.: A framework for behavioural change through incentivization in a collaborative virtual power plant ecosystem. In: Camarinha-Matos, L., Farhadi, N., Lopes, F., Pereira, H. (eds.) DoCEIS 2020. IFIP Advances in Information and Communication Technology, vol. 577, pp. 31–40. Springer, Cham (2020). https://doi.org/10.1007/978-3-030-45124-0_3K
8. Fathy, Y., Jaber, M., Nadeem, Z.: Digital twin-driven decision making and planning for energy consumption. J. Sens. Actuator Netw. **10**(37), 1–33 (2021). https://doi.org/10.3390/jsan10020037
9. Henzel, J., Wróbel, Ł, Fice, M., Sikora, M.: Energy consumption forecasting for the digital-twin model of the building. Energies **15**(12), 4318 (2022). https://doi.org/10.3390/en15124318
10. Tan, Y., Cheng, P., Shou, W., Sadick, A.-M.: Digital Twin-driven approach to improving energy efficiency of indoor lighting based on computer vision and dynamic BIM. Energy Build. **270**, 112271 (2022). https://doi.org/10.1016/j.enbuild.2022.112271
11. Kharlamova, N., Traholt, C., Hashemi, S.: A digital twin of battery energy storage systems providing frequency regulation. In: SysCon 2022 - 16th Annual IEEE International Systems Conference, Proceedings (2022). https://doi.org/10.1109/SysCon53536.2022.9773919
12. You, M., Wang, Q., Sun, H., Castro, I., Jiang, J.: Digital twins based day-ahead integrated energy system scheduling under load and renewable energy uncertainties. Appl. Energy **305**, 117899 (2022). https://doi.org/10.1016/j.apenergy.2021.117899
13. The European Parliament and the Council of the European Union: Directive (EU) 2018/2001 of the European Parliament and of the Council on the promotion of the use of energy from renewable sources. Official Journal of the European Union (2018). https://eur-lex.europa.eu/legal-content/EN/TXT/PDF/?uri=CELEX:32018L2001&from=fr. Accessed 07 Mar 2022
14. Adu-Kankam, K.O., Camarinha-Matos, L.M.: Towards collaborative virtual power plants: trends and convergence. Sustain. Energy Grids Netw. **626**, 217–230 (2018). https://doi.org/10.1016/j.segan.2018.08.003

15. IBM: What is a digital twin? https://www.ibm.com/topics/what-is-a-digital-twin. Accessed 30 Jun 2022
16. Sala Lizarraga, J.M.P., Picallo-Perez, A.: Exergy Analysis and Thermoeconomics of Buildings: Design and Analysis for Sustainable Energy Systems. Butterworth-Heinemann, Oxford (2019)
17. Mark, J., Hufnagel, P.: The IEEE 1451. 4 Standard for Smart Transducers. IEEE Standard Association (1996). https://standards.ieee.org/wp-content/uploads/import/documents/tutorials/1451d4.pdf. Accessed 28 Jun 2022
18. Geyser, W.: What is an Influencer? - Social Media Influencers Defined. Influencer Marketing Hub (2022). https://influencermarketinghub.com/what-is-an-influencer/. Accessed 23 Jun 2022
19. Chen, W., Lakshmanan, L.V.S., Castillo, C.: Information and influence propagation in social networks. In: Özsu, M.T. (ed.) Synthesis Lectures on Data Management, vol. 5, no. 4, pp. 1–177. Morgan & Claypool Publishers, Williston (2013)
20. Hugo, O., Garnsey, E.: The emergence of electronic messaging and the growth of four entrepreneurial entrants. New Technology Based Firms New Millenium, vol. 2, pp. 97–123 (2002)
21. AnyLogic: AnyLogic: Simulation Modeling Software Tools & Solutions for Business (2018). https://www.anylogic.com/. Accessed 27 Apr 2020
22. Adu-Kankam, K.O., Camarinha-Matos, L.M.: Modelling 'cognitive households digital twins' in an energy community. In: Bendaoud, M., Wolfgang, B., Chikh, K. (eds.) ICESA 2021, pp. 67–79. Springer, Singapore (2022). https://doi.org/10.1007/978-981-19-0039-6_6
23. Zimmermann, J.-P., et al.: Household electricity survey: a study of domestic electrical product usage. Intertek Report R66141 (2012). https://www.gov.uk/government/uploads/system/uploads/attachment_data/file/208097/10043_R66141HouseholdElectricitySurveyFinalReportissue4.pdf. Accessed 05 Sep 2021
24. Adu-Kankam, K.O., Camarinha-Matos, L.M.: Modelling mutual influence towards sustainable energy consumption. In: Camarinha-Matos, L.M. (ed.) DoCEIS 2022. IFIP Advances in Information and Communication Technology, vol. 649, pp. 3–15. Springer, Cham (2022). https://doi.org/10.1007/978-3-031-07520-9_1

SHPIA: A Low-Cost Multi-purpose Smart Home Platform for Intelligent Applications

Florenc Demrozi[ID] and Graziano Pravadelli[(✉)][ID]

Department of Computer Science, University of Verona, 37134 Verona, Italy
{florenc.demrozi,graziano.pravadelli}@univr.it

Abstract. Nowadays, smart devices have invaded the market and consequently our daily life. Their use in smart home contexts, to improve the quality of life, specially for elderly and people with special needs, is getting stronger and stronger. Therefore, many systems based on smart applications and intelligent devices have been developed, for example, to monitor people's environmental contexts, help in daily life activities, and analyze their health status. However, most of the existing solutions present disadvantages regarding accessibility, as they are costly, and applicability, due to lack of generality and interoperability.

This paper is intended to tackle such drawbacks by presenting SHPIA, a multi-purpose smart home platform for intelligent applications. It is based on the use of a low-cost Bluetooth Low Energy (BLE)-based devices, which "transforms" objects of daily life into smart objects. The devices allow collecting and automatically labelling different type of data to provide indoor monitoring and assistance. SHPIA is intended, in particular, to be adaptable to different home-based application scenarios, like for example, human activity recognition, coaching systems, and occupancy detection and counting.

The SHPIA platform is open source and freely available to the scientific and industrial community.

Keywords: Smart home platform · Automatic data annotation · Automatic data collection · Human activity recognition

1 Introduction

Nowadays, smart systems have invaded our daily lives with a plethora of devices, mainly from consumer electronics, like smartwatches, smartphones and personal assistants, and domestic appliances with intelligent capabilities to autonomously drive modern homes. These are generally based on wireless protocols, like WiFi, Bluetooth Low Energy (BLE) and ZibBee, low-cost sensing components, including Passive InfraRed (PIR) and Radio Frequency Identification (RFID)-based technologies, and several other kinds of environmental sensors. These devices communicate with each other without the need for human intervention, thus

© IFIP International Federation for Information Processing 2022
Published by Springer Nature Switzerland AG 2022
L. M. Camarinha-Matos et al. (Eds.): IFIPIoT 2022, IFIP AICT 665, pp. 217–234, 2022.
https://doi.org/10.1007/978-3-031-18872-5_13

contributing to the implementation of the Internet of Things (IoT) paradigm. Their number is continuously increasing, and their versatility enables several opportunities for different scenarios, ranging from simple environmental monitoring solutions to more complex autonomous control systems, in both private life (i.e., at home) and public contexts (i.e., social and working environments). Without claiming to be exhaustive, examples of applications can be found in healthcare [3,16] and elderly assistance [21,22], in smart building for Human Activity Recognition (HAR) [5], and energy management [11,20], as well as in smart industries [12] and smart cities [18].

In particular, concerning private life, in the last decade, the idea of a smart home has become of central interest, where its main aim concerns the recognition of the activities performed by the environment occupants (e.g., cooking, sitting down, sleeping, etc.), and the detection of changes in the environmental status due to such activities (e.g., temperature variation related to the opening or closing of a window) [2,7]. The concept of home, indeed, includes different connotations, and according to [13], it is characterized as a place for a) security and control, b) activity, c) relationships and continuity, and d) identity and values. Thus, to guarantee and promote these peculiarities, the design of a smart home cannot ignore the need of implementing the capability of recognizing human activities through HAR systems to provide real-time information about people's behaviors. HAR algorithms are based on pattern recognition models fed with data perceived by on-body sensors, environmental sensors, and daily life smart devices [2,9]. HAR algorithms and smart devices provide, then, the basics for implementing and integrating intelligent systems, which autonomously take decisions and support life activities in our homes.

1.1 Related Works

The literature concerning smart home platforms is extremely vast and differentiated, which makes impossible to exhaustively summarize them in a few lines. Among the cheapest solutions, we can cite the CASAS platform proposed in [6]. It integrates several ZigBee-based sensors for door, light, motion, and temperature sensing, with a total cost of $2,765. Based on the data collected by the platform, the authors were able to recognize ten different Activities of Daily Life (ADLs) executed by the environment occupants achieving, on average, approximately 60% accuracy.

In a similar way, in [19], the authors proposed a HAR model, fed with data collected through a smart home platform based on motion, door, temperature, light, water, and bummer sensors, to classify more than ten ADLs, achieving approximately 55% accuracy.

In [24], a study is presented where the authors installed a sensor network, composed of motion sensors, video cameras, and a bed sensor that measures sleep restlessness, pulse, and breathing levels, in 17 flats of an aged eldercare facility. They gathered data for 15 months on average (ranging from 3 months to 3 years). The collected information was used to prevent and detect falls and recognize ADLs by identifying anomalous patterns.

In [28], the authors used an application to continually record raw data from a mobile device by exploiting the microphone, the WiFi scan module, the device heading orientation, the light proximity, the step detector, the accelerometer, the gyroscope, the magnetometer, and other built-in sensors. Then, time-series sensor fusion and techniques such as audio processing, WiFi indoor positioning, and proximity sensing localization were used to determine ADLs with a high level of accuracy.

When developing a strategy to deploy technology for discreet in-home health monitoring, several questions arise concerning, for example, the types of sensors that should be used, their location, and the kind of data that should be collected. In [26], the authors deeply studied such issues, pointing out that no clear answer can be identified, but the perceived data must be accurately evaluated to provide insights into such questions.

Recently, relevant pilot projects have been developed and presented, such as HomeSense [25, 27], to demonstrate seniors' benefits and adherence response to the designed smart home architecture. HomeSense exposes the visualization of activity trends over time, periodic reporting for case management, custom real-time notifications for abnormal events, and advanced health status analytics. HomeSense includes magnetic contact, passive infrared motion, energy, pressure, water, and environmental sensors.

However, all these innovative systems and applications frequently present disadvantages in terms of accessibility and applicability. In several cases, they are based on ad-hoc and costly devices (e.g., cameras) which are not accessible to everyone. In fact, as shown in [14], among 844 revised works, the system cost is the principal reason for the failure of projects concerning the design of smart health/home systems.

Some projects targeting the definition of low-cost solutions have been also proposed, but they are generally devoted to monitoring or recognizing single activities and/or specific use-case scenarios, thus lacking generality, or requiring the final users to install several non inter-operable solutions in their homes. For example, in [4] a set of very low-cost projects focusing on solutions for helping visually-impaired people are presented. Less effort has been spent, instead, designing solutions that use low-cost objects of daily life (ODLs) to monitor and recognize people's activity in general.

Finally, a further limitation of the existing smart home environments regards the necessity of annotating the collected data based on the video registration of the environment for training the pattern recognition algorithms, which is of central importance for the implementation of efficient HAR algorithms. Unfortunately, the annotation process is generally a very time-consuming and manual activity, while only a few prototypical automatic approaches are currently available in the literature [8].

1.2   Paper Contribution

According to the previous considerations and the limitation of existing solutions, this paper presents SHPIA, an open-source multi-purpose smart home platform for intelligent applications. It is based on the use of low-cost Bluetooth Low Energy (BLE)-based devices, which "transform" objects of daily life into smart objects. The devices allow collecting and automatically labeling different types of data to provide intelligent services in smart homes, like, as example, indoor monitoring and assistance. Its architecture relies on the integration among a mobile Android application and low-cost BLE devices, which "transform" objects of daily life into smart objects. By exploiting these devices, SHPIA flexibly collects and annotates datasets that capture the interaction between humans and the environment they live in, and then the related behaviors. These datasets represent the basics for implementing and training HAR-based systems and developing intelligent applications for different indoor monitoring and coaching scenarios. SHPIA can be set up with less than $200 and operates in a ubiquitous and not invasive manner (i.e., no camera is required). SHPIA's software is available to the scientific community through a public GitHub repository [1].

1.3 Paper Organization

The rest of the paper is organized as follows. Section 2 introduces preliminary information concerning the devices and the communication protocols used in SHPIA. Section 3 details the SHPIA architecture and describes how it enables data collection and labeling. Section 4 showcases and discusses the experimental results and application scenarios. Finally, Sect. 5 concludes the paper with final remarks.

2   Preliminaries

SHPIA is based on the use of the Nordic Thingy 52 device shown in Fig. 1. The choice of using such a device to implement the SHPIA platform has been made on the basis of its versatile and complete set of characteristics, which are summarized below in this section. However, this device can be easily replaced, without affecting SHPIA functionalities, with many other BLE-based inertial measurement units available on the market, provided that they allow to collect a similar set of data through their sensors.

The Nordic Thingy 52 is a compact, power-optimized, multi-sensor device designed for collecting data of various type based on the nRF52832 System on Chip (SoC), built over a 32-bit ARM CortexTM-M4F CPU. The nRF52832 is fully multiprotocol, capable of supporting Bluetooth 5, Bluetooth mesh, BLE, Thread, Zigbee, 802.15.4, ANT, and 2.4 GHz proprietary stacks. Furthermore, the nRF52832 uses a sophisticated on-chip adaptive power management system achieving exceptionally low energy consumption. This device integrates two types of sensors: i) environmental and ii) inertial. Environmental concern temperature, humidity, air pressure, light intensity, and air quality sensors (i.e., CO_2 level). Instead, inertial concerns accelerometer, gyroscope, and compass sensors. Besides the data directly measured by the integrated sensors, the Thingy computes over the edge the following information: quaternion, rotation matrix, pitch, roll, yaw, and step counter. Concerning the communication capabilities, Thingy 52 instantiates a two-side BLE communication with the data aggregator device, unlike BLE beacons. The communication between Thingy 52 and the data aggregator occurs at a frequency that goes from 0.1 Hz to 133 Hz, making SHPIA adaptable to applications scenarios were high sampling frequencies are required. Moreover, since the BLE provides the possibility to send more than just one value into every single transmitted package, the sensor's sampling frequency is not limited 133 Hz (i.e., the maximal frequency of the BLE communication), but it enables the sensor to sample at higher frequencies.

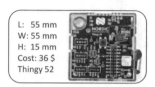

Fig. 1. SHPIA compatible device: Nordic Thingy 52.

Fig. 2. Schematic view of the SHPIA platform.

3   SHPIA Architecture

This section introduces the core of the SHPIA platform, which is shown in Fig. 2. In particular, it describes the principal agents composing its architecture, and how a smart home environment can be defined and configured for enabling data collection and annotation.

3.1   Agents

The agents involved in the SHPIA architecture are classified as *abstract agents* and *real agents*. The abstract agents are necessary to analyze the status of the environment (in terms of included objects and environmental conditions) and the status of people living in it (in terms of presence, quantity, movements, and accomplished actions). On the other side, real agents are represented by the people occupying the environment, their smartphones, and the Thingy 52 devices. SHPIA enables communication capabilities among real agents as described below in the paper.

3.2   Environment Definition

Concerning the home environment, SHPIA defines it as a set composed of the home itself, people inside it, and available ODLs. In particular, ODLs enclose mobile objects (bottles, pills container, keys, etc.) and motionless objects (e.g., doors, desks, coffee machine, etc.) present inside the environment, as those shown in Fig. 2.

Therefore, given a set of mobile ODLs (M) and a set of motionless ODLs (Ml), the environment (E) is formally defined as:

$$E = \{\{M \cup Ml\}, f_s, f_l, T, D\}, \text{with}$$
$$f_s : M \longrightarrow T$$
$$f_l : Ml \longrightarrow T$$

where, T is a set of Thingy 52 devices, D is a data aggregator node, while f_s and f_l are functions that associate, respectively, a Thingy 52 device to each mobile (M) and motionless (Ml) ODL. The data aggregator D identifies the device that collects the data perceived by the Thingy 52 devices, behaving as a gateway towards a Cloud database. SHPIA uses an Android smartphone as data aggregator.

3.3   Environment Configuration

To handle the definition of the environment, we designed the Android application shown in Fig. 3. It allows the users to create one or more environments and associate a single specific Thingy 52 to each ODL of interest. In addition, this application allows real-time visualization of the perceived data and enables the smartphone to operate as the data aggregator.

Figure 4 presents the steps that the user has to perform in order to configure the smart environment by means of the mobile application. They work as follows.

Fig. 3. SHPIA Android mobile application.

Fig. 4. SHPIA environmental configuration work-flow.

User Account Creation: In this first step, the SHPIA application allows, if not already existing, the creation of a user profile to associate the collected data. Once the user is verified, she/he can set the IP address of a Cloud-based NoSQL database from the setting page, to which the data will be transmitted. We want to emphasize that the transmitted data can be saved at any NoSQL database deployed on such IP. Users, for analysis purposes, need only to know the format that the SHPIA mobile application uses to save the data.

Create Environment: Once authenticated, the user can create one or more environments, as introduced in Sect. 3.2, by defining its name (i.e., *env_id*) and geographical address (i.e., *address*). Alternatively, if the environment already exists, the user can share it with other SHPIA users (Fig. 3(a) and Fig. 3(b)).

Create Sub-environment: SHPIA users can create as many environments as needed, and an environment is typically composed of other sub-environments (Fig. 3(c)). For example, an apartment consists of a lounge, a kitchen, two bedrooms, and two bathrooms. SHPIA does not present any limit in the depth of nested sub-environments (i.e., it can configure sub-environments of a sub-environment of ... of an environment). This specific feature has been developed by considering the possibility of adopting SHPIA also in industrial, scholastic, or smart city scenarios. Moreover, SHPIA can be used also for not environmental-related contexts. For example, the users can adopt it for implementing a wireless body area network by associating the Thingy 52 devices to body parts instead of environments or ODLs, as in [15]. Overall, environments and sub-environments are described as shown in the example of Listing 1.1. Besides, *env_id* and *address*, the environments and sub-environments are identified by *owner*, *creation_time*, list of *sub_environments* and a brief *description*.

```
{
    "env_id": "Home_1",
    "description": "master bedroom",
    "owner": "florenc.demrozi@univr.it",
    "address": "Strada le Grazie 15, Verona, Italy",
    "creation_time":'27/12/2021 15:13:52.085',
    "sub_environments": ["Sub_Home_1","Sub_Home_2","
    Sub_Home_3","Sub_Home_4"]
}
```

Listing 1.1. Example of environment description in SHPIA.

Create Smart ODLs: Once the environment has been created, the user can finally attach a Thingy 52 device to each mobile or motionless ODL of interest to transform it into a smart ODL. At this point, the user is required to move his/her smartphone close (<10 cm) to the ODL equipped with the Thingy 52 to allow SHPIA to recognize it. SHPIA automatically associates the ODL with the nearest Thingy 52 device by exploiting the Received Signal Strength Indicator

(RSSI) measurement (Fig. 3(d)). RSSI, often used in Radio Frequency (RF)–based communication systems, is related to the power perceived by a receiver. In particular, it provides an indication of the power level at which the data frames are received. The rationale is that the higher the RSSI value, the stronger the signal and the closer the receiver and the emitter. The RSSI is used to reduce possible wrong associations in the presence of a high number of BLE devices distributed in the environment.

Data Collection: After the environment definition and the association of ODLs to Thingy 52 devices, the SHPIA mobile app will start collecting data from them (Fig. 3(e) and Fig. 3(f)). The data perceived by the smartphone are internally stored as JSON documents. As soon as an Internet connection is available, all data are saved on the remote NoSQL database (Fig. 3(g)). Listing 1.2 shows an example of the data perceived by the Thingy 52 device.

```
{
    "deviceID": "00:00:5e:00:53:af",
    "on_device_time":'27/12/2021 15:13:52.085',
    "on_aggreg_time":'27/12/2021 15:13:52.155',
    "parent_env_id": "Sub_Home_1"
    "ODL":       "Description",
    "temp":      23.8,
    "light":     43,
    "pressure": 101.325,
    "CO2": 56,
    "accel": [{
            "X":   0.0226898,
            "Y":  -0.382233,
            "Z":   9.54773,
        }],
    "gyro": [{
            "X":   15.022791,
            "Y":  -12.233382,
            "Z":    3.73547,
        }],
    "comp": [{
            "X":   0.6898022,
            "Y":  -2.233382,
            "Z":   5.385477,
        }],
    "quaternion": [{
            "a":   0.02,
            "b":  -0.38,
            "c":   9.54,
            "d":   5.47,
        }],
    "other": [{
            "pitch": 8.2,
            "roll": -3.8,
```

```
        "yaw":    9.54773,
    }],
  "rssi":    -65
}
```

Listing 1.2. Data format of Thingy 52 device.

Attributes *deviceID*, *on_aggreg_time* and *on_device_time* uniquely identify the document; the rest represents the data perceived by the device's sensors and the RSSI value measured by the smartphone. The *on_aggreg_time* variable represents the timestamp when the aggregator receives the data. Instead, *on_device_time* represents the timestamp when the data is perceived on the Thingy 52 device. Finally, *parent_env_id* is used to identify the (sub-)environment to which the device is collected. We want to emphasize that the transmitted data can be saved at any NoSQL database deployed on the target IP (Fig. 3(g)). Users, for analysis purposes, need only to know the data format (i.e., Listings 1.2) that the SHPIA mobile application adopts to save the data.

4   SHPIA Evaluation

This section deals with the evaluation of the performance of the SHPIA data aggregator to show the lightweight of the Android application in terms of power consumption and use of resources. In addition, it illustrates four application scenarios where SHPIA can operate. Such scenarios do not require any modification of the SHPIA platform, thus proving its versatility.

4.1   Data Aggregator Performance Evaluation

The performances of three Android smartphones with different characteristics and prices have been evaluated while acting as data aggregators for the SHPIA platform. The characteristics of the tested smartphones are reported in Table 1. Instead, Table 2 presents the results of profiling the data aggregator nodes over a collection phase of 4/4/4 h, by using five Thingy 52 with sensors sampling data set 50 Hz, 100 Hz, 200 Hz. The data aggregator nodes were placed over a table at the height of 100 cm. Instead, the Thingy devices were associated with different desks. The distance between the data aggregator and the thingy nodes varied between 2 and 7 m. Overall, the average RAM use per hour was <116 Mbh, the storage memory use was <126 Mbh[1], and the battery usage was <680 mAh[2]. On average, CPU usage and data loss were respectively 37% and 0%.

It is worth noting that smartphones executing an Android version older than v11 can be connected simultaneously with up to seven Thingy 52. Instead, smartphones running Android v11 can support the simultaneous connection with up

---

[1] Cumulative, if Internet connection is missing, e.g., 1260 Mb in 10 h without connectivity.
[2] 270 mAh excluding the results of the Honor 7S smartphone.

Table 1. Characteristics of the tested data aggregator nodes.

Model	RAM (GB)	Storage (GB)	Battery (mAh)	Weight (g)	Price ($)	Android version
Honor 7S	2	16	3020	142	78	8.1
LG X Power 2	2	16	4500	164	89	8.1
Galaxy S9	4	64	3000	163	262	10.0

Table 2. Data aggregators profiling.

	Honor 7S			Galaxy S9 Edge			LG X Power 2		
Frequency (Hz)	50	100	200	50	100	200	50	100	200
RAM (MB/h)	93	93	92	127	132	140	100	100	110
Storage (MB/h)	50	100	196	48	99	198	104	127	219
CPU (%)	35	46	55	19	21	23	40	50	50
Battery (mAh)	1150	1208	1389	360	360	390	225	450	630
Data loss (%)	0	0	0	0	0	0	0	0	0

to eleven Thingy 52. To overcome this limitation, SHPIA implements a computation balancing module that allows different smartphones (thus, different users sharing the same environment) to automatically balance the number of Thingy 52 devices connected to them and save their information on the same dataset. Thus, in practice, SHPIA can handle more than 11 Thingy devices by jointly using more than one smartphone. Moreover, this balancing process helps to further reduce smartphone battery consumption.

These results show that the proposed platform works well on different data aggregator nodes, proving there is no need to buy costly top-level smartphones to run the SHPIA application. Concerning the Thingy 52, they can efficiently operate for more than three days without recharging the battery. In addition, a lower sampling frequency would further extend the battery life consistently for both smartphone and BLE nodes [17].

4.2 SHPIA Application Scenarios

In the following, we provide an overview of four different applications exploiting the SHPIA platform: a) environmental monitoring, b) occupancy detection and counting, c) automatic data annotation of ADLs, and finally, d) virtual coaching.

Environmental Monitoring: The primary use of SHPIA is that of collecting data concerning environmental conditions. For example, we used SHPIA to monitor a working office, shown in Fig. 5, shared by ten persons. We associated the Thingy 52 devices with 5 motionless nodes (indicated by red arrows in Fig. 5) and six mobile nodes (indicated by green arrows in Fig. 5) to perceive the environment status. The Honor 7S smartphone, permanently connected to the electric current, described in Table 1 acted as a data collector. The Thinghy 52 associated with the motionless nodes were placed as follows: one at the office door, two on the windows, one on the desk at the office center, and one inside the locker. Instead, the mobile nodes were used to monitor different ODLs and the activity that employees performed on them (e.g., one Thingy 52 was attached to a bottle of water). The data collection process was conducted for two consecutive weeks.

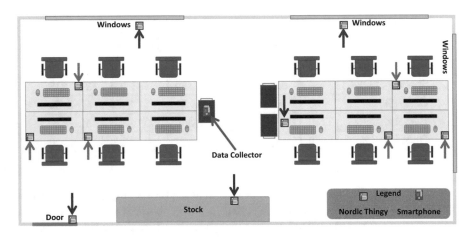

Fig. 5. Office 1.71. Motionless (red) and mobile (green) nodes and data collector (grey). (Color figure online)

Table 3 shows an overview of the collected data. The first column introduces the used sensors. The second and third columns show the sensor sampling frequency and the measurement unit. Column four shows the number of samples collected by the system during the two weeks (i.e., 1209600 s). Column five identifies the number of data sources (BLE Thingy 52 nodes). Finally, the last column shows the memory space required to store the sensed data. The last row concerns the collection of RSSI data, since the data collector extracts and associates the reception timestamp, the RSSI measure, and the emitter identity to each received BLE packet.

Once collected through SHPIA, such data were successfully used by a HAR-based analyzer to perform environmental monitoring, recognition of people's actions (e.g., drinking), and localization of ODLs and people in the environment. Because of the adopted low sampling frequency, the mobile and motionless BLE nodes perfectly worked for the overall duration of the experiments (2 weeks) without being recharged.

Occupancy Detection and Counting: Occupancy detection and counting represent a fundamental knowledge for implementing smart energy management

Table 3. Results of data collection.

Sensor type	Frequency (Hz)	Measure unit	# of samples	# of BLE devices	Stored data
Temperature	0.33	Celsius	2016000	5	≈ 15Mb
Pressure	0.33	Bar	2016000	5	≈ 15Mb
Brightness	0.33	Lux	2016000	5	≈ 15Mb
Acceleration	10	m/s^2	133056000	11	≈ 1Gb
RSSI	10	dBm	133056000	11	≈ 1Gb

Table 4. Distance estimation results based on RSSI measurements captured 60 Hz.

Regression model	5 m				3 m				2 m			
	Raw data		Features		Raw data		Features		Raw data		Features	
	RMSE	MAE	RMSE	MAE	RMSE	MAE	RMSE	MAE	RMSE	MAE	RMSE	MAE
Gradient Boosting	51	31	57	33	17	12	30	15	12	9	30	15
Random Forest	51	31	55	28	17	12	25	8	12	9	25	8
Linear	74	58	104	79	27	22	80	60	22	16	80	60
Ridge	74	58	69	45	27	22	60	39	22	16	60	39
RANSAC	84	54	113	86	28	21	85	59	43	26	82	59
Bayesian	74	58	233	158	27	22	229	171	22	16	229	171
TheilSen	78	54	96	70	29	21	89	65	24	18	89	65

systems, as well as solutions for security and safety purposes [23]. Existing techniques for occupancy detection and counting can be categorized as a) not device free [29] and b) device free [30]. The SHPIA platform provides the capability to implement both categories.

Concerning the former, SHPIA can detect a user inside an environment by estimating the distance between the user's smartphone and a Thingy 52 device associated with the environment itself, based on the RSSI measurement. To test this scenario, we evaluate the accuracy of the distance estimation between the user's smartphone and ODLs equipped with Thingy 52 node. The evaluation has been performed on three different distance ranges: a) 0–5 m, b) 0–3 m, and c) 0–2 m by using two opposite setups: i) the smartphone in the user's hand and the ODL in a fixed position, and ii) the ODL on the user's hand and the smartphone in a fixed position.

Table 4 presents the results obtained by seven different regression models trained on RSSI data perceived 60 Hz. The models were trained in two ways: by using the raw data, and by using features extracted from one-second RSSI time windows. The quality of the achieved results is shown in terms of Root Mean Square Error (RMSE) and Mean Absolute Error (MAE) while estimating the distance in centimeters between the emitter and the receiver. The Random Forest model achieved the lowest RMSE/MAE value in both the raw and the feature-based data representation. The second most performing model was Gradient Boosting. Overall, we achieved an RMSE on raw RSSI data of 51 cm in the range 0–5 m, 17 cm in the range 0–3 m, and 12 cm in the range 0–2 m. Moreover, in terms of MAE, the features performed better than the raw data: 28 cm (range 0–5 m), 8 cm (range 0–3 m), and 8 cm (range 0–5 m). Furthermore, the most essential characteristics of these regression models regard the reduced memory and computation requirements, making them suitable for running on mobile and hardware-constraint devices.

The second category of occupancy detection and counting systems behave more intelligently. In fact, users do not need to carry any device. By using SHPIA, we can detect their presence and number based on the variations of the RSSI measurements associated with the BLE signals received by the data aggregator from Thingy 52 located in the environment. The idea is that RSSI measurement fluctuations are generated by people's presence and movements inside the environment. Figure 6 shows very clearly the difference between nocturnal (red plot [8:00 PM–8:00 AM]) and diurnal (blue plot [8:00 AM–8:00 PM]) RSSI observations at the office shown in Fig. 5. The same concept is applied as regards the occupancy counting scenario (aka., identification of the number of people present inside or in the environment).

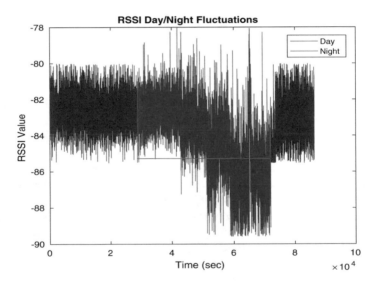

Fig. 6. Office 1.71. RSSI fluctuation between night and day for occupancy detection. (Color figure online)

We carried out tests in a university classroom (8.8 m × 8.6 m) with 15 study stations (chairs + tables) involving six different subjects. One female (29 years, 1.58 m height) and five males (25–29 years, 1.75–1.95 m height) were involved in the experiment. Subjects entered and left the environment in an undefined order with the only constraint that they must stay in the environment at least for one minute. Besides, the following environmental situations were recreated: i) all standing still, ii) all standing in motion, iii) all seated, and iv) some standing in motion and some sitting.

Table 5 presents the achieved results by using five different BLE nodes connected to SHPIA. Tests were performed over five different well-known classification models[3]. Columns two to five show results in terms of specificity, sensitivity, precision, and comprehensive accuracy. Overall, the SVM model with a linear kernel achieved the most noticeable results. Among all the other models, such a model requires higher computational capabilities; however, the Keras library provides a Quasi-SVM model implementation for Android-based mobile devices, thus enabling the SHPIA data collector recognition capabilities. By verifying the classification errors in detail, we observed that the incorrectly classified samples are related to the situation in which people inside the environment are all seated, independently by their number.

Table 5. Occupancy detection results.

Model	Specificity	Sensitivity	Precision	Accuracy
kNN	98.72%	99.10%	99.10%	99.10%
WkNN	98.29%	99.02%	99.03%	99.10%
LDA	99.83%	99.70%	99.70%	99.70%
QLDA	99.78%	99.77%	99.77%	99.77%
SVM	99.82%	99.86%	99.81%	99.82%

Table 6. Occupancy estimation results.

Regression model	Raw data		Features	
	RMSE	MAE	RMSE	MAE
Gradient Boosting	0.9	0.6	0.5	0.3
Random Forest	0.7	0.4	0.5	0.3
Linear	1.4	1.0	1.3	1.0
Ridge	1.4	1.0	2.5	4.2
RANSAC	1.8	1.3	3.3	3.3
Bayesian	1.4	1.0	2.1	2.1
TheilSen	1.9	1.2	2.0	1.8

Table 6 presents the results obtained on raw and features data concerning the occupancy counting scenario. The outcome is an estimation of the number of persons in the environment. The lower the RMSE, the higher the estimation accuracy. In particular, the proposed occupancy counting system, given a set of features identifying a one-second time window of RSSI measurements, estimates the number of people in the environment with an RMSE of 0.5 and an MAE of

---

[3] k-Nearest Neighbor (kNN), Weighted kNN (WkNN), Linear Discriminant Analysis (LDA), Quadratic LDA (QLDA), Support Vector Machine (SVM).

0.3. Using the raw dataset, we achieved an RMSE of 0.7 and an MAE of 0.4. As for the occupancy detection scenarios, the estimation error is amplified when all people inside the environment are sitting down.

Automatic Annotation of ADLs: As already mentioned in Sect. 1, one of the most significant limitations in the HAR research area concerns the creation of the learning dataset through a data annotation process. This process usually requires extensive manual work, during which at least two annotators associate data samples (e.g., perceived through inertial sensors) with labels that identify the activity (e.g., sleeping, eating, drinking, cooking, and many others) based on a video recording of the context. SHPIA can automatically annotate these activities by assigning a Thingy 52 device to specific objects or locations in the environment (e.g., by associating the Thingy 52 to the eating table, to the working desk, the bottle of water, the bed, etc.) and by estimating the distance between the data collector (i.e., the smartphone that the user is carrying) and the Thingy 52. Thus, when the user is eating, SHPIA assigns the label "eating" to the data collected from the smartphone, based on the estimated distance between the nearest Thingy 52 (i.e., the one on the table) and the user's smartphone. Preliminary results in this direction [8] showed that the approach works properly for activities requiring more than 30 s to be performed (e.g., intensively washing hands, or cooking).

Virtual Coaching: Virtual coaching capabilities can be easily supported by the SHPIA platform. A virtual coaching system (VCS) is an ubiquitous system that supports people with cognitive or physical impairments in learning new behaviors and avoiding unwanted ones. By exploiting SHPIA, we set up a VCS comprising a set of smart objects used to identify the user needs and to react accordingly. For example, let us imagine a person requiring a new medical treatment based on pill's assumption that initially forgets to respect the therapy. By attaching a BLE tag to the pills container SHPIA can monitor pills assumption. The user carries the smartphone (e.g., into the pocket), and when he/she approaches the pills container, SHPIA estimates the distance between the user and the container. It can also understand when the user opens and closes the cap based on the received motion information emitted by the BLE tag attached to the container. Thus, it is possible to understand, with greater accuracy, whether the user has taken medicines or not. If the person does not take medicines, the system warns him. Otherwise, the system remains silent. A prototype of such a system has been proposed in [10].

5   Conclusions

This paper presented SHPIA, a platform exploiting low-cost BLE devices and an Android mobile application that transforms ODLs into smart objects. It allows effective and efficient data collection for implementing various solutions in smart home and HAR scenarios. SHPIA works in a ubiquitous and non-invasive way, using only privacy-preserving devices such as inertial and environmental sensors. Its versatility has been evaluated by discussing four monitoring scenarios concerning the automatic data annotation of ADLs, occupancy detection and counting, coaching systems, and environmental monitoring. Moreover, despite the mentioned scenarios, SHPIA can be easily used in other scenarios such as industrial, smart buildings, smart cities, or human activity recognition. Nevertheless, although we have already implemented a computation balancing system that overcomes SHPIAs scalability issue, further work is required to overcome such weakness. Therefore, besides making open-source SHPIA, we intend to integrate BLE broadcasting communication technology in future developments, thus increasing the number of supported BLE devices per smartphone to hypothetically infinite.

References

1. SHPIA (2022). https://github.com/IoT4CareLab/SHPIA/
2. Abdallah, Z.S., Gaber, M.M., Srinivasan, B., Krishnaswamy, S.: Activity recognition with evolving data streams: a review. ACM Comput. Surv. (CSUR) **51**(4), 71 (2018)
3. Acampora, G., Cook, D.J., Rashidi, P., Vasilakos, A.V.: A survey on ambient intelligence in healthcare. Proc. IEEE **101**(12), 2470–2494 (2013)
4. Balakrishnan, M.: ASSISTECH: an accidental journey into assistive technology. In: Chen, J.-J. (ed.) A Journey of Embedded and Cyber-Physical Systems, pp. 57–77. Springer, Cham (2021). https://doi.org/10.1007/978-3-030-47487-4_5
5. Bouchabou, D., Nguyen, S.M., Lohr, C., LeDuc, B., Kanellos, I., et al.: A survey of human activity recognition in smart homes based on IoT sensors algorithms: taxonomies, challenges, and opportunities with deep learning. Sensors **21**(18), 6037 (2021)
6. Cook, D.J., Crandall, A.S., Thomas, B.L., Krishnan, N.C.: Casas: a smart home in a box. Computer **46**(7), 62–69 (2013)
7. Cook, D.J., et al.: Mavhome: an agent-based smart home. In: Proceedings of the First IEEE International Conference on Pervasive Computing and Communications (PerCom 2003), pp. 521–524. IEEE (2003)
8. Demrozi, F., Jereghi, M., Pravadelli, G.: Towards the automatic data annotation for human activity recognition based on wearables and BLE beacons. In: 2021 IEEE International Symposium on Inertial Sensors and Systems (INERTIAL), pp. 1–4. IEEE (2021)
9. Demrozi, F., Pravadelli, G., Bihorac, A., Rashidi, P.: Human activity recognition using inertial, physiological and environmental sensors: a comprehensive survey. IEEE Access **8**, 210816–210836 (2020)
10. Demrozi, F., Serlonghi, N., Turetta, C., Pravadelli, C., Pravadelli, G.: Exploiting bluetooth low energy smart tags for virtual coaching. In: 2021 IEEE 7th World Forum on Internet of Things (WF-IoT), pp. 470–475. IEEE (2021)
11. Ehlers, G.A., Beaudet, J.: System and method of controlling an HVAC system, US Patent 7,130,719, 31 October 2006
12. Fernández-Caramés, T.M., Fraga-Lamas, P.: A review on human-centered IoT-connected smart labels for the industry 4.0. IEEE Access **6**, 25939–25957 (2018). https://doi.org/10.1109/ACCESS.2018.2833501

13. Gram-Hanssen, K., Darby, S.J.: Home is where the smart is? Evaluating smart home research and approaches against the concept of home. Energy Res. Soc. Sci. **37**, 94–101 (2018)
14. Granja, C., Janssen, W., Johansen, M.A.: Factors determining the success and failure of ehealth interventions: systematic review of the literature. J. Med. Internet Res. **20**(5), e10235 (2018)
15. Jeong, S., Kim, T., Eskicioglu, R.: Human activity recognition using motion sensors. In: Proceedings of the 16th ACM Conference on Embedded Networked Sensor Systems, pp. 392–393 (2018)
16. Keller, M., Olney, B., Karam, R.: A secure and efficient cloud-connected body sensor network platform. In: Camarinha-Matos, L.M., Heijenk, G., Katkoori, S., Strous, L. (eds.) IFIP International Internet of Things Conference, pp. 197–214. Springer, Cham (2021). https://doi.org/10.1007/978-3-030-96466-5_13
17. Kindt, P.H., Yunge, D., Diemer, R., Chakraborty, S.: Energy modeling for the bluetooth low energy protocol. ACM Trans. Embed. Comput. Syst. (TECS) **19**(2), 1–32 (2020)
18. Kirimtat, A., Krejcar, O., Kertesz, A., Tasgetiren, M.F.: Future trends and current state of smart city concepts: a survey. IEEE Access **8**, 86448–86467 (2020)
19. Krishnan, N.C., Cook, D.J.: Activity recognition on streaming sensor data. Pervasive Mob. Comput. **10**, 138–154 (2014)
20. Pourbehzadi, M., Niknam, T., Kavousi-Fard, A., Yilmaz, Y.: IoT in smart grid: energy management opportunities and security challenges. In: Casaca, A., Katkoori, S., Ray, S., Strous, L. (eds.) IFIPIoT 2019. IAICT, vol. 574, pp. 319–327. Springer, Cham (2020). https://doi.org/10.1007/978-3-030-43605-6_19
21. Rachakonda, L., Mohanty, S.P., Kougianos, E.: cStick: a calm stick for fall prediction, detection and control in the IoMT framework. In: Camarinha-Matos, L.M., Heijenk, G., Katkoori, S., Strous, L. (eds.) IFIP International Internet of Things Conference, pp. 129–145. Springer, Cham (2021). https://doi.org/10.1007/978-3-030-96466-5_9
22. Rashidi, P., Mihailidis, A.: A survey on ambient-assisted living tools for older adults. IEEE J. Biomed. Health Inform. **17**(3), 579–590 (2013)
23. Salimi, S., Hammad, A.: Critical review and research roadmap of office building energy management based on occupancy monitoring. Energy Build. **182**, 214–241 (2018)
24. Skubic, M., Alexander, G., Popescu, M., Rantz, M., Keller, J.: A smart home application to eldercare: current status and lessons learned. Technol. Health Care **17**(3), 183–201 (2009)
25. VandeWeerd, C., et al.: Homesense: design of an ambient home health and wellness monitoring platform for older adults. Heal. Technol. **10**(5), 1291–1309 (2020)
26. Wang, J., Spicher, N., Warnecke, J.M., Haghi, M., Schwartze, J., Deserno, T.M.: Unobtrusive health monitoring in private spaces: the smart home. Sensors **21**(3), 864 (2021)
27. Wang, Y., Yalcin, A., VandeWeerd, C.: Health and wellness monitoring using ambient sensor networks. J. Ambient Intell. Smart Environ. **12**(2), 139–151 (2020)
28. Wu, J., Feng, Y., Sun, P.: Sensor fusion for recognition of activities of daily living. Sensors **18**(11), 4029 (2018)
29. Yang, J., et al.: Comparison of different occupancy counting methods for single system-single zone applications. Energy Build. **172**, 221–234 (2018)
30. Zou, H., Zhou, Y., Yang, J., Spanos, C.J.: Device-free occupancy detection and crowd counting in smart buildings with WiFi-enabled IoT. Energy Build. **174**, 309–322 (2018)

A Visible Light Communication System to Support Indoor Guidance

Manuela Vieira[1,2,3](✉) ⓘ, Manuel Augusto Vieira[1,2] ⓘ, Paula Louro[1,2] ⓘ,
and Pedro Vieira[1,4] ⓘ

[1] Electronics Telecommunication and Computer Department, ISEL, Lisboa, Portugal
mv@isel.ipl.pt
[2] CTS-UNINOVA, Caparica, Portugal
[3] DEE-FCT-UNL, Caparica, Portugal
[4] Instituto de Telecomunicações, IST, Lisboa, Portugal

Abstract. Toward supporting people's wayfinding activities, we propose a Visible Light Communication (VLC) cooperative system with guidance services and fog/edge based architectures. The dynamic navigation system is made up of several transmitters (ceiling luminaries) that transmit map information and path messages for wayfinding. Each luminaire includes one of two types of controller: a "mesh" controller that communicates with other devices in its vicinity, effectively acting as a router for messages to other nodes in the network, or a "mesh/cellular" hybrid controller that communicates with the central manager via IP. Edge computing can be performed by these nodes, which act as border routers. Mobile optical receivers, using joint transmission, collect the data at high frame rates, extracts theirs location to perform positioning and, concomitantly, the transmitted data from each transmitter. Each luminaire, through VLC, reports its geographic position and specific information to the users, making it available for whatever use. A bidirectional communication process is carried out and the optimal path through the venue is determined. Results show that the system offers not only self-localization, but also inferred travel direction and the ability to interact with received information optimizing the route towards a static or dynamic destination.

Keywords: Visible Light Communication · Assisted indoor navigation · Bidirectional communication · Optical sensors · Transmitter/receiver · Edge-Fog architecture

1 Introduction

The main goal is to specify the system conceptual design and define a set of use cases for a VLC based guidance system to be used by mobile users inside large buildings.

With the increasing shortage of radio frequency spectrum and the development of Light-Emitting Diodes (LEDs), VLC has attracted extensive attention. Compared to conventional wireless communications, VLC has higher rates, lower power consumption, and less electromagnetic interferences. VLC is a data transmission technology that can

L. M. Camarinha-Matos et al. (Eds.): IFIPIoT 2022, IFIP AICT 665, pp. 235–252, 2022.
https://doi.org/10.1007/978-3-031-18872-5_14

easily be employed in indoor environments since it can use the existing LED lighting infrastructure with simple modifications [1, 2].Visible light can be used as an Identifier (ID) system and can be employed for identifying the building itself. The main idea is to divide the service area into spatial beams originating from the different ID light sources and identify each beam with a unique timed sequence of light signals. The signboards, based on arrays of LEDs, positioned in strategic directions [3], are modulated acting as down- and up-link channels in the bidirectional communication. For the consumer services, the applications are enormous. Positioning, navigation, security and even mission critical services are possible use cases that should be implemented. The use of white polychromatic LEDs offers the possibility of Wavelength Division Multiplexing (WDM), which enhances the transmission data rate. A WDM receiver based on tandem a-SiC:H/a-Si:H pin/pin light controlled filter can be used [4, 5] to decode the received information. Here, when different visible signals are encoded in the same optical transmission path, the device multiplexes the different optical channels, performs different filtering processes (amplification, switching, and wavelength conversion) and finally decodes the encoded signals recovering the transmitted information.

In this paper, a VLC based guidance system to be used by mobile users inside large buildings is proposed. After the Introduction, in Sect. 2, a model for the system is proposed and the communication system described. In Sect. 3, the main experimental results are presented, downlink and uplink transmission is implemented and the best route to navigate calculated. In Sect. 4, the conclusions are drawn.

1.1 Background on Wireless Guidance Services

Interaction between planning, control, and localization is important. The localization (Where am I?) senses the environment and computes the user position, the planning (Where am I going?) computes the route to follow from the position, and the control (How do I get there?) moves the user in order to follow the route. A destination can be targeted by user request to the Central Manager (CM).

Geolocation refers to the identification of the geographic location of a user or computing device via a variety of data collection mechanisms. Multi-device connectivity can tell users, from any device, where they are, where they need to be and what they need to do after arrival. Typically, most geolocation services use network routing addresses or internal Global Positioning System (GPS) devices to determine location. With the help of the GPS, outdoor positioning becomes full-fledged and can be regarded as accurate in most application scenarios. However, indoor positioning is still far from maturity, because of the complex indoor electromagnetic propagation environment. Indoor positioning methods are mainly based on Wi-Fi, Bluetooth, Radio-Frequency Identification (RFID) and Visible Light Communications (VLC) [6, 7, 8]. Accurate and reliable indoor positioning services will change the living habits of mobile users. Moreover, there is a growing consensus that accurate indoor positioning might not be viable by solely utilizing RF communications. Such application is highly expected to be realized in the next 6th Generation (6G) era, giving birth to more advanced non-RF communication technologies.

With the rapid increase in wireless mobile devices, the continuous increase of wireless data traffic has brought challenges to the continuous reduction of radio frequency (RF) spectrum, which has also driven the demand for alternative technologies [9, 10]. In order to solve the contradiction between the explosive growth of data and the consumption of spectrum resources, VLC has become the development direction of the next generation communication network with its huge spectrum resources, high security, low cost, and so on [11, 12].

To conduct the research, the following questions are considered: Would it be possible to implement a reliable VLC system to support indoor guidance? Can the combined VLC location of modulated LED ceiling luminaires and the stored network edge data from different users provide valuable information about users' movements within a public building? How can lighting plans and building models affect multi-person cooperative localization and guidance?

The proposed guidance system considers wireless communication, computer based algorithms, smart sensor and optical sources network, which stands out as a transdisciplinary approach framed in cyber-physical systems.

2   System Model

The main goal is to specify the system conceptual design and define a set of use cases for a VLC based guidance system to be used by mobile users inside large buildings.

2.1   Communication System

The system model is composed by two modules: the transmitter and the receiver. The block diagram is presented in Fig. 1. Both communication modules are software defined, where modulation/demodulation can be programed.

Data from the sender is converted into an intermediate data representation, byte format, and converted into light signals emitted by the transmitter module. The data bit stream is input to a modulator where an ON–OFF Keying (OOK) modulation is utilized. On the transmission side, a modulation and conversion from digital to analog data is done. The driver circuit will keep an average value (DC power level) for illumination, combining it with the analog data intended for communication. The visible light emitted by the LEDs passes through the transmission medium and is then received by the MUX device.

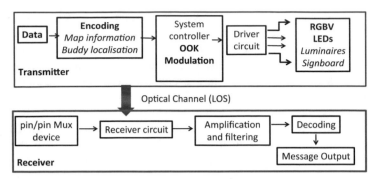

Fig. 1. Block diagram. System model of the proposed control scheme applied to OOK modulation.

To realize both the communication and the building illumination, white light tetra-chromatic sources (WLEDs) are used providing a different data channel for each chip. The transmitter and receiver relative positions are displayed in Fig. 2a.

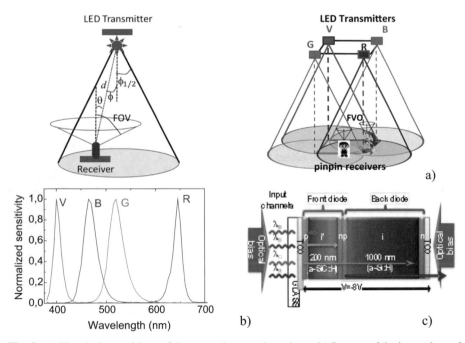

Fig. 2. a) 3D relative positions of the transmitters and receivers. b) Spectra of the input channels. c) Configuration and operation of the pin/pin Mux device. (Color figure online)

Each luminaire is composed of four polichromatic WLEDs framed at the corners of a square. At each node, only one chip is modulated for data transmission (see Fig. 2b), the Red (R: 626 nm, 25 μW/cm^2), the Green (G: 530 nm, 46 μW/cm^2), the Blue (B: 470 nm, 60 μW/cm^2) or the Violet (V, 400 nm, 150 μW/cm^2). Data is encoded, modulated and converted into light signals emitted by the transmitters. Modulation and digital-to-analog conversion of the information bits is done using signal processing techniques. An OOK modulation scheme was used to code the information. This way digital data is represented by the presence or absence of a carrier wave.

The signal is propagating through the optical channel, and a VLC receiver, at the reception end of the communication link, is responsible to extract the data from the modulated light beam. It transforms the light signal into an electrical signal that is subsequently decoded to extract the transmitted information. The obtained voltage is then processed, by using signal conditioning techniques (adaptive bandpass filtering and amplification, triggering and demultiplexing), until the data signal is reconstructed at the data processing unit (digital conversion, decoding and decision) [13]. At last, the message will be output to the users.

In the receiving system, a MUX photodetector acts as an active filter for the visible spectrum. The integrated filter consists of a p-I'(a-SiC:H)-n/p-i(a-Si:H)-n heterostructure with low conductivity doped layers [7] as displayed in Fig. 2c. Independent tuning of each channel is performed by steady state violet optical bias ($\lambda_{bias} = 2300\ \mu W/cm^2$) superimposed from the front side of the device and the generated photocurrent measured at -8 V. The generated photocurrent is processed using a transimpedance circuit obtaining a proportional voltage. Since the photodetector response is insensitive to the frequency, phase, or polarization of the carriers, this kind of receiver is useful for intensity-modulated signals. After receiving the signal, it is in turn filtered, amplified, and converted back to digital format for demodulation. The system controller consists of a set of programmable modules.

In this system model, there are a few assumptions that should be noted: The channel state information is available both at the receiver and the transmitter; compared with the direct light, the reflected light is much weaker in the indoor VLC systems; only the Line Of Sight (LOS) path is considered and the multipath influence is not considered in the proposed indoor VLC system.

The received channel can be expresssed as:

$$y = \mu hx + n \tag{1}$$

where y represents the received signal, x the transmitted signal, μ is the photoelectric conversion factor which can be normalized as $\mu = 1$, h is the channel gain and n is the additive white Gaussian noise of which the mean is 0.

The LEDs are modeled as Lambertian sources where the luminance is distributed uniformly in all directions, whereas the luminous intensity is different in all directions. The luminous intensity for a Lambertian source is given by Eq. 2 [14]:

$$I(\emptyset) = I_N \cos(\emptyset)^m;\ m = \frac{\ln(2)}{\ln(\cos(\phi_{1/2}))} \tag{2}$$

I_N is the maximum luminous intensity in the axial direction, ϕ is the angle of irradiance and m is the order derived from a Lambertian pattern. For the proposed system, the commercial white LEDs were designed for illumination purposes, exhibiting a wide half intensity angle ($\phi_{1/2}$) of 60°. Thus, the Lambertian order m is 1. Friis' transmission equation is frequently used to calculate the maximum range by which a wireless link can operate. The coverage map is obtained by calculating the link budget from the Friis Transmission Equation [15]. The Friis transmission equation relates the received power (P_R) to the transmitted power (P_E), path loss distance (L_R), and gains from the emitter (G_E) and receiver (G_R) in a free-space communication link.

$$P_{R\,[dBm]} = P_{E\,[dBm]} + G_{E\,[dB]} + G_{R\,[dB]} - L_{R\,[dB]} \tag{3}$$

Taking into account Fig. 2a, the path loss distance and the emitter gain will be given by:

$$L_{R[dB]} = 22 + 20\ln\frac{d}{\lambda} \tag{4}$$

$$G_{E\,[dB]} = \frac{(m+1)A}{2\pi d_{E-R}^2}I(\varnothing)\cos(\theta) \tag{5}$$

With A de area of the photodetector and d_{E_R} the distance between each transmitter and every point on the receiver plane. Due to their filtering properties of the receptors the gains are strongly dependent on the wavelength of the pulsed LEDs. Gains (G_R) of 5, 4, 1.7 and 0.8 were used, respectively, for the R, G, B and V LEDs. I_N of 730 mcd, 650 mcd, 800 mcd and 900 mcd were considered.

Taking into account Eqs. 1–5, the coverage map for a square unit cell is displayed in Fig. 3. All the values were converted to decibel (dB).

In order to receive information from several transmitters, the receiver must position itself so that the circles corresponding to the range of each transmitter overlap (Fig. 2a). This results in a multiplexed (MUX) signal that acts both as a positioning system and as a data transmitter. The grid sizes were chosen to avoid overlap in the receiver from adjacent grid points. The nine possible overlaps (#1–#9), defined as fingerprint regions, as well as receiver orientations (2–9 steering angles; δ) are also pointed out for the unit square cell, in Fig. 3, respectively.

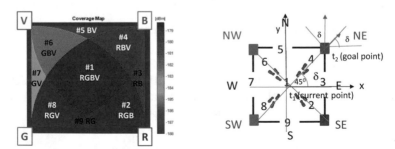

Fig. 3. Illustration of the coverage map in the unit cell: footprint regions (#1–#9) and steering angle codes (2–9).

The input of the aided navigation system is the pose, $q(t) = q(x(t), y(t), z(t), \delta(t))$, a coded signal sent by the transmitters to an identified user (I2D), which includes its position in the network and the steering angle, δ, which directs the user along the path at the given moment, t. The device receives multiple signals, finds the centroid of the received coordinates, and stores it as the reference point position. Nine reference points, for each unit cell, are identified giving a fine-grained resolution in the localization of the mobile device across each cell.

2.2 Lighting Plan Layout and Building Model

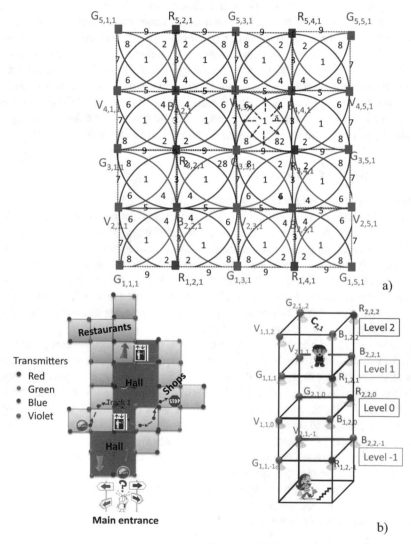

Fig. 4. a) Illustration of the optical scenarios (RGBV = modulated LEDs spots). Clusters of cells in square topology. b) Indoor layout and proposed scenario.

In VLC geotracking, geographic coordinates are generated, but the feature's usefulness is enhanced by using them to determine a meaningful location, to guide the user through an unfamiliar building, or to lead him to his desired meeting destination.

Lighting in large environments is designed to illuminate the entire space in a uniform way. Ceiling plans for the LED array layout is shown in Fig. 4a. A square lattice topology was considered. Here, cells have squares shapes to form an orthogonal shaped constellation with the modulated RGBV LEDs at the nodes.

Building a geometry model of buildings' interiors is complex. Each room/crossing/exit represents a node, and a path as the links between nodes. The proposed scenario is illustrated in Fig. 4b. The user positions can be represented as P (x, y, z) by providing the horizontal positions (x, y) and the correct floor number z. The ground floor is level 0 and the user can go both below $(z < 0)$ and above $(z > 0)$ from there. In this study, the 3D model generation is based on footprints of a multi-level building that are collected from available sources (luminaires), and are displayed on the user receiver for user orientation. It is a requirement that the destination can be targeted by user request to the CM and that floor changes are notified. Each unit cell can be referred as $C_{i,j,k}$ were i, j, k are the x, y position in the square unit cell of the top left node (Fig. 4b).

2.3   Architecture and Geolocation

Fog/Edge computing bridges the gap between the cloud and end devices by enabling computing, storage, networking, and data management on network nodes within the close vicinity of IoT devices. Fog computing has advantages since it provides moderate availability of computing resources at lower power consumption. Computing resources may be used for caching at the edge of the network, which enables faster retrieval of content and a lower burden on the front-haul. A hybrid Edge/Fog Computing is as effective as the Cloud even considering that it has less available data and less computational power. In edge computing, the computation is done at the edge of the network through small data centers that are close to users [16].

A mesh cellular hybrid structure to create a gateway-less system is proposed. This architecture consists of VLC-ready access equipment, that provide the computing resources, end devices, and a controller that is in charge of receiving service requests and distributing tasks to fog nodes. The luminaires, are equipped with one of two types of controllers: A "mesh" controller that connects with other nodes in its vicinity and can forward messages to other devices (I2D) in the mesh, effectively acting like routers nodes in the network. A "mesh/cellular" hybrid controller, that is also equipped with a modem providing IP base connectivity to the central manager services (I2CM). These nodes act as border-routers and can be used for edge computing. So, edge computing is located at the edge of the network close to end-user devices. A mesh network is a good fit since it dynamically reconfigures itself and grows with the size of any installation. In Fig. 5 the proposed architecture is illustrated.

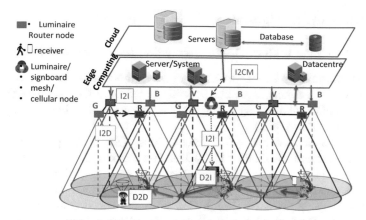

Fig. 5. Mesh and cellular hybrid architecture.

A user navigates from outdoor to indoor. It sends a request message to find the right track (D2I) and, in the available time, he adds customized points of interest (wayfinding services). The requested information (I2D) is sent by the emitters at the ceiling to its receiver. Under this architecture, the short-range mesh network purpose is twofold: enable edge computing and device-to-cloud communication, by ensuring a secure communication from a luminaire controller to the edge computer or datacenter (I2CM), through a neighbor luminaire/signboard controller with an active cellular connection; and enable peer-to-peer communication (I2I), to exchange information.

The polychromatic WLEDs are placed on the ceiling in a square lattice topology (see Fig. 4), but only one, chip is modulated (R, G, B, V). The principle is that each WLED transmits a VLC signal with a unique identifier. The optical receiver uses this information and a position algorithm, based on the received joint transmission, calculates the track of the user.

The indoor route throughout the building (track; $q(x, y, z, \delta, t)$) is presented to the user by a responding message (I2D) transmitted by the ceiling luminaires that work also either as router or mesh/cellular nodes.

Two-way communication (D2I-I2D) between users and the infrastructure is carried out through a neighbor luminaire/signboard controller with an active cellular connection (I2CM). With this request/response concept, the generated landmark-based instructions help the user to unambiguously identify the correct decision point where a change of direction (pose, $q_i(x, y, z, \delta, t)$) is needed, as well as offer information for the user to confirm that he/she is on the right way.

3 Geotracking, Navigation and Route Control

3.1 Communication Protocol, Coding/Decoding Techniques and Error Control

To code the information, an On-Off Keying (OOK) modulation scheme was used and it was considered a synchronous transmission based on a 64- bits data frame. This modulation, despite not allowing a high bit rate, benefits from a better performance in terms of Bit Error Rate (BER).

The frame is divided into six different blocks (Sync, ID, pin1/pin2, Angle δ, Request/Response and Wayfinding Data).The first block is the synchronization block [10101], the last is the payload data (traffic message) and a stop bit ends the frame. The second block, the ID block, $4 + 4 + 4$ bits, gives the geolocation (x, y, z coordinates) of the emitters inside the array ($X_{i,j,k}$). Cell's IDs are encoded using a 4 bits binary representation for the decimal number. When bidirectional communication is required, the user has to register by choosing a user name (pin_1) with 4 decimal numbers, each one associated to a RGBV channel. If buddy friend services are required a 4-binary code of the meeting (pin_2) has to be inserted. The δ block (steering angle (δ)) completes the pose in a frame time q(x, y, δ, t). Eight steering angles along the cardinal points are possible from a start point to the next goal (Fig. 3). The codes assigned to the pin_2 and to δ are the same in all the channels. If no wayfinding services are required these last three blocks are set at zero and the user only receives its own location. The last block is used to transmit the wayfinding message.

Using the photocurrent signal measured by the photodetector, it is necessary to decode the received information. A calibration curve is previously defined to establish this assignment [17]. As displayed in Fig. 6a, calibration curves make use of 16 distinct photocurrent thresholds which correspond to a bit sequence that allows all the sixteen combinations of the four RGBV input channels (2^4). If the calibrated levels (d_0–d_{15}) are compared to the different four-digit binary codes assigned to each level, then the decoding is obvious, and the message may be read. The correct use of this calibration curve demands a periodic retransmission of curve to ensure an accurate correspondence to the output signal and an accurate decoding of the transmitted information.

Due to the proximity of successive levels occasional errors occur in the decoded information. A parity check is performed after the word has been read [18]. The parity bits are the SUM bits of the three-bit additions of violet pulsed signal with two additional RGB bits and defined as:

$$P_R = V \oplus R \oplus B; P_G = V \oplus R \oplus G; P_B = V \oplus G \oplus B \qquad (6)$$

In Fig. 6a, the MUX signal that arises from the transmission of the four calibrated RGBV wavelength channels and the MUX signal that results from the generation of the synchronized parity MUX are displayed. On the top the seven bit word [R,G,B,V, P_R, P_G, P_B] of the transmitted inputs guides the eyes. The colors red, green, blue and violet were assigned respectively to P_R, P_G and P_B. For simplicity the received data ($d_{0–15}$ levels) is marked in the correspondent MUX slots as well as the parity levels marked as horizontal lines. On the top the decoded 7-bit coded word is exhibited. In the right side 4-bit binary codes assigned to the eight parity sublevels are inserted.

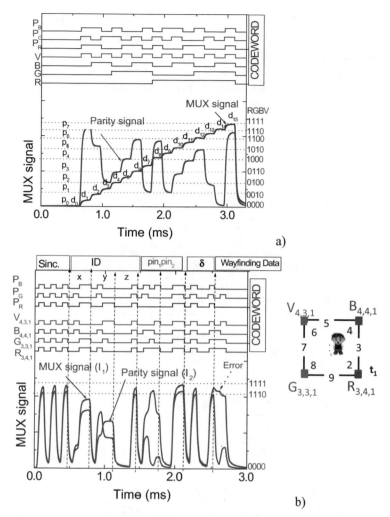

Fig. 6. Code and parity MUX/DEMUX signals. On the top the transmitted channels [R G B V: P_R P_G P_B] are shown. a) Calibrated cell. b) Error control assigned to a request from user "7261" at $C_{4,3,1}$; #1 N.

The traffic message is revealed by decoding MUX signals and considering the frame structure, pose, and transmitter type [19]. In Fig. 6b we illustrate how error control is achieved using check parity bits. A request from user "7261" is shown at $C_{4,3,1}$; #1 N, along with the matching parity signal. Results show that without check parity bits, decoding was difficult primarily when levels were close together (dotted arrow).

To automate the process of recovering the original transmitted data, an algorithm was developed. The transmitted data is decoded by comparing the code MUX signal with the parity MUX levels. The decoding algorithm is based on a proximity search [20]. For each time slot, the data are translated into a vector in multidimensional space, which is determined by the signal currents I_1 and I_2, where I_1 is the d level and I_2 is the p level for the 4-bit codeword (RGBV). The corresponding parity levels, [P_R, P_G P_B] in the respective time slot are also obtained and are assumed to be correct. The result is then compared with all vectors resulting from the calibration sequence (Fig. 6a) where each code level, d (0–15) is assigned the corresponding parity level, p (0–7). Eucledian metrics are used to calculate distances.

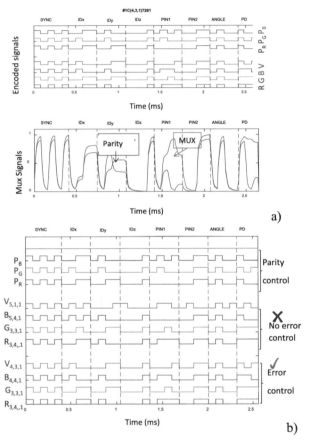

Fig. 7. Encoding/decoding process with and without check parity error. a) Transmitted code signals [R G B V: P_R P_G P_B] and received MUX and Parity signals. b) Decoded information with and without error control assigned to a request from user "7261" at cell $C_{4,3,1}$ #1 NE.

The tests were done with a variety of random sequences, and we were able to recover the original colour bits, as shown in the top of the figure. In Fig. 7 illustrates the encoding/decoding process with and without check parity error. In Fig. 7a, the encoded optical signals (codewords) and the experimental received signals are depicted. After encoding, Fig. 7b shows how information can be recovered with and without error control. The encoded signals transmitted by the LEDs are determined through the interpolation of the signals received by the photodiode, (Mux and Parity, Fig. 6b), with the calibration curves (Fig. 6a). According to the results for the analysing cases, the BER is high (4.6%) without error correction while it is negligible with error correction.

3.2 Fine-Grained Indoor Localization and Navigation

In Fig. 8, the MUX received signal and the decoding information that allows the VLC geotracking and guidance in successive instants (t_0, t_1, t_2) from user "7261" guiding him along his track is exemplified. The visualized cells, paths, and the reference points (footprints) are also shown as inserts.

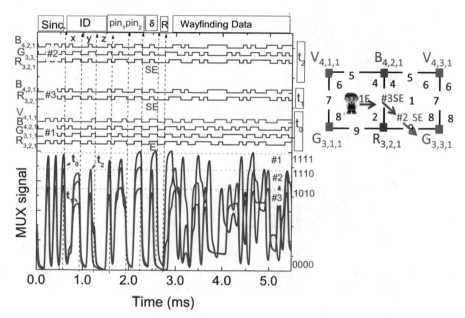

Fig. 8. Fine-grained indoor localization and navigation in successive instants. On the top the transmitted channels packets are decoded [R, G, B, V].

Data shows that at t_0 the network location of the received signals is $R_{3,2,1}$, $G_{3,1,1}$, $B_{4,2,1}$ and $V_{4,1,1}$, at t_1 the user receives the signal only from the $R_{3,2,1}$, $B_{4,2,1}$ nodes and at t_2 he was moved to the next cell since the node $G_{3,1,1}$ was added at the receiver. Hence, the mobile user 7261 begins his route into position #1 (t_0) and wants to be directed to his goal position, in the next cell (# 9). During the route the navigator is guided to E (code 3) and, at t_1, steers to SE (code 2), cross footprint #2 (t_3) and arrives to #9. The ceiling lamps (landmarks) spread over all the building and act as edge/fog nodes in the network, providing well-structured paths that maintain a navigator's orientation with respect to both the next landmark along the path and the distance to the eventual destination. Also, the VLC dynamic system enables cooperative and oppositional geolocation. In some cases, it is in the user's interest to be accurately located, so that they can be offered information relevant to their location and orientation (pin_1, pin_2 and δ blocks). In other cases, users prefer not to disclose their location for privacy, in this case these last three blocks are set at zero and the user only receives its own location.

3.3 Multi-person Cooperative Localization and Guidance Services

Via the control manager, a handheld device with VLC connectivity communicates bidirectionally with a signboard receiver in each unit cell (#1). Each user (D2I) uplinks to the local controller a "request" message with the pose, q_i (t), (x, y, z, δ), user code (pin$_1$) and also adds its needs (code meeting and wayfinding data). For route coordination the CM, using the information of the network's VLC location capability, downlinks a personalized "response" message to each client at the requested pose with his wayfinding needs (I2D).

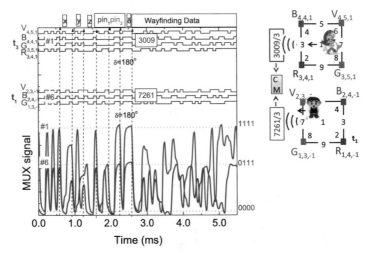

Fig. 9. MUX/DEMUX signals assigned requests from two users ("3009" and "7261") at different poses ($C_{4,4,,1}$; #1W and $C_{2,3,-1}$; #6 W) and in successive instants (t_1 and t_3).

In Fig. 9, the MUX synchronized signals received by two users that have requested guidance services, at different times, are displayed. We have assumed that a user located at $C_{2,3,-1}$, arrived first (t_1), auto-identified as ("7261") and informed the controller of his intention to find a friend for a previously scheduled meeting (code 3). A buddy list is then generated and will include all the users who have the same meeting code. User "3009" arrives later (t_3), sends the alert notification ($C_{4,4,1}$; t_3) to be triggered when his friend is in his floor vicinity, level 1, identifies himself ("3009") and uses the same code (code 3), to track the best way to his meeting.

Upon receiving this request (t_3), the buddy finder service uses the location information from both devices to determine the proximity of their owners (q_{ij} (t)) and provides the best route to the meeting, avoiding crowded areas.

The pedestrian movement along the path can be thought as a queue, where the pedestrians arrive at a path, wait if the path is congested and then move once the congestion reduces. In Fig. 10, a graphical representation of the simultaneous localization and mapping problem using connectivity as a function of node density, mobility and transmission range is illustrated.

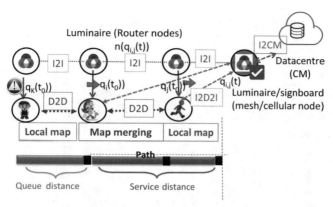

Fig. 10. Graphical representation of the simultaneous localization and mapping problem using connectivity as a function of node density, mobility and transmission range.

The following parameters are therefore needed to model the queuing system: The initial arrival time (t_0) and the path, defined as the time when the pedestrian leaves the previous path and the actual movement along the path, q_i (t, t'). Here, the service time is calculated using walking speed and distance of the path. The number of service units or resources is determined by the capacity of the pathway, $n(q_i$ $(x, y, z, \delta, t))$ and walking speed which depends on the number of request services, and on the direction of movement along the pathway q_i (x, y, z, δ, t). The pedestrians are served as soon as the request message is appended by the CM (response message).

If the number of pedestrians exceeds the path capacity, a backlog is automatically formed until the starting node. The hybrid controller integrates the number of requests and individual positions received during the same time interval. Once the individual positions are known, q_i (t), the relative positions are calculated, q_{ij} (t). If the relative position is less than a threshold distance (around 2 m), a crowded region locally exists, and an alert message is sent for the users. An example of the MUX signals assigned to a request/response received by user "3009" during his path to reach user "7261" is displayed in Fig. 11. In the top of the figure, the decoded information is shown and the simulated scenario is inserted to guide the eyes.

The "request" message includes, beyond synchronism, the identification of the user ("3009"), its address and orientation, $q_i(t)$, ($C_{4,4,1}$, #1W) and the help requested (Wayfinding Data). Since a meet-up between users is expected, its code was inserted before the right track request. In the "response", the block CM identifies the CM [0000] and the next blocks the cell address ($C_{4,4,1}$), the user (3009) for which the message is intended and finally the requested information: meeting code 3, orientation NE (code 4) and wayfinding instructions.

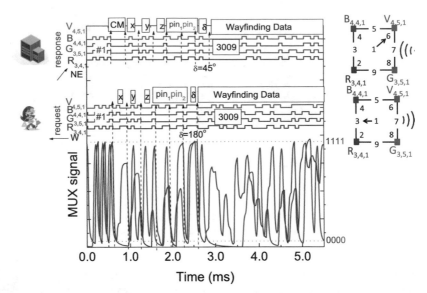

Fig. 11. a) Request from user "3009" and response from the CM to him. On the top the transmitted channels packets are decoded [$X_{i,j,k}$].

Every time a user switches floors he has to notify the CM. In response to the estimated relative pose position, $q_{i,j}$ (t), between the users with the same meeting code, the CM sends a new alert that takes into account the occupancy of the service areas along the paths, q_i (x, y, z, δ, t), which optimizes the path without crowding the users.

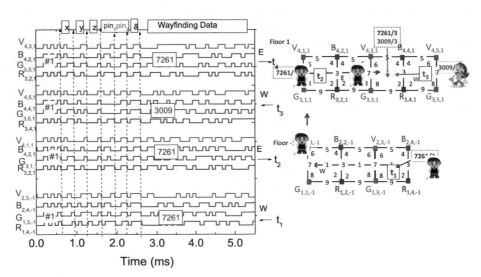

Fig. 12. Decoded messages from the two users as they travel to a pre-scheduled meeting.

Whenever the CM sends users wayfinding service alerts, it recalculates the best route in real time, so that users are not directed to crowded areas. In Fig. 12, the decoded messages from the two users as they travel to the pre-scheduled meeting is displayed. Decoded data shows that user "7621" starts (t_1) his journey on floor -1, $C_{2,3,-1}$; #1W, goes up to floor 1 in $C_{2,1,-1}$ and at t_2 he arrives at $C_{4,1,1}$ heading for E. During his journey, user "3009" from $C_{4,4,1}$ #1 asks the CM (t_3) to forward him to the scheduled meeting and follows course to W. At t_4 both friends join in $C_{4,3,1}$. Results show that, with VLC's dynamic LED-aided guidance system, users can get accurate route guidance and perform navigation and geotracking. Users of VLC in large buildings will be able to find the shortest route to their destination, providing directions as they go.

4 Conclusions

We have proposed and characterized a VLC-based guidance system for mobile users inside large buildings. A mesh cellular hybrid structure was chosen as the architecture, and the communication protocol was defined for a multi-level building scenario.

In the encoding/decoding process, the check parity error is evaluated and for the analyzed cases, the BER is high without correction whereas it is negligible with correction. An analysis of bidirectional communication between the infrastructure and the mobile receiver was conducted. According to global results, the location of a mobile receiver is found in conjunction with data transmission. The dynamic LED-aided guidance system provides accurate route guidance, allows navigation, and keeps track of the route. Localization tasks are automatically rescheduled in crowded regions by the cooperative localization system, which provides guidance information and alerts the user to reschedule.

Acknowledgements. This work was sponsored by FCT – Fundação para a Ciência e a Tecnologia, within the Research Unit CTS – Center of Technology and Systems, reference UIDB/00066/2020.

References

1. Tsonev, D., et al.: A 3-Gb/s single-LED OFDM-based wireless VLC link using a Gallium Nitride μLED. IEEE Photon. Technol. Lett. **26**(7), 637–640 (2014)
2. O'Brien, D.H., et al.: Indoor visible light communications: challenges and prospects. Proc. SPIE **7091**, 709106 (2008)
3. Park, S.B., et al.: Information broadcasting system based on visible light signboard. In: Presented at Wireless and Optical Communication 2007, Montreal, Canada (2007)
4. Vieira, M., Louro, P., Fernandes, M., Vieira, M.A., Fantoni, A., Costa, J.: Three transducers embedded into one single SiC photodetector: LSP direct image sensor, optical amplifier and demux device. In: Advances in Photodiodes InTech, Chap. 19, pp. 403–425 (2011)
5. Vieira, M.A., Louro, P., Vieira, M., Fantoni, A., Steiger-Garção, A.: Light-activated amplification in Si-C tandem devices: a capacitive active filter model. IEEE Sens. J. **12**(6), 1755–1762 (2012)
6. Yang, C., Shao, H.R.: WiFi-based indoor positioning. IEEE Commun. Mag. **53**(3), 150–157 (2015)

7. Lin, X.Y., Ho, T.W., Fang, C.C., Yen, Z.S., Yang, B.J., Lai, F.: A mobile indoor positioning system based on iBeacon technology. In: Proceedings of the International Conference on IEEE Engineering in Medicine and Biology Society, pp. 4970–4973 (2015)
8. Huang, C.H., Lee, L.H., Ho, C.C., Wu, L.L., Lai, Z.H.: Real-time RFID indoor positioning system based on kalman filter drift removal and heron-bilateration location estimation. IEEE Trans. Instrum. Meas. **64**(3), 728–739 (2015)
9. Zafar, F., Karunatilaka, D., Parthiban, R.: Dimming schemes for visible light communication: the state of research. IEEE Wirel. Commun. **22**, 29–35 (2015)
10. Khan, L.U.: Visible light communication: applications, architecture, standardization and research challenges. Digit. Commun. Netw. **3**, 78–88 (2017)
11. Hassan, N.U., Naeem, A., Pasha, M.A., Jadoon, T., Yuen, C.: Indoor positioning using visible led lights: a survey. ACM Comput. Surv. **48**, 1–32 (2015)
12. Ozgur, E., Dinc, E., Akan, O.B.: Communicate to illuminate: state-of-the-art and research challenges for visible light communications. Phys. Commun. **17**, 72–85 (2015)
13. Vieira, M.A., Vieira, M., Louro, P., Vieira, P.: Bi-directional communication between infrastructures and vehicles through visible light. In: Proceedings of the SPIE 11207, Fourth International Conference on Applications of Optics and Photonics, 112070C, 3 October 2019 (2019). https://doi.org/10.1117/12.2526500
14. Zhu, Y., Liang, W., Zhang, J., Zhang, Y.: Space-collaborative constellation designs for mimo indoor visible light communications. IEEE Photonics Technol. Lett. **27**(15), 1667–1670 (2015)
15. Friis, H.T.: A note on a simple transmission formula. Proc. IRE **34**, 254–256 (1946)
16. Yousefpour, A., et al.: All one needs to know about fog computing and related edge computing paradigms: a complete survey. J. Syst. Architect. **98**, 289–330 (2019)
17. Vieira, M., Vieira, M.A., Louro, P., Fantoni, A., Vieira, P.: Dynamic VLC navigation system in crowded buildings. Int. J. Adv. Softw. **14**(3&4), 141–150 (2021)
18. Vieira, M.A., Vieira, M., Silva, V., Louro, P., Costa, J.: Optical signal processing for data error detection and correction using a-SiCH technology. Phys. Status Solidi C **12**(12), 1393–1400 (2015)
19. Vieira, M., Vieira, M.A., Louro, P., Fantoni, A., Vieira, P.: Geolocation and communication in unfamiliar indoor environments through visible light. Proc. SPIE 11706, Light-Emitting Devices, Materials, and Applications XXV, 117060P (2021)
20. Vieira, M.A., Vieira, M., Louro, P., Silva, V., Costa, J., Fantoni, A.: SiC multilayer structures as light controlled photonic active filters. Plasmonics **8**(1), 63–70 (2013). https://doi.org/10.1007/s11468-012-9422-9

Development, Engineering, Machine Learning

Semantic Inferences Towards Smart IoT-Based Systems Actuation Conflicts Management

Gérald Rocher$^{(\boxtimes)}$, Jean-Yves Tigli, and Stéphane Lavirotte

I3S Laboratory, Université Côte d'Azur, CNRS, Sophia-Antipolis, France
{gerald.rocher,Jean-yves.tigli,
Stephane.lavirotte}@univ-cotedazur.fr

Abstract. IoT-based systems have long been limited to collecting field information via sensors distributed at the edge of their infrastructure. However, in many areas such as smart home, smart factory, etc. these systems include devices that interact with the physical environment via common actuators. Throughout the lifecycle of these systems, from design, to deployment to operation, the ability to avoid actuation conflicts, both in terms of the commands that actuators receive (direct conflicts) and the effects that they produce (indirect conflicts), is a new challenge in the realm of trustworthy Smart IoT-based Systems (SIS). As part of the European project ENACT, which aims to provide full DevOps support for trustworthy SIS, we present a lightweight ontology that provides SIS designers with (1) a semantic metamodel to formally describe SIS subsystems and the actuators they interact with, and (2) a set of SWRL (Semantic Web Rule Language) inference rules to automatically identify and semi-automatically resolve actuation conflicts. Consistent with the best practices of the DevOps approach, a particular emphasis is placed on facilitating the use and interpretation of inference results. To provide insight into the appropriateness of the proposed approach in the context of SIS, rule processing times for different actuation conflict configurations are provided.

Keywords: Actuation · Conflict · Identification · Resolution · Ontology · Internet of Things · DevOps

1 Introduction

DevOps is one of the best practices in software engineering today [1]. The method aims to harmonize software development (Dev) and software operations (Ops) in a collaborative framework. It facilitates all phases of a system lifecycle, from design, development, integration, testing and deployment, to runtime monitoring and behavioural analysis, with the latter phases introducing a new design phase into a perpetual, incremental and agile development cycle. If DevOps is obvious today, it is thanks to a number of technical enablers, such as infrastructures that enable and facilitate the deployment of systems designed on the basis of *convergence* and *virtualization* hypotheses. A backend is deployed in a cloud while the frontend relies on web interfaces supported by similar

L. M. Camarinha-Matos et al. (Eds.): IFIPIoT 2022, IFIP AICT 665, pp. 255–273, 2022.
https://doi.org/10.1007/978-3-031-18872-5_15

target devices such as smartphones, PCs, tablets, SmartTVs, interactive terminals etc. at the price of some web responsive design configurations.

However, in the context of the Internet of Things (IoT), these hypotheses are undermined by the strong heterogeneity and dynamics of the infrastructure. This heterogeneity can be divided into two types. The first type of heterogeneity is that of computational targets, embodied in a three-tier infrastructure vision: cloud but also edge and IoT devices. Consideration of computational and storage constraints along with the locality of edge and IoT device targets is critical here. The second type of heterogeneity concerns the wide variety of IoT devices, which by their nature cannot benefit from the well-known convergence phenomenon in the evolution of IT media. This new characteristic is intrinsically linked to their vocation and results from the natural evolution of digital systems, which has been observed from the 90s onwards: *"Silicon-based information technology [...] is far from having become part of the environment"* (Mark Weiser). While Pervasive Computing and Ambient Intelligence (AmI) have reinforced the idea that modern computing is not only confronted with the distribution, the availability (*everytime*) and the mobility of their supports (everywhere), it must now be recognized that modern computing is also confronted with the great diversity of IoT devices and their variability in terms of *sensors* and *actuators* (everything).

While many IoT-based systems focus on massively collecting field data from sensors, their scope becomes increasingly complex once they are able to act on the physical environment using actuators shared by multiple independent subsystems. The management of such devices becomes critical, as their sharing or simultaneous use potentially leads to the occurrence of conflicts that can result in user dissatisfaction at best and dramatic consequences in the field at worst. From a design standpoint, managing actuation conflicts is made difficult by the complexity of so-called Smart IoT-based Systems (SIS) and the large number of shared actuators they may rely on at the edge of the infrastructure. As we move towards trustworthy SIS, it is imperative to provide DevOps stakeholders with tools that can support both the identification of actuation conflicts and their resolution through the instantiation of Actuation Conflicts Managers (ACM) *at relevant conflict points in the design*. The local nature of ACM here suggests the possibility of their reuse which is relevant in the context of DevOps best practices because it enables continuous and rapid deployment.

Given this context, this paper makes a threefold contribution:

1. We present a lightweight ontology that provides DevOps stakeholders with a *semantic metamodel* for formally describing Smart IoT-based Systems (SIS) and the actuators with which they interact. The formal description is automatically obtained from the deployment and implementation models provided as part of the DevOps framework,
2. The identification and resolution of actuation conflicts are *automatically* and *systematically* derived from SWRL rules (Semantic Web Rule Language) used in conjunction with a Description Logic (DL) reasoner. Special attention is paid to facilitating the use and interpretation of inference results:

    a. Detected conflicts are clarified by special instances, and querying the knowledge base after inference is not required,

b. ACM components are automatically instantiated at relevant conflict points in the design. They make their inputs and outputs explicit for further use. As such, ACM components are black boxes whose associated resolution logic must be selected by designers from off-the-shelf reusable solutions or designed as needed,
c. Specific object properties are derived to help designers understand the reasons for identified conflicts.

3. Performance metrics for different actuation conflict configurations are provided. They provide insight into the relevance of the proposed approach to the targeted SIS, which can range from a few dozen (smart-home) to tens of thousands of actuators (smart-city).

The paper is organized as follows. In Sect. 2, we discuss direct and indirect actuation conflicts and review some relevant work that uses semantic web languages to identify and resolve them. In Sect. 3, we describe a lightweight ontology and 6 SWRL rules for automatic identification and semi-automatic resolution of actuation conflicts. In Sect. 4, we use the Stanford Protégé tool to illustrate the proposed ontology and associated SWRL rules with a small example. In Sect. 5, we present performance results for different actuation conflict configurations. In Sect. 6, we discuss future work.

2   Related Works

Potential actuation conflicts are likely to occur whenever independent subsystems compete for access to common actuators (*direct actuation conflicts*) or common physical properties through different actuators (*indirect actuation conflicts*). There is a rich literature and culture on *feature interaction* in telecommunication systems, in software systems and, more recently, in IoT-based systems [2].

However, as highlighted in [2], the proposed methods mainly consider the identification and resolution of direct conflicts. Indirect actuation conflicts can be subtle, making them difficult to detect. For example, a ventilation system *indirectly* affects physical properties such as temperature and humidity by influencing airflow. A TV, understood primarily as an entertainment device, can also be understood as an actuator that affects sound, brightness, and, to a lesser extent, temperature. Indirect actuation conflicts involve non-trivial semantic and subjective considerations and are therefore difficult to resolve automatically while still satisfying all SIS end users. For example, if one user wants to increase the temperature in a room while another wants to increase the airflow in the same room by opening a window and then possibly lower the temperature, what must be the resolution strategy that satisfies both? In this context, the use of semantic web formal description languages [4] and their reasoning capabilities seems to be a relevant approach for describing SIS, identifying and resolving their actuation conflicts.

Some research has been done in this direction recently. In [5], the authors propose a generic knowledge graph to represent the relations between IoT services and environment entities. The indirect actuation conflicts are then identified based on Event-Condition-Action (ECA) automation rules defined by end-users. No resolution is proposed in this work. In [6] the authors present A3ID, an automatic indirect actuation conflicts detection method based on IF-This-Then-That (IFTTT) rules and knowledge graphs that capture the functionality, effect and scope of the devices involved in the design. No resolution method is proposed in this work. In [7], the authors consider the case where different end-users interact with a Building Automation System (BAS). End-user requirements are encoded by an ontology model that provides semantic information about the physical environment. Identification of indirect conflicts is achieved by SPARQL queries [3] to this model, while resolution operations are performed using constraint solving.

Most of these approaches are based on knowledge of the functional logic of the systems under consideration, end-user requirements, rules and policies. SIS, as defined in this paper, may be large-scale systems (e.g., smart city) built on highly dynamic subsystems (e.g., cloud services, containerized microservices, embedded software, heterogenous edge devices, etc.) whose functional logic (hardware and software) is not necessarily under the control of the DevOps stakeholders. The knowledge is therefore limited to the structural interactions between subsystems and the actuators they act upon at the edge of the infrastructure provided by deployment and implementation models as part of the DevOps approach (e.g., [8, 9]). By focusing on the structural interactions, the identification of potential actuation conflicts can be done systematically, and their resolution applied locally through reusable ACM that implement different resolution strategies, in line with DevOps best practices.

Finally, none of the above approaches provides processing time data for managing actuation conflicts. For example, in [6], although the authors conducted experiments with 11,859 IFTTT-like rules with up to 99 actuators, no performance data is provided.

3   A Lightweight Ontology for Identifying and Resolving Actuation Conflicts

The Semantic Web can be defined as "*a vision for the future of the Web in which information is given explicit meaning, making it easier for machines to automatically process and integrate information available on the Web*" [10]. In this context, explicit meaning is provided by semantically rich metadata that relies on *ontologies*. An ontology (a.k.a. vocabulary) is a meta-model that defines concepts and relationships used to describe and represent a particular domain[1]. It is based on logic-based knowledge representation languages such as RDF (Resource Description Framework), RDFS (RDF-Schema) [11] and OWL-* family of languages [12] (OWL-LITE, OWL-DL and OWL-FULL), each providing different levels of expressiveness for asserting facts or axioms.

What makes ontologies interesting is their capacity, from their underlying logic-based knowledge representation languages, to derive logical consequences (i.e., implicit assertions) from a set of asserted facts or axioms (i.e., explicit assertions). However, the derivational capacity is limited by the expressive capacity of the language in question. The greater the expressive capacity of the language, the lower the inference and the computability [13]. For example, OWL-LITE and OWL-DL are decidable and correspond to $\mathcal{SHIF}$ and $\mathcal{SHOIN}$ Description Logics (DL) respectively, with $\mathcal{SHOIN}$DL providing higher expressivity than $\mathcal{SHIF}$DL. OWL-FULL, provides the highest expressivity, but is not decidable.

---

[1] https://www.w3.org/standards/semanticweb/ontology.

In the context of SIS and DevOps, the use of semantic web technologies seems to be relevant assuming:

1. Explicit statements describing (1) the structural relationships between SIS subsystems and the actuators they interact with, (2) the actuators (at least, their localization and the physical properties they act upon), can be extracted from DevOps deployment and implementation models,
2. The knowledge representation language is expressive enough to identify direct and indirect actuation conflicts and guide DevOps stakeholders towards their resolution from inference under constraint of decidability.

Based on these assumptions, a lightweight OWL-DL ontology is presented below for automatically identifying and semi-automatically resolving actuation conflicts.

It includes the following concepts and relationships whose individuals are taken from DevOps deployment and implementation models, shown in green in Fig. 1:

Entity - An entity is an abstract element,

Subsystem - A subsystem is an entity that sends commands to an entity,

Physical Property - A physical property is any observable and measurable property whose value characterizes a state of a physical system [14] (e.g. temperature, brightness, humidity, pressure, sound, etc.),

Context - A context can be any abstract, spatially bounded physical system (e.g. kitchen, living room, etc.) whose state can be characterized by physical properties,

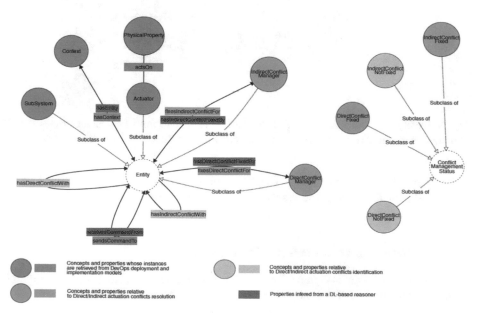

Fig. 1. Concepts and object properties of the proposed lightweight ontology.

Actuator - An actuator is an entity that has exactly one context, acts on (i.e. changes) at least one physical property and receives commands from at least one subsystem.

On this basis, an example of a knowledge description is given below, the graphical representation of which is shown in Fig. 2 is given below:

```
<!-- An actuator -->
<rdf:Description rdf:about="#TV">
  <hasContext rdf:resource="#Livingroom"/>
  <actsOn rdf:resource="#Luminosity"/>
  <actsOn rdf:resource="#Sound"/>
</rdf:Description>
<!-- A SubSystem -->
<rdf:Description rdf:about="#RemoteControl">
  <sendsCommandTo rdf:resource="#TV"/>
</rdf:Description>
<owl:AllDifferent>
<owl:distinctMembers rdf:parseType="Collection">
  <rdf:Description rdf:about="#TV"/>
  <rdf:Description rdf:about="#RemoteControl"/>
</owl:distinctMembers>
</owl:AllDifferent>
```

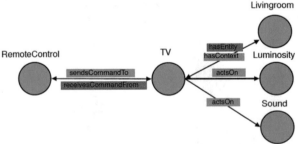

Fig. 2. Example of semantic description that can be expressed from DevOps deployment and implementation models (properties depicted in yellow are inferred from a DL-based reasoner).

This structured representation of knowledge provides a formal description of SIS and a basis for identifying and resolving direct and indirect actuation conflicts from inferences.

3.1 Automatic Actuation Conflicts Identification

The proposed ontology is equipped with the following concepts and properties related to the identification of direct and indirect conflicts (shown in pink in Fig. 1):

DirectConflictNotFixed - The individuals of this concept correspond to all actuators that are potentially subject to a direct actuation conflict.

→An actuator is potentially subject to a direct conflict if it receives its commands from at least two different entities,

IndirectConflictNotFixed - The individuals of this concept correspond to all actuators that are potentially subject to an indirect actuation conflict.

→An actuator is potentially subject to an indirect conflict if it shares its context with at least one other actuator acting on the same physical property.

While OWL-DL ontologies provide simple, reusable, and easy-to-understand models of domain knowledge, they lack the declarative expressiveness that rules provide, especially when it comes to designing complex assertions of facts that go beyond the simple declaration of domain concepts, as is the case with the above concepts [15]. The Semantic Web Rule Language (SWRL) [16] enables declarative assertions using OWL concepts. By combining first-order Horn logic (HL) and DL-based reasoners such as Pellet, Fact++, etc., it achieves higher expressive power and reasoning capacity. In this paper, the proposed ontology is SWRL-enabled, i.e. it contains a set of Horn clause rule axioms (Table 1 and Table 2) that conform to DL-*Safety* (i.e. rule axioms contain only known concepts, which makes them decidable [17]).

Table 1. Horn-clause axioms for Direct/Indirect actuation conflicts identification

1	An actuator **?act** is subject to a direct conflict if it receives its commands from at least two different entities:

```
Actuator(?act) ^ sendsCommandTo(?ent1,?act) ^ receivesCom-
mandFrom(?act,?ent2) ^ differentFrom(?ent1,?ent2) →
hasDirectConflictWith(?act,?ent1)
```

2	An actuator **?act1** is subject to an indirect conflict if it shares its context with at least one other actuator **?act2** acting on the same physical property:

```
hasContext(?act1,?ctx) ^ receivesCommandFrom(?act1,?ent1) ^
hasEntity(?ctx,?act2) ^ receivesCommandFrom(?act2,?ent2) ^
actsOn(?act1,?eff) ^ actsOn(?act2,?eff) ^ differ-
entFrom(?act1,?act2) ^ differentFrom(?ent1,?ent2) → hasIndi-
rectConflictWith(?act1,?act2)
```

The identification of actuation conflicts is then done in two steps:

1. The first step consists in asserting the object properties **hasDirectConflictWith** and **hasIndirectConflictWith** to each actuator that is potentially subject to direct and/or indirect conflicts. This step is achieved thanks to the axioms of the Horn-clause rule defined in Table 1,
2. The second step relies on a DL-based reasoner, i.e. **DirectConflictNotFixed** individuals are derived from actuator individuals that have the **hasDirectConflictWith** property. The same is true for **IndirectConflictNotFixed** individuals.

An example is shown in Fig. 3 where the TV instance has direct conflict with **RemoteControl#1** and **RemoteControl#2** instances. So far, no ACM has been instantiated to fix this conflict (**DirectConflictNotFixed**).

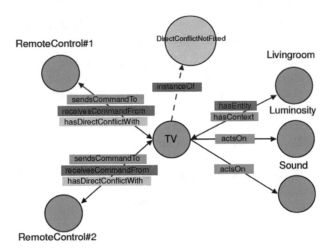

Fig. 3. Example of direct actuation conflicts identification

3.2 Semi-automatic Actuation Conflicts Resolution

Based on the assertions derived during the actuation conflicts identification phase, a means should be proposed to resolve the conflicts identified semi-automatically. For this purpose, the proposed ontology is equipped with additional concepts and properties, shown in purple in Fig. 1. Besides these concepts and properties, four additional Horn-clause rule axioms are defined in the ontology (cf. Table 2). In particular, rule 3 and rule 4 are used to instantiate individuals of the concepts **DirectConflict-Manager** and **IndirectConflictManager** at relevant points in the design. The instantiation of these individuals is done automatically thanks to the built-in SWR-LAPI extension swrlx:makeOWLThing, which can be used to create new individuals directly from a rule, where a **DirectConflictManager** is instantiated for each actuator that have the property **hasDirectConflictWith** asserted (rule 3); an **IndirectConflictManager** is instantiated for each actuator that have the property **hasIndirectConflictWith** asserted (rule 4).

Table 2. Horn-clause axioms for Direct/Indirect actuation conflicts resolution

3	Whenever an actuator **?act** has the property **hasDirectCon-flictWith(?act,?ent)** asserted, a direct ACM ?acm is instantiated with the property **fixesDirectConflictFor(?acm,?act)** asserted. The entity **?ent** sending commands to actuator **?act**, whose direct actuation conflict is fixed by the direct conflict manager **?acm**, also send commands to **?acm**:

```
Actuator(?act) ^ hasDirectConflictWith(?act,?ent) ^
swrlx:makeOWLThing(?acm,?act) → DirectConflictManager(?acm) ^
fixesDirectConflictFor(?acm,?act) ^ sendsCommandTo(?ent,?acm)
```

4	Whenever an actuator ?act1 has the property **hasIndirectCon-flictWith(?act1,?act2)** asserted, an indirect ACM **?acm**, associated to the pair PhysicalEffect/Context, is instantiated with the property **fixesIn-directConflictFor(?acm,?act1)** asserted:

```
PhysicalProperty(?eff1) ^ Context(?ctx) ^
hasEntity(?ctx,?act1) ^ Actuator(?act1) ^ actsOn(?act1,?eff1)
^ hasIndirectConflictWith(?act1,?act2) ^ actsOn(?act2,?eff2) ^
sameAs(?eff1,?eff2) ^ swrlx:makeOWLThing(?acm,?eff1,?ctx) →
IndirectConflictManager(?acm) ^ fixesIndirectConflict-
For(?acm,?act1)
```

5	Each entity **?ent** sending commands to actuator **?act**, whose indirect actuation conflict is fixed by an indirect conflict manager **?acm**, also send commands to **?acm**:

```
fixesIndirectConflictFor(?acm, ?act) ^ receivesCom-
mandFrom(?act, ?ent) → sendsCommandTo(?ent,?acm)
```

6	Direct/Indirect conflict managers are merged whenever they fix actuation conflict for the same actuators:

```
fixesDirectConflictFor(?acm1, ?act) ^ fixesIndirectConflict-
For(?acm2, ?act) → sameAs(?acm1, ?acm2)
```

In rule 3, **DirectConflictManager** individuals are created once per actuator (`swrlx:makeOWLThing(?acm,?act)`) while in rule 4, **IndirectCon-flictManager** individuals are created once for each pair (physical effect, context) (`swrlx:makeOWLThing(?acm,?eff,?ctx)`). This prevents ACM from being duplicated. As shown in Fig. 4, each instance of a direct/indirect ACM is bound to subsystems that send commands to the faulty actuators and to the faulty actuators themselves by asserting the **fixesDirectConflictFor** or **fixesIndirectCon-flictFor** properties depending on whether the ACM in question targets a direct or an indirect actuation conflict (rules 3, 4 and 5). In line with DevOps best practices, this approach enables the *systematic* implementation of *local* and *reusable* ACM whose integration into the deployment and implementation models can be greatly facilitated thanks to their associated properties.

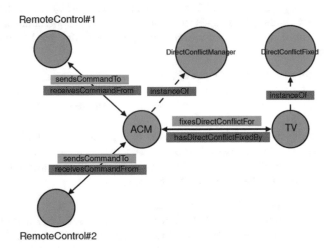

Fig. 4. Example of direct actuation conflicts resolution.

One special case must still be considered in order for the proposed actuation conflict resolution to be complete. This is the case when an actuator is subject to both direct and indirect conflicts. An example can be found in Fig. 5 where the TV receives its commands from two different entities and both TV and Lamp have the same context Livingroom and act on the same physical property (Luminosity).

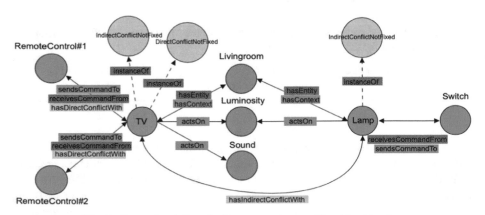

Fig. 5. Example of direct/indirect actuation conflicts identification.

In such a configuration, two ACM individuals must be created, a **DirectConflictManager** and an **IndirectConflictManager**, as shown in Fig. 6. Here, both individuals must be *merged* to prevent an indirect actuation conflicts from occurring between them. The solution to this is to consider both individuals as identical. This is achieved by the rule 6 defined in Table 2 and the use of the property owl:sameAs.

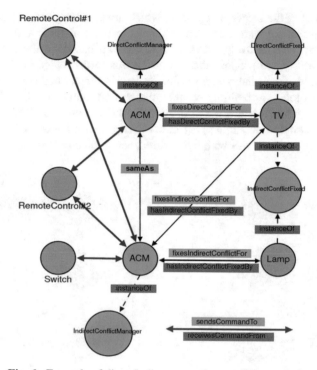

Fig. 6. Example of direct/indirect actuation conflicts resolution.

As such, actuation conflict managers are not yet associated with conflict resolution logic; they are *black boxes*. Concrete actuation conflict managers must be selected by designers from off-the-shelf reusable solutions, hence the semi-automatic qualification of the proposed resolution approach. We will have the opportunity to return to this point in the perspectives of this research. Finally, the counterparts of the concepts **Direct-ConflictNotFixed** and **IndirectConflictNotFixed**, are provided in the proposed ontology:

DirectConflictFixed - Individuals of this concept correspond to all actuators that are potentially subject to a direct actuation conflict and for which the property **hasDirectConflictFixedBy** is asserted, derived from <owl:inverseOf rdf:resource="fixesDirectConflictFor"/>,

IndirectConflictFixed - Individuals of this concept correspond to all actuators that are potentially subject to an indirect actuation conflict and for which the property **hasIndirectConflictFixedBy** is asserted, derived from <owl:inverseOf rdf:resource= "fixesIndirectConflictFor"/>.

4   Identifying and Resolving Actuation Conflicts with the Stanford Protégé Tool

This work is part of the DevOps approach, which aims, among other things, to enable continuous and fast software deployment thanks to a set of tools and models shared by all actors involved in the process. In this context, based on the semantic model described previously, we propose the use of the Stanford Protégé [18] tool to reason about the knowledge and analyze the results. Protégé is a free, open-source platform that provides a set of tools for building domain models and knowledge-based applications with ontologies[2]. The Protégé SWRLTab supports the execution of SWRL Horn-clause rules using the Drools rule engine [19] in conjunction with Fact++ DL reasoner [20]. As an example, consider a SIS with five indirect actuation conflicts, as shown in Fig. 7 below.

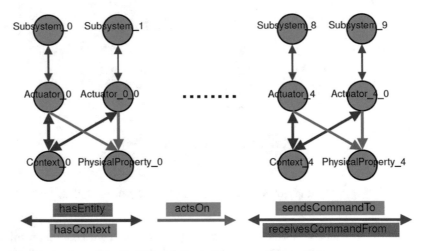

Fig. 7. SIS with five indirect actuation conflicts.

Initially, only the rules for identifying actuation conflicts identification are enabled (rule 1 and rule 2 in Table 1). Executing these rules in conjunction with the Fact++ reasoner produces the results shown in Fig. 8 and Fig. 9. Actuators that are subject to indirect actuation conflicts are identified as individuals of the concept **Indirect-ConflictNotFixed** (Fig. 8). Object properties associated with each actuator give designers the opportunity to better understand the cause of the conflicts (Fig. 9).

Now, the rules for resolving actuation conflicts are activated (rule 3, rule 4, rule 5 and rule 6 defined in Table 2). Executing these rules in conjunction with the Fact++ reasoner produces the results shown in Fig. 10. Actuator individuals that are subject to an indirect actuation conflict are now individuals of the **IndirectConflictFixed** concept. Individuals of **IndirectConflictMager** have been created automatically, as shown in Fig. 11.

---

[2] https://protege.stanford.edu.

Fig. 8. Actuator individuals potentially subject to indirect conflicts are made directly available under the concept **IndirectConflictNotFixed**.

Fig. 9. Object properties associated with each actuator make the cause of conflict clear.

Fig. 10. Actuator individuals whose indirect conflicts is fixed by an ACM are directly made available under the concept **IndirectConflictFixed**.

Fig. 11. ACM Individuals are made available under the concept **IndirectConflictManager**.

The object properties associated with each ACM give designers a better understanding of the actuators involved (Fig. 12). Since ACM are bound to conflicting actuators (**fixesIndirectConflictFor**) and their associated subsystems (**receivesCommandFrom**), this facilitates their integration into DevOps deployment and implementation models.

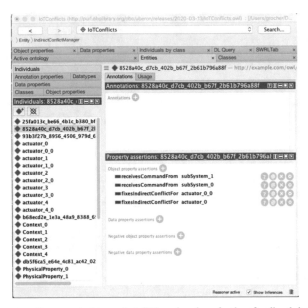

Fig. 12. Object properties asserted to each ACM make clear further feedback in deployment and implementation models.

5 Performance Analysis

SIS can be implemented from a few dozen (smart homes) to thousands of actuators (smart cities). In this context, it is important to evaluate the performance of the proposed approach to gain insight into its relevance against the targeted SIS. To this end, we propose a set of synthetic actuation conflict configurations that serve as a reference for experiments and benchmarks, divided into four categories defined as follows:

1. The first category represents SIS that have only direct actuation conflicts and follow the pattern below, which is duplicated as many times as the number of direct conflicts requires:

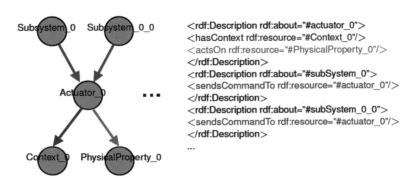

2. The second one represents SIS that have only indirect actuation conflicts, following the pattern below duplicated as often as the number of indirect conflicts requires:

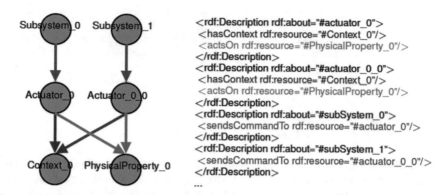

```
<rdf:Description rdf:about="#actuator_0">
<hasContext rdf:resource="#Context_0"/>
<actsOn rdf:resource="#PhysicalProperty_0"/>
</rdf:Description>
<rdf:Description rdf:about="#actuator_0_0">
<hasContext rdf:resource="#Context_0"/>
<actsOn rdf:resource="#PhysicalProperty_0"/>
</rdf:Description>
<rdf:Description rdf:about="#subSystem_0">
<sendsCommandTo rdf:resource="#actuator_0"/>
</rdf:Description>
<rdf:Description rdf:about="#subSystem_1">
<sendsCommandTo rdf:resource="#actuator_0_0"/>
</rdf:Description>
...
```

3. The third category corresponds to SIS that have both direct and indirect actuation conflicts, which are duplicated as many times as the number of indirect conflicts requires, according to the pattern below:

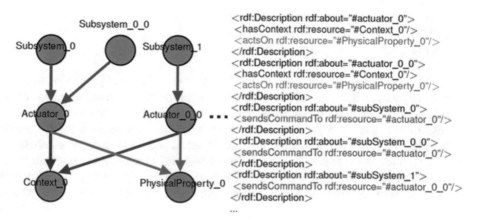

```
<rdf:Description rdf:about="#actuator_0">
<hasContext rdf:resource="#Context_0"/>
<actsOn rdf:resource="#PhysicalProperty_0"/>
</rdf:Description>
<rdf:Description rdf:about="#actuator_0_0">
<hasContext rdf:resource="#Context_0"/>
<actsOn rdf:resource="#PhysicalProperty_0"/>
</rdf:Description>
<rdf:Description rdf:about="#subSystem_0">
<sendsCommandTo rdf:resource="#actuator_0"/>
</rdf:Description>
<rdf:Description rdf:about="#subSystem_0_0">
<sendsCommandTo rdf:resource="#actuator_0"/>
</rdf:Description>
<rdf:Description rdf:about="#subSystem_1">
<sendsCommandTo rdf:resource="#actuator_0_0"/>
</rdf:Description>
...
```

4. The fourth category corresponds to SIS that have no actuation conflict and are duplicated as many times as the number of actuators requires:

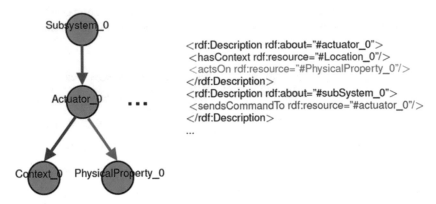

The experiments are conducted using the Protégé tool with either only the actuation conflicts identification rules (rule 1 and rule 2 in Table 1) or both the actuation conflict identification and resolution rules (rules 1, 2, 3, 4, 5 and 6 in Table 1 and Table 2) enabled. The complete experimental setup is defined as follows:

**Macbook pro Quad-Core i7 2.8 GHz,
16 GB RAM 2133 Mghz LPDDR3,
Protégé 5.5.0,
(OWL API 4.5.9.2019-02-01T07:24:44Z),
(SWRLTab Protege 5.0+ Plugin (2.0.6)),
Fact++ 1.6.5.**

The performance results are shown in Fig. 13 and indicate that processing time of the rules depends on the number of actuation conflicts to be identified and resolved. Without actuation conflicts, the performance results are mainly determined by the number of actuators involved in SIS. These results suggest that the proposed approach is suitable for SIS with no more than a few thousand actuators and a few hundred conflicts (e.g., smart homes, smart buildings, etc.). It should be noted that the DevOps approach is an agile and incremental approach. Due to the consecutive design loops, it is unlikely that the number of potential conflicts detected in the design will be more than a few hundred.

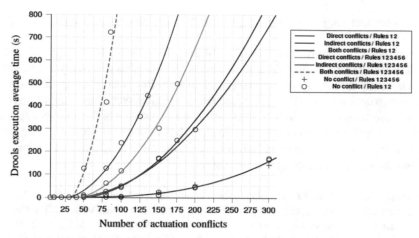

Fig. 13. SWRL rule performance results for different actuation conflict configurations.

6 Future Work

While the identification of actuation conflicts is automatic, their resolution is semi-automatic. Actuation Conflicts Managers (ACM) are automatically instantiated to resolve conflicts at relevant points in the design. However, these ACM are black boxes and require designers to manually select concrete ACM from a set of available off-the-shelf ACM. To better assist designers in this task, we plan to extend the proposed ontology with additional semantics that allow selection of relevant off-the-shelf ACM based on their configuration (input/output types, command types, etc.).

Performance wise, we plan to compare the SWRL-based approach with an approach based on Shapes Constraint Language (SHACL) [21]. SHACL is a standard validation language that allows to define rules whose violations are formalized into reports. It also can be used as a modelling language through SPARQL-based constructs.

Finally, the proposed ontology is simple enough to have its concepts and relationships aligned with those from existing ontologies. For example, we plan to align the proposed ontology with the Smart Applications REFerence ontology (SAREF) and its extensions [22].

7 Conclusion

In the realm of trustworthy Smart IoT-based Systems (SIS), the implementation of actuators at the edge of their infrastructure requires new development tools to help DevOps stakeholders detect and resolve actuation conflicts that can lead to unexpected and potentially harmful behavior as early as possible. While much work as gone into identifying and resolving direct actuation conflicts (concurrent access to a common actuator), little attention has been paid to the indirect conflicts (concurrent access to physical properties) introduced by SIS and the devices they implement at the edge of their infrastructure. These conflicts can be subtle, making them difficult to detect. Their resolution must take into account subjective knowledge related to the context of use of SIS and user expectations.

In this context, a lightweight ontology was proposed to provide DevOps stakeholders with (1) a semantic meta-modelling framework to formally describe SIS and the actuators with which they interact from deployment and integration models; (2) a set of 6 SWRL rules used in conjunction with a DL-based reasoner to automatically identify and semi-automatically resolve actuation conflicts. Performance analysis of the proposed approach for different configurations of actuation conflicts has shown that it is acceptable for SIS with up to a thousand actuators and a few hundred actuation conflicts, making it suitable for smart home, smart building, etc. use-cases.

Acknowledgment. The research leading to these results has received funding from the European Commission's H2020 Program under grant agreement numbers 780351 (ENACT). This work was conducted using the Protégé resource, which is supported by grant GM10331601 from the National Institute of General Medical Sciences of the United States National Institutes of Health.

References

1. Ebert, C., Gallardo, G., Hernantes, J., Serrano, N.: DevOps. IEEE Softw. **33**, 94–100 (2016)
2. Ibrhim, H., Hassan, H., Nabil, E.: A conflicts' classification for IoT-based services: a comparative survey. PeerJ Comput. Sci. **7**, 480 (2021)
3. Harris, S., Seaborne, A., Prud'hommeaux, E.: SPARQL 1.1 query language. W3C Recommendation **21**, 778 (2013)
4. Euzenat, J., Rousset, M.-C.: Semantic web. In: Marquis, P., Papini, O., Prade, H. (eds.) A Guided Tour of Artificial Intelligence Research, pp. 181–207. Springer, Cham (2020). https://doi.org/10.1007/978-3-030-06170-8_6
5. Huang, B., Dong, H., Bouguettaya, A.: Conflict detection in IoT-based smart homes. arXiv: 2107.13179 (2021)
6. Xiao, D., Wang, Q., Cai, M., Zhu, Z., Zhao, W.: A3ID: an automatic and interpretable implicit interference detection method for smart home via knowledge graph. IEEE Internet of Things J. **7**, 2197–2211 (2019)
7. Camacho, R.J.L.: Intelligent actuation in home and building automation systems. Master's thesis (2014)
8. Rocher, G., et al.: An actuation conflicts management flow for smart iot-based systems. In: 7th International Conference on Internet of Things: Systems, Management and Security (IOTSMS) (2020)
9. Ferry, N., et al.: Genesis: continuous orchestration and deployment of smart IoT systems. In: IEEE 43rd Annual Computer Software and Applications Conference (COMPSAC), pp. 870–875 (2019)
10. Heflin, J.: OWL web ontology language-use cases and requirements. W3C Recommendation (2004)
11. McBride, B.: The resource description framework (RDF) and its vocabulary description language RDFS. In: Staab, S., Studer, R. (eds.) Handbook on Ontologies, pp. 51–65. Springer, Heidelberg (2004). https://doi.org/10.1007/978-3-540-24750-0_3
12. Van Harmelen, F., McGuinness, D.L.: OWL web ontology language overview. World Wide Web Consortium (W3C) Recommendation (2004)

13. Colomo-Palacios, R.: Semantic competence pull: a semantics-based architecture for filling competency gaps in organizations. In: Global, I. (ed.) Semantic Web for Business: Cases and Applications, pp. 321–335 (2009)
14. Mark, B.: Theory of Knowledge: Structures and Processes. World scientific (2016)
15. Lawan, A., Rakib, A.: The semantic web rule language expressiveness extensions-a survey. arXiv preprint arXiv:1903.11723 (2019)
16. Horrocks, I., et al.: SWRL: a semantic web rule language combining OWL and RuleML. W3C Member Submission **21**, 1–31 (2004)
17. Rosati, R.: Semantic and computational advantages of the safe integration of ontologies and rules. In: Fages, F., Soliman, S. (eds.) PPSWR 2005. LNCS, vol. 3703, pp. 50–64. Springer, Heidelberg (2005). https://doi.org/10.1007/11552222_6
18. Musen, M.A.: The protégé project: a look back and a look forward. AI Matters **1**, 4–12 (2015)
19. Browne, P.: JBoss Drools Business Rules. Packt Publishing Ltd. (2009)
20. Tsarkov, D., Horrocks, I.: FaCT++ description logic reasoner: system description. In: Furbach, U., Shankar, N. (eds.) IJCAR 2006. LNCS (LNAI), vol. 4130, pp. 292–297. Springer, Heidelberg (2006). https://doi.org/10.1007/11814771_26
21. Knublauch, H., Kontokostas, D.: Shapes constraint language (SHACL). W3C Recommendation (2017)
22. Daniele, L., Hartog, F., Roes, J.: Created in close interaction with the industry: the smart appliances reference (saref) ontology. In: Cuel, R., Young, R. (eds.) FOMI 2015. LNBIP, vol. 225, pp. 100–112. Springer, Cham (2015). https://doi.org/10.1007/978-3-319-21545-7_9

Trade-Off Analysis of Pruning Methods for Compact Neural Networks on Embedded Devices

Sebastiaan B. H. C. Hofstee$^{(\boxtimes)}$ and Duc V. Le

Faculty of Electrical Engineering, Mathematics and Computer Science Faculty Office,
University of Twente, P.O. Box 217, 7500AE Enschede, The Netherlands
s.b.h.c.hofstee@student.utwente.nl, v.d.le@utwente.nl
https://www.utwente.nl/en/eemcs

Abstract. Pruning of neural networks is a technique often used to reduce the size of a machine learning model, as well as to reduce the computation cost for model inference. This research provides an analysis on four current pruning techniques that theoretically efficiently reduce the machine learning model size, where efficiency is defined by the relation between the compression of the model and the accuracy of the model. Furthermore, this research will assess in what way these four neural network pruning techniques affect the total energy consumption during model inference on a Raspberry Pi 4B board, applied to MobileNetV2, a machine learning model architecture optimized for image classification on embedded devices. Lastly, the research will analyze the trade-offs between energy consumption, model size and model accuracy for each of the assessed pruning algorithms applied to one of the most commonly used neural network architectures, MobileNetV2, on a Raspberry Pi 4B prototyping board. The research is expected to provide engineers a reference providing guidance upon deciding what pruning technique to use for a machine learning model to be deployed on an embedded device.

Keywords: Pruning · Neural networks · Machine learning · Deep learning · Embedded devices · Energy consumption · Efficiency

1 Introduction

Machine learning models have grown increasingly large over the past years [12], while at the same time increasingly often machine learning models are used on

This work is supported by the InSecTT project, https://www.insectt.eu/, funded by the ECSEL Joint Undertaking (JU) under grant agreement No 876038. The JU receives support from the European Union's Horizon 2020 research and innovation programme and Austria, Sweden, Spain, Italy, France, Portugal, Ireland, Finland, Slovenia, Poland, Netherlands, Turkey. The document reflects only the author's view and the Commission is not responsible for any use that may be made of the information it contains.

embedded devices [20]. As embedded devices often have very limited resources, pruning algorithms can be used to effectively reduce the size of a model, as well as lower the model inference time [1]. There are various novel pruning techniques proposed [6, 22, 26] which allow for significant reduction of model size while keeping the accuracy of a model acceptable.

Blalock et al. [1] show that existing work analyzing individual pruning techniques, often has shortcomings, among other things regarding the identification of experiment setups and metrics, the usage of too few combinations of datasets and architectures as well as failure to control confounding variables. As the scope of this research is somewhat limited due to time constraints, it is not possible to analyze a vast set of (dataset, architecture) combinations. Regardless of this, the work of Blalock et al. still provides valuable insights regarding the analysis of pruning methods.

While research has been done evaluating the energy consumption of classification algorithms [24], as well as on minimizing the energy consumption of embedded neural networks by introducing quantized neural networks (QNNs) [19], there appears to be, to the best of our knowledge, only little research done on the impact of algorithms on the energy consumption of embedded devices. The work that has been done however, is laid out in the related work section of this paper.

Furthermore, García-Martín et al. [7] have shown in their analysis on the (often theoretical) estimation of energy consumption in machine learning that merely the number of weights in a machine learning model is too simplistic and cannot be seen as a good estimator for the energy consumption of a machine learning model. Something which was also subscribed in research by Yang et al. [25], in which is stated that not only computation, but also memory access affects the total energy consumption of a neural network, where it is important to note that fetching data from memory takes multiple order of magnitudes more energy than the energy required for the computation itself, as shown by Horowitz in 2014 [10]. Additionally, Molchanov et al. point out in their 2017 paper [18] that since modern hardware utilizes regularities in computation, the size of a model may not directly infer faster inference speeds.

Based on this, it appears reasonable to assume that the energy consumption of a machine learning model does not only depend on the model size, and that further research into the real-world energy consumption of different pruning algorithms on embedded devices, which is the focus of this paper, is relevant.

This work identifies a number of neural network pruning techniques currently exist that efficiently reduce the model size (efficiency is in this case defined by the relation between the compression of the model and the accuracy of the model) and provides a trade-off analysis of four different commonly used pruning methods of two different categories applied to MobileNetV2, regarding energy consumption, model size and accuracy based on real-world tests. This paper furthermore tries to generalize, where appropriate, the results to be able to make a possible prediction about other, not touched upon pruning techniques and model architectures based on for example the properties of said techniques and architectures. This paper could be used by engineers as a reference providing insight and guidance upon deciding what pruning technique to apply to a machine learning model to be deployed on an embedded device, depending on accuracy, energy consumption and model size requirements.

2   Related Work

Neural network pruning has been around since the late 1980s [11,13] and much research has since been done in the field.

Blalock et al. [1] provides a very useful view into the state of neural network pruning and its references provide an excellent collection of novel pruning techniques [6,9,22,26]. The paper furthermore looks into how one can systematically compare different pruning methods by laying out a list of best practices, and shows that many novel pruning techniques have not been compared according to these best practices.

Molchanov et al. show in their 2017 paper [18] that pruning entire feature maps from CNN's based on a Taylor expansion-based criterion is a promising pruning method, showing significant improvement in the total estimated number of floating point operations (FLOPs) required for inference over other criteria such as the norm of kernel weights. Their paper quantifies the improvement by stating the total estimated number of FLOPs required for inference, as well as by stating the inference time (speedup). In contrast to [18], our work does not compare different criteria for pruning entire feature maps (a form of structured pruning), but rather aims to identify the trade-offs present between fundamentally different pruning methods. Furthermore, while likely related, our work does not make the assumption that energy consumption is directly related to the estimated number of FLOPs or time required for inference. Although pruning feature maps based on the criterion proposed in the work by Molchanov et al. [18] is not a pruning method analyzed in this work, it is certainly of interest to see if their proposed structured pruning method shares high-level patterns with results obtained from analysis done on different structured pruning methods in this paper.

Research on the energy consumption of pruned neural networks has mostly been done in a theoretical way, and seems to mainly focus on estimating the overall energy consumption of a model as a whole, as has been done in work by Cai et al. in 2017 [2], which makes use of a regression based approach. An excellent overview of the state of the art of such theoretical energy consumption models can be found in the work of Garciá-Mártin et al. in 2019 [7].

One of the few researches that focus on the energy consumption of pruning algorithms however, is a very interesting paper by Yang et al. [25], which proposes a novel pruning algorithm for Convolutional Neural Networks, Energy-aware Pruning, and approximates the energy consumption by means of a model which takes into account the computation and memory accesses, and uses values for energy which are extrapolated from hardware measurements in the real-world, making the approximation for the energy usage more accurate. In their research, their novel pruning algorithm is compared to magnitude-based pruning [8] and using no pruning algorithm at all. While it is still mostly theoretical and only compares the novel pruning algorithm to one other, more common pruning algorithm, this research is of great value for the research to be conducted and provides a useful reference regarding the analysis of obtained data for the energy consumption of different pruning algorithms.

Moreover, work from Mirmahaleh and Rahmani in 2019 [17] proposes a novel pruning method for Deep Neural Networks which relies on pruning weights, layers and neurons based on the minimum distance error, and shows to speed up inference by approximately 22.56%–77% and a reduction in energy consumption by 65.94%–88.54% as compared to not utilizing the novel pruning algorithm based on simulations. Even though Mirmahaleh and Rahmani their work does not provide a comparison with other pruning algorithms, it does show interest in the topic, which is of relevance to this work.

As the differences in the energy consumption and inference time of different pruning algorithms on embedded devices seem to not have been explored much, and as to the best of our knowledge no thorough real-world analysis has been composed that can be used by engineers as a reference providing guidance upon deciding what pruning technique to use for a machine learning model to be deployed on an embedded device, there appears to be ample scientific value to this work.

3   Preliminaries

The idea of pruning neural networks, in the sense that one removes parameters that are deemed unimportant, has been around for quite some time since it was first proposed by Lecun et al. in 1989 [14].

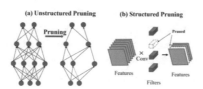

Fig. 1. **(a)** For unstructured pruning, individual connections between neurons are removed. **(b)** The structured pruning example shows an entire convolution filter being pruned [3].

As the pruning of parameters in a machine learning model generally results in the accuracy of a machine learning model decreasing, pipelines have been devised to minimize this accuracy loss. In particular, model fine tuning is often applied as to regain a certain degree of accuracy after pruning a model. This fine tuning entails retraining the model after pruning the network, as proposed by Han et al. in 2015 [8]. The retraining phase might be implemented in several ways, among which the approach used in this work, which was originally proposed by Frankle et al. in their 2019 work [5]. This approach entails rewinding the weight values to those before the pruning took place for those parameters left unpruned, and retrain the model starting from those values rather than resetting them to the values they had at the first iteration.

Furthermore, there is two main categories of pruning techniques: unstructured pruning, which relies on the removal of individual connections between neurons, and structured pruning, which relies on the pruning of entire convolution channels, filters or layers. In Fig. 1, originally presented in [4], this difference between these two fundamentally different pruning techniques is made clear.

As to obtain somewhat of an insight on the difference between these two categories of pruning methods, this work analyses two structured pruning techniques as well as two unstructured pruning techniques.

Regarding the unstructured pruning techniques, the first pruning technique to be analyzed is unstructured global magnitude pruning, introduced by Han et al. in 2015 [8]. This pruning method relies on pruning weights in a neural network based on their magnitude, where the lowest magnitude weights are set to zero. The second unstructured pruning technique that is analyzed in this work is unstructured random pruning. This pruning method serves as a baseline to compare other pruning techniques to and provides an hence excellent sanity check when analyzing pruning techniques (does a technique perform better than random pruning).

Regarding the structured pruning techniques, the first pruning technique to be analyzed is structured L1-norm filter pruning, introduced by Li et al. in 2016 [15], which relies on pruning CNN filters that are identified as having only a very limited effect on the accuracy of the model. In their work, Li et al. mention that magnitude based pruning of weights might not reduce the inference cost, and hence the energy consumption, to a large enough extent despite the significant pruning of weights due to the irregular nature of its sparsity. The second structured pruning technique to be analyzed is network slimming, introduced by Liu et al. in 2017 [16]. This pruning method is based on automatically identifying insignificant channels and immediately pruning these during training. The significance of channels is determined by analyzing the scaling factors in batch normalization, and removing those channels with scaling factors near zero.

The choice of pruning techniques is not arbitrary, as disregarding the random unstructured pruning baseline, the selected pruning methods are among those referenced the most. With Han et al. their global unstructured magnitude pruning [8] being referenced almost five thousand times, L1-norm filter pruning introduced by Li et al. [15] being referenced more than two and a half thousand times and network slimming introduced by Liu et al. [16] being referenced over one and a half thousand times.

As these pruning methods appear to be of such popularity, it appears likely that these methods are among the most relevant methods to analyze in this work.

A number of neural network architectures optimized for edge devices have been identified in recent work by Chen et al. in 2020 [4]. These compact architectures make use of specific design strategies, such as but not limited to reducing the size of convolutional filters, introducing shortcut connections to building blocks (as is the case for MobileNetV2 [21]) and channel shuffling.

An overview of a selection of compact neural network architectures as presented in [4] can be seen in Fig. 2

The reason why for this work, MobileNetV2 was selected to apply the analyzed pruning methods on is because the goal of this work is to provide an analysis of the pruning methods that is as relevant as possible. As MobileNetV2 has by far, the most citations out of all architectures presented in Fig. 2, with over ten thousand citations to the original paper [21], and hence appears to be the most relevant architecture to apply the pruning methods to. Moreover, MobileNetV2 is relatively similar in structure when compared to some other, often used compact neural network architectures such as MobileNet, ShuffleNet, ShuffleNetV2 and IGCV3, as can be seen in Fig. 2. Due to this similarity to other common compact neural network architectures, conclusions based on results from this work might be more generally valid.

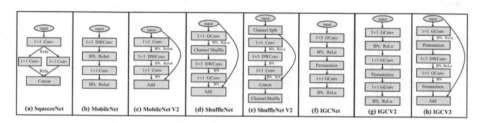

Fig. 2. An overview of compact neural network architectures as presented in [4]. **a** SqueezeNet, **b** MobileNet, **c** MobileNetV2, **d** ShuffleNet, **e** ShuffleNetV2, **f** IGCNet, **g** IGCV2, **h** IGCV3.

4   Methodology

In this section, the exact approach to come to a valid trade-off analysis regarding accuracy, energy consumption and model size will be laid out.

4.1   Implementing Pruning Algorithms

The pruning algorithms that have been analyzed in this work, global unstructured random weight pruning, global unstructured magnitude pruning [8], L1-norm filter pruning [15] and network slimming [16], as well as the MobileNetV2 network have all been implemented in PyTorch. This is due to the fact that for two structured pruning methods, existing PyTorch implementations exist which are based directly on their respective original papers. These implementations have been adapted for the purpose of this paper, and can be accessed through a special GitHub repository.

4.2 Training and Pruning MobileNetV2

MobileNetV2 has been trained on the CIFAR-10 dataset, in PyTorch, through the Jupyter notebook hosted by the University of Twente. It was chosen to use this Jupyter notebook as it gives access to high-performance GPU equipment that is able to quickly and efficiently train, convert and prune models CIFAR-10 was chosen as a dataset to train MobileNetV2 on for this work, as it appears to be widely used in literature, as shown in [1], as a dataset used to train neural network architectures on for the purpose of assessing the (theoretical) performance of pruning networks. Furthermore, CIFAR-10 is a convenient as it is of a relatively manageable size (163 MB) and hence does not require extremely high-performance equipment to utilize it for training neural networks, which is among other things beneficial for the reproducibility of this work. The unpruned MobileNetV2 network trained on CIFAR10 acts as the baseline of the experiment, to which all pruning algorithms have been applied. After applying a pruning technique, fine-tuning is used to improve the overall accuracy of the pruned model. This fine-tuning entails retraining unpruned parameters from their final trained values.

4.3 Determining Model Accuracy

To be able to determine the accuracy of the (pruned) models, the model is evaluated by using PyTorch model inference on the CIFAR-10 test set, and then use the standard formula for accuracy:

$$Accuracy = \frac{TruePositive + TrueNegative}{TruePositive + TrueNegative + FalsePositive + FalseNegative} \quad (1)$$

4.4 Exporting the Model

The model is exported by first converting the model to an Open Neural Network Exchange (ONNX) format. The ONNX platform allows one to interchange machine learning models between various frameworks. In the case of this work, the ONNX platform is used to export the original PyTorch model into a TensorFlow Lite model. TensorFlow Lite is a frame work that is often used to deploy machine learning models on edge devices, and is the format to which the PyTorch models are converted before being loaded on the testboard in this work.

4.5 Energy Consumption Measurements

For measuring the energy consumed, the following setup will be used: An arduino Uno, which is connected to an INA219 current sensor [23], as well as the prototyping board, a Raspberry Pi 4B, of which the VCC line from the power supply will be routed through the INA219 chip by means of connecting it to the V_{in} and V_{out} of the INA219 chip, hence connecting the INA219 chip in series with the prototpying board. The Arduino Uno can then report the measured values for the current and the voltage, together with a timestamp to the computer that is connected by means of a Serial connection. A schematic of the circuit can be seen in Fig. 3.

The values for the voltage (which stays approximately constant) and current, will provide one with a power consumption in mW for each timestamp at which a measurement has been taken.

The INA219 chip has, according to its specification, a current and bus voltage accuracy measurement error of typically ±0.2% with a maximum of ±0.5%. Furthermore, the chip has a 12-bit ADC resolution.

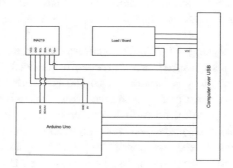

Fig. 3. Circuit of current measurement setup.

5 Experiments

Each pruning algorithm has been applied to the MobileNetV2 model trained on CIFAR-10 with exactly five different sparsity levels, namely, 0.4, 0.5, 0.6 and 0.8 sparsity. It is important to define the sparsity level, as the term has been ambiguously used throughout literature, as pointed out by Blalock et al. [1]. In this work, the sparsity level is referred to as the fraction of the network parameters that has been pruned:

$$Sparsity level = \frac{\#Parameters pruned}{\#Total parameters} \tag{2}$$

For each sparsity level of each pruning method, the pruned model accuracy (after finetuning) is determined.

Furthermore, the total energy consumed for exactly 2000 inferences is determined by taking a sample of the current energy consumption, as described in the methodology section, every 0.5 s. The start and end time of the inference (in miliseconds) is recorded, and each energy consumption data point is tagged with a timestamp. By means of this, it is possible to synchronize this data (required as the energy consumption is recorded on a separate board) and determine which energy consumption data points have been recorded during inference. After this, trapezoidal numerical integration is used to approximate the total amount of energy consumed during inference. The trapezoidal integration for N points can be described by the following formula:

$$\int_a^b f(x)\,dx = \frac{1}{2} \sum_{n=1}^{N} (x_{n+1} - x_n)[f(x_n) + f(x_{n+1})] \tag{3}$$

6   Results

In this subsection, the experimental results shall be presented in various graphs and tables. These results shall be analyzed in this section, whereas further discussion based on results presented in this section shall be made in the discussion section.

Firstly, when analyzing Fig. 4a, it becomes apparent that when increasing sparsity, global unstructured random pruning as well as L1-norm pruning lose accuracy rather rapidly as compared to the Network Slimming and global unstructured magnitude pruning approaches. Now, it is expected that the global unstructured random pruning method loses accuracy rapidly, as to be pruned weights are, as its name suggests, selected randomly. Hence for global unstructured random pruning, there is a possibility that weights closer to one rather than those closer to zero are pruned, as is the case with the unstructured magnitude pruning. Furthermore, from this figure it becomes apparent that when requiring a sparsity larger than 60% on MobileNetV2 and still requiring acceptable accuracy, which we shall define as 50%, one might choose Network Slimming or global unstructured magnitude pruning over the other two pruning methods.

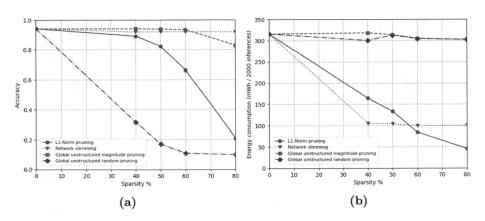

Fig. 4. (a) Model accuracy for various sparsities per pruning method, (b) Model energy consumption for various sparsities per pruning method.

Next, when analyzing Fig. 4b, it becomes apparent that the energy consumption of the unstructured pruning methods stays rather constant, whereas the structured pruning methods significantly decrease the energy consumption when increasing the sparsity of the model. A possible explanation for this could be, as previously referred to in this paper, the theory by Li et al., who mentions that magnitude based pruning of weights might not reduce the inference cost, and hence the energy consumption, to a large enough extent despite the significant pruning of weights due to the irregular nature of its sparsity. This result obtained from real-world inference data seems to support this theory. Another interesting pattern that can be seen in Fig. 4b is that the Network Slimming pruning methods appears to converge around 100 mWh/2000 inferences. It could be a variation on the theory by Li et al. mentioned above for the structure pruning methods, and that there might be a certain degree of irregular sparsity of channels at which the phenomenon occurs, which from this data appears to be before or around 40% sparsity. Future research might give insight in this matter by pruning a model at lower sparsity levels to see from what point this behaviour occurs, and possibly find the cause of why the behaviour occurs.

Now, let us examine Fig. 5a, which shows the relation between the model sparsity and the size of the model. It appears that all pruning methods except for the Network Slimming, have some sort of linear relation between the sparsity of the model and the real-world model size. This is of course expected as one is removing data completely, or in the case of structured data, replacing near-zero weights by zero, allowing for efficient compression of the model. Like the apparent plateau that could be seen in Fig. 4b, again a plateau can be seen for the Network Slimming pruning method. As previously mentioned, a possible explanation for the observed phenomenon could be the fact that there might be a certain degree of irregular sparsity of channels at which the phenomenon occurs. Again, this phenomenon would need to be investigated further to be able to produce a theory that bears more certainty than the speculation presented.

Despite the cause for the plateau behaviour not being known for certain, linking the graphs together, which has been done in Fig. 5b, which compares the real-world model size with the energy consumed per 2000 inferences. At first sight, for the structured pruning methods, there appears to be evidence for a linear relation existing between the size of the model and the energy consumed by the model, however the data for the L1-Norm pruning method in Fig. 5b could also be considered to be somewhat concave upward, which is a possibility somewhat reinforced by the L1-Norm method data in Fig. 5c, which will be discussed in a later part of this section. Furthermore, from this figure it becomes clear that the energy consumption of models pruned with the unstructured pruning methods, does not significantly change when the model size changes as compared to the changes in model energy consumption of models pruned with the structured pruning methods when the model size changes. It seems to make intuitive sense that a model uses less energy when its models size is smaller. Especially for structured pruning methods, it would make sense that when removing complete parts of the network, there is simply less calculations to be done. Now, a possible explanation on why the unstructured pruning algorithms do not use significantly less energy when their model size decreases, could firstly be due to the theory by Li et al., proposing that magnitude based pruning of weights might not reduce the inference cost, and hence the energy consumption, to a large enough extent despite the significant pruning of weights due to the irregular nature of its sparsity. Secondly, a possible reason why the energy consumption does not decrease significantly when the model size decreases, is that because the pruned weights are set to be zero, they might be easily compressed, reducing the model size, however the calculations that need to be done, might still cost the same amount of energy i.e. the calculation $0 \cdot 256$ might cost the same amount of energy as the calculation $42 \cdot 256$.

Next, figure Fig. 5c shows an interesting relation between the sparsity of the model against the energy consumption per Megabyte of the model. This relation is interesting as it gives insight if pruning the model to a higher sparsity, is more or less expensive in terms of energy consumption per MB of the model size. To explain this relation further, imagine a horizontal line in Fig. 5c. Such horizontal line would mean that whenever the sparsity changes, the amount of energy consumed for each MB of the model size stays the same, or in other words, when the model size gets multiplied by x, the energy consumption also gets multiplied by x Now, imagine a line trending downwards. This would mean that when the sparsity increases, the model uses less energy per MB of model size. In other words, when the model size increases by x, the energy consumption increases by $a \cdot x \mid a > 1$.

When looking at the data for the pruning methods in this figure, the first observation is that it appears that the amount of energy consumed per MB by the structured pruning methods increases exponentially when the sparsity of the model increases. This is an indication that, if one would like to reduce the energy consumption of a model by means of decreasing its model size, this is not the best approach for these two pruning methods when using MobileNetV2.

Furthermore, it appears that for the Network Slimming method, the energy consumption per MB of model size is roughly constant. As in the original data, the model size as well as the energy consumption stay roughly constant when changing the sparsity of the network, the ratio between these two variables also stays constant when sparsity changes, hence the curve (or lack thereof) in the figure produced by the data on the Network Slimming pruning method is trivial based on the original data.

Lastly, and most interestingly, the data in Fig. 5c shows, after pruning (from 40% sparsity onwards), a possible, alebeit slight, negative linear relation. This would mean that when the sparsity increases by say x, the the energy consumption decreases by $a \cdot x \mid a < 1$. This is additional evidence to the previously mentioned idea that the relation between the energy consumption and actual model size in MB for the L1-Norm pruning method is not strictly linear, but rather slightly upward concave. This could be useful if one would want to decrease the energy consumption of a model by means of decreasing its model size, as a model size reduction would result in a reduction in energy consumption greater than the magnitude by which the model size was reduced. To be able to confirm this proposed theory however, further research that focuses on this exact relation is required.

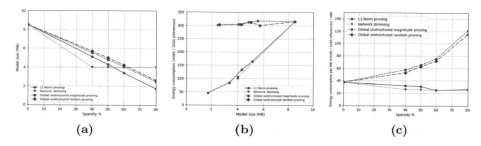

Fig. 5. (a) Model size for various sparsities per pruning method, **(b)** Model energy consumption for different model sizes, **(c)** Model energy consumption per MB for various sparsities per pruning method.

Now, when analyzing Fig. 6a, showing the energy consumption per percentage point of accuracy for each of the sparsity levels used for the experiments, it is apparent that the lowest amount of energy consumed per percentage point gained is the Network Slimming method. The L1-Norm pruning method appears to consume somewhat more energy per accuracy percentage point gained as compared to the Network Slimming method, however the global weight pruning method consumes even more energy for each percentage point of accuracy gained. Lastly, the global random unstructured pruning method appears to firstly, consume significantly more energy per percentage point of model accuracy, and secondly appears to consume more energy per percentage point of accuracy when the sparsity of the model increases. A possible explanation for this behaviour could be derived from Fig. 4a and Fig. 4b. Namely, it appears from Fig. 4b that when the sparsity of the model pruned with the global unstructured random pruning increases, the model energy consumption does not decrease significantly, which could be explained by the previously mentioned theory by Li et al. [15]. At the same time, when increasing the sparsity of the model, the accuracy of the model appears to decrease drastically for the global random unstructured pruning method, as can be seen in Fig. 4a. A combination of both a drastically decreasing accuracy and a model energy consumption that stays approximately the same with increasing sparsity, results in relatively more energy being consumed for each accuracy percentage point for higher sparsities as compared to the energy consumption per percentage point of accuracy for lower sparsities.

Next, when analyzing Fig. 6b, which gives insight in the model accuracy percentage points for each MB of the model size for each of the sparsities experimented with. This is an interesting insight when one wants to maximize accuracy and minimize the model size in MB. One can see that, until about 50% model sparsity, network slimming provides the most accuracy percentage points per MB of the model size. At the same time, around this level of sparsity, L1-norm pruning and global unstructured magnitude pruning seem to provide approximately the same amount of accuracy percentage points per MB of their respective model sizes. All but the global unstructured magnitude pruning method appear to be somewhat constant (L1-Norm pruning and global unstructured random pruning do appear to have more variance however, but they do not appear to display a certain pattern). The global unstructured magnitude pruning method does however appear to show an upward concave, which would mean that for every scaling factor f the network size gets multiplied by, the accuracy decreases with a factor $p \mid p < f$. This would mean that if one wants to decrease the model size as much as possible and keep the accuracy as high as possible at the same time (keeping the energy consumption of the model out of the equation), it would be beneficial to select the global unstructured magnitude pruning as a pruning method from a set of the four methods analyzed in this work on MobileNetV2. Furthermore, the global random unstructured pruning method consistently has a fraction of the accuracy percentage points per MB of the model size compared to the other pruning techniques analyzed.

Lastly, in Table 1, average values over all tested sparsities have been laid out regarding the energy consumption per percentage point of accuracy of a pruned model, as well as the average amount of percentage points of accuracy against the model size in MB of the pruned model. Analyzing Table 1, provides one with similar insights to those already mentioned above when analyzing Fig. 6a and Fig. 6b. It must be noted however that Table 1 does not provide one insights into possible patterns in data, such as the apparent increase of energy consumption per percentage point of accuracy when the sparsity increases for the global unstructured random pruning method and the increase in the amount of accuracy percentage points for each MB of the model size for the global unstructured magnitude pruning method.

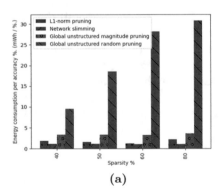 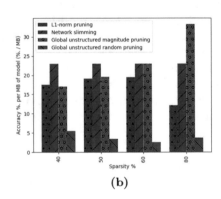

(a)   (b)

Fig. 6. (a) Energy consumption per accuracy %. for various sparsities (lower is better), (b) Accuracy %. per MB of model for various sparsities (higher is better).

Table 1. Average energy per accuracy percent point and average percent point per MB of model size.

Pruning method	Average mWh/2000 inferences per %. (lower is better)	Average %. per MB of model size (higher is better)
L1-Norm pruning	1.73	17.03
Network slimming	1.11	22.98
Global unstructured weight pruning	3.41	20.78
Global unstructured random weight pruning	21.94	3.79

7 Discussion

From the obtained data it has become clear that each pruning method that has been analyzed has its own trade offs regarding accuracy, energy consumption and model size. Network Slimming appears to be decreasing the model energy consumption by almost three times, and has a consistently high model accuracy of about 91%, regardless of the sparsity level. Although this method appears to reach some plateau for firstly the model size, and to a certain extent the model energy consumption from at least 40% sparsity onward. Due to these plateaus, despite the method's relatively constant high accuracy, excellent average energy consumption per 2000 inferences as well as a very acceptable average amount of accuracy percentage points per MB of the model size and on the lowest energy consumption per MB across almost all sparsity levels, it appears to not be possible to prune the model to achieve a model size lower than 4 MB or a model energy consumption of less than approximately 100 mWh per 2000 inferences. For this reason, if one's main goal is to decrease the model size as much as possible as well as if one's main goal is to achieve a minimal energy consumption, one has to take into account that if one's required model size or energy consumption is lower than the plateau values, one should most likely consider an alternative pruning approach. The relatively consistent high accuracy seen in the experiments conducted in this work, is similar to the accuracy behaviour observed in experiments done on VGGNet, DenseNet-40 and ResNet-164 trained on the CIFAR-10 dataset in the paper in which the method was originally proposed [16]. The model size and energy consumption plateauing behaviour is however not observed the original paper, which does not report a real-world energy consumption and model size, but rather reports the theoretical number of float point operations and sparsity. From this work, it appears that the theoretical sparsity and theoretical amount of float-point-operations required for model inference does not necessarily reflect the real-world model size and energy consumption respectively. This could possibly be due to the framework used for the real-world experiments in this work, Tensorflow Lite, being unable to compress the network architecture further due to for example a certain degree of irregular sparsity of channels, as theorized above as a possible adaptation of the theory proposed by Li et al. [15].

Next, L1-Norm pruning appears to be very effective in decreasing the model energy consumption when model sparsity is increased, even below the earlier mentioned Network Slimming plateau value of around 100 mWh per 2000 inferences. The energy consumption of the L1-Norm pruning per MB, as can be seen in Fig. 5c, is furthermore comparable to that of the Network Slimming pruning method. The largest trade off of using the L1-Norm pruning method however is the model accuracy, which as can be seen in Fig. 4a decreases significantly more than all other pruning methods, with the exception of the global unstructured random pruning method. Furthermore, the energy consumption appears to decrease approximately linearly with the model size and the energy consumption per MB across all sparsity levels is not much higher than that of the Network Slimming pruning method. It appears that if one would like to effectively decrease model size and/or the energy consumption beyond the plateau level to which the Network Slimming approach seems to be constrained, and if a relatively low model accuracy compared to Network Slimming and global unstructured magnitude pruning (<60%) is not an issue for the implementation, then using L1-Norm pruning to prune a MobileNetV2 model could be a beneficial choice. The results obtained from the experiments in this work regarding L1-Norm pruning appears to largely correspond to the paper originally introducing the pruning method [15]. In said paper, the curve describing the model accuracy compared to the sparsity for VGG-16 trained on CIFAR-10 is largely similar in its shape as to the curve seen in this work. The main difference between this work and the original paper being the real-world accuracy being lower, despite the trade-off curve between accuracy and sparsity being of approximately the same shape. This could possibly be due to a dissimilarity in the amount of training epochs or hyperparameter values between the two papers. Furthermore, the theoretical reduction in the number of float point operations described in the original paper, seems to be of similar magnitude for a given sparsity as the real-world reduction in energy consumption seen in this work. From the similarities between the two works, it appears that the theoretical performance of L1-Norm pruning is somewhat similar to its performance in the real world and that real world frameworks such as Tensorflow do not significantly seem to affect the performance of said pruning technique.

Global unstructured magnitude pruning has shown to be highly accurate even at high levels of sparsity, while not having the plateau constraint that Network Slimming has. Furthermore, the method appears to have a an upward concave relation between the amount of accuracy percentage points per MB of the model size and the sparsity of the model, making it an excellent pruning method for effectively reducing the size of a model, while retaining high accuracy. The major downside to the global unstructured magnitude pruning method is however its energy consumption, which appears to stay unchanged at all tested sparsity levels as compared to the unpruned network. A possible explanation for the lack of energy consumption reduction is the in the results section previously mentioned theory by Li et al. [15], in which it is proposed that possibly, magnitude pruning of wights might not reduce energy consumption due to the irregular nature of the sparsity. This appears to make the pruning method unsuitable when one's objective is to reduce the energy consumption. The method is however of great use when one intends to decrease the size of a model by the largest possible amount, while retaining a relatively high accuracy on MobileNetV2. In the paper in which the pruning method was originally proposed [8], one can see that the amount by which the number of weights decrease when the sparsity decreases, is three times as large as the amount by which the inference cost in float point operations drops when the sparsity increases by the same amount when applied to AlexNet trained on ImageNet. This behaviour would in itself lead to an increase in energy consumption per MB of model size when the sparsity increases, and is observed in the results of this work. It appears that in this work however, the behaviour that can be seen in Fig. 5c is, despite it appearing a reasonable possibility when looking at the theoretical results from the original paper, not only due to the nature of the model as can be seen from its theoretical behaviour in [8], but also due to the theory by Li et al. described above as there appears to not simply be a smaller decrease in model energy consumption as compared to the decrease in model size when sparsity increases, but there seems to be no decrease in energy consumption at all.

Global unstructured random pruning, shows similar energy consumption concerns as global unstructured magnitude pruning. It seems plausible that, looking at the data regarding energy consumption for each of the tested sparsity levels as well as looking at the previously mentioned theory by Li et al. [15], that this might be the case for all unstructured pruning methods on MobileNetV2, and possibly other networks as well. To confirm such hypothesis however, further research into this matter is required. Furthermore, global unstructured random pruning appears to decrease in accuracy very significantly, with at a sparsity level of 40%, the model accuracy being 58%. less accurate than the pruning method with the next lowest accuracy at 40% sparsity, L1-Norm pruning. The model accuracy loss for global unstructured random pruning is of such magnitude, that it appears that beyond 60% sparsity, the method converges to an accuracy of approximately 10%, which for CIFAR-10, with 10 different classes to identify, means that the performance of the pruning method is as good as simply guessing of what category an image might be. As, when increasing the sparsity, the accuracy drops significantly while the energy consumption stays approximately constant, the energy consumption per accuracy percentage point, as is shown in Fig. 6a increases in a concave down fashion (as the model accuracy eventually converges to 10%) and is almost an order of magnitude worse performing as compared to all other pruning methods.

Now, global unstructured random pruning was introduced as a baseline for other pruning techniques to compare to. After all, if a pruning method would perform worse than random pruning, it is likely not a very useful pruning method. Therefore, it was expected that all other pruning techniques would outperform this global unstructured random pruning method.

When comparing the results from this work with results obtained in the work by Molchanov et al. from 2017 [18], which analyzes pruning entire feature maps based on different criteria (structured pruning), it becomes apparent that from a high-level perspective, disregarding the plateauing behaviour observed for Network Slimming, it appears that in general structured pruning methods decrease the energy required for inference when sparsity increases (a decrease in FLOPs required for inference is in this case assumed analogous to a decrease in inference energy consumption, regardless of their exact relation). Unstructured pruning techniques however, while very effective in decreasing the model size as subscribed in [18], appear to not necessarily decrease the energy consumption required for inference, which is a theory supported by literature [15,18].

Furthermore, as there appears to be a number of similarities between the theoretical performance of the analyzed pruning techniques on network architectures other than MobileNetV2 and their real-world performance obtained from the results of this work, there is reason to believe that similar real-world behaviour might be observed on models other than MobileNetV2, especially those with relatively similar network structures, as can be seen in Fig. 2, such as MobileNet, Shufflenet, ShuffleNetV2 and IGCV3. The effect of the pruning methods analyzed in this work on networks that are more dissimilar to MobileNetV2 might still behave similar to the behaviour seen in this work, although there might be more dissimilarities due to differences in the ability of TensorFlow Lite to compress pruned models in the real world caused by the nature of the sparsity induced by the pruning method on a specific network architecture, which is behaviour that is theorized to be observed in this work when applying Network Slimming on MobileNetV2. Further research on this topic, analyzing the real-world trade-offs of the pruning methods analyzed in this work on network architectures other than MobileNetV2 would however be required to confirm this hypothesis and to possibly generalize any conclusions across multiple network architectures.

8   Conclusion and Future Work

Firstly, the conducted research has been able to provide one with highly useful insights regarding the trade-offs between accuracy, energy consumption and model size between unstructured global magnitude pruning, Network Slimming, L1-Norm structured pruning and random pruning on MobileNetV2, and attempts to generalize obtained results where reasonable. Results from this work could well be used as a reference providing insight and guidance upon deciding what pruning technique to apply to a machine learning model to be deployed on an embedded device, depending on accuracy, energy consumption and model size requirements.

Despite this however, there is a number of questions that are still left to be answered. Firstly, the previously discussed behaviour observed for the Network Slimming pruning method, where a plateau is reached for both the model size as well as the model energy consumption, should be further investigated. Additionally, the original theory posed by Li et al. regarding the inference cost of models pruned with unstructured pruning methods could furthermore be investigated further. This work adds a certain degree of credibility to this theory as no significant decrease in model energy consumption is observed when increasing the sparsity of the network for models pruned with any of the two unstructured pruning methods analyzed in this work.

Furthermore, by conducting the experiments carried out in this work on architectures other than MobileNetV2, it might be possible to generalize conclusions based on observations done to a large range of architectures, as discussed in the discussion section of this paper.

Lastly, by conducting the experiments carried out in this work a large number of times (i.e. measure the energy consumption of a certain model pruned with a certain pruning method 50 times), which due to the time frame of this research was not possible, based on the variance of the data, conclusions presented in this work might become more sound and statistically valid.

References

1. Blalock, D., Gonzalez Ortiz, J.J., Frankle, J., Guttag, J.: What is the state of neural network pruning? Proc. Mach. Learn. Syst. **2**, 129–146 (2020)
2. Cai, E., Juan, D.C., Stamoulis, D., Marculescu, D.: NeuralPower: predict and deploy energy-efficient convolutional neural networks. In: Asian Conference on Machine Learning, pp. 622–637. PMLR (2017)
3. Chen, L., Chen, Y., Xi, J., Le, X.: Knowledge from the original network: restore a better pruned network with knowledge distillation. Complex Intell. Syst. **8**(2), 709–718 (2022)
4. Chen, Y., Zheng, B., Zhang, Z., Wang, Q., Shen, C., Zhang, Q.: Deep learning on mobile and embedded devices: state-of-the-art, challenges, and future directions. ACM Comput. Surv. (CSUR) **53**(4), 1–37 (2020)
5. Frankle, J., Dziugaite, G.K., Roy, D.M., Carbin, M.: Stabilizing the lottery ticket hypothesis. arXiv preprint arXiv:1903.01611 (2019)
6. Gale, T., Elsen, E., Hooker, S.: The state of sparsity in deep neural networks. arXiv preprint arXiv:1902.09574 (2019)
7. García-Martín, E., Rodrigues, C.F., Riley, G., Grahn, H.: Estimation of energy consumption in machine learning. J. Parallel Distrib. Comput. **134**, 75–88 (2019)
8. Han, S., Pool, J., Tran, J., Dally, W.: Learning both weights and connections for efficient neural network. In: Advances in Neural Information Processing Systems, vol. 28 (2015)
9. He, Y., Zhang, X., Sun, J.: Channel pruning for accelerating very deep neural networks. In: Proceedings of the IEEE International Conference on Computer Vision, pp. 1389–1397 (2017)
10. Horowitz, M.: 1.1 computing's energy problem (and what we can do about it). In: 2014 IEEE International Solid-State Circuits Conference Digest of Technical Papers (ISSCC), pp. 10–14. IEEE (2014)
11. Janowsky, S.A.: Pruning versus clipping in neural networks. Phys. Rev. A **39**(12), 6600 (1989)
12. Jordan, M.I., Mitchell, T.M.: Machine learning: trends, perspectives, and prospects. Science **349**(6245), 255–260 (2015)

13. Karnin, E.D.: A simple procedure for pruning back-propagation trained neural networks. IEEE Trans. Neural Netw. **1**(2), 239–242 (1990)
14. LeCun, Y., Denker, J., Solla, S.: Optimal brain damage. In: Advances in Neural Information Processing Systems, vol. 2 (1989)
15. Li, H., Kadav, A., Durdanovic, I., Samet, H., Graf, H.P.: Pruning filters for efficient convnets. arXiv preprint arXiv:1608.08710 (2016)
16. Liu, Z., Li, J., Shen, Z., Huang, G., Yan, S., Zhang, C.: Learning efficient convolutional networks through network slimming. In: Proceedings of the IEEE International Conference on Computer Vision, pp. 2736–2744 (2017)
17. Mirmahaleh, S.Y.H., Rahmani, A.M.: DNN pruning and mapping on NoC-based communication infrastructure. Microelectron. J. **94**, 104655 (2019)
18. Molchanov, P., Tyree, S., Karras, T., Aila, T., Kautz, J.: Pruning convolutional neural networks for resource efficient inference. arXiv preprint arXiv:1611.06440 (2016)
19. Moons, B., Goetschalckx, K., Van Berckelaer, N., Verhelst, M.: Minimum energy quantized neural networks. In: 2017 51st Asilomar Conference on Signals, Systems, and Computers, pp. 1921–1925. IEEE (2017)
20. Murshed, M.S., Murphy, C., Hou, D., Khan, N., Ananthanarayanan, G., Hussain, F.: Machine learning at the network edge: a survey. ACM Comput. Surv. (CSUR) **54**(8), 1–37 (2021)
21. Sandler, M., Howard, A., Zhu, M., Zhmoginov, A., Chen, L.C.: MobileNetV2: inverted residuals and linear bottlenecks. In: Proceedings of the IEEE Conference on Computer Vision and Pattern Recognition, pp. 4510–4520 (2018)
22. Suau, X., Zappella, L., Apostoloff, N.: Network compression using correlation analysis of layer responses (2018)
23. Texas Instruments: INA219 Zerø-Drift, Bidirectional Current/Power Monitor with I2C Interface (2015). Latest rev
24. Venkataramani, S., Raghunathan, A., Liu, J., Shoaib, M.: Scalable-effort classifiers for energy-efficient machine learning. In: Proceedings of the 52nd Annual Design Automation Conference, pp. 1–6 (2015)
25. Yang, T.J., Chen, Y.H., Sze, V.: Designing energy-efficient convolutional neural networks using energy-aware pruning. In: Proceedings of the IEEE Conference on Computer Vision and Pattern Recognition, pp. 5687–5695 (2017)
26. Yu, R., et al.: NISP: pruning networks using neuron importance score propagation. In: Proceedings of the IEEE Conference on Computer Vision and Pattern Recognition, pp. 9194–9203 (2018)

Low-Code Internet of Things Application Development for Edge Analytics

Hafiz Ahmad Awais Chaudhary[1,4(✉)], Ivan Guevara[1,4], Jobish John[2,4],
Amandeep Singh[1,5], Tiziana Margaria[1,3,4,5], and Dirk Pesch[2,4]

[1] University of Limerick, Limerick, Ireland
{ahmad.chaudhary,ivan.guevara,amandeep.singh,tiziana.margaria}@ul.ie
[2] University College Cork, Cork, Ireland
{j.john,d.pesch}@cs.ucc.ie
[3] Lero - The Software Research Centre, Limerick, Ireland
[4] Confirm Centre for Smart Manufacturing, Limerick, Ireland
[5] Centre for Research Training in Artificial Intelligence (CRT AI), Limerick, Ireland

Abstract. Internet of Things (IoT) applications combined with edge analytics are increasingly developed and deployed across a wide range of industries by engineers who are non-expert software developers. In order to enable them to build such IoT applications, we apply low-code technologies in this case study based on Model Driven Development. We use two different frameworks: DIME for the application design and implementation of IoT and edge aspects as well as analytics in R, and Pyrus for data analytics in Python, demonstrating how such engineers can build innovative IoT applications without having the full coding expertise. With this approach, we develop an application that connects a range of heterogeneous technologies: sensors through the EdgeX middleware platform with data analytics and web based configuration applications. The connection to data analytics pipelines can provide various kinds of information to the application users. Our innovative development approach has the potential to simplify the development and deployment of such applications in industry.

Keywords: Low code · Model driven development · Edge analytics

1 Introduction

The Internet of Things (IoT) enables the communication between integrated infrastructure of connected sensors, devices and systems with the aim to provide innovative solutions to various data acquisition and decision challenges across different domains. Research [14] has shown a substantial rise in adoption of a wide range of IoT devices and platforms over the past few years. 29.4 billion IoT devices are expected by 2030 according to [31], a twofold increase compared to the expected number at the end of this year. There is a growing necessity for these

Published by Springer Nature Switzerland AG 2022
L. M. Camarinha-Matos et al. (Eds.): IFIPIoT 2022, IFIP AICT 665, pp. 293–312, 2022.
https://doi.org/10.1007/978-3-031-18872-5_17

different devices and solutions from different service providers to seamlessly work together, as each vendor provides support for its own devices and infrastructure, leading to interoperability issues in the overall ecosystem.

Software development cycles, in the context of IoT applications, are becoming more complex as the challenge for interoperability increases. The complexity across several functional layers composing novel IoT architectures requires deep technical knowledge and cross-functional integration skills for each bespoke system. The learning curve presented by this kind of heterogeneous system development demands simplification of their design, construction, and maintenance. IoT middleware platforms have become an essential part of the IoT ecosystem, as they provide a common interface between the different sensors, computing devices, and actuators. As shown in Ali et al. [3] these platforms fulfil different types of requirements, which leads adopters to perform an exhaustive analysis before choosing and implementing a specific type of architecture. From the perspective of application developers, incompatibility between IoT platforms results in adapting their application to the platform-specific API and information models of each different platform, which makes cross-platform development harder and time-consuming.

We present a low code approach designed to simplify the development of IoT applications. For this we adopt EdgeX Foundry [9] as our example integration platform as it is a well-known, highly flexible open-source software framework addressing the challenge of interoperability between a heterogeneous set of devices, protocols and IoT objects. EdgeX provides a way to homogenize the data sent from different protocols, providing a single data structure that facilitates the way we retrieve information from the Edge. The framework is structured in different layers, each composed of multiple microservices.

In the context of smart manufacturing, we are working on a Digital Thread platform [18] based on model driven development, that provides automatic code generation and deployment of heterogeneous applications that require the interoperability across different systems, technologies and programming paradigms. We choose model types with formal semantics, so that they are amenable to formal verification and analysis. This choice is due to the fact that we believe in the benefits of early validation and verification at the model level and automated support for syntactic and semantic correctness.

In this study, we work with the low/no-code development environments DIME [5] and Pyrus [35], and follow the native library approach [6] to extend the range of systems and domain-specific functionalities that they provide. Figure 1 shows the current architecture of the Digital Thread platform, where the modelling layer provides the essential application modelling capabilities e.g. GUI, data persistence etc. The Process layer, in combination with already implemented common DSLs and External Native DSLs, models the business logic to the application. The integration of different frameworks and technologies is encapsulated in the External Native DSLs and orchestrated in the Process models.

In the following, Sect. 2 summarizes related work, Sect. 3 gives an overview of the software and hardware technologies and tools adopted for the use case,

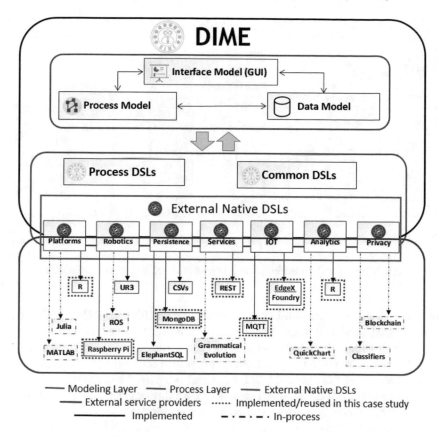

Fig. 1. Architecture overview of the digital thread platform

Sect. 4 details the architecture and the new functionalities in the system, Sect 5 describes the application development and the processes, Sect. 6 discusses the results, and Sect. 7 concludes and sketches future work.

2   Related Work

Low-code platforms are becoming a key technology in the IT industry. They enable a more straightforward workflow to generate highly complex solutions, hiding implementation details and relying on a model-like paradigm, putting the focus on composing behaviours instead of boilerplate code. Many benefits and opportunities are provided by these types of technologies. It is estimated that the global low-code platform market revenue will reach approximately 65 billion U.S. dollars in 2027, having generated 13 billion U.S. dollars in 2020 [30]. This clearly demonstrates the capabilities and potential of these technologies in the context of a competitive and dynamic market. Despite the predominant position of programming languages and frameworks, several solutions can be

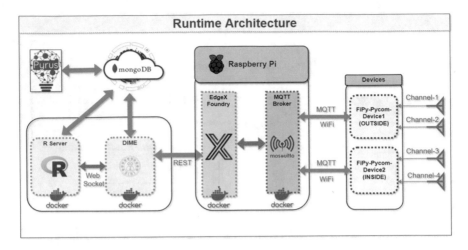

Fig. 2. The runtime architecture: infrastructure and communications

found nowadays with this kind of approach: next to CINCO/DIME [5,24], which have a formal model at their core, several industrial solutions are coming forward, among which Tines [10] specializing in security workflow automation, PTC ThingWorx [25], AWS IoT [4] and Microsoft Azure IOT Suite [23] specializing in IoT and Industrial IoT, H2o.ai [13] for general purpose AI and ML, and Siemens MindSphere [28] for industrial IoT as a Service solutions, that uses analytics and AI to power IoT solutions from the edge to the cloud.

The industrial solutions do not have so far formal models, but they resort instead to the combination of the visual composition of the orchestrations, which is more intuitive than code, with traditional debugging and testing. This can be onerous if one is more remote from the code that is actually running, and has no access to it. Several approaches support dataflow models or control-flow models, but not both. Our choice of models combines the visual appeal of the block-based composition with formal semantics [19,20], and we carry out the data analytics twice: with DIME (control and data flow) and Pyrus (only dataflow).

3   Overview of Tools and Technologies

Figure 2 shows the runtime architecture of the end-to-end application under consideration. Accordingly, in this section, we briefly present the software and hardware platforms that it encompasses.

3.1   Software Platforms

In the following, we present a brief overview of the different software platforms we have integrated to create our low code IoT application development workflow.

EdgeX Foundry. EdgeX Foundry [9] is one of the Industrial IoT middleware platforms that is being widely adopted by industry, especially for industrial automation applications to exploit the benefits of edge compute and edge intelligence. EdgeX Foundry is a highly flexible hardware-agnostic platform consisting of loosely coupled microservices. The docker deployable microservices required to handle a particular application can be broadly categorised into four service layers. The device service layer provides the required connectors used to provision and connects the external hardware devices/objects such as sensors, actuators, machines, cameras etc. These connectors translate the data coming from a wide variety of devices, each possibly using different protocols, into a common data structure/format that is understood by the microservices in all the different layers. The core services layer holds the most knowledge about the EdgeX system deployment, such as which things are connected, how they are configured, what data is flowing through them, etc. The supporting service layer consists of microservices that provide services such as alerts, edge analytics, scheduling, data clean up etc. The application service layer provides a means to export/send the data from EdgeX to other external software applications such as on-premise applications or cloud platforms like AWS IoT or Google IoT for additional processing. A detailed description of all the layers and associated microservices can be found in some of our prior work [15, 16]. While we have chosen EdgeX for this work, similar IoT middleware or integration platforms offering a microservice architecture with REST interfaces would be similarly suitable to our approach described in this paper.

DIME. DIME [5] is an Eclipse based programming-less graphical modelling environment for prototype driven web application development. It follows the OTA (One Thing Approach) [20] and the XMDD (eXtreme Model-Driven Design) [22] paradigms to modelling and development, and it empowers domain experts to model an end-to-end web application with little or no programming experience. To cover the different aspect of web application, DIME provides a family of native DSLs that provide collections of ready to use functionalities, and it supports the development of new applications via different model types that refer to each other and whose consistency is checked largely automatically. GUI models are structural descriptions of UIs that use basic UI components with data bindings. GUI models cover a range of various basic to complex UI elements, that ease the development of user interfaces that are highly customizable at runtime. Data Models cover the persistency needs of applications, on the basis of UML-type structures. In addition to built-in primitive data types, users can define complex and enum data types, and perform aggregation on attributes and associations. Process models express the most often hierarchical business logic, and detail both the data and control flow. Finally, a DIME application descriptor (DAD) model specifies the needed artefacts for an application, including relevant domain models and an interaction process that serves as the landing page for the project. We use DIME for the development of new applications, that we model with the help of natively supported and newly developed DSLs.

MongoDB Database. The Atlas NoSQL cloud database by MongoDB offers an optimised solution for JSON-like optional schemas [1]. It natively supports complex data objects occurring in IoT architectures, like time series data. Atlas can handle operational data in real-time with seamless accessibility across heterogeneous systems and stakeholders. This capability addresses a core need of IoT applications, hence we use MongoDB to store the data collected from the Pycom FiPy light sensors. The communication between the application and the cloud instance of the database is implemented in DIME as a MongoDB-specific DSL.

R Infrastructure. R is a free programming language specifically for statistical and numerical computations and data visualization [33]. We use the *R-serve* package to provide support to the R language in DIME using the TCP/IP protocol [29]. We use R to analyse and visualize the time-series data from the FiPy light sensors. Several packages are imported in the R environment to import data from MongoDB, analyse the time series, and then visualize the data.

Docker. Docker is an open software platform successfully used to deploy applications as *containers*. Using Docker, applications can be built, tested, deployed and scaled into many environments because it includes support for libraries, system tools, code, and various runtimes [8]. We use Docker here to securely deploy frameworks, services and platforms in separate containers. These containers communicate with each other via different protocols such as MQTT, REST, etc.

Pyrus. Pyrus [35] is a web based special purpose graphical modelling tool for Data Analytics. It bridges the gap between Python-based established platforms like Jupyter [2] and workflows in a data-flow driven fashion. The single Python functions are implemented and stored in Jupyter, special signature annotations are added to these functions, so that the functions can be identified by the Pyrus web-based orchestration tool, where the pipelines are composed. From the pipelines, Pyrus generates the Python code for the orchestration and configuration, which is again stored and executed in Jupyter. This separation of concerns decouples the coding and development of the single functionalities from the data analytics orchestration modelling, which happens in accordance with model driven engineering principles [21].

3.2   Hardware Platforms

Here, we discuss the various hardware components that are used for the system implementation. We run EdgeX Foundry on the well-known, and widely used single-board computer, the Raspberry Pi (RPi). We use the 4th generation model B RPi boards with 4 GB memory running Ubuntu server as the operating system (OS). There is no particular reason behind our choice of hardware/OS

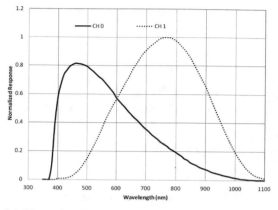

(a) Normalized spectral response of the light sensor [17]

(b) Experimental set up installation

Fig. 3. MQTT based Pycom IoT module

platform other than simplicity, low cost and open-source nature. Any other suitable hardware or OS platform that supports docker based microservices can be used based on specific application demands.

The external "thing" or IoT device we use in our evaluation is the "FiPy" [26] wireless module by Pycom. The device is mounted on a "Pysense" [27] expansion board, also from Pycom. FiPy is a micro python enabled ESP32 microcontroller-based IoT module that supports several wireless connectivity options, including WiFi. We refer to the FiPy module and the Pysense board as "pycom device" in the discussions below. The pycom device acts as an external IoT device that communicates with the EdgeX middleware platform over the MQTT protocol. The provisioning of the pycom MQTT device to EdgeX is done using its device profile, which is a YAML file following the similar procedure as detailed in one of our prior works [16]. The pycom device has different sensors, but we use the light sensor(LTR329ALS01) as an example in this work. The LTR329ALS01 [17] is a dual light sensor that provides digital outputs for external light levels. The sensor periodically reports the light detected at two different wavelengths (blue, red) as Channel 0 and Channel 1 outputs, and the spectral response is shown in Fig. 3a. Thus, we consider the pycom device as an MQTT device having two resources, and we name them as light_ch0 and light_ch1. The remaining sensors may be added as additional resources in the device. However, the approach is the same, hence, we do not include further details in this work.

4   Architectural View: The System of Systems

4.1   The System Architecture

As mentioned earlier, Fig. 2 shows the runtime infrastructure of the end-to-end application under development. Here, two pycom devices with two light channels

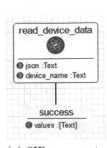

(a) SIB representation in DIME

(b) Java implementation of the body

Fig. 4. read_device_data SIB in the EdgeX collection

each (right) capture the light in different environments. They send that data via MQTT protocol to a MQTT broker running on a Raspberry Pi (middle). The EdgeX Foundry listener reads this data from the MQTT broker and stores it in a local schema.

On the left side, the low-code Web application developed using the DIME model driven development framework runs in a Docker container. The web application initiates the communication with the EdgeX Foundry over a REST protocol, it reads the device data from the local schema of the EdgeX Foundry and does further processing. In this case, it stores the data into a MongoDB NoSQL database, instructs the R server to perform analytics computations on this data, and then sends back the results to the Web application for their visualization and presentation to the users in a graphical format.

Altogether, we see here a variety of systems and subsystems, spanning various hardware and software platforms, protocols, runtimes, and programming languages, that are successfully orchestrated to produce a visualization, an understanding and an interpretation of the data, in two different ways. The key points of this low-code approach are

- the ease of producing virtualized representatives of the disparate system's capabilities in the MDD environments: following the "write once" principle, the Native Service Independent Building Blocks(SIBs) delivers this convenient abstraction, followed by the
- reusability of these ready-made SIBs in many applications, potentially across application domains.

4.2   Integration of the Heterogeneous Subsystems: The Native SIBs

Figure 4a shows how a typical SIB looks like when it is used in a process model. This specific SIB is the read_device_data SIB that belongs to the EDGEX.sibs

Fig. 5. Native SIBs collections (SIB palette developed) and processes in DIME

palette shown in Fig. 5. From this visual representation we see that it requires two inputs, json and device_name, that are fed to this block as either a static value or from another component, as shown via the data flow arrows. The body of the SIB is shown in Fig. 4b. At runtime, this backend functionality is invoked, and upon successful execution the outgoing control branch labelled success is taken, with the corresponding data output to be used later in the workflow. If there are runtime issues, an error branch is followed instead. Every SIB has an error branch to deal with exceptions. The error branches typically output messages and/or take corrective/mitigation actions. They are not shown in this picture nor in the processes, where we concentrate on the normal behaviour. Extending the capabilities of the platform through this integration when developing a new application is the low-code part of the development process: only missing functionalities need to be added, and this happens in a local, small scale development that uses the programming language and runtime of the target system.

4.3 No-Code Reuse Through the Native SIB Palettes

In Fig. 5 we see the collections of new SIBs developed for this application, categorised in their respective Native DSL. This way it is easy to find the Native

DSL to access EdgeX devices, MongoDB, the R platform, REST services etc., that grow with the growth of the platform. Every SIB is developed once, made available to the platform, for further reuse. This is the ease of no-code reuse, so that over time the development of applications that involve systems for which the integration is already available becomes increasingly a no-code task, with low-code new integrations only required for new systems, or when new functionalities for existing systems are added.

5   Application Development: The Processes

At the bottom of Fig. 5 we see the list of processes that have been developed for this application: the Data Acquisition process and the Analytics Dashboard process. We describe them in detail, together with an alternative implementation of the analytics in Pyrus.

5.1   Data Acquisition from IoT Devices

Figure 6 shows the business logic of the web application for the data acquisition from the IoT devices and ingestion into MongoDB. Our fully functional process is rather simple and typical of such applications. It is intended to be used as a demonstrator, as a blueprint for subsequent applications, as well as for application development training purposes.

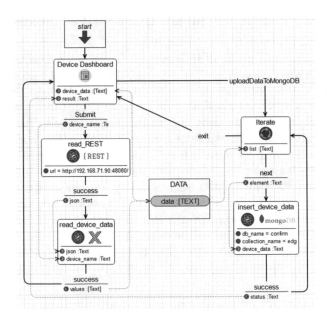

Fig. 6. Data acquisition from EdgeX foundry and data ingestion into MongoDB - process in DIME

Fig. 7. IoT web application: the device name input GUI

The start SIB indicates that we have here a stand-alone process, that does not receive any inputs from the context. The application displays the Device Dashboard shown in Fig. 7, implemented through a GUI model, where a user writes the name of the IoT device of interest. On clicking submit on the GUI, the control flow moves to successive SIB read_REST that has the server url as static value. This SIB reads the device data from the EdgeX Foundry instance running on the Raspberry Pi, and retrieves the corresponding JSON. The SIB read_device_data, the SIB we presented in Sect. 4.2, parses the JSON received from EdgeX Foundry and extracts the device related instances, which are passed as input to this SIB from the GUL SIB. We see here that the dataflow and the control flow differ: while so far we have a linear pipeline in the control flow, the data for some SIBs is provided by various components, at various times. It is therefore useful for the developer to be able to see and design or check separately both the control flow (the logic of what is done, step by step) and the flow of data, which is typically prepared in a number of steps and then consumed by a SIB that collects a number of inputs and processes them.

At this point, the control flow and dataflow return to the GUI, where the extracted data is displayed on the web page. If the user decides to store this data, by clicking on the Upload button, the control flow proceeds to the right side of the Process in Fig. 6: the iterate goes through all the tuples of the dataset and inserts them into the MongoDB cloud database. For this, input parameters provide the given database connection string, the collection name, the device. Upon completion, the control returns to the GUI SIB, to display on the webpage the status of the workflow, and to be ready to accept further inputs.

There is no end SIB as this Web application does not terminate its execution: it is always available, as part of a device command and monitoring infrastructure.

5.2   Analytics Dashboard in R

For numerical and statistical analytics on the data, the Analytics Dashboard process shown in Fig. 9 implements a second web application. When the workflow starts, the SIB connection_mongoDB sends instructions to the R server along with the required inputs: connection string, database name and collection name of

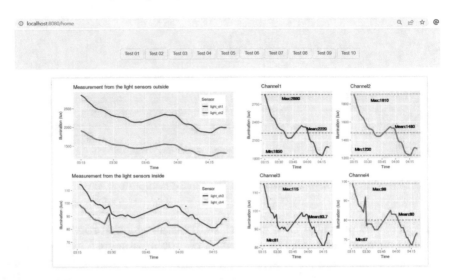

Fig. 8. IoT web application: the data visualization dashboard

the MongoDB database. The R environment reads the dataset in JSON format using the *mongolite* package and returns the file handler for the dataframe. This file handler is passed to the split_data_frame SIB along with the column names that require splitting. The R server splits the master dataframe into multiple dataframes according to the given inputs. In our case they are light_ch1, light_ch2, light_ch3 and light_ch4, corresponding to the four channels in the two devices, two per each device. The file handler for the list of these four dataframes is passed to the next SIBs, plot_dual_linechart and plot_quad_summary_charts along with the variable names for the x and y axes. These SIBs use the four dataframes to generate the plots shown in Fig. 10 and Fig. 11. The plots are then shared with the analytics_dashboard GUI SIB that displays them on the web application dashboard, as shown in Fig. 8.

This is a simple pipeline in R that is easily extensible to more elaborate computations and visualizations. The advantage of having the data in the cloud is that it can be made accessible also to other analytics systems. We show how we carry out essentially the same computations in Python using another Low-code/no-code platform: Pyrus.

5.3   Analytics Dashboard in Python

Figure 12 shows an alternative data analytics processing workflow pipeline that we implemented in the Pyrus platform, this time using Python as the language and platform of choice. The logic is similar to that in the DIME pipeline, but it is worth noting that Pyrus is itself a web application, and its pipeline modelling style is purely dataflow. In this sense, it is simpler to learn and has simpler models, but it is also far less expressive and thus less powerful than DIME. Here,

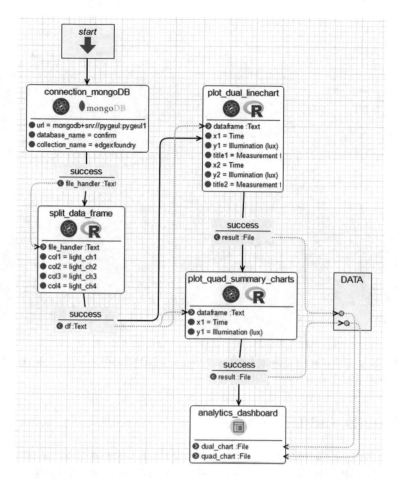

Fig. 9. Analytics dashboard in R: the process in DIME

the Pyrus pipeline establishes a connection to the MongoDB database with the connection_to_mongoDB block, whose required inputs (i.e. MongoDB database URL, database name and collection) are provided as constant strings, which are the grey input blocks in the model. It fetches the requested data in JSON format and uses the Pandas package to create a dataframe. This dataframe is passed for preprocessing to the next block, convert_to_datetime: it converts the time of observation column to the correct time format for ease of analysis and for later plotting. The dataframe and the names of the channels are then passed to the block dataframe_split in order to create a separate dataframe for each light channel. Finally, the plot_all_data block plots them as graphs in the dashboard, as shown in Fig. 13. Here we see the same dual line plot and quad summary with minimum, maximum and mean value as in Figs. 10 and 11.

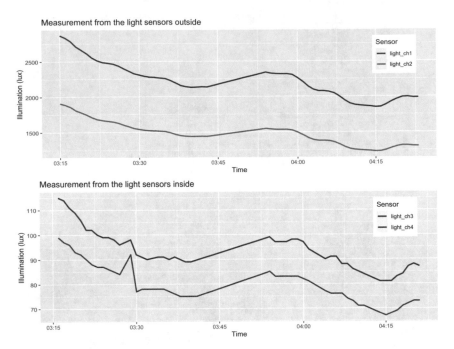

Fig. 10. Dual line plot - generated using R and the DIME DSLs and processes. Outside sensor (top) and inside sensor (bottom)

6   Results and Discussion

The case study described in this paper concretizes a heterogeneous architecture proposal for the development of low-code IoT applications involving cross-edge analytics. In this real-world use case, two devices interact with an orchestrator (here a simple Raspberry Pi) and an analytics server that includes a NoSQL database for storing the unstructured data. The purpose is to create several communication channels to send/receive data from the devices, and eventually provide a data analytics decision-making process that enables supervisors or an automated procedure to take decisions according to established criteria. In this particular case, we send instructions to different devices to start taking observations. We retrieve the observation data from the Pycom FiPy devices 1 and 2, and we show two alternative solutions for the analytics and graphical visualization: an R Server accessed through DIME processes, and a Python/Jupyter notebook server accessed through a Pyrus pipeline.

In the experimental setting, two Pycom FiPy devices installed in the Lero building at the University of Limerick record the observations at fixed intervals. FiPy-Pycom 1 collects light illumination measurements outside the building on channels light_ch1 and light_ch2, while FiPy-Pycom 2 collects the respective light illumination measurements inside the room on light_ch3 and light_ch4. This data is sent to a MQTT Broker that is part of the EdgeX Foundry framework, running

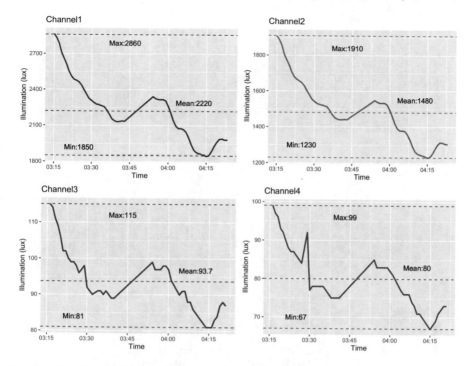

Fig. 11. Quad summary line plot – generated using R and the DIME DSLs and processes. Individual channel plots, same colours as in Fig. 10

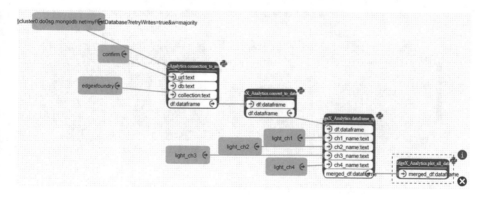

Fig. 12. Analytics dashboard in Python: the Pyrus pipeline

at the edge, in the orchestrator device which is the Raspberry Pi. When the data enters the EdgeX framework, we retrieve it through a REST API call and send it to an analytics pipeline where MongoDB (Fig. 6) stores the data, and then both an R and a Python servers provide the graphics interpretation, within a DIME process (Fig. 9) and a Pyrus process (Fig. 12, respectively. The presented use case shows the ease of modifying the requested features in a simple way:

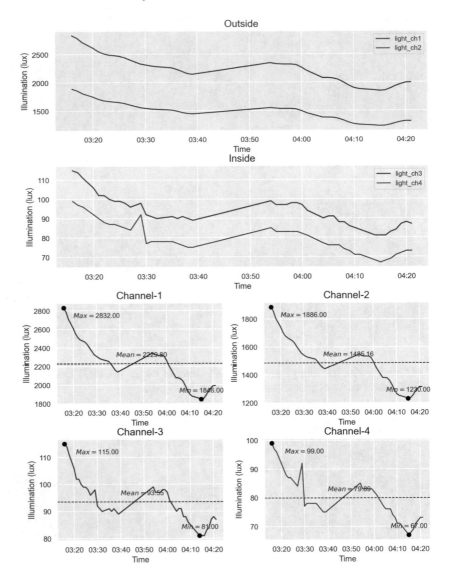

Fig. 13. Analytics visualizations - generated using Python and Pyrus

one only needs to modify the parameters of the SIBs, in a no-code way. This effectively converts the use case into an EAaaS (Edge Analytics as a Service), a service created by low-code/no code applications, which is a novelty in the research field.

The importance of this approach lies in its contribution to the Digital Thread Platform of Fig. 1: we have extended the Native DSLs for EdgeX Foundry, REST, R, and MongoDB. We have also addressed MQTT and Raspberry Pi, but without the need to create specific native SIBs as they are covered by the EdgeX Foundry platform: from the DIME processes we simply communicate with the EdgeX Foundry services via REST, and we do not need to manually integrate them into DIME. As EdgeX Foundry runs on the Raspberry Pi within a docker container, the management is greatly simplified. For the light sensors, we use bespoke Python code that captures the light data from embedded digital light sensor and then sends this data to EdgeX foundry server using the MQTT protocol over WiFi.

The power of abstraction experienced through the use of EdgeX Foundry is again leveraged at the application design level through DIME: we create web applications without writing a single line of GUI code, we have as well reused several SIBs that were preexisting, for REST services and R, so that the combination of EdgeX Foundry and DIME appears as a powerful combination to provide a Digital Thread platform that supports low-code Internet of Things application development for Edge analytics. The quality and completeness of the base platforms are validated via empirical research, both within the open source community and with the adopters in academia [11,22], industry [7], specifically also including manufacturing [34] and security [12]. The core approach for all these specific tools and applications is the language driven engineering (LDE) of [32]: it addresses the principles and the tools for balancing general purpose vs. purpose-specific design of languages and the generation of corresponding Integrated Modeling Environments, of which DIME and Pyrus are the ones we currently use most extensively. The more Native DSLs are included in DIME, the more diverse the systems it integrates, and the more applications are created, the more functionalities in each system, server, platform are made available for others to reuse.

In terms of relevance for the IoT user communities, this is a transformative contribution: instead of needing expertise in a large number of diverse technologies, the users needs to be only trained on these low code platforms. These tools leverage the opportunity to be more productive, efficient, and cost-effective delivering a solution, as the learning curve for abstractions is simpler than the one for programming languages. After initial training, IoT application developers can design, deploy, maintain and evolve their applications with less effort, in a uniform environment, at a more convenient abstraction level, and with better tool support for the code generation and deployment through platforms like DIME and Pyrus.

The goal of supporting non-experts in a specific domain or technology to achieve nevertheless good results in use cases that exceed their expertise is also important: with the proposed approaches, experts of some of the needed technologies create complex, heterogeneous applications using components produced and provided to the platforms by experts of other technologies and domains, widely extending their range of action and confidence.

7   Conclusion and Future Work

Domain specific languages in a low code, model driven paradigm have become a popular approach to design and develop heterogeneous systems. They empower non-software domain experts to participate in the development process. In this case study, we developed and deployed an IoT enabled edge analytics web application in two low code development environments. We used DIME for the application design and implementation of IoT and edge aspects as well as analytics in R, and Pyrus for data analytics in Python, demonstrating how such domain engineers can build innovative IoT applications without having full coding expertise. Our innovative platforms and development approach have the potential to simplify the development and deployment of such applications in industry.

Our next steps include the refinement of the baseline architecture and further extension of the supported devices, protocols and services. Particularly interesting are a DSL for orchestrating the EdgeX Foundry "cr" rule-based engine, which defines rules in a SQL-like syntax and creates streams to retrieve data from the Edge, as well as an extension to work with other orchestration engines like eKuiper from within DIME applications.

Acknowledgements. This project received funding from the European Union's Horizon 2020 research and innovation programme under the Marie Skłodowska-Curie Smart 4.0 Co-Fund, grant agreement No. 847577; and research grants from Science Foundation Ireland (SFI) under Grant Number 16/RC/3918 (CONFIRM Centre), 13/RC/2094-1 (Lero, the Software Research Centre) and 18/CRT/6223 (SFI Centre of Research Training in AI).

References

1. MongoDB Atlas Database—Multi-Cloud Database Service. https://www.mongodb.com/atlas/database. Accessed Mar 2022
2. The Jupyter Notebook. https://jupyter.org. Accessed Mar 2022
3. Ali, O., Ishak, M.K., Bhatti, M.K.L., Khan, I., Kim, K.I.: A comprehensive review of internet of things: technology stack, middlewares, and fog edge computing interface. Sensors **22**(3), 995 (2022)
4. AWS: Amazon Web Services IoT. https://aws.amazon.com/iot/. Accessed Mar 2022
5. Boßelmann, S., et al.: DIME: a programming-less modeling environment for web applications. In: Margaria, T., Steffen, B. (eds.) ISoLA 2016, Part II. LNCS, vol. 9953, pp. 809–832. Springer, Cham (2016). https://doi.org/10.1007/978-3-319-47169-3_60
6. Chaudhary, H.A.A., Margaria, T.: Integration of micro-services as components in modeling environments for low code development. Proc. Inst. Syst. Prog. RAS **33**(4), 19–30 (2021)
7. Chaudhary, H.A.A., Margaria, T.: DSL-based interoperability and integration in the smart manufacturing digital thread. Electron. Commun. EASST **80** (2022)
8. Docker Inc.: Docker. https://www.docker.com/. Accessed Mar 2022
9. EdgeX Foundry: The preferred edge IoT plug and play ecosystem - open source software platform. https://www.edgexfoundry.org/. Accessed Mar 2022
10. Hinchy, E., Kinsella T.: Tines. http://www.tines.com. Accessed Mar 2022
11. Gossen, F., Kühn, D., Margaria, T., Lamprecht, A.L.: Computational thinking: learning by doing with the Cinco adventure game tool. In: 2018 IEEE 42nd Annual Computer Software and Applications Conference (COMPSAC), vol. 1, pp. 990–999. IEEE (2018)

12. Gossen, F., Margaria, T., Neubauer, J., Steffen, B.: A model-driven and generative approach to holistic security. In: Flammini, F. (ed.) Resilience of Cyber-Physical Systems. ASTSA, pp. 123–147. Springer, Cham (2019). https://doi.org/10.1007/978-3-319-95597-1_6
13. H2o.ai: H2o.ai. https://www.h2o.ai/. Accessed Mar 2022
14. Irmak, E., Bozdal, M.: Internet of things (IoT): the most up-to-date challenges, architectures, emerging trends and potential opportunities. Int. J. Comput. Appl. **975**, 8887 (2017)
15. John, J., Ghosal, A., Margaria, T., Pesch, D.: DSLs and middleware platforms in a model-driven development approach for secure predictive maintenance systems in smart factories. In: Margaria, T., Steffen, B. (eds.) ISoLA 2021. LNCS, vol. 13036, pp. 146–161. Springer, Cham (2021). https://doi.org/10.1007/978-3-030-89159-6_10
16. John, J., Ghosal, A., Margaria, T., Pesch, D.: DSLs for model driven development of secure interoperable automation systems with EdgeX foundry. In: 2021 Forum on Specification and Design Languages (FDL), pp. 1–8 (2021)
17. LITEON: Digital ambient light sensor. https://www.mouser.ie/datasheet/2/239/liteon_LTR-329ALS-01-1175539.pdf. Accessed Mar 2022
18. Margaria, T., Chaudhary, H.A.A., Guevara, I., Ryan, S., Schieweck, A.: The interoperability challenge: building a model-driven digital thread platform for CPS. In: Margaria, T., Steffen, B. (eds.) ISoLA 2021. LNCS, vol. 13036, pp. 393–413. Springer, Cham (2021). https://doi.org/10.1007/978-3-030-89159-6_25
19. Margaria, T., Steffen, B.: Lightweight coarse-grained coordination: a scalable system-level approach. Int. J. Softw. Tools Technol. Transf. **5**(2), 107–123 (2004). https://doi.org/10.1007/s10009-003-0119-4
20. Margaria, T., Steffen, B.: Business process modeling in the jABC: the one-thing approach. In: Handbook of Research on Business Process Modeling, pp. 1–26. IGI Global (2009)
21. Margaria, T., Steffen, B.: Continuous model-driven engineering. Computer **42**(10), 106–109 (2009)
22. Margaria, T., Steffen, B.: eXtreme Model-Driven Development (XMDD) technologies as a hands-on approach to software development without coding. In: Tatnall, A. (ed.) Encyclopedia of Education and Information Technologies, pp. 732–750. Springer, Cham (2020). https://doi.org/10.1007/978-3-319-60013-0_208-1
23. Microsoft: Azure IoT. https://www.microsoft.com/. Accessed Mar 2022
24. Naujokat, S., Lybecait, M., Kopetzki, D., Steffen, B.: CINCO: a simplicity-driven approach to full generation of domain-specific graphical modeling tools. Int. J. Softw. Tools Technol. Transf. **20**(3), 327–354 (2017). https://doi.org/10.1007/s10009-017-0453-6
25. PTC: ThingWorx. https://www.ptc.com/. Accessed Mar 2022
26. Pycom: FiPy development modules. https://docs.pycom.io/datasheets/development/fipy/. Accessed Mar 2022
27. Pycom: Pysense shield expansion module. https://docs.pycom.io/datasheets/expansionboards/pysense/. Accessed Mar 2022
28. Siemens: Siemens MindSphere. https://siemens.mindsphere.io/. Accessed Mar 2022
29. Urbanek, S.: Rserve - Binary R server - Rforge.net. https://www.rforge.net/Rserve/. Accessed Mar 2022
30. Statista: Low-code development global platform market revenue. https://www.statista.com/statistics/1226179/low-code-development-platform-market-revenue-global/. Accessed Mar 2022

31. Statista: Number of internet of things (IoT) connected devices worldwide from 2019 to 2030. https://www.statista.com/statistics/1183457/iot-connected-devices-worldwide/. Accessed Mar 2022
32. Steffen, B., Gossen, F., Naujokat, S., Margaria, T.: Language-driven engineering: from general-purpose to purpose-specific languages. In: Steffen, B., Woeginger, G. (eds.) Computing and Software Science. LNCS, vol. 10000, pp. 311–344. Springer, Cham (2019). https://doi.org/10.1007/978-3-319-91908-9_17
33. The R Foundation: R: The R project for statistical computing. https://www.r-project.org/. Accessed Mar 2022
34. Wortmann, N., Michel, M., Naujokat, S.: A fully model-based approach to software development for industrial centrifuges. In: Margaria, T., Steffen, B. (eds.) ISoLA 2016, Part II. LNCS, vol. 9953, pp. 774–783. Springer, Cham (2016). https://doi.org/10.1007/978-3-319-47169-3_58
35. Zweihoff, P., Steffen, B.: Pyrus: an online modeling environment for no-code data-analytics service composition. In: Margaria, T., Steffen, B. (eds.) ISoLA 2021. LNCS, vol. 13036, pp. 18–40. Springer, Cham (2021). https://doi.org/10.1007/978-3-030-89159-6_2

Applications

Adaptive Traffic Control Using Cooperative Communication Through Visible Light

Manuel Augusto Vieira[1,2(✉)] , Manuela Vieira[1,2,3] , Paula Louro[1,2] ,
Pedro Vieira[1,4] , and Rafael Fernandes[1]

[1] Electronics Telecommunications and Computer Deptartment ISEL/IPL Lisboa, Lisboa, Portugal
mv@isel.pt
[2] CTS-UNINOVA, Caparica, Portugal
[3] DEE-FCT-UNL, Caparica, Portugal
[4] Instituto de Telecomunicações, IST, Lisboa, Portugal

Abstract. The purpose of this study is to develop a Visible Light Communication (VLC) system that facilitates safe vehicle management through intersections using Vehicle-to-Vehicle, Vehicle-to-Infrastructure, and Infrastructure-to-Vehicle communications. By using the headlights, streetlights and traffic signaling to broadcast information, the connected vehicles interact with one another and with the infrastructure. Using joint transmission, mobile optical receivers collect data, calculate their location for positioning and, concomitantly, read the transmitted data from each transmitter. In parallel with this, an intersection manager coordinates traffic flow and interacts with the vehicles via Driver Agents embedded in them. A communication scenario is stablished, and a "mesh/cellular" hybrid network configuration proposed. Data is encoded, modulated and converted into light signals emitted by the transmitters. As receivers and decoders, optical sensors with light filtering properties, are used. Bidirectional communication between the infrastructure and the vehicles is tested. To command the passage of vehicles crossing the intersection safely queue/request/response mechanisms and temporal/space relative pose concepts are used. Data shows that the adaptive traffic control system in the Vehicle to Everything environment can collect detailed data, including vehicle position, speed, queue length, and stopping time. The short-range mesh network ensures a secure communication from streetlamp controllers to the edge computer through the neighbor traffic light controller and enables peer-to-peer communication.

Keywords: Vehicular communication · Traffic control · Light controlled intersection · Queue distance · Pose connectivity · White LEDs transmitters · SiC photodetectors · OOK modulation scheme · "mesh/cellular" hybrid network

1 Introduction

The main objective of the Intelligent Transport System (ITS) technology is to optimize traffic safety and efficiency on public roads by increasing situation awareness and mitigating traffic accidents through vehicle-to-vehicle (V2V) and vehicle-to-infrastructure

L. M. Camarinha-Matos et al. (Eds.): IFIPIoT 2022, IFIP AICT 665, pp. 315–331, 2022.
https://doi.org/10.1007/978-3-031-18872-5_18

(V2I) communications [1–3]. The goal is to increase the safety and throughput of traffic intersections using cooperative driving [4, 5]. For self-localization the precise knowledge of the own motion and position, is important. By knowing, in real time, the location, speed and direction of nearby vehicles, a considerable improvement in traffic management is expected.

This work focuses directly on the use of Visible Light Communication (VLC) as a support for the transmission of information providing guidance services and specific information to drivers. VLC is an emerging technology [6, 7] that enables data communication by modulating information on the intensity of the light emitted by LEDs. VLC has a great potential for applications due to their relatively simple design for basic functioning, efficiency, and large geographical distribution. In the case of vehicular communications, the use of VLC is made easier because all vehicles, streetlights, and traffic lights are equipped with LEDs, using them for illumination. Here, the communication and localization are performed using the streetlamps, the traffic signaling and the head and tail lamps, enabling the dual use of exterior automotive and infrastructure lighting for both illumination and communication purposes [8, 9]. VLC enables a more accurate measurement of the distance and position of vehicles with sub-meter resolution given the high directivity of visible light.

The paper is organized as follows. After the introduction, in Sect. 2, the V-VLC system is described and the scenario, architecture, communication protocol, coding/decoding techniques analyzed. In Sect. 3, the experimental results are reported, and the system evaluation performed. A phasing traffic flow diagram based on V-VLC is developed, as a Proof of Concept (PoC). Finally, in Sect. 4, the main conclusions are presented.

1.1 Background Theory on Adaptive Traffic Control

The traffic data collected by the current traffic control system using induction loop detector and other existing sensors is limited. With the advancement of the wireless communication technologies and the development of the V2V and V2I systems, called Connected Vehicle (CV) [10], there is an opportunity to optimize the operation of urban traffic network by cooperation between traffic signal control and driving behaviors. Besides, it will also provide a technical support for the development of Vehicle-to-X systems and autonomous driving industries. A real-time detection of the spatial and temporal data from the network traffic status of urban roads can provide rich and high-quality basic data and a fine-grained assessment of traffic control effects. A closed-loop feedback self-adaptive control system with better uncertainty response capability and higher intelligent decision-making level are inevitable results of the objective needs of the development and application of traffic control and advanced infrastructure technologies. The main difference between the existing self-adaptive traffic control systems is that it relies on traffic control data gathered via a data-driven approach. Also, it can provide support for the interaction between the traffic control system and the traffic flow.

Our adaptive traffic control strategy aims to respond to real-time traffic demand through current and predicted future traffic flow data modeling. Compared with the traffic flow and occupancy information provided by the fixed coil detector in the traditional traffic environment, the adaptive traffic control system in V2X environment can collect more detailed data such as vehicle position, speed, queuing length, and stopping time. While V2V links are particularly important for safety functionalities such as pre-crash sensing and forward collision warning, I2V links provide the CV with a variety of useful information [11, 12]. Since the information network of CVs affects driving behavior and the need for traffic stream control, more research is required on the theory of multimodal traffic control.

To conduct the research, the following questions are considered: Is it possible to implement a reliable VLC system using the proposed I2X vehicular visible communication model, in traffic controlled intersections? Using a network simulator, how can VLC be implemented in a traffic control intersection? By employing VLC at a traffic control intersection, what effects does it have on traffic performance parameters in an urban traffic scenario?

The proposed smart vehicle lighting system considers wireless communication, computer based algorithms, smart sensor and optical sources network, which stands out as a transdisciplinary approach framed in cyber-physical systems.

1.2 V-VLC Communication Link

A Vehicular VLC system (V-VLC) consists of a transmitter to generate modulated light and a receiver to detect the received light variation located at the infrastructures and at the driving cars. Both the transmitter and the receiver are connected through the wireless channel. Line of Sight (LoS) is mandatory.

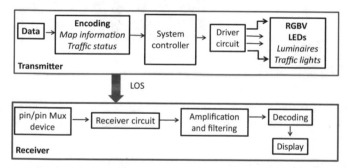

Fig. 1. Generic design of VLC system: data transmission and reception. Block diagram of the VLC link.

Figure 1 illustrates the basic architecture of a V-VLC system. Both communication modules are software defined, where modulation/ demodulation can be programed.

The VLC emitter has a dual purpose, emits light, and transmits data instantaneously by using the same optical power without any noticeable flickering. The digital VLC emitter module converts the binary data to intensity modulated light waves for transmission. A driving circuit controls the switching of the LED according to the incoming binary data at the given data rate, generating an amplitude modulated light beam. Here, the light produced by the LED is modulated with ON–OFF-keying (OOK) amplitude modulation [13].

White light tetra-chromatic (WLEDs) sources, framed at the corners of a square (see Fig. 2a) are used providing a different data channel for each chip. They consist of red, green, blue and violet chips and combine the lights in correct proportion to generate white light. At each node, only one chip of the LED is modulated for data transmission, the Red (R: 626 nm), the Green (G: 530 nm), the Blue (B: 470 nm) or the Violet (V: 390 nm). Modulation and digital-to-analog conversion of the information bits is done using signal processing techniques. Parasitic capacitance (traces and support circuitry) plays an important role in increasing the RC time constant and thus slowing transitions. However, the typical bit rates that can be supported by fast moving vehicles is usually limited by channel conditions, not by the switching speed of the LED.

Transmitters and receiver's 3D relative positions is displayed in Fig. 2a. The LEDs are modeled as Lambertian sources where the luminance is distributed uniformly in all directions, whereas the luminous intensity is different in all directions [14]. The coverage map for a square unit cell is displayed in Fig. 2b. All the values were converted to decibel (dB). The nine possible overlaps (#1–#9), defined as fingerprint regions, as well as the possible receiver orientations (steering angles; δ) are also pointed out for the unit square cell.

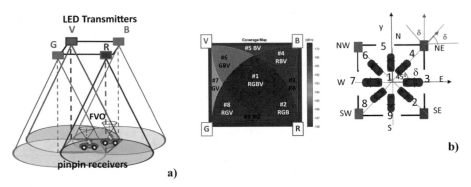

Fig. 2. a) Transmitters and receivers 3D relative positions. b) Illustration of the coverage map in the unit cell: footprint regions (#1–#9) and steering angle codes (2–9).

The visible light emitted by the LEDs passes through the transmission medium and is received by the MUX photodetector that acts as an active filter for the visible region of the light spectrum [15]. The MUX photodetector multiplexes the different optical channels, perform different filtering processes (amplification, switching, and wavelength conversion) and decode the encoded signals, recovering the transmitted information. The received channel can be expresssed as $y = \mu h x + n$ where y represents the received signal, x the transmitted signal, μ is the photoelectric conversion factor which can be normalized as $\mu = 1$, h is the channel gain and n is the additive white Gaussian noise of which the mean is 0. The responsivity of the receiver depends on its physical structure and on the effective area collection. After receiving the signal, it is in turn filtered, amplified, and converted back to digital format for demodulation. The received signal power includes both the energy transmitted from the transmitter and from ambient light. The device receives multiple signals, finds the centroid of the received coordinates, and stores it as the reference point position. Nine reference points, for each unit cell, are identified giving a fine-grained resolution in the localization of the mobile device across each cell (see Fig. 2b). The input of the guidance system is the coded signal sent by the transmitters to an identify vehicle (I2V), and includes its position in the network $P(xi, yj)$, inside the unit cell (#1–#9) and the steering angle, δ (2–9) that guides the driver orientation across his path.

2   Scenario, Environment and Architecture

2.1   Traffic Controlled Intersection

Four-legged intersections are usually two-way-two-way intersections (four-legged intersections), which are connected by eight incoming and eight exiting roads to North, West, South, and East. The simulated scenario is a four-legged traffic light-controlled intersection as displayed in Fig. 3.

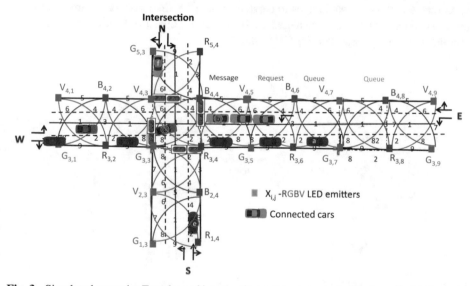

Fig. 3. Simulated scenario: Four-legged intersection and environment with the optical infrastructure (X_{ij}), the generated footprints (1–9) and the CV.

An orthogonal topology based on clusters of square unit cells was considered. The grid size was chosen to avoid an overlap in the receiver from the data in adjacent grid points. Each transmitter, $X_{i,j}$, carries its own color, X, (RGBV) as well as its horizontal and vertical ID position in the surrounding network (i, j). During the PoC, it was assumed that the crossroad is at the intersection of line 4 and column 3. Located along the roadside are the emitters (streetlamps). Thus, each LED sends an I2V message that includes the synchronism, its physical ID and the traffic information. When a probe vehicle enters the streetlight's capture range, the receiver replies to the light signal, and assigns a unique ID and a traffic message [16].

Four traffic flows were considered. One is coming from West (W) with seven vehicles approaching the crossroad: five a_i Vehicles with straight movement and three c_i Vehicles with left turn only. In the second flow, three b_i Vehicles from East (E) approach the intersection with left turn only. In the third flow, e Vehicle, oncoming from South (S), has right-turn approach. Finally, in the fourth flow, f Vehicle coming from North, goes straight. Road request and response segments, offer a binary (turn left/straight or turn right) choice. According to the simulated scenario, each car represents a percentage of traffic flow.

2.2 Architecture

The term "Intelligent Control System" refers to any combination of hardware and software, which operates autonomously according to the information received and processed. After processing, it is able to act towards the desired control through rational choices. In this case, it is intended to apply an ITS to the CV systems.

The computing and communication workload for CVs may also vary over time and locations, which poses challenges to capacity planning, resource management of computation nodes, and mobility management of the CVs. Thus, a well-designed computing architecture is very important for CV systems.

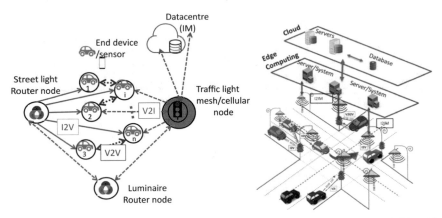

Fig. 4. Representation of the Edge Computing infrastructure. Mesh and cellular hybrid architecture.

Figure 4 presents a draft of a mesh cellular hybrid structure that can be used to create a gateway-free system. As illustrated the streetlights are equipped with one of two types of nodes: A "mesh" controller that connects with other nodes in its vicinity. These controllers can forward messages to the vehicles (I2V) in the mesh, acting like routers nodes in the network. The other one is the "mesh/cellular" hybrid controller that is also equipped with a modem provides IP base connectivity to the Intersection Manager (IM) services. These nodes act as border-router and can be used for edge computing [16].

This architecture enables edge computing and device-to-cloud communication (I2IM) and enables peer-to-peer communication (I2I), to exchange information. It performs much of the processing on embedded computing platforms, directly interfacing to sensors and controllers. It supports geo-distribution, local decision making, and real-time load-balancing.

As exemplified in Fig. 5, the vehicle movement along the road can be thought as a queue, where the vehicles arrive at a lane, wait if the lane is congested and then move once the congestion reduces.

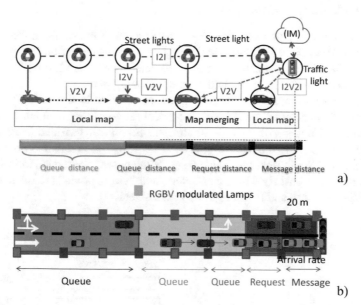

Fig. 5. a) Graphical representation of the simultaneous localization as a function of node density, mobility and transmission range. b) Design of the state representation in the west arm of the intersection, with cells length.

For the intersection manager crossing coordination, the vehicle, and the IM exchange information through two types of messages, "request" (V2I) and "response" (I2V). Inside the request distance, an approach "request" is sent, using as emitter the headlights. The "request" contains all the information that is necessary for a vehicle's space-time reservation for its intersection crossing (flow's direction and its own and followers' speeds). IM uses this information to convert it in a sequence of timed rectangular spaces that each assigned vehicle needs to occupy the intersection. The objective is to let the IM knows the position of vehicles inside the environment at each step t. It includes only spatial information about the vehicles hosted inside the environment, and the cells used to discretize the continuous environment.

A highly congested traffic scenario will be strongly connected. To determine the delay, the number of vehicles queuing in each cell at the beginning and end of the green time is determined by V2V2I observation, as illustrated in Fig. 5. The distance, d, between vehicles can be calculated based on a truncated exponential distribution [17]. An IM acknowledge is sent, "response" from the traffic signal over the facing receiver to the in-car application of the head vehicle. Once the response is received (message distance in Fig. 5), the vehicle is required to follow the provided occupancy trajectories (footprint regions, see Fig. 2 and Fig. 3). If a request has any potential risk of collision with all other vehicles that have already been approved to cross the intersection, the control manager only sends back to the vehicle (V2I) the "response" after the risk of conflict is exceeded.

2.3   Color Phasing Diagram

The specification of the phasing plan requires that each of the traffic movements to be accommodated be assigned to one of the timing functions to produce the desired sequence of displays. The choice of treatments used will determine which timing functions will be activated and which will be omitted from the phasing plan.

A color phasing diagram for a four-legged intersection is shown in Fig. 6. It was assumed four "color poses" linked with the radial range of the modulated light in the RGBV crossroad nodes [13]. The West straight, South left turn and West right turn maneuvers correspond to the "Green poses". "Red poses" are related to South straight, East left turn, and South right turn maneuvers. "Blue poses" are related to East straight, North left turn, and East right turn maneuvers, and "violet poses" are related to North straight, West left turn, and North right turn maneuvers.

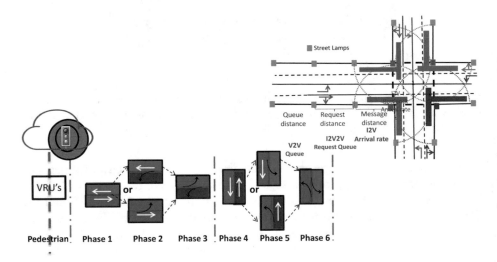

Fig. 6. Color phasing diagram in a four-legged intersection.

In the phasing diagram, Phase 2 and Phase 5 offer two alternatives. Only one of which may be displayed on any cycle. Vehicles are stopped on all approaches to an intersection while pedestrians are given a WALK indication, the phasing is referred to as "exclusive". Functional barriers (dash dot lines) exist between exclusive pedestrian and Phase 1and Phase 6.

The problem that the IM has to solve is, in fact, allocating the reservations among a set of drivers in a way that a specific objective is maximized. Signal timing involves the determination of the appropriate cycle length (i.e., the time required to execute a complete sequence of phases) and apportionment of time among competing movements and phases. The timing apportionment is constrained by minimum green times that must be imposed to provide for pedestrians and to ensure that motorist expectancy is not violated.

2.4 Multi-vehicle Cooperative Localization

There are critical points where traffic conditions change: the point at which a vehicle begins to decelerate when the traffic light turns red (message distance), the point at which it stops and joins the queue (queue distance), the point at which it starts to accelerate when the traffic light turns green (request distance) or the points at which the coming vehicle is slowed by the leaving vehicle (see Fig. 5). As a result, the road resistances can be calculated dynamically based on the relative pose positions of the vehicles and the traffic signal phase at intersections. With V2I2V communication, the travel time that influences traffic channelization in different routes can be calculated and real-time data about speed, spacing, queues, and saturation can be collected across the queue, request and message distances.

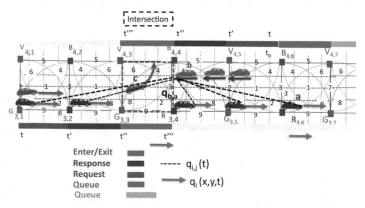

Fig. 7. Movement of the cars, in the successive moments, with their colorful poses (color arrows) and $q_{i,\ j}$ spatial relative poses (dot lines).

In Fig. 7, the movement of the cars in successive moments is depicted with their colored poses (colored arrows) and $q_{i,j}$ spatial relative poses (dot lines).

We denote $q(t)$, $q(t')$, $q(t'')$, $q(t''')$ as the vehicle pose estimation at the time t, t', t'', t''' (request, response, enter and exit times), respectively. All the requests contain vehicle positions and approach speeds. If followers exist, the request message from its leader includes the position and speed previously received by V2V. This information alerts the controller to a later request message (V2I), confirmed by the follow vehicle.

The vehicle speed can be calculated by measuring the actual travelled distance overtime, using the ID's transmitters tracking. Two measurements are required: distance and elapsed time. The distance is fixed while the elapsed time varies and depends on the vehicle's speed and is obtained through the instants where the footprint region changes. The receivers compute the geographical position in the successive instants (path) and infer the vehicle's speed. When two vehicles are in neighborhood and in different lanes, the geometric relationship between them ($q_{i, j}$) can be inferred fusing their self-localizations via a chain of geometric relationships among the vehicles poses and the local maps. For a vehicle with several neighboring vehicles, the mesh node (Fig. 3 and Fig. 4) uses the indirect V2V relative pose estimations method taking advantage of the data of each neighboring vehicle [18].

3   VLC Evaluation

In the PoC (see Fig. 3) it is assumed that a_1, b_1, and a_2, make up the top three requests, followed by b_2, a_3, and c_1 in fourth, fifth and sixth place, respectively. In seventh, eighth and nineth request places are b_3, e and a_3, respectively, followed in tenth place, by c_2. In penultimate request is a_5, and in the last one is f. So, $t_{a1} < t_{b1} < t_{a2} < t_{b2} < t_{a3} < t_{c1} < t_{b3} < t_e < t_{a4} < t_{c2} < t_{a5} < t_f$. According to our assumptions, 540 cars approach the intersection per hour, of which 80% come from east and west. Then, 50% of cars will turn left or right at the intersection and the other 50% will continue straight. There is only one episode per scenario and the cars cycle in the same order every time.

3.1   Communication Protocol and Coding/Decoding Techniques

To code the information, an On-Off keying (OOK) modulation scheme was used, and it was considered a synchronous transmission based on a 64- bits data frame.

As exemplified in the top part of Fig. 8, the frame is divided into four, if the transmitter is a streetlamp or headlamp, or five blocks, if the transmitter is the traffic light. The first block is the synchronization block [10101], the last is the payload data (traffic message) and a stop bit ends the frame. The second block, the ID block gives the location (x, y coordinates) of the emitters inside the array ($X_{i, j}$,). Cell's IDs are encoded using a 4 bits binary representation for the decimal number. The δ block (steering angle (δ)) completes the pose in a frame time $q(x, y, \delta, t)$. Eight steering angles along the cardinal points gives the car direction, and are coded with the same number of the footprints in the unit cell (Fig. 2) are possible. If the message is diffused by the IM transmitter, a pattern [0000] follows this identification, if it is a request (R) a pattern [00] is used. The traffic message completes the frame.

Because the VLC has four independent emitters, the optical signal generated in the receiver can have one, two, three, or even four optical excitations, resulting in 2^4 different optical combinations and 16 different photocurrent levels at the photodetector.

As an example, in in Fig. 8 Vehicle c_1 receives two response MUX signals as it crosses the intersection. This vehicle, driving on the left lane, receives order to enter the intersection in # 7, turning left (NE) and keeps moving in this direction across position #1 toward the North exit (Phase2, violet pose). In the right side, the received channels are identified by its 4-digit binary codes and associated positions in the unit cell. On the top the transmitted channels packets [R, G, B, V] are decoded.

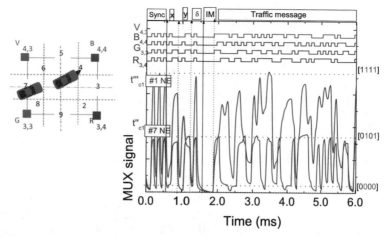

Fig. 8. MUX signal responses and the assigned decoded Inside the intersection; messages acquired by vehicle c_1, poses #7NE, #1NE. On the top the transmitted channels packets [R, G, B, V] are decoded.

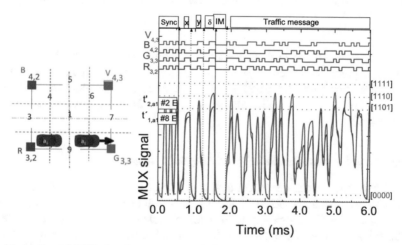

Fig. 9. Normalized MUX signal responses and the assigned decoded messages acquired by vehicles a_1 at different response times. Message distance, Poses #8E and #2E.

3.2 Adaptive Traffic Control

In Fig. 9 and Fig. 10 the normalized MUX signals and the decoded messages assigned to IM received by Vehicle a_1, a_5, b_2, b_3 at different response times are shown. On the top the transmitted channels [R, G, B, V] are decoded. In the right side, the received channels for each vehicle are identified by its 4-digit binary codes and associated positions.

Figuring out Fig. 3 and Fig. 6, Fig. 9 shows the MUX signals assigned to response messages received by Vehicle a_1, driving the right lane, that enters Cell $C_{4,2}$ in #2 (t'_1, Phase1, green pose), goes straight to E to position #8 (t'_2, Phase1, green pose). Then, this vehicle enters the crossroad through #8 and leaves it in the exit #2 keeping always

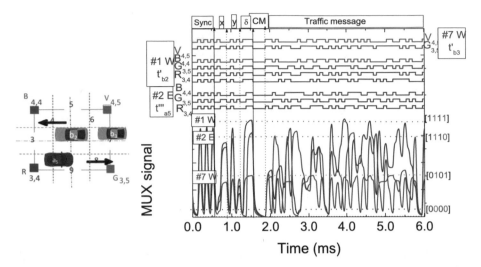

Fig. 10. Normalized MUX signal responses and the assigned decoded messages acquired by vehicles a_5, b_2, b_3 at different response times. Vehicle a_5, pose #2E, and Vehicle b_2 poses #7W and, b_3 at #1W.

the same direction (E). In Fig. 10, vehicle b_2 and b_3 approaches the intersection after having asked permission to cross. It only receives authorization when the vehicle a_5 has left the intersection (end of Phase 2). Then, Phase 3 begins with vehicle b_1 heading to the intersection (W) (pose red) while vehicles a_i ($1 < i < 5$) follows its destination towards E (pose green).

3.3 Queuing System: Dynamic Traffic Signal Phasing

The traffic controller uses queue, request and response messages, from the a_i, b_i, c_i, e_i and f_i vehicles, fusing the self-localizations $q_i(t)$ with their space relative poses $q_{ij}(t)$ to generate phase durations appropriate to accommodate the demand on each cycle.

The following parameters are therefore needed to model the queuing system: The initial arrival time (t_0) and velocity (v) in each the occupied section. The initial time is defined as the time when the vehicles leave the previous section (queue, request or message distances) and move along the next section, $q_i(t, t')$. The service time is calculated using vehicle speed and distance of the section. The number of service units or resources is determined by the capacity of the section, $n(q_i (x, y, \delta, t))$ and vehicle speed which depends on the number of request services, and on the direction of movement along the lane $q_i (x, y, \delta, t)$.

To each driving Vehicle, x_i, is assigned the unique time at which it must enter the intersection, $t''[x_i]$. The phase flow of the PoC intersection is shown in Fig. 11 according to the phasing diagram. In this diagram, the cycle length is composed of 5 of the 7 phases contemplated (see Fig. 6) and divided in 16 time sequences. The exclusive pedestrian phase contains the *"0"*, the *"1"* and the *"16"* sequences. The cycle's top synchronism starts with sequences "*1*". The first, second, third, and fourth phases contain sequences between "*2*" and "*15*" and control traffic flow.

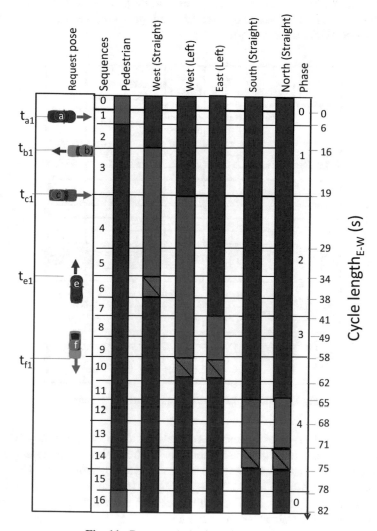

Fig. 11. Requested phasing of traffic flows.

The vehicle movement along the lane can be thought as a queue, where the vehicles arrive, wait if the lane is congested and then move once the congestion reduces. In Fig. 5, a graphical representation of the simultaneous localization and mapping problem using connectivity as a function of node density, mobility and transmission range was illustrated.

The matrix of states allows the user to view, enter, or modify the division of an intersection into states, as shown in Fig. 12. The matrix shows the durations of the states for a given cycle. In this matrix, each element represents the lighting state of the traffic light (if it is selected, the light is green) for the corresponding state. Columns represent the duration of the states in the different arms of the intersection, from cycle minimum [fluid traffic] to cycle maximum [dense traffic]. For a medium traffic scenario, three distinct cycles are considered based on the higher volume traffic in the request directions (N-S, W-E straight or left).

Sequences	Low-traffic scenario (s)	N-S medium traffic scenario (s)	E-W medium traffic scenario (Left) (s)	E-W medium traffic scenario (Straight) (s)	High traffic scenario (s)	Fixed time (s)
0	9	3	3	3	3	
1	0	6	6	6	6	
2						10
3						3
4	0	8	7	10	12	
5						5
6						4
7						3
8	3	3	8	8	10	
9	3	3	9	9	8	
10						4
11						3
12	3	6	3	3	7	
13	3	8	3	3	9	
14						4
15						3
16	0	4	4	4	6	
Cycle lenght	60	80	82	85	100	39

Fig.12. Matrix of states at a four-legged intersection.

The column on the right of the matrix is called the column of fixed times. A fixed time is filled in when a state has the same duration for all the cycles of the lighting plan. The durations of movable states can be entered for any state at a dynamic time. The following operations can be performed by the IM depending on the requests information: modify the durations of cycle; enter the fixed times; change the durations of states with the transportable from any state at a dynamic time or modify the intersection coordination offset.

The objective is to maximize the traffic flow through the intersection over time. For traffic coordination, in the scenario presented (Fig. 3), the IM receives requests for access to the intersection from all the leading cars at different times. t_{x1} (Fig. 10). This type of information (V2I) enables the IM to know the precise location and the speed of all the leader vehicles, as well as the location and speed from their followers that was sent to the leaders through V2V. This data helps previewing the initial arrival times and speeds at the different sections. The IM has to minimize accumulated total waiting time $aTwt$ in each arm of the intersection defined as [19]:

$$aTw_t = \sum_{xi=1}^{n} (awt)_{xi,t}$$

(1)

where *awt (xi,t)* is the amount of time in seconds a vehicle x_i has a speed of less than 0.1 m/s at step t and n represents the total number of vehicles in the environment at step t. When the speed is less than 0.1 m/s a queue alert is generated. If:

$$r_t = aTw_t - aTw_{(t-1)} \qquad (2)$$

$aTwt_t$ and $aTwt_{t-1}$ represent the accumulated total waiting time of all the cars in the intersection captured respectively at step t and $t - 1$. If r_t is negative more vehicles in queues are added compared to the situation in the previous step $t - 1$, resulting in higher waiting times compared to the previous step.

The PoC assumes that all the leaders approach the intersection with similar velocities at different times (Fig. 11). There is only one episode per scenario and the cars cycle in the same order every time. Vehicle a_1 was the first to request to cross the intersection and informed IM about its position and also that four others follow it at their positions with their speeds (see Fig. 9). Phase 1, sequence 3, therefore, begins at $t'a_1$. Vehicle b_1 requests access later and includes the mappings of its two followers in its request. As the order to cross conflicts with a_i movement, he and his followers will pile up on the stop line increasing the total waiting time of the b_i cars. The fourth sequence, is an adaptive sequence (Fig. 12). Due to the presence of a medium E-W traffic scenario, the IM extends the green time in order to accommodate the passage of all the a_i followers as well as the simultaneous passage of the arriving c_i (Fig. 8). From the capacity point of view, it is more efficient, if Vehicle c_1 is given access (Phase 2) before Vehicles b_i, and Vehicle c_2 is given access before Vehicle e, forming a west left turn of set of vehicles (platoon) before giving way to the fourth phase with north and south conflicting flows, as stated in Fig. 6. Meanwhile, the speed of Vehicle e was reduced, increasing the total accumulated time in the S-N arm.

Adaptive sequences 8 and 9 kick off Phase 3 (Fig. 11) and the sequence times will be adjusted according to the variation of r_t for the left turn of the b_i cars. A new phase, Phase 4, begins and includes two adaptive sequences, sequence 12 and 13. Their time intervals will be as short as possible, which will free up capacity in the cycle for the E-W flows that are heavily loaded. Taking into account the accumulated total waiting time in each arm an 85-s cycle is recommended for this type of flow. The times associated with each sequence can be visualized in Fig. 11.

So, the real-time detection of the spatiotemporal data based on urban road network traffic status can provide rich and high-quality basic data and fine-grained assessment of control effects for traffic control.

Safety and privacy are also the key requirements for the V-VLC. It is important to improve the coding techniques, in the future, in order to allow only the legitimate receivers to process secure request/response messages. Here, the security is embedded in the physical transmission. In the LoS channel no information can be made available by the eavesdropper, i.e., he is completely passive. Using the street lamp positions to determine vehicular flow eliminates the need for certificates or passwords from the network and replaces them with statistical secrecy.

4 Conclusions

With V-VLC-ready connected cars, we propose optimizing urban traffic network operation by integrating traffic signal control and driving behavior. For managing intersections, the adaptive traffic control system uses a queue/request/response approach. An architecture, scenario, environment, and hybrid mesh/cellular network configuration were developed and proposed. The V2I2V communications enable real-time monitoring of queues, requests, and messages, along with the travel times necessary to synchronize traffic routing in various routes. The vehicles are controlled in their arrival time and scheduled to cross intersections at predetermined times to reduce traffic delays. In order to demonstrate the concept, a phasing diagram and matrix of states are proposed based on the total accumulated time. Results show that the adaptive traffic control in a V2X environment can collect more detailed data, such as vehicle position, speed, queue length, and stopping time, than the traffic flow and occupancy information provided by fixed coil detectors. The traffic light phase is adjusted to the traffic scenario and the duration of the traffic light is changed dynamically which reduces travel times and unnecessary waiting for the green phase, leading to optimized traffic flow. The introduction of VLC between connected vehicles and the surrounding infrastructure allows the direct monitoring of critical points that are related to the queue formation and dissipation, relative speed thresholds and inter-vehicle spacing increasing the safety.

Acknowledgements. This work was sponsored by FCT – Fundação para a Ciência e a Tecnologia, within the Research Unit CTS – Center of Technology and Systems, reference UIDB/00066/2020.

References

1. Elliott, D., Keen, W., Miao, L.: Recent advances in connected and automated vehicles. J. Traffic Transp. Eng. **6**(2), 109–131 (2019)
2. Bajpai, J.N.: Emerging vehicle technologies & the search for urban mobility solutions. Urban Plann. Transp. Res. **4**(1), 83–100 (2016)
3. Wang, N., Qiao, Y., Wang, W., Tang, S. Shen, J.: Visible light communication based intelligent traffic light system: designing and implementation. In: 2018 Asia Communications and Photonics Conference (ACP)(2018). https://doi.org/10.1109/ACP.2018.8595791
4. Cheng, N., et al.: Big data driven vehicular networks. IEEE Netw. **32**(6), 160–167 (2018)
5. Singh, P., Singh, G., Singh, A.: Implementing visible light communication in intelligent traffic management to resolve traffic logjams. Int. J. Comput. Eng. Res **5**(9), 1–5 (2015)
6. O'Brien, D., et al.: Indoor visible light communications: challenges and prospects. Proc. SPIE **7091**(709106), 60–68 (2008)
7. Parth, H., Pathak, X., Pengfei, H., Prasant, M.: Visible light communication, networking and sensing: potential and challenges. IEEE Commun. Surv. Tutorials Fourthquarter **17**(4), 2047–2077 (2015)
8. Nawaz, T., Seminara, M., Caputo, S., Mucchi, L., Catani, J.: Low-latency VLC system with Fresnel receiver for I2V ITS applications'. J. Sensor Actuator Netw. **9**(3), 35 (2020)
9. Caputo, S., Mucchi, L., Cataliotti, F., Seminara, M., Nawaz, T., Catani, J.: Measurement-based VLC channel characterization for I2V communications in a real urban scenario. Veh. Commun. **28**, 100305 (2021)

10. Yousefi, S., Altman, E., El-Azouzi, R., Fathy, M.: Analytical model for connectivity in vehicular Ad hoc networks. IEEE Trans. Veh. Technol. **57**(6), 3341–3356 (2008)
11. Pribyl, O., Pribyl, P., Lom, M., Svitek, M.: Modeling of smart cities based on ITS architecture. IEEE Intell. Transp. Syst. Mag. **11**(4), 28–36 (2019)
12. Miucic, R.: Connected Vehicles: Intelligent Transportation Systems. Springer, Cham, Switzerland (2019). https://doi.org/10.1007/978-3-319-94785-3
13. Vieira, M.A., Vieira, M., Louro, P., Vieira, P.: Bi-directional communication between infrastructures and vehicles through visible light. In: Proceeding SPIE 11207, Fourth International Conference on Applications of Optics and Photonics, 112070C, 3 October 2019 (2019). https://doi.org/10.1117/12.2526500
14. Zhu, Y., Liang, W., Zhang, J., Zhang, Y.: Space-collaborative constellation designs for MIMO indoor visible light communications. IEEE Photonics Technol. Lett. **27**(15), 1667–1670 (2015)
15. Vieira, M.A., Vieira, M., Vieira, P., Louro, P.: In: Optical signal processing for a smart vehicle lighting system using a-SiCH technology. In: Proceeding SPIE 10231, Optical Sensors 2017, 102311L (2017)
16. Yousefpour, A., et al.: All one needs to know about fog computing and related edge computing paradigms: a complete survey. J. Syst. Architect. **98**, 289–330 (2019)
17. Momeni, S., Wolfinger, B.E.: Availability evaluations for IPTV in VANETs with different types of access networks. EURASIP J. Wirel. Commun. Netw. **2014**(1), 1–11 (2014). https://doi.org/10.1186/1687-1499-2014-117
18. Vieira, M.A., Vieira, M., Louro, P., Vieira, P.: Cooperative vehicular communication systems based on visible light communication. Opt. Eng. **57**(7), 076101 (2018)
19. Vidali, A., Crociani, L., Vizzari, G., Bandini, S.: A deep reinforcement learning approach to adaptive traffic lights management. In: WOA 2019, pp. 42–50, June 26 (2019)

An Edge Computing Approach for Autonomous Vehicle Platooning

Omkar Dokur$^{(\boxtimes)}$ ⓘ, Gustavo Olenscki ⓘ, and Srinivas Katkoori ⓘ

University of South Florida, Tampa, FL 33620, USA
{omkardokur,gustavo12,katkoori}@usf.edu

Abstract. One of the recent advancements in Internet of Things (IoT) is connected vehicles (CV), where each vehicle can connect to the things or vehicles nearby using wireless networks such as Dedicated Short Range Communication (DSRC). This gives rise to many vehicular applications such as platooning. A group of vehicles can negotiate and drive jointly close to each other in a cooperative manner to form a platoon. Using connected and automated driving systems, platooning can aid in cutting total fuel costs, reducing CO_2 emissions, improving efficiency, decreasing traffic congestion, increasing safety, and providing comfort for the drivers. The existing work on platooning assumes sensors besides DSRC sensors which may not be reliable in extremely poor weather conditions. In this work, we propose DSRC only based platoon negotiation where each vehicle is an edge node. A vehicle that is interested in platooning can broadcast a DSRC message and interesting vehicles can establish communication to negotiate their route. Then, in a series of transactions over the DSRC channel they can agree upon the leader position as well as the follower position(s). We employ the relative position estimation technique we proposed in prior work. The host vehicle (HV) computes the relative angle with the remote vehicle (RV) to accurately estimate its relative position based on Basic Safety Messages (BSMs) only. In this paper, we propose a new platoon negotiation algorithm based only on DSRC communication messages that works well in any weather condition. To test this, we extend CARLA, an autonomous driving simulator to support IoT connectivity as well as platooning. We implemented DSRC agent class for connectivity that can be instantiated for every vehicle in the simulation. The proposed edge node negotiation algorithms include platoon-ready, pre-negotiation, negotiation resolver, and platoon member algorithms. We experimented with a two-vehicle case scenario in the platoon negotiation phase and validated the algorithms in simulation.

Keywords: Internet of Things (IoT) · Connected vehicles · Autonomous vehicles · Platooning · CARLA · Simulation

1 Introduction and Motivation

Internet of Things (IoT) refers to an exchange of information between physical objects connected over the internet. IoT is experiencing a rapid increase in the

© IFIP International Federation for Information Processing 2022
Published by Springer Nature Switzerland AG 2022
L. M. Camarinha-Matos et al. (Eds.): IFIPIoT 2022, IFIP AICT 665, pp. 332–349, 2022.
https://doi.org/10.1007/978-3-031-18872-5_19

number of physical objects getting connected [1]. Many IoT architectures have been proposed so far. Hanes *et al.* [2] presented a simplified IoT architecture in their book consisting of edge, fog, and cloud layers from bottom to top which is briefly discussed below:

– Edge Layer: Contains smart objects, sensors, and actuators also known as edge nodes. Computing is performed by IoT devices here also known as edge computing.
– Fog Layer: Contains communication and processing units with network connectivity also known as fog nodes. Data from edge nodes is uploaded to the cloud through fog nodes also known as fog computing.
– Cloud Layer: In this layer, data from fog nodes is used to develop applications and analytics.

The above concept of IoT can be applied in the field of transportation to autonomous vehicles (AVs) [3] where each AV can act as an edge node to solve many problems. According to American Trucks Association (ATA), trucks transported about 72.5% of the nation's total freight while consuming 45.6 billion gallons of fuel in 2019 [4]. Lately, travel by passenger cars and light-duty trucks has increased by 48% in 2019. U.S. Environment Protection Agency (EPA) reported that greenhouse gas emissions due to transportation are the largest accounting for 29% of the total in 2019 with an increasing trend from 1990 to 2019 [5]. This problem can be solved by platooning where vehicles travel in a group to achieve more fuel efficiency [6]. A lot of companies such as Tesla, Waymo, Uber, etc. are working towards making autonomous driving technology available to the general public. Government agencies are working together to test the connected vehicle (CV) technology through various pilot deployment programs [7]. These two technologies are combined to achieve more efficiency and safety in transportation. Various vehicular applications are under development, and platooning is certainly one them [8]. Driver Assistive Truck Platooning (DATP) Pilot is a Florida Department of Transportation (FDOT) led project to illustrate platoon operations only in a specified set of weather scenarios [9,10]. International projects like Konvoi and SARTRE were not verified over broad weather scenarios [11]. However, the United States is home to a wide variety of weather conditions like rain, snow, fog, etc., and platooning cannot be operated in these conditions. Therefore, there is a need to support platooning even in these situations. This motivated us to apply our relative angle approach to support the existing platoon design.

The contributions of this work are: (1) an IoT-based message exchange algorithm that can be extended to n number of unique messages; (2) Dedicated Short Range Communication (DSRC) Basic Safety Message (BSM) based communication with the neighboring vehicles to initiate a platoon; and (3) extension of CARLA simulator to support IoT connectivity. The proposed algorithm is currently demonstrated in a two-vehicle scenario which will be extended to multiple vehicles in future work. The current scope of this work is to demonstrate successful platoon negotiation without consideration of safety issues. In the near future, we plan to address them.

The remainder of the paper is laid out as follows. Section 2 provides an overview of Automated Driving System (ADS), Connected Automated Vehicles (CAVs), an IoT vision for platooning, and CARLA Simulator. Section 3 discusses the current research in platooning along with its limitations. Section 4 presents platoon-ready, pre-negotiation, negotiation resolver, and Platoon Member (PM) algorithms for various platoon scenarios. Section 5 implements the proposed algorithms and demonstrates the experimental results conducted through the CARLA simulator. Lastly, Sect. 6 summarizes the findings from our experiments and discusses future work.

2   Overview

In this section, an overview on ADS, CAVs, an IOT vision for platooning, and CARLA simulator is provided.

2.1   Automated Driving System

An ADS on a vehicle is equipped with a suite of sensors such as LIDAR, camera, radars, etc. There are six levels of autonomy, according to the Society of Automotive Engineers (SAE), with level zero indicating no autonomy and level five indicating complete autonomy [12]. At level five, ADS is capable of performing all the driving tasks in all situations without human intervention. Baude et al. [13] provided a typical architecture of ADS consisting of perception and decision-making systems. These two modules work together to generate necessary brake, throttle, and steering wheel commands. From Yurtsever et al. [14], although ADS guarantees a safe, efficient, and comfortable driving experience yet the number of causalities are ascending. Level four and above autonomy is still an open and challenging problem. Thakurdesai et al. [15] presented in detail the technical, moral, and legal issues faced by ADS. Further, most of the existing approaches are ego-only and there is not one functional CAV on the road [14].

2.2   Connected Automated Vehicles (CAVs)

A CAV can depend on other vehicles or infrastructure on the roads to carry out the functionalities of an ADS. This design is believed to be autonomous driving's future. Through vehicle-to-vehicle (V2V), vehicle-to-infrastructure (V2I), and vehicle-to-everything (V2X) communications, CAVs will be able to access a huge amount of data which could be used to remove the flaws in the current ego-only design [14,16]. The two main components of CV technology are On-Board Unit (OBU) and Road-Side Unit (RSU) representing an edge and a fog node respectively in an IoT framework as shown in Fig. 1. RSUs are installed on road infrastructure such as traffic lights, current poles, etc., while OBUs are installed inside the vehicles. These units communicate through DSRC. Vehicle information such as speed, location, heading, etc., is collected by OBUs which is then transmitted to RSUs and OBUs several times per second in the form of a BSM. Data from fog nodes or RSUs is then transmitted to the central server or cloud layer to perform data analytics.

Therefore, when CV technology is deployed within ADS, it becomes a CAV that can access a huge amount of traffic data to provide improved safety, efficiency, and mobility [16].

2.3   An IoT Vision for Platooning

Platooning is defined as a group of vehicles that drive together cooperatively at a very small inter-vehicle gap through a local ad-hoc network (such as DSRC) [6,17]. A typical platoon consists of a Platoon Leader (PL) and PM where the PL leads and PM follows the PL as shown in Fig. 2. Platoon speed, number of members, and permit for entry or exit of the platoon are controlled and tracked by the PL. The instructions from PL are followed by PM who in turn provides its status back to PL. The inter-vehicle gap is calculated and maintained by Adaptive Cruise Control (ACC) using LIDAR, radar, camera sensors., etc. while the PL and PM communication is achieved by V2V. Platooning is made possible through a Cooperative ACC (CACC), i.e. combination of V2V communication in CV and ACC in ADS [18]. Stages involved in platooning are briefly discussed below [19]:

- Find - A vehicle uses V2V or V2I communication to find an available platoon.
- Join - A vehicle negotiates with the PL on how to join the detected platoon.
- Maintain - After joining, the inter-vehicle gap between PL and PMs is maintained here.
- Leave and Dissolve - PM can move out of the platoon to either end or join another platoon.

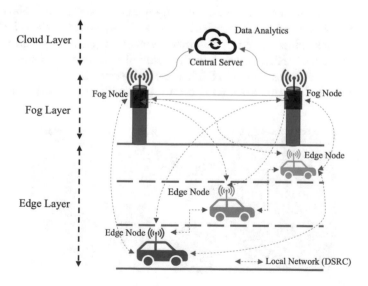

Fig. 1. Vehicles connected through local ad-hoc network (DSRC)

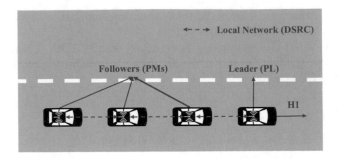

Fig. 2. Platoon illustration through DSRC communication

There are various vehicle-dependent factors such as inter-vehicle gap, platoon-dependent factors such as platoon size, and external factors such as weather that influence a platoon. All of these factors are discussed in detail in [19]. This paper focuses on finding a vehicle willing to platoon, negotiating with it to join a platoon, determining a PL and PM, and instructing PM to drive into the PL lane using BSMs only. To achieve this, we use the relative angle approach for CVs proposed in our previous work [20]. The relative angle 'θ' can be computed between HV and RV by calculating the angle between the HV heading and a new vector drawn between HV and RV positions. Similarly, relative angle 'θ' between HV and PL (an RV here) can be acquired by calculating the angle between HV and the new vector joining HV and PL as shown in Fig. 3.

2.4   CARLA

CARLA (Car Learning to Act), an open-source simulator platform for autonomous driving built on Unreal Engine 4 (UE4) enables basic NPC logic, real-time physics, plug-in interoperability, and cutting-edge rendering quality [21]. This enabled CARLA to realistically simulate various scenarios present in the "real world". Furthermore, CARLA is a client-server interface that allows an agent, the vehicles, in this case, to communicate with the dynamic world. The

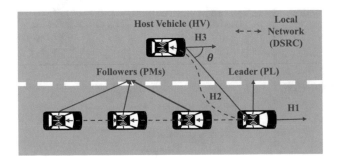

Fig. 3. Relative angle approach for platooning

client oversees the interaction between an agent and the server using a Python Application Programming Interface, (API) while the server is responsible for scene rendering and simulation control. The client sends out commands to control the vehicles present in that scenario, and meta-commands adjust the behavior of the server, which will result in sensor readings. Moreover, vehicle commands include steering, braking, and accelerating, whereas the meta-commands will reset the simulation, set up new environments, and configure sensors such as GPS, IMU, LIDAR, and camera. It is also possible to develop custom sensors that can be used in simulated vehicles. In other words, an agent will behave according to how these "classes" are written. These functionalities may be used to mimic autonomous vehicles and get data related to the position, velocity, direction, and other parameters. All this information, which composes the BSMs, concerning different agents within the simulation is then shared among vehicles using the client API. Consequently, CARLA is a reliable framework for studying and developing different CV applications. CARLA is extended to model vehicular communication, or connection, that are not present in the framework. In Sect. 5, we go through this in-depth.

3   Related Research

There have been many platoon research projects while some are still ongoing. They all have various objectives such as truck platooning, mixed vehicles platooning, etc. They either assume vehicles to be fully autonomous or PL to be driving manually [19]. One such project is CARMA (Cooperative Automation Research Mobility Applications). CARMA is a U.S. Department of Transportation (USDOT) initiative that is developed by the Federal Highway Administration (FHWA) [22]. CARMA3 is the latest version of CARMA and is equipped with ADS and V2X capabilities to achieve Cooperative Driving Automation (CDA). Cruising, yielding, lane changing and merging, speed harmonizing, and platooning are the various CDA features available within CARMA [8]. CARMA allows to develop and tests the CDA features through an open-source approach by collaborating with academic institutions. While CARMA is paving the way to further research and development (R&D) in CDA, there are a lot of problems yet to be solved.

The implementation of IoT within vehicles has been given increasing attention over the years. Petrov et al. [23] have developed a framework for message exchange and relay-based data processing in order to alleviate the overhead of data processing in edge nodes. In other words, the authors use Narrowband IoT Technology (NB-IoT) in order to take advantage of a concept known as *crowd-sensing*, where multiple devices (in this case the vehicles) collectively process desired data. Another significant benefit covered in this research work is the mobility as well as the higher power availability in vehicles compared to static conventional edge nodes. Similarly, Wang et al. [24] at Ibaraki University, Japan, addressed the impact of latency of message exchange in the safety of platooning. The authors observed that message delay was decreased in V2V communication

Table 1. Comparison of ADS sensors

Sensor	Influenced by light	Influenced by weather
LIDAR	No	Yes
Radar	No	No
Ultrasonic	No	No
Camera	Yes	Yes
Stereo camera	Yes	Yes
Flash camera	Yes	Yes
Event camera	Limited	Yes
Thermal camera	No	Yes

by the use of directional antenna. Although it is still effective for high traffic, directional antenna usage has shown to be advantageous for vehicles or beacons that are close to one another. Sodhro *et al.* [25] study aims to tackle the decrease in QoS (Quality of Service) due to the high mobility of vehicles as nodes in an IoT network. A QoS-aware, green, sustainable, reliable, and available (QGSRA) algorithm is then developed to reduce the latency of message exchange, power consumption, and improve the reliability of the service. The authors also propose the development of metrics for features such as power consumption.

Finally, it is also important to point out the emerging technologies that may dramatically improve the overall quality of not only the proposed V2V application but also of countless other IoT-related technologies. Artificial Intelligence of Things (AIoT) has the capability to benefit IoT in terms of data processing and analytics, which will in turn optimize the reliability and efficiency of Platooning negotiation, formation, and maintenance [26]. Applying AI combined with Blockchain technology may also improve vehicular IoT applications such that it can offer decentralized network management, interoperability across nodes, as well as traceability and reliability of the data being exchanged [27]. Additionally, Blockchain can also be utilized as a tool for many security issues in V2X applications [28].

So far, extensive research is done in platooning that relies on on-board sensors of ADS such as radar, LIDAR, cameras, etc. But these sensors may lead to failure during bad weather conditions [29]. Adverse weather conditions such as rain, snow, or fog may lead to a limited view for platooning [19]. Table 1 compares exteroceptive sensors used in ADS to better understand their functionality during poor light and bad weather conditions [14]. All the sensors except radar and ultrasonic are affected either by light or weather. And one cannot rely on these two sensors as they help only to calculate distances of objects ahead but cannot provide the lane information or relative position of the platoon. From [30], DSRC communication is not affected by the change in air density that occurs during foggy weather. University of Michigan Transportation Research Institute

(UMTRI) led Safety Pilot Model Deployment (SPMD) project with about 2800 vehicles installed with OBU devices along with 25 RSU devices [31]. The data collected from this study is used to investigate the impact of weather conditions on DSRC communication. A sample size containing 2,581 clear weather days, 114 rainy days, and 227 snowy days showed that adverse weather conditions have negligible impact on DSRC performance. This evaluation makes DSRC a promising and reliable technology in any kind of a weather scenario. This motivated us to propose an approach that relies on DSRC communication for platoon negotiation without depending on LIDAR, radar, or camera sensors.

4 Negotiation Algorithms on Edge Nodes

In this section, we discuss the algorithms implemented within edge nodes (vehicles) responsible for achieving platoon negotiation to determine PL and PM. We then proposed a PM algorithm using the relative angle θ approach. For this, we assume that the vehicles are connected through DSRC communication and automated. Algorithms are derived for vehicles heading to the same destination and different destinations with a common path. Negotiations happen in the open first and then a PlatoonKey system from [32] or FlowMiner from [33] can be implemented in the future for secure platoon-based V2V communication. Various stages namely platoon-ready, pre-negotiation, and negotiation resolver are involved for which the algorithms are proposed. These algorithms run independently on each vehicle using data from BSM messages. Finally, the PM algorithm is proposed through which PM can start following the PL. Further, experiments are conducted in Sect. 5 to validate them. Also, a discussion on edge-cases of the algorithms is provided in Sect. 4.5.

4.1 Platoon-Ready Algorithm

Here, individual vehicles check if they are ready to platoon. Several criteria can be set to accomplish this. The criteria we set here is that the platoon be turned on and the vehicle be driving on a road at a certain speed, for example driving at a speed greater than 40 km/h. If these conditions are met, the vehicle is ready to platoon. Figure 4 shows the flowchart illustrating the platoon-ready condition. Once the vehicle is ready to platoon, pre-negotiation transactions are carried out before the actual negotiation.

4.2 Pre-negotiation Transactions

Once the vehicles are ready to platoon, they broadcast willingness to platoon with their destination and global route set by the autonomous feature. In the meantime, individual vehicles check if this information is also available in the received BSMs from nearby vehicles. If available, the destinations are compared to check if they both are heading to the same destination. If not, their paths are

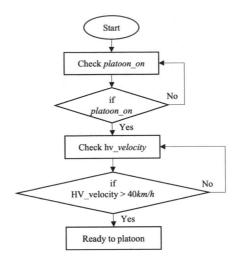

Fig. 4. Platoon-ready flowchart

compared to find a maximum match. Once a common destination is found, the vehicle starts negotiating.

Figure 5 clearly illustrates pre-negotiation transactions over the time occurring between Vehicle 1 and Vehicle 2 after they are platoon-ready. Once Vehicle 1 is platoon-ready, it broadcasts its destination and route via BSMs to Vehicle 2. Now, Vehicle 1 keeps checking if Vehicle 2 destination and the route are available. Once available, Vehicle 1 compares its destination against Vehicle 2 destination. If they do not match, their global route is compared to find a maximum match. After a match is found, Vehicle 1 starts negotiating by sending a Platoon Join Request (PJRQ) negotiation. The same logic runs in the Vehicle 2 which is illustrated on the right side of Fig. 5 and starts negotiating once a match is found. Once the vehicles start negotiating, these are resolved through the negotiation resolver algorithm which is explained in Sect. 4.3.

4.3   Negotiation Resolver Algorithm

Once the vehicle is ready to platoon as well as to start to negotiate, a PJRQ negotiation is sent to other vehicles through BSMs. The structure of the negotiation contains a *negotiation, sender_id,* and *receiver_id.* A *negotiation* can be either a PJRQ, a Platoon Accepted (PA), a Platoon Join Ready (PJRY), or a Platoon Leader Request (PLR). Currently, the algorithm handles these four negotiations, and logic to handle more negotiations can be included in the future. Other variables *sender_id* and *receiver_id* are host vehicle id and remote vehicle id respectively. This way the negotiation messages can be processed by interacting parties only and not others. Negotiations received through the BSMs are processed by the negotiation resolver that runs separately on each vehicle.

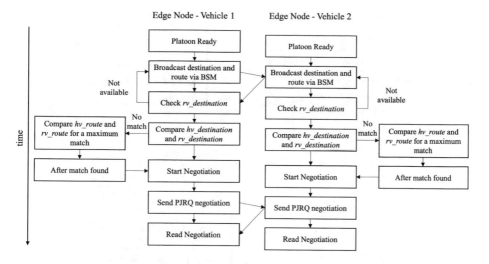

Fig. 5. Pre-negotiation transactions

The resolver reads these negotiations and processes them accordingly as shown in Fig. 6.

Vehicles process the received BSMs and once a negotiation is read from the BSM, *receiver_id* in it is compared against the current vehicle's id 'current_veh_id' or HV id that is processing the negotiation. If the current_veh_id is the same as the *receiver_id*, the received negotiation is further processed. If the *negotiation* is a PJRQ, the algorithm accepts it and a PA negotiation is sent back to the above *sender_id* or RV id. While sending a PA negotiation back, the current HV id becomes the new *sender_id* and the RV id becomes the new *receiver_id*. This concept is similar to the rest of the negotiations. Next, if *negotiation* is a PA, a PJRY negotiation is acknowledged back to the above *sender_id* or RV id. At this state, both vehicles have acknowledged each other that they are ready to start a platoon. The next negotiations would be to determine who would be the leader of the platoon. For this, we assume that all the PJRY state vehicles declare themselves to be PL and send PLR negotiations. While processing, if the negotiation is a PLR, the current vehicle or HV compares its velocity against the sender vehicle's or RV's velocity. If *hv_velocity* is less than *rv_velocity*, meaning that it is driving slower than the remote, it becomes a PM. The criteria set to become a PL here are arbitrary and can be changed according to the requirements. This way a negotiation resolver is implemented to settle the negotiations between the vehicle to initiate platooning.

4.4   Platoon Member Algorithm

Once PM and PL are determined, this logic is used by PM to follow PL based on the relative angle 'θ'. Figure 7a, 7b, 7c shows when PL is on right, left, and same lanes of PM respectively. Here, we assume that H1 is the heading angle

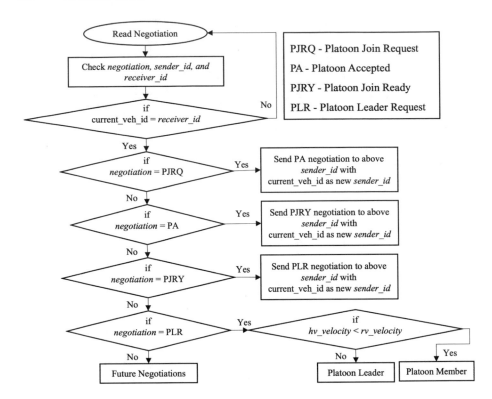

Fig. 6. Negotiation resolver flowchart

of PM, H2 is the heading angle of new vector AB joining PM and PL, and H3 is the heading angle of PL. Relative angle θ is the difference between H1 and H2. First, we check if both PM and PL are heading in the same direction by calculating 'α', the difference in their heading angles (H1–H3). When mod α is less than 5° meaning PM and PL are heading in the same direction, the relative angle θ between PM and PL is computed. PM and PL are in the same lane when mod θ is less than 1°. In this scenario, PM will follow PL in the same lane as shown in Fig. 7c. PM and PL are in different lanes when mod θ is greater than 1°. PL is on the right lane of PM when θ is positive or greater than 0°. In this case, PM will drive to its right lane to follow PL as shown in Fig. 7a. Lastly, PL is on the left lane of PM when θ is negative or less than 0°. Here, PM will drive to its left lane to follow PL as shown in Fig. 7b. Figure 8 shows the above logic in a flowchart.

This way vehicles can negotiate with each other to find a platoon and then join using BSM information only. Further, we have conducted experiments to evaluate the above algorithm and the results are shown in Sect. 5.

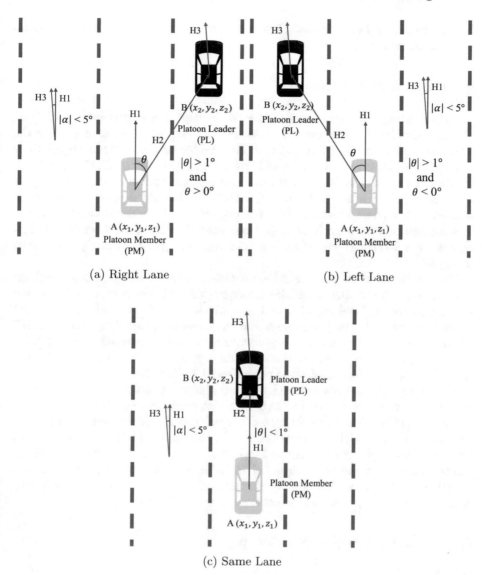

Fig. 7. PM illustration when PL in right lane, left, and same lanes respectively

4.5   Discussion

There could be several edge cases during the negotiation as well as while platooning. One such scenario is that during negotiation there could be denial to platoon by a vehicle. In such a situation, the vehicles trying to form the platoon will register this and stop communicating with the vehicle. In another scenario, there could be an abrupt disruption of communication during platooning. In this case, all the vehicles will break out of platooning and act as individual AVs.

Re-negotiation and re-platooning can occur on the restoration of communication between the vehicles.

5   Experimental Results

In this section, the algorithms discussed in Sect. 4 are implemented in the CARLA simulator and various experiments are conducted to demonstrate the proposed approach. We chose CARLA Town06 for testing platoon negotiations as it has long highways with a lot of highway entrances and exits that are feasible for this application. To drive the vehicles between source and destination, we used the behavior agent (BA) from CARLA's python API client. BA is implemented as a Python class and for each vehicle, a BA object is created that is independent of others. Each BA object contains all of the above-mentioned algorithms from Sect. 4, as well as the logic for computing relative angle θ as shown in Fig 9.

We developed a custom sensor i.e. OBU sensor to get all the required vehicle information. All the spawn vehicles are equipped with this sensor to collect the location, velocity, heading, etc., of the vehicle. By default, CARLA does not support connectivity or platooning. For this reason, we implemented a DSRC agent to connect the vehicles in simulation. Vehicles spawned from CARLA client send and receive BSMs through this agent. Also in Sect. 3, we showed that the DSRC communication is not affected by the weather conditions. The following steps explain how connectivity and platooning are achieved in CARLA. In step one, each vehicle in the CARLA client reads its own negotiation set in the previous time and forwards it to other vehicles if any through the BSM. In step two, all the vehicle information, destination and route (if platoon-ready), and negotiation (if any) are sent to the DSRC agent. In step three, each vehicle receives BSM from the DSRC agent. Lastly, in step four, all of the information is sent to individual BA objects to run the platoon algorithms as shown in Fig. 9. The following experiments are conducted using the above setup.

5.1   Same Destination Experiment

In this experiment, two vehicles are spawned in two different lanes with the same destination as shown in Fig. 10. The following vehicle is HV while the leading vehicle is an RV on the right lane to HV. Here, RV started first and reached a speed of 40 km/h before HV. At this stage, RV is ready to platoon and started to broadcast its destination. Similarly, HV started to broadcast its destination once the speed criteria is met. At this stage, both HV and RV received destinations of each other. Since the destinations are the same, a PJRQ negotiation is set in its BA object that can be read from the CARLA client in the future. First, RV gets its negotiation for HV and publishes it to the DSRC agent through the BSM. The same is repeated for HV. Now, both HV and RV receive their BSMs from the DSRC agent and send this to their BA object which also contains negotiations this time. The negotiation resolver reads this and processes them

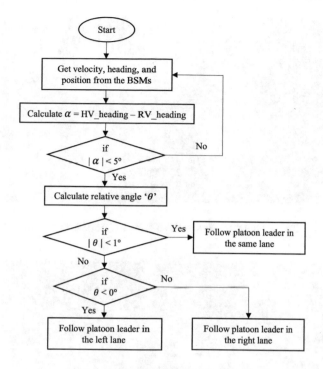

Fig. 8. Platoon member flowchart

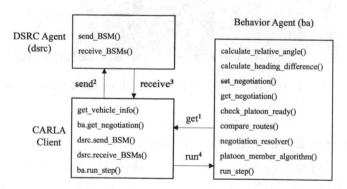

Fig. 9. Connectivity architecture implemented in CARLA

according to the logic discussed in Fig. 6. When both vehicles are at PJRY state, a PLR request is sent and whoever has a higher speed becomes a PL. In this case, RV speed is greater than HV and assigned as PL while HV is assigned as a PM. Once PL and PM are determined, heading angle difference α, and relative angle θ are compared. After checking, PM joins the platoon with PL by driving to the right lane as shown in Fig. 10.

Fig. 10. PM driving at speed of 46 km/h to join PL on the right lane at an angle of θ = 10.12° ahead of PM

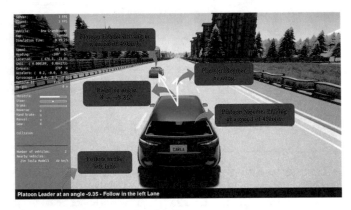

Fig. 11. PM driving at speed of 45 km/h to join PL on the left lane at an angle of θ = −9.35° ahead of PM

5.2   Different Destination Experiment

This experiment is the same as the experiment in Sect. 5.1 except that the vehicles are spawned with different destinations. In this scenario, a common match is found using the *compare_routes()* function in the individual BA object. After successful negotiations, RV becomes PL while HV becomes PM. Once PL and PM are known, heading angle difference α, and relative angle θ are compared. After checking, PM joins the platoon with PL by driving to the left lane as shown in Fig. 11.

5.3   Same Lane Experiment

This experiment is the same as the experiment in Sect. 5.1 except that the vehicles are spawned in the same lanes. In this scenario, vehicles start negotiations once after their destinations are matched. After successful negotiations,

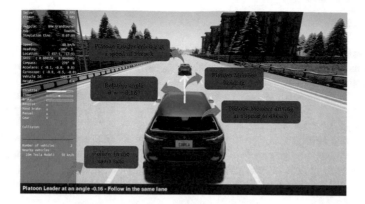

Fig. 12. PM driving at speed of 49 km/h to join PL on the same lane at an angle of $\theta = -0.16°$ ahead of PM

RV becomes PL while HV becomes PM. Once PL and PM are known, heading angle difference α, and relative angle θ are compared. After checking, PM joins the platoon with PL by driving in the same lane as shown in Fig. 12.

6 Conclusions and Future Work

The applications of IoT are increasing at a very fast pace and this work presents how the concept of IoT can be applied to approach existing problems in the transportation field. Through this work, platooning with respect to IoT is researched and a simplified IoT architecture is applied to approach this problem. There are many advantages due to platooning. It can lower fuel costs, enhance safety, and improve the efficacy of the energy. Existing work on platooning is limited to certain weather conditions and the proposed work paves the way to implement this feature even under adverse weather conditions. The related research in this work shows that the DSRC communication is not affected by uncertain weather conditions which is the key in the negotiation exchange. The presented algorithms to find a platoon are derived from BSMs only and negotiations are carried out further to determine PL and PM. We see that the PM algorithm can accurately determine the relative position of PL using the relative angle without the use of any camera or LIDAR sensor. We successfully extended the CARLA simulator to include platooning negotiation which is explained in detail in Sect. 5.

Furthermore, the algorithms and simulations presented in this paper will be the basis for further development of cooperative driving. The future work includes testing the proposed algorithm with more than two vehicles, testing in dense traffic, extending the algorithm to support complete platoon formation with more use cases, platoon safety, usage of RSUs (fog nodes) connected to the central server in order to perform data analytics and provide better accuracy, and tackle the security aspects of this application.

References

1. Al-Fuqaha, A., Guizani, M., Mohammadi, M., Aledhari, M., Ayyash, M.: Internet of things: a survey on enabling technologies, protocols, and applications. IEEE Commun. Surv. Tutor. **17**(4), 2347–2376 (2015)
2. Hanes, D., Salgueiro, G., Grossetete, P., Barton, R., Henry, J., Trollope, R.: IOT Fundamentals Networking Technologies, Protocols, and Use Cases for the Internet of Things. Cisco Press, Indianapolis (2017)
3. Pawar, N., Bourgeau, T., Chaouchi, H.: Study of IoT architecture and application invariant functionalities. In: 2021 IFIP/IEEE International Symposium on Integrated Network Management (IM), pp. 667–671 (2021)
4. American Trucking Associations: Economics and Industry Data (2020). Accessed 06 Feb 2022
5. U. S. Environmental Protection Agency: Sources of Greenhouse Gas Emissions. Accessed 06 Feb 2022
6. Bergenhem, C., Shladover, S., Coelingh, E., Englund, C., Tsugawa, S.: Overview of platooning systems. In: Proceedings of the 19th ITS World Congress, 22–26 October 2012 Vienna, Austria (2012)
7. U.S. Department of Transportation: Connected Vehicle Pilot Deployment Program. Accessed 06 Feb 2022
8. Lochrane, T., Dailey, L., Tucker, C.: CarmaSM: driving innovation. Public Roads **83**(4), 28–31 (2020)
9. Florida Department of Transportation: Driver Assisted Truck Platooning (DATP) Pilot. Accessed 07 Feb 2022
10. Crane, C., Bridge, J., Bishop, R.: Driver assistive truck platooning: considerations for Florida state agencies, January 2018. Accessed 06 Feb 2022
11. Foreman, C., Keen, M., Petrella, M., Plotnick, S.: FHWA research and technology evaluation: truck platooning. FHWA-HRT-20-071, Technical report, June 2021
12. SAE: Taxonomy and definitions for terms related to driving automation systems for on-road motor vehicles. SAE J3016. Technical report (2018)
13. Badue, C., et al.: Self-driving cars: a survey. Expert Syst. Appl. **165**, 113816 (2021)
14. Yurtsever, E., Lambert, J., Carballo, A., Takeda, K.: A survey of autonomous driving: common practices and emerging technologies. IEEE Access **8**, 58443–58469 (2020)
15. Thakurdesai, H.M., Aghav, J.V.: Autonomous cars: technical challenges and a solution to blind spot. In: Gao, X.-Z., Tiwari, S., Trivedi, M.C., Mishra, K.K. (eds.) Advances in Computational Intelligence and Communication Technology. AISC, vol. 1086, pp. 533–547. Springer, Singapore (2021). https://doi.org/10.1007/978-981-15-1275-9_44
16. Kim, N., Karbowski, D., Jeong, J., Rousseau, A.: Simulation of heavy-duty vehicles in platooning scenarios. In: 2018 21st International Conference on Intelligent Transportation Systems (ITSC), pp. 1604–1610 (2018)
17. Strunz, M., Heinovski, J., Dressler, F.: CoOP: V2V-based cooperative overtaking for platoons on freeways. In: 2021 IEEE International Intelligent Transportation Systems Conference (ITSC), pp. 1090–1097 (2021)
18. Ghosal, A., Sagong, S.U., Halder, S., Sahabandu, K., Conti, M., Poovendran, R., Bushnell, L.: Truck platoon security: state-of-the-art and road ahead. Comput. Netw. **185**, 107658 (2021)
19. Sturm, T., Krupitzer, C., Segata, M., Becker, C.: A taxonomy of optimization factors for platooning. IEEE Trans. Intell. Transp. Syst. **22**(10), 6097–6114 (2020)

20. Dokur, O., Katkoori, S.: Three connected V2V applications based on DSRC basic safety messages. In: 2022 International Conference on Connected Vehicle and Expo (ICCVE), pp. 1–6 (2022)
21. Dosovitskiy, A., Ros, G., Codevilla, F., Lopez, A., Koltun, V.: CARLA: an open urban driving simulator. In: Proceedings of the 1st Annual Conference on Robot Learning, pp. 1–16 (2017)
22. U.S. Department of Transportation: CARMA. Accessed 06 Feb 2022
23. Petrov, V., et al.: Vehicle-based relay assistance for opportunistic crowdsensing over narrowband IoT (NB-IoT). IEEE Internet Things J. 5(5), 3710–3723 (2018)
24. Wang, X., Wang, D., Ariyasu, N., Umehira, M.: Better platooning toward autonomous driving: inter-vehicle communications with directional antenna. China Commun. 18(7), 44–57 (2021)
25. Sodhro, A.H., et al.: Quality of service optimization in an IoT-driven intelligent transportation system. IEEE Wirel. Commun. 26(6), 10–17 (2019)
26. Sigov, A., Ratkin, L., Ivanov, L.A., Xu, L.D.: Emerging enabling technologies for industry 4.0 and beyond. Inf. Syst. Front. 1–11 (2022). https://doi.org/10.1007/s10796-021-10213-w
27. Guo, F., Yu, F.R., Zhang, H., Li, X., Ji, H., Leung, V.C.M.: Enabling massive IoT toward 6G: a comprehensive survey. IEEE Internet Things J. 8(15), 11891–11915 (2021)
28. Eltahlawy, A.M., Azer, M.A.: Using blockchain technology for the internet of vehicles. In: 2021 International Mobile, Intelligent, and Ubiquitous Computing Conference (MIUCC), pp. 54–61 (2021)
29. Kouchak, S.M., Gaffar, A.: Determinism in future cars: why autonomous trucks are easier to design. In: 2017 IEEE SmartWorld, Ubiquitous Intelligence Computing, Advanced Trusted Computed, Scalable Computing Communications, Cloud Big Data Computing, Internet of People and Smart City Innovation (SmartWorld/SCALCOM/UIC/ATC/CBDCom/IOP/SCI), pp. 1–6 (2017)
30. El-Said, M., Bhuse, V., Arendsen, A.: An empirical study to investigate the effect of air density changes on the DSRC performance. Proc. Comput. Sci. 114, 523–530 (2017)
31. Huang, X., Zhao, D., Peng, H.: Empirical study of DSRC performance based on safety pilot model deployment data. IEEE Trans. Intell. Transp. Syst. 18(10), 2619–2628 (2017)
32. Li, K., Lu, L., Ni, W., Tovar, E., Guizani, M.: Cooperative secret key generation for platoon-based vehicular communications. In: ICC 2019–2019 IEEE International Conference on Communications (ICC), pp. 1–6 (2019)
33. Ahmed, M.R., Zheng, H., Mukherjee, P., Ketkar, M.C., Yang, J.: Mining message flows from system-on-chip execution traces. In: 2021 22nd International Symposium on Quality Electronic Design (ISQED), pp. 374–380 (2021)

Development of a Smart Insole
for Baropodometric and Gait Analysis

Misael Elias de Morais[1]([⊠]) (iD), Lauriston Medeiros Paixão[1] (iD),
Katia Elizabete Galdino[1] (iD), Vivian Cardoso de Morais Oliveira[1] (iD),
Raphael Sousa Santos[3] (iD), José Eugênio Eloi Moura[2] (iD),
and Carlúcia Ithamar Fernandes Franco[2] (iD)

[1] Center of Strategic Technologies in Health, Campina Grande, Brazil
moraiscg@gmail.com
[2] State University of Paraiba, Campina Grande, Brazil
[3] Amsterdam, The Netherlands

Abstract. With recent technological advances, in-soles or smart insoles have been designed, with a different arrangement of sensors. The objective of this project is to develop a new model of smart, wearable insole composed of hardware with twelve resistive force sensors, FSR® 402 short, coupled to an ESP-WROOM-32 embedded microprocessor module for wireless data acquisition, processing, storage and transmission, integrated with Android application software for data reading, sensor fusion and creation of dashboards to be displayed on an interface. The results of the concept validation tests in the laboratory have demonstrated that this new device can be used in future clinical studies as a tool for real-time baropodometric and motion analysis in various daily life, work and sport activities, with respect to injury prevention, disease assessment and diagnosis, and rehabilitation support.

Keywords: Smart insole · Wearable devices · Baropodometry

1 Introduction

According to Shumway-Cook and Woollacott [25] for postural control, constant neuromuscular adjustments are required, through the processing of information from the visual, vestibular and somatosensory systems (proprioceptive, joint and cutaneous receptors). The plantar region of the feet also plays a fundamental role in stabilizing the body, as they contribute to the distribution of weight in the orthostatic position and influence postural control and gait parameters [30].

In the standing position, balance is controlled by muscular action, which moves the distribution of plantar pressure, changing the rotation of the foot around the ankle (anterior-posterior) and the distribution of total body weight on both sides. Feet (side) [6]. The heads of the 1st and 5th metatarsals and the calcaneal tuberosity support greater

---

R. S. Santos—Independent Researcher.

© IFIP International Federation for Information Processing 2022
Published by Springer Nature Switzerland AG 2022
L. M. Camarinha-Matos et al. (Eds.): IFIPIoT 2022, IFIP AICT 665, pp. 350–360, 2022.
https://doi.org/10.1007/978-3-031-18872-5_20

pressure [11]. These stability limits change constantly depending on the task, the biomechanics of the person and the support surface, which can be stable or unstable, depending on the type of footwear.

In this way, the foot is considered a link between an imbalance of high origin and the ground, which will always adapt to neutralize the support, and can be considered the terminal cap of the postural system, in descending postural alterations, or the initial one, in the ascending postural alterations [5]. Foot and ankle disorders are prevalent in the general population and one of the main motivations for primary care consultations, usually these disorders are associated with the type of plantar pressure distribution [14].

The measurement of plantar pressure is generally confined to a laboratory environment, primarily through pressure platform systems, also known as baropodometers. However, in recent years, with recent advances in sensor technology and mobile devices, in-shoes or smart insoles have been designed, each with a different arrangement of sensors [20]. Despite this variety of models, it was found that the main benefit observed in smart insoles is the continuous monitoring of functional, occupational and sports activities in real time.

Several studies with populations at risk have already been carried out using smart insoles, with the aim of evaluating the plantar pressure of hemiplegics [8, 10, 22]; in the postural control of children with Cerebral Palsy [17]; to detect when excessive pronation occurs in patients with hallux valgus [3]; in the treatment of Parkinson's Disease [28]; alcohol-induced gait disorders [19]; as well as in the prevention and healing of pressure ulcers in individuals with diabetic neuropathy [1, 16, 23, 26].

Some studies [15, 27, 32] used smart insoles to analyze the gait pattern, whose main parameters are: stride duration, cadence, stride length and gait speed. Substantial evidence on cognitive neuroscience and motor control suggests that gait parameters can reveal important factors that determine general health and well-being [2], with gait speed being considered a sixth vital sign because it has been validated as a marker of frailty and mortality in the elderly [4].

Smart insoles are flexible, portable and comfortable for gait analysis and can monitor plantar pressure in real time by means of built-in sensors that convert the applied pressure into an electrical signal that can be displayed and analyzed later. Several research teams are still working to improve the insole features, such as size, sensitivity of the insoles' sensors, durability, and the use of artificial intelligence to monitor and control the gait of subjects, providing recommendations to improve gait performance.

Therefore, the objective of this research is the development of a new model of smart insole, composed by force sensors, coupled to an embedded system for acquisition, processing, storage and wireless transmission of data, integrated to a software for reading the data, fusion of sensors and creation of dashboards that will be displayed in an interface.

This new device could become an objective and low-cost tool for real-time baropodometric and movement analysis in various daily, work and sports activities, regarding injury prevention, evaluation and diagnosis of diseases and support for rehabilitation of osteomyoarticular pathologies related to stepping and gait pattern.

2 Methodology

When a new technology is created or conceptualized, it must go through delimited, described and standardized maturity levels, until it is ready for use and commercialization. The Technological Maturity Level (TML) is a systematic metric, with nine levels, developed in 1974 by Stan Sadin, a senior scientist at the National Aeronautics and Space Administration (NASA), which allows the assessment, at a given moment, of the maturity level of a particular technology or the comparison of maturity levels between different types of technologies, as well as the entire context of a specific system, its application and its operating environment [29].

Based on the TML scale, a strategic plan was organized focusing on the feasibility of the concept and product development. This project reached level 4 of technological maturity, including the validation of the prototype in the Laboratory of Biomedical Instrumentation and Electronic Tests of the Nucleus of Strategic Technology in Health (NUTES) of the State University of Paraíba (UEPB).

The dimensions of the smart insole correspond to number 40 according to the Brazilian standard of measurements, with approximately 265 mm in length, 90 mm in width and 3 mm in thickness. The structure of the insole has three layers: two layers of armor composed of Ethylene Vinyl Acetate (EVA) and Corotex; and a conductive layer for connecting the sensors, consisting of a double-faced copper plated phenolite. The printed circuit manufacturing process was carried out by machining in a CNC milling machine, through copper grinding.

Shielding layers are important to increase the durability of the insole, once they protect the sensors from mechanical damage and from the influence of environmental factors such as temperature and humidity. The material indicated by the FSR datasheet [12] to be used in the shielding layers is a thin elastomer (3 mm), as it allows a better sensor repeatability.

For plantar pressure sensing, FSR® 402 short resistive force sensors manufactured by Interlink Electronics (Canada) were used. The FSR® exhibits a decrease in resistance with increasing pressure applied to the sensor's active area (12.70 mm). The sensitivity range of the FSR® 402 short ranges from 0.1 Kgf/cm^2 to 10 Kgf/cm^2, with an accuracy of ±5 to ±25% depending on measurement system consistency, repeatability tolerance and device calibration [13].

Regarding the choice of types of pressure sensors, according to Razak and collaborators it appears that force-sensitive resistance sensors, especially the FSR 402, are the most used in smart insoles projects, especially because of the following characteristics: low cost, low hysteresis, low temperature sensitivity, linear response and a pressure sensitivity range from 0.1 Kgf/cm^2 to 10 Kgf/cm^2 [20].

This sensor also meets the recommended size in systematic reviews which is 5 mm × 5 mm, as a larger sensor may underestimate peak pressure, and with a smaller sensor it is difficult to control the displacement of pressure points of interest during gait, therefore, smaller sensors are recommended for use in an array system, such as pressure platforms [20, 21].

Twelve sensors were used in this smart insole, which are positioned in specific areas of the plantar region: four sensors in the rearfoot (1–4), region of the calcaneal bone;

two sensors in the midfoot (5–6), medial and lateral longitudinal arch region; and six sensors in the forefoot (7–12), region of the metatarsal bones and phalanges (Fig. 1).

In the literature, there is no consensus between the quantity and positioning of sensors in the smart insole to obtain a better measurement of plantar pressure. According to Razak and collaborators [20] this determination depends on which clinical and functional analyzes will be performed by the smart insole and is limited to different sizes of feet, since the position of the pressure points changes. However, the literature indicates that the minimum number of sensors per insole is between three and four, due to the main pressure areas in the plantar region, which includes the heel, the head of the first and fifth metatarsals and the hallux, such as observed in the studies [10, 11].

Shu and collaborators [24] mentioned that the plantar region of the foot can be divided into 15 areas: heel (area 1–3), midfoot (area 4–5), forefoot, on the metatarsal heads (area 6–10) and phalanges (area 11). -15). These areas support most of the body weight and are adjusted by the body's balance. Therefore, ideally fifteen pressure sensors are needed to cover most body weight changes based on foot anatomy.

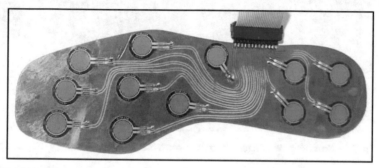

Fig. 1. - Positioning of the FSR® 402 short sensors on the smart insole. (Source: Author's own data)

In this project the sensors are connected in an "n + 1" line structure to build a sensor array. The use of matrices has the advantage of not having to make any a priori decisions about the areas to be monitored, since a larger area of the plantar surface can be accessed at once. [20]. Line "1" connects the set of sensors to the ground (GND) and line "n" represents the output of each sensor. By combining several force sensors, it is possible to measure force at a single point, as well as distributions by region. To connect the sensors to the conditioning circuit, a flat cable was used due to its flexibility, malleability and viable thickness for application [18].

For data acquisition, processing, storage and transmission, an ESP-WROOM-32 microcontroller manufactured by Espressif Systems (China) was chosen, with the following characteristics: low cost; small size, measuring just 18mm x 25.5mm and pin spacings at 1.27 mm pitch; Tensilica Xtensa 32-bit LX6 dual core microprocessor; adjustable clock from 80 MHz to 240 MHz; has 512 KB SRAM and 32 Mb external flash memory; 36 general purpose GPIO ports; SPI interface; 18 ADC pins; WiFi and Bluetooth communication [9].

In order to physically protect the embedded system, a protective case was designed, manufactured by additive manufacturing in the LT3D Laboratory (NUTES/UEPB), so the embedded system can be protected, isolating the possibility of any physical contact between the user and the board and the electrical supply system (battery). For the device's power system, a 3.7 v, 1500 mAh, 2-Wire Lithium Battery was used. Charging time for this battery varies from 3 h in fast mode and from 2 to 6 h in standard mode.

Voltage signals in the FSR® 402 short sensors are extracted from voltage dividers (R = 10 kΩ) and then sent to the 12-bit analog-to-digital (A/D) channels (0 to 4095) of the ESP-WROOM microcontroller −32 via a flat cable and then transmitted to a mobile device such as a smartphone or tablet via Bluetooth transmission (Fig. 2). The software is an Android application, capable of processing and reading the collected data, merging the force sensors and plotting all the data in images.

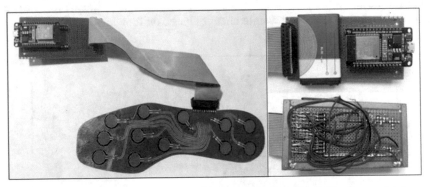

Fig. 2. - Smart insole integrated circuit prototype. (Source: Author's own data)

For software development, Flutter was used, which is an Open Source SDK (Software Development Kit) or user interface (framework) toolkit developed by Google, to build natively compiled applications on iOS and Android, for mobile devices, web and desktop from a single codebase.

3   Results and Discussion

The results of the proof-of-concept tests with the electronic components and the smart insole system were carried out in the following stages: 1st) test of the FSR® 402 short sensors; 2nd) sensor integration test to the ESP-WROOM-32; 3rd) test of data transmission via Bluetooth; and the 4th) application functionality tests.

To analyze the responses of the FSR® 402 short sensors and their operating range, tests were performed by applying pressure directly to the active area of the sensor. Each sensor was subjected to increasing loads from 1 to 10 kg, using metal washers as they are standardized and easy to handle. In order to verify the responses to the applied loads, the output voltage was measured on the FSR, using a Minipa Digital Multimeter, model ET-1100A, and using the Arduino analog reading (Fig. 3).

Fig. 3. Bump test of FSR® 402 short sensors. (Source: Author's own data)

Seeking to ensure that the correct weight was added only in the active area of the sensor, an instrument with two metal plates and a fixed rod with two magnet tips of different dimensions was designed and manufactured by the Machining Center of NUTES/UPEB, adapt to different types of sensors (Fig. 4).

Fig. 4. Instrument developed for testing the response of the FSR® 402 short. (Source: Author's own data)

To measure the pressure through an FSR, the values read in the range of 0 V to the voltage of 3.3 V were mapped. The regression curve relating the force/pressure and tension of each FSR can be obtained from the information contained in its datasheet [11] and represented in Eq. 1:

$$F(kgf) = 511{,}6 \times V_{fsr}^{-1{,}683} - 22{,}75 \tag{1}$$

In Fig. 5 it is possible to observe the comparative graph between the points obtained from the datasheet and the regression curve of Eq. 1, with a correlation coefficient (R2) of 0.9991.

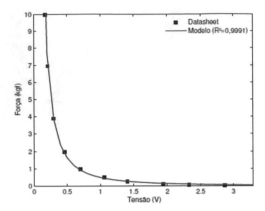

Fig. 5. Comparative graph between the datasheet points and the force/pressure regression curve in relation to the FSR voltage.

In the tests of hardware integration with the embedded system, it was evidenced that the ESP-WROOM-32's 12-bit ADC has an output signal that can vary from 0 to 4026 as the sensor is pressed. This range represents the voltage variation on the analog port, which can also be interpreted as a variation range from 0 to 3.3 V, according to the sensor resistance variation.

The sampling period is shaped by the processing time and data acquisition, where the 12 sensors are read in a time of 10 ms, so the device can operate with a sampling frequency of 100 Hz. The data transmission time is determined by the ESP-WROOM-32 Bluetooth version 4.2 bit rate per second which is approximately 1 Mbps with a sampling rate of 2.45 GHz, 1,200 data per second are generated depending on of the sampling time of 10 ms. The sensors were read continuously during the tests, allowing the evaluator to visualize in real time the pressure distribution in the plantar region.

Regarding the baropodometric variable analyzed in the Application, it concerns the distribution of plantar pressure, expressed by the Engineering Unit kilogram-force per square centimeter (kgf/cm^2), which will be displayed in the interface in the form of images with chromatic spectrum, to demonstrate the variations in pressure levels in each sensor and by plantar area, taking as an example the commercial software of baropodometers (Fig. 6).

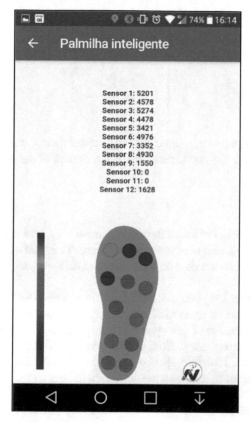

Fig. 6. Smart Insole Application. (Source: Author's own data).

The color spectrum is divided into six colors that represent the pressure ranges of each sensor:

a) Dark blue: 0–1,6 kgf/cm^2
b) Light blue: 1,6–3,3 kgf/cm^2
c) Green: 3,3–4,5 kgf/cm^2
d) Yellow: 4,5–5,9 kgf/cm^2
e) Orange: 5.9–6,8 kgf/cm^2
f) Red: 6.8–10 kgf/cm^2

With the values obtained it is also possible to manually calculate the maximum pressure (1), average pressure (2) and center of pressure (3) using the following equations [33]:

$$Peak = Max(p_1, \ldots p_i, \ldots, p_n) \tag{2}$$

$$Mean = \frac{1}{n} \sum_{i=1}^{n} p_i \tag{3}$$

$$
\begin{cases}
X_{cop} = \dfrac{\sum\limits_{i=1}^{n} X_i P_i}{\sum\limits_{i=1}^{n} P_i} \\[4ex]
Y_{cop} = \dfrac{\sum\limits_{i=1}^{n} Y_i P_i}{\sum\limits_{i=1}^{n} P_i}
\end{cases}
\tag{4}
$$

where p is the plantar pressure, n indicates the total number of sensors, i denotes the i-th sensor, and X and Y are the coordinates of the entire area of the foot.

4   Conclusion

This project had as main objective the development of a new model of smart insole, whose system is divided into hardware and software. The hardware collects, stores and transmits the plantar pressure data on the feet to the software, which saves and displays the data in an interface.

In the conceptualization phases of the insole, the resistive force sensors of the FSR® 402 short type were chosen to be used in the measurement of plantar pressure, as they meet the main requirements of this system, among which its linear response, low hysteresis stand out, operating range from 0.1 Kgf/cm^2 to 10 Kgf/cm^2 and an active area diameter of 0.5 inches. It should also be noted that the number of twelve sensors and their respective locations in the smart insole proved to be effective for the features of this device, given that these specifications were determined based on the areas of greatest plantar pressure through a review in studies with baropodometric analysis.

The collection, storage and transmission of output signals from the sensors by the embedded system containing an ESP-WROOM-32, showed correct functioning in the hardware feasibility tests. The data transmission rate of this smart insole is 100 Hz, which allows its application in various clinical gait analysis tests at different speeds.

The power system with a 3.3 V battery allowed energy autonomy to isolate the individual from the electrical network, as well as not limiting its use in relation to the structure in the environment (socket, cables, etc.), and still responded efficiently to the energy consumption of the smart insole, as it did not interrupt data collection for at least three hours of system use with the battery at full charge.

As this project is still in the prototype phase, the hardware design and the types of materials used in the manufacture can be modified after technical evaluation, to make this device even more comfortable, light and flexible. In addition, it is intended to develop several sizes of insoles, in order to adjust their use by individuals of different age groups and sex, adapted to foot sizes and types of shoes.

For this system, a graphical interface of the Android application type compatible with smartphone was developed, allowing a better display and reading of the data of each sensor, which were represented numerically and by figures with chromatic spectrum.

As the results of this project only showed the feasibility of the concept with laboratory tests, it is necessary in future works to validate this prototype through clinical studies in various environments, considering changes in temperature and humidity, with the performance of several functional tasks (work, sports and daily activities), both for healthy individuals of different ages, and for the evaluation and diagnosis of diseases.

A suggestion for future work is to add to the hardware a 9-axis MPU 9250 type IMU (InvenSense Inc., USA) with inertial sensors accelerometer, gyroscope and magnetometer, enabling the evaluation of all spatio-temporal parameters of gait, as well as tracking the angular and rotational movement of the ankle joint during locomotion.

Furthermore, we will try to implement more functions in the software such as: analysis of maximum and average pressure by region; stabilometry; step count; gait speed; ankle angulation; warning signs to prevent injury hazards, detect a pre-fall condition or pathological gaits. One can also think about the use of appropriate and efficient algorithms to relate the pathologies to the sensor signals. Therefore, the objectives of this work were achieved, regarding the characterization and development of a new smart insole and its demonstration in the laboratory through concept validation tests.

References

1. Alfonso, A.R., et al.: Novel pressure-sensing smart insole system used for the prevention of pressure ulceration in the insensate foot. Plast. Reconstr. Surg. – Glob. Open **5**(12), 1–4 (2017)
2. Avvenuti, M., et al.: Smart shoe-assisted evaluation of using a single trunk/pocket-worn accelerometer to detect gait phases. Sens. (Basel, Switz.) **18**(11), 3811–3820 (2018)
3. Berengueres, J., Fritschi, M., Mcclanahan, R.: A smart pressure-sensitive insole that reminds you to walk correctly: an orthotic-less treatment for over pronation. In: 36th Annual International Conference of the IEEE Engineering in Medicine and Biology Society, Chicago, pp. 2488–2491 (2014)
4. Binotto, M.A., Lenardt, M.H., Rodriguez-Martinez, M.C.: Fragilidade física e velocidade da marcha em idosos da comunidade: uma revisão sistemática. Rev. esc. enferm. USP, **52** (2018)
5. Bricot, B.: Posturologia Clínica. 1nd. edn. Andreoli, São Paulo (2011)
6. Christovão, T.C.: Effect of different insoles on postural balance: a systematic review. J. Phys. Ther. Sci. **25**(10), 1353–1356 (2013)
7. Das, R., Kumar, N.: Investigations on postural stability and spatiotemporal parameters of human gait using developed wearable smart insole. J. Med. Eng. Technol. **39**(1), 75–78 (2015)
8. Davies, R.J., et al.: A personalized self-management rehabilitation system for stroke survivors: a quantitative gait analysis using a smart insole. JMIR Rehabil. Assist. Technol. **3**(2), 1–11 (2016)
9. Espressif Systems, ESP32 Series Datasheet. https://www.espressif.com/en/support/documents/technical-documents. Accessed 20 May 2021
10. Fulk, G.D., et al.: Identifying activity levels and steps of people with stroke using a novel shoe-based sensor. J. Neurol. Phys. Ther. **36**(2), 100–107 (2012)
11. Ghaida, H.A., Mottet, S., Goujon, J.M.: Plantar pressure cartography reconstruction from 3 sensors. In: 36th Annual International Conference of the IEEE Engineering in Medicine and Biology Society EMBC 2014, pp. 578–581 (2014)
12. Interlink Eletronics, FSR Integration Guide and Evaluation Parts Catalog. https://www.sparkfun.com/datasheets/Sensors/Pressure/fsrguide.pdf. Accessed 31 Jan 2021
13. Interlink Eletronics, FSR 400 Series Datasheet. https://cdn2.hubspot.net/hubfs/3899023/Interlinkelectronics%20November2017/Docs/Datasheet_FSR.pdf. Accessed 31 Jan 2021
14. Magee, D.J. Avaliação Musculoesquelética. 5nd. edn. Manole, São Paulo (2010)

15. Min, S.D., Wang, C., Park, D.-S., Park, J.H.: Development of a textile capacitive proximity sensor and gait monitoring system for smart healthcare. J. Med. Syst. **42**(4), 1–12 (2018). https://doi.org/10.1007/s10916-018-0928-3
16. Najafi, B., et al.: Smarter sole survival: will neuropathic patients at high risk for ulceration use a smart insole-based foot protection system? J. Diabetes Sci. Technol. **11**(4), 702–713 (2017)
17. Neto, H.P.: Effect of posture-control insoles on function in children with cerebral palsy: randomized controlled clinical trial. BMC Musculoskelet. Disord. **13**, 193–199 (2012)
18. Orlin, M.N., Mcpoil, T.G.: Plantar pressure assessment. Phys. Ther. **80**(4), 399–409 (2000)
19. Park, E., et al.: Unobtrusive and continuous monitoring of alcohol-impaired gait using smart shoes. Methods. Inf. Med. **56**(1), 74–82 (2017)
20. Razak, A.H.A., et al.: Foot plantar pressure measurement system: a review. Sens. (Switz.) **12**(7), 9884–9912 (2012)
21. Ramirez-Bautista, J.A., Chaparro-Cárdenas, S.L.: A review in detection and monitoring gait disorders using in-shoe plantar measurement systems. IEEE Rev Biomed. Eng. **10**(22), 299–309 (2017)
22. Sanghan, S., Chatpun, S., Leelasamran, W.: Plantar pressure difference: decision criteria of motor relearning feedback insole for hemiplegic patients. Int. Proc. Chem. Biol. Environ. Eng. **29**, 29–33 (2012)
23. Sheibani, S., et al.: Single chip interrogation system for a smart shoe wireless transponder. In: 36th Annual International Conference of the IEEE Engineering in Medicine and Biology Society EMBC 2014, pp. 3150–3153 (2014)
24. Shu, L., et al.: In-shoe plantar pressure measurement and analysis system based on fabric pressure sensing array. IEEE Trans. Inf. Technol. Biomed.sss **14**, 767–775 (2009)
25. Shumway-Cook, A., Woollacott, M.H.: Controle motor : teoria e aplicações práticas. 3nd. edn. Manole, Barueri (2010)
26. Telfer, S., et al.: Virtually optimized insoles for offloading the diabetic foot: a randomized crossover study. J. Biomech. **60**, 157–161 (2017)
27. Truong, P.H., et al.: Stride counting in human walking and walking distance estimation using insole sensors. Sens. (Switz.) **16**(6), 1–15 (2016)
28. Tsiouris, K.M., et al.: PD Manager: an mHealth platform for Parkinson's disease patient management. Healthc. Technol. Lett. **4**(3), 102–108 (2017)
29. Velho, S.R.K., et al.: Nível de Maturidade Tecnológica: uma sistemática para ordenar tecnologias. Parc. Estrat. **22**(45), 119–140 (2017)
30. Wafai, L.: Identification of foot pathologies based on plantar pressure asymmetry. Sens. (Basel, Switz.) **15**(8), 20392–20408 (2015)
31. Wang, W., et al.: Self-powered smart insole for monitoring human gait signals. Sensors **19**(24), 5336–5345 (2019)
32. Wang, C., Kim, Y., Min, S.D.: Soft-material-based smart insoles for a gait monitoring system. Materials **11**(12), 2435–2449 (2018)
33. Zhao, S.: Flexible sensor matrix film-based wearable plantar pressure force measurement and analysis system. PLoS One **15**(8), 1–16 (2020)

Author Index

Printed in the United States
by Baker & Taylor Publisher Services